south essex college
FURTHER & HIGHER EDUCATION
SOUTHEND CAMPUS

Sociological

The Sociological Review Monographs

Since 1958, *The Sociological Review* has established a tradition of publishing one or two Monographs a year on issues of general sociological interest. The Monograph is an edited book length collection of research papers which is published and distributed in association with Wiley-Blackwell. We are keen to receive innovative collections of work in sociology and related disciplines with a particular emphasis on exploring empirical materials and theoretical frameworks which are currently under-developed.

If you wish to discuss ideas for a Monograph then please contact the Monographs Editor, Chris Shilling, School of Social Policy, Sociology and Social Research, Cornwallis North East, University of Kent, Canterbury, Kent CT2 7NF, C.Shilling@kent.ac.uk

Our latest Monographs include:

Nature after the Genome (edited by Sarah Parry and John Dupré)
Nature, Society and Environmental Crisis (edited by Bob Carter and Nickie Charles)
Space Travel & Culture: From Apollo to Space Tourism (edited by David Bell and Martin Parker)
Un/Knowing Bodies (edited by Joanna Latimer and Michael Schillmeier)
Remembering Elites (edited by Mike Savage and Karel Williams)
Market Devices (edited by Michel Callon, Yuval Millo and Fabian Muniesa)
Embodying Sociology: Retrospect, Progress and Prospects (edited by Chris Shilling)
Sports Mega-Events: Social Scientific Analyses of a Global Phenomenon (edited by John Horne and Wolfram Manzenreiter)
Against Automobility (edited by Steffen Böhm, Campbell Jones, Chris Land and Matthew Paterson)
A New Sociology of Work (edited by Lynne Pettinger, Jane Parry, Rebecca Taylor and Miriam Glucksmann)
Contemporary Organization Theory (edited by Campbell Jones and Rolland Munro)
Feminism after Bourdieu (edited by Lisa Adkins and Beverley Skeggs)
After Habermas: New Perspectives on the Public Sphere (edited by Nick Crossley and John Michael Roberts)

Other Monographs have been published on consumption; museums; culture and computing; death; gender and bureaucracy; sport plus many other areas.

Sociological Routes and Political Roots

edited by Michaela Benson and Rolland Munro

Wiley-Blackwell/The Sociological Review

BLACKWELL PUBLISHING
350 Main Street, Malden, MA 02148–5020, USA
9600 Garsington Road, Oxford OX4 2DQ, UK
550 Swanston Street, Carlton, Victoria 3053, Australia

First published in 2011 by Blackwell Publishing Ltd

Library of Congress Cataloging-in-Publication Data

Sociological routes and political roots / edited by Michaela Benson and Rolland Munro.
    p. cm. – (Sociological review monographs ; 6)
    Includes bibliographical references and index.
    ISBN 978-1-4443-3813-3 (pbk.)
    1. Politics, Practical–Social aspects.   I. Benson, Michaela.
II. Munro, Rolland.
   JF799.S63   2011
   306.2–dc22

                                              2011012324

A catalogue record for this title is available from the British Library

Set by Toppan Best-set Premedia Limited

Printed and bound in the United Kingdom

by Page Brothers, Norwich

For further information on Monograph Series, please visit:
http://www.wiley.com/WileyCDA/Section/id-324292.html

Contents

Unfolding social construction: sociological routes and political roots

Rolland Munro

Introduction

Sociology is re-creating itself into one of the most diverse fields of modern study. After 20th-century debate more or less abandoned society as a holistic unit of analysis, key notions such as 'the social' and 'social facts' have been gradually unpacked, continually creating a plenitude of themes and complex issues for study. The resulting lines and directions of analysis – our sociological routes – reach out in ways that now far exceed the scope of the functional sub-division of the discipline into such areas as criminology, education, family, government, industry, medicine, and social policy.

As foolhardy as it would be to attempt to explain what binds all these different writings together, questions persist as to what makes writing *sociological*. Much of the recent sense of sociological solidarity, for instance, occurred in the wake of notions of social construction and, while many authors still report their work in this way, any collective glue appears nonetheless to be vapourizing. The consequence is that dissipation and fragmentation are once more germane issues. If a focus on 'little narratives' offers sociology too few overlaps in direction to speak any longer of 'the mainstream', are we just to suppose that current research adds up to just so many potatoes in a sack?

Any picture of expansion can mask internal conflict, in which it becomes hard to keep separate the 'politics of sociology' (disputes among ourselves about how we conduct research and how we report it) from the 'sociology of politics' (broadly understood as a focus on others and how they conduct their conflicted affairs). The interplay here is critical as targets for sociological dominance now reach far beyond the domain of knowledge – the main focus of Berger and Luckmann (1967). In a collapsing of borders between nature and culture on the one hand, and knowledge and practice on the other, authors have gone on to expand the sociological universe by arguing, for instance, that such matters as gender and age are social; as well as to identify primary materials, from mathematics (Bloor, 1976) to the gene (Rabinow, 1996), as to be taken first and foremost as social.

We want, in all this, to suggest a slightly different thesis: that it is this very diversity of sociological routes that is helping to open up the political. Current research is not only broadening our understandings of politics beyond the work-ings of politicians, but also sometimes facilitating a coming together of different, if overlapping, intellectual developments. Yes, there is in an 'unfolding' of the *social*, particularly in terms of the greater awareness of the diverse materials and relations making up its fabric. Yet, accompanying this are deeper, more intricate ways of thinking about *construction*, particularly in terms of power and organization. We can revise conceptions about what is making up the social beyond the human, and amend ideas of how different forms of power interact – and organize themselves – without succumbing to the humanist dogma that everything *is* socially constructed and *only* socially constructed.

In this introduction we explore some of the more perennial routes by which researchers are currently making links between the social and the political. These include: work on *borders*, inevitably a topic that sharpens thinking about its political roots; field studies on *belonging*, a topic which is currently enjoying a renaissance; discussions about *theory*, a space in which the political can easily be elided; writings on *discourse*, one of the most fruitful topics in which to explore the political; and pieces on *social movements*, the area in which politics is perhaps most explicit. As we hope our discussion shows, there is of course much overlap between all these topic, so that field studies on belonging engage thematically with borders and vice versa. So, too, work on discourse invariably engages thematically with social movements.

Borders and conflict

Sociology is not without help in covering the diverse fields that constitute its interests. It has always kept itself open to other human sciences, with researchers in geography perhaps able to claim as much influence nowadays as those in anthropology. The question remains as to what such perennial drawing on other disciplines does for sociology? Is this, for instance, to be viewed as a strength or a weakness? The issue is neither perlucid nor straight-forward. On the one hand, failing to patrol vigorously its boundaries and borders leaves any field open to dismissal as a discipline. On the other, it is fair to add that over-policing the state is always more likely to lead to repression and calcification than truth and clarity.

Keeping open 'sociological routes' to the ideas and methods of other disci-plines is crucial, we suggest, not least because the discipline is bringing back into the fold much of its founding 'roots'. For instance, classic themes, such as capitalism and the division of labour, may spring out of the work of economists, but in a turning of the tables that evokes the spirit of Weber on capitalism and Durkheim on the division of labour, recent work is re-examining economics – together with its fabric of markets – as social material and as social phenomena (Callon, 1998). Similarly science, whose images still dominate conceptions of rigour and knowledge, has been re-examined in terms of communities (Kuhn, 1970), culture (Barnes, 1974) and laboratories (Latour and Woolgar, 1979).

These examples are more than border raids. They register the extent to which sociology is imperialistic in its tendencies; as envisaged by one of the founders of the discipline, Comte. To add to the sociology of religion and the sociology of work, to name but two more long-standing specialisms, sociologists now make regular and often aggressive incursions into the fields of aesthetics, emotions, entertainment, food, media, museums, prisons, shopping, space, sport, tourism, urban planning and what has become known as bio-science. Whereas much economics maroons itself in mathematical abstractions about markets, and much psychology contains itself to laboratory studies of cognition, there appears to be no stop on sociology.

If this crossing of borders has tended to proliferate 'sociologies' of anything and everything, much of the permission to colonize new pastures and re-claim older ground is owed to the 1960s turn in sociology towards the 'everyday'. Rather than erecting walls in which to keep out what is non-sociological, as has happened often in the past in a search for disciplinary boundaries, or keeping for itself a kind of sovereignty in deciding the 'exception' (Schmitt, 1996), sociology has instead 'leapt the fence', to draw on William Kent's apt phrase, and now views a common landscape in which it is *everyday practice* that creates the exception.

Attention to everyday matters is not of course particularly novel, given the early theoretical work of Simmel (1972) and Schutz (1967), the mass observation studies in the UK (now part of the 'Le Play' archive funded by *The Sociological Review*), the field studies of the Chicago school in the US, especially in studies of city life by Robert Park, and Whyte's (1949) influential *Street Corner Society*. Yet in their different, if overlapping ways, Goffman's close study of 'facework' in interaction (1959) and Garfinkel's (1967) documenting of members having 'methods', provided a new impetus that moved sociology on and away from the 'functional' theories of Talcott Parsons.

The revolution in terrain, if it is this, has not been easy. The subsequent dubbing of studies of the everyday as 'micro-sociology' (Collins and Munro, 2010) created a false division that misled scholars of different persuasions into erecting phantom borders around research considered political and that which wasn't. Yet it is a fallacy to believe that the study of the everyday signifies a straight-forward shift from macro abstraction towards field studies. Nor need it represent an inversion in scale, from the production of general theory to the behaviour patterns of individuated actors. Such a wholesale reduction in ambition would not only throw away the possibility of systems like money being particular kinds of 'social facts'. It would also bury persons in the solipsism of choice, separating them off from all reference to system and structure in the lifeworld.

Everday life incorporates everything back into itself and collapses taken-for-granted distinctions between nature and culture, as Michael Schillmeier and Wiebke Pohler's paper in this volume underlines by their opening up the politics

3

of the Danube. It does not reduce to a dualistic partition, say, between 'systems' – abstractions such as the nation state or world economy – and the agency of 'individuals' – such as can be found in theories of rational choice. Yes, understanding the everyday requires marginalizing precepts like 'structure' on the one hand, and bodies like the 'actor' on the other. But it seems imperative to set aside these units of analysis (favoured by macro and micro analysts alike) and explore instead the many, many ways in which everday conduct helps re-create the very *institutions* that facilitate the day-to-day's taking place.

To paraphrase William James, it is institutions 'all the way down'. It is institutions that help body forth the social, from corporate bodies like parliament to transitory phenomena like queues. It was institutions that made it possible to keep strangers in the city (Derrida, 2000), even if these territories are today being subdivided in the name of security into gated communities and unfenced slums. It was the institutions of train times, lists of names and 'due process' which made it possible to build the death camps (Bauman, 1989) and it is institutions like passports and CVs that enable the few to enjoy the much vaunted global mobility while the majority are made immobile in 'enclaves' (Turner, 2007) by the absence of educational institutions and barriers to job opportunities.

In this respect it is pertinent to point back to Goffman's meticulous attention to the variety and scope of institutional settings. Goffman's (1964) 'neglected situation' is often underplayed in readings that privilege a theatrical emphasis on facework as little more than impression management. Similarly, inasmuch as power can be garnered together within groups, the possibilities for sanctions may hang on better understandings of 'account-giving' (Garfinkel, 1967) as the medium with which everyday actors co-construct mutuality in their lifeworlds.

It is unfortunate therefore that pundits deemed this renewed attention to the everyday to be silent about power. Claims that studies of the everyday are unable to address the 'macro' topics of domination and legitimation overlooked the extent to which power is at its most effective when 'running silently' (Giddens, 1968). Power, as Parsons himself recognized, works best as a consequence of its being deeply embedded within day-to-day conduct. And, as Barbara Grüning's analysis of German unification in Part 1 of this volume makes vivid, far from the political being 'absent' from the mundane, aspects of humiliation and appropriation are often best illustrated by stories of the everyday.

Our point then is not to raise flags here over motifs like 'power is in the capilliaries', as this too easily echoes a micro-macro split. The key issue is that the study of everyday life involves unravelling the *inter*dependence and *inter*-twining of all kinds of institutions, broadly understood, from occasions like festivals to family meals. Nor are we attempting to hoist ourselves on the petard of 'cultural sociology'. Far from reinventing issues of structure and agency, concepts like conduct and culture permeate all boundaries. Not only is everday conduct, as Simmel pointed out, interpellated by systemic matters like money; so, too, issues like class and gender are percolated by cultural performances that can owe as much to locally accomplished 'ways of doing' as to mass mediums like television (Skeggs, 2004).

Belonging and its political 'roots'

Border raids and skirmishes in the expansion of empire are not the only matters to engage sociologists. Sociology, if for nothing else, is marked by its preponderance of debates, few of which ever become resolved. Some of these debates preoccupy a whole generation of sociologists, such as the macro-micro controversies discussed earlier. Others reduce to trench warfare, as happened between the 'ethnos' and the Marxists during the 1970s and 1980s. In a subject area that prides itself on its roots, and in particular on its *political* roots, it is difficult not to feel a 'punctualizing' of identity (Munro, 2004a) in the call to arms issued by one side or another.

One of the longest-running of these debates is staged between the logics of rationalism and community, a split whose roots only partially reach back to Tönnies's famous distinction between Gesellschaft and Gemeinschaft. This 'division', which often misplaces Weber with bureaucracy on one side and Durkheim with ritual and belonging on the other, continues today between those who champion decision-making and choice and others who defer to custom and precedent. Given the prominence of visions of utopia within sociology, it is also possible to frame aspects of this debate as taking place between those who subscribe to *design* – albeit with all-seeing humans rather than an omniscient God (cf Fuller, 2006) – and those who draw succour from *custom* – with or without Darwinian overtones of 'evolution' (Runciman, 2008).

During the last century this debate increasingly polarized between 'traditionalists', who are typically branded as outmoded and reactionary, and 'modernizers', who pose as the forces of progress and enlightenment. That this divison continues to operate even today is evident in Part 2 of this volume, for example in displaced communities as Oscar Forero and Graham Smith identify in the case of the Ukrainian diaspora living in Bradford. The high point came, however, with Bell and Newby's (1971) dismissal of ideas of belonging and community, particularly the rural model of arcadia, as just so much 'nostalgia'. A whole raft of studies of community, from Frankenberg (1966) onwards, were suddenly disenfranchised and – with key exceptions in anthropology such as Cohen (1982) – the political issues that could be caught under the tag of belonging were abandoned until critiques of the so-called 'collapse of community' (Spencer and Pahl, 2006) co-incided with the communitarian revival in the 1990s.

In seeming to be unafraid to question the very roots of the discipline, Bell and Newby had caught winds of change that were developing into a wider programme of attacks on institutions – the very framework on which sociology had founded itself. In turning to the mundane and the everyday, for instance, sociologists had already embarked on a process of challenging monopolies of power by 'demystifying' the professions through field studies, particulary medicine (eg

Becker *et al.*, 1961) – with the demystification of science, as mentioned above, not far behind. So, too, the examination of community within these establishments proceeded apace, especially in terms of the study of closed or 'total institutions' (eg Goffman, 1961), including schools, factories, prisons and hospitals – each of which was shown to be failing on many counts.

The upshot of all this critique, which Giddens and others sought to capture under the rubric of 'detraditionalization', was to encourage a more general unmasking of institutions as reproducing elites, building on Mills (1956), and as being hotbeds of discrimination (Jeffery, 1979). The unchallengible thesis was that establishments like hospitals, schools and universities are intrinsically involuted and are invariably stuck in the mud of so much habit and routine. The unintended consequence of reform, however, was to give impetus to one particular form of organization – namely bureaucracy – as the machinery by which 'informal' forms of organization were to be made transparent; and by which fairness and equality could be more firmly established.

If sociology is nothing without its respect for institutions being at the heart of the lifeworld – as we are pressing – then even greater care has to be taken over valorizing certain forms of order over others. Some forms of organizing can help re-generate feelings of belonging and value; other forms, such as fashion and media, may help drive it out. This is an issue explored in Part 2, with Maria Adamczyk recollecting her feelings as she enters a website forum for people who see themselves cast out as ugly. And nostalgia may yet have its place in the generation of a sense of belonging, as Michaela Benson in her paper in this volume illustrates. Yet as these and other papers indicate, the exact ways in which organization of one sort or another affect feelings of belonging are still poorly understood.

In ways that chime with both Benson's and Adamczyk's emphasis on the imaginary, Cohen's (1985, 1987) retheorizing of belonging around symbols has helped Savage *et al.* (2005) posit a notion of 'elective belonging'. As Cohen (1985: 118) argues '[p]eople construct community symbolically, making it a resource and repository of meaning, and a referent of their identity'. As he goes on to argue, elasticity in the use of symbols stems from their intrinsic ambiguity in meaning. This has helped others to challenge the classic distinction of community sociology (the division between insiders and outsiders) and question ideas of globalization (especially the supposition that locality no longer matters). Feeling at home in a neighbourhood remains crucial even if, as Savage *et al.* argue, in their key study on the middle classes in the Manchester region, it is no longer a product of having been born and bred there.

In their gloss on community, Bell and Newby not only failed to distinguish between different forms of community and friendship, but also conflated the workings of different kinds of institutions. Specifically, in eliding the ties that link feelings of belonging to mundane institutions and everyday practices, such as opening doors for others, they had neither absorbed the importance of Goffman and Garfinkel, nor understood the lessons of Dalton's (1959) and Gouldner's (1955) work on organization and bureaucracy. Instead, in harbouring utopian ideals of progress, they naïvely assumed that more 'rational' practices could simply be identified and put in place with broad consent. In their picking up and running with the threads of a nascent managerialism, it is difficult today to see Bell and Newby, and the many who followed their lead, as other than unthinking 'modernizers'.

More worryingly perhaps, the chance for sociologists to unpick the emerging division of labour between *policy* and *practice* had slipped away. It is this distinction which creates the 'fence' (cf Agamben, 1998) between the strategic and the mundane, between what is inside and what is outside political and managerial attention. And it is this distinction which simultaeously organizes power for managers, by reserving for them the sovereign capacity to decide 'the exception': what is to be lifted into the realms of policy and what isn't.

The subsequent institutionalization of this separation – across every form of organization, from the business corporation and offices of government to the community shop and local charity – has eclipsed even the macro-micro divisions that preceded it. In its place, an hierarchization of policy over practice rules supreme and unchallenged. In so doing it has not only granted managers a new source for identity (and belonging) in 'strategy' (cf Knights and Morgan, 1991), but reinforced the manifold possibilities for discrimination in terms of class and gender. The utopian maps on which managers walk the talk of their policies is bought at the expense of dystopian worlds for employees to work within.

A consequence for sociologists in all this is not simply a widening of the split between those who feel they belong to the world of critique and those who identify themselves with policy-linked research. The separation of policy from practice has been hardening into a partition that has helped to lift much policy-setting debate out of the academy into the hallowed ground of government funding circles – and in ways that simultaneously relegate research to 'practical' field studies. The world of policy-making and studies of worlds of practice are now sealed apart in separate sets of referents, a segregation in which 'reform' of research practice is always going to be held to be necessary as the only means for 'moving forward'; and over which even more *management* of policy-driven research is to be the only solution on offer.

Left unchallenged, these arrangements are likely to wither away our 'political roots', once so vital to the growth of sociology, as our political masters seek to re-direct our sociological routes. If it was ever possible to decide among ourselves germane issues covered by the 'politics of sociology', that luxury is now in the process of being eviserated by universitities having to follow the money and further 'fence' its academics into the enclave of delivering to the commisioning policy-makers more and more 'evidence-based research'.

Theory and critique

As part of these changes, theory and critique appear to be in process of being downgraded, at least in the eyes of UK policy-makers (from research to 'scholarship'). Yet in spite of this, theory remains a key *resource* in debate as well as being a key *topic* in sociological work. What we mean by this is that there is now general agreement in the sociological community that research has to be 'theoretically informed'. In this way, 'informing' ideas are not only now acknowledged more explicitly, rather than being left implicit; the iteration and circulation of certain preferred ideas, such as Bourdieu's habitus, and not others, say 'figuration' in Elias, also is made more evident.

At a minimum sociological papers are expected to demonstrate a reflexivity about the sets of ideas and presuppositions they are operating within. What Kuhn (1970) called paradigms, and Foucault terms 'truth regimes', are to be taken seriously as setting up competing schools and possibly incommensurable research programmes. Surveys and other forms of empirical research – whether policy-driven or not – cannot bootstrap themselves for publication, but typically have to sound out their findings within the realms of 'extant' theory. Concommitantly, theory-oriented papers are expected to ground their argument in examples drawn from field studies of the lifeworld and not in the time-worn dilemmas of armchair philosophy (Kilminster, 2011).

Even more pungently, as all three papers in Part 3 illustrate, post-colonial debates are having their effect. For many writers this may simply mean little more than a political correctness in phrasing things to obscure the more obvious forms of ideological domination. For others, as in the comparative piece in this volume by John Law and Wen-yuan Lin, which explores the 'disconcertment' experienced in an apparent reversed clash between East and West, such work represents a genuine attempt to 'work backwards' to unpick *thinking* from what Heidegger (1962) calls our 'thrownness'; the way in which each of us is brought up to consider things – and pre-judge matters as if it were thought – long before we are able to wake up to issues of prejudice and oppression.

Consequently, as Celine-Marie Pascale brings out in her discussion in Part 3 on 'porosity' in the social world, sharp distinctions between theory and the empirical, or even ontology and epistemology, are increasingly less tenable. This is not, though, to register a complete shift away from the more empiricist decades of the 1960s and 1970s. Yes, there is now considerable scepticism about facts standing by themselves. Yet, as the paper by Derek Robbins brings out in a wide-ranging and incisive critique on Bourdieu, there is equally strong resistance among sociologists towards any attempts to recentralize the role of theory – at least in the way 'totalizing' pronouncements on theory were encouraged and allowed to dominate in earlier parts of the 20th century.

For all this, discussions about theory, one way or another, continue to form a set of important routes by which sociological thought develops. Our emphasis though has to be firmly on the multiplicity of sociological routes. There is no royal road to Rome. What has changed is precisely the idea that theory is nomothetical. Theory no longer lives in some hierarchical vacuum, caught between the once and future truth that is yet to be thought and the burial grounds of the 'rubbish' people are held to have believed in earlier times. Consequently, even if certain journals, particularly those in the US, have re-doubled their efforts in the way of censorship over what they take to be sociologically relevant, there are fewer autocratic pronouncements about what the world is and fewer normative papers making general statements about how we should study it.

Against notions of top-down theory, sociological thought mainly finds its way into print, as the papers in the volume illustrate, through the medium of sociological debate. Instead of leaving empirical findings inert, or building theory out of the ruins of other theories, researchers typically presage their findings by addressing what they call 'theoretical considerations' (or some similar rubric) in order to turn their field material critically upon the theory they find churned up from earlier debates. Progress in sociology is seen to be conducted, variously, on the one hand through longstanding wrangles over the classic topics of class, gender, ethnicity and age and on the other through emergent issues, such as globalization, liberalization, managerialization, medicalization, migration, secularization and universal rights – each of these having already having been creamed off as topics in their own right.

In all this a generic and positive move towards *theorizing* fieldwork can be detected that is no longer beholden to the division of *either* testing theory *or* applying theory. Theoretically informed or not, it is self-evident that some sociological work is more theoretically *engaged* than others. Yet, this said, to highlight theory in various ways does not entail a return to 'grand theory' as Giddens contended. To the contrary, the 'agonistics' (Lyotard, 1984) of repeated entry and re-entry through the back door of debate, means that work on 'theory' is, and remains as is discussed next, largely *interpretive*. Setting out one's understandings of the arguments of this or that theorist, however provisional, entails that the originating propositions and premises are always being recast – as each author struggles to make the connection (or disconnection) that evinces the point they are seeking to establish.

The power of discourse

This general re-positioning of theory is linked to the 20th century turn to language. The well-accepted idea is that we are always in *interpretation*; and perhaps further that interpretation is all we are ever 'in'. This is not just to assert that theory has always to be 'interpreted', rather than be 'applied' as was previously assumed. It is particularly germane to our point about the re-locating of theory within the medium of sociological debate, rather than above it. It is our contention that this creates an on-going interpretative process in which, in sociology at least, theory is always being reworked and rethought.

The idea that there is no exit from language (Barthes, 1967) – and further that we can only move from one truth regime to another – is perhaps what most foxes those who want to partition theory from empirics, values from facts, things from thoughts – to mention a few of the usual suspects by which epistemological 'representationalism' (realism by another name) is protected. If we can wean ourselves off attempts to reduce ontology to a facticity of the 'ontic', the meaningless checking off of the mere existence of things (cf Munro, 2004b), then we can open up our work instead to the manifold connections and mutual interrelations that help create and sustain our 'worlds' as we live and breathe in them.

A key direction for this resurgence in the importance of language has coalesced in the study of everyday conversation and in the study of institutionally-embedded narratives. Technically both of these forms are known as discourse, and while all three papers in Part 4 are particularly concerned to explore the interplay of each with the other, it is the formation of the latter which has drawn primarily on the work of Michel Foucault. With the rise of medicine, psychiatry and criminology, *discourse* – previously understood to be conversation writ large – becomes segmented, sedimented and stabilized. Foucault's argument is that power and knowledge are interpenetrated with each other, especially within the 'total institutions' of the clinic, the asylum and the prison. It is here, through this circulation and iteration of discourse, that power and knowledge – together – are understood to be 'exercised'.

Interpreted as a circulatory medium within which power is exercised as knowledge, these initial cuts at formulating 'discourse' reflect the earlier shift from a (proto-Durkheimian) holistic study of society towards the (neo-Weberian) analysis of its parts. Understood to be composed of the major institutions making up its workings, society is more or less divided up into autonomous establishments, such as Weber's separation of politics from science. To give another instance, Luhmann (1982), in his analysis of communication, argues that 'semi-closed systems', like the law, media and government, have their own ways of communicating that leave each establishment talking past the other.

As such this particular concept of discourse – as stable and standardized – offers a meso-level of analysis that accepts that key establishments, once legitimated by the state, are subject to domination by a power elite. And it should not escape notice, in passing, that this particular version of discourse has suited the fragmentation of sociology, already noted, into the 'expert' areas of criminology, education, family, government, industry, medicine, and social policy. Somewhat arbitrarily, an analysis developed for the level of the nation state is adapted (down) to the level of these meso-institutions – albeit one reduced in scale – with the advantage that each 'sociology' can bask in the supposed autonomy of the institutions underpinning their functional area.

As each specialism in sociology emerges, though, more is at stake. As Bernhard Weicht explains in this volume over the hagiography of 'independence' and the concomitant stigma of 'dependence', there is a sedimentation in language as words take on particular meanings and specific phrasings come to be repeated more than others. But given the prevalence of mimesis (Taussig, 1990) – the readiness to imitate and 'copy' – what is going on here in terms of iteration and denigration cannot just be explained by recourse to the notion that everyday accounts 'reflect' ideology. Nor is it straightforwardly a matter of action being 'institututionalised' by virtue of habit and routine. Rather the point here lies at the heart of another aspect of the 20th century turn to language. This revolves around the Foucauldian insight that 'ways of saying' are made *subject* to processes of surveillance and discipline. It is this cutting edge that opens up much of the study of discourse to its political roots and helps explain how the issue of sanctions runs deep within mundane and everyday practices.

In Foucault's (1973) analysis 'ways of saying' become 'ways of seeing'; and vice versa. On the one hand, and bearing in mind Derrida's (1982) arguments about iteration, the speaker gains '*author*-ization' and '*author*-ity' by stepping into the 'place of the king' and saying 'what is to be seen' (Foucault, 1970). As Callon (1988) has also noted, such feigning to 'represent' things – the scallops in his case – is a political act by virtue of *representing* things as their 'spokes-person'. On the other, though, this very act of speaking out, acting as a 'spokes-person', opens up the speaker to techniques of surveillance – since each occasion is always a 're-presenting' of the putative facts and acts therefore as a test, or *examination* (Hoskin, 1996), of membership in the eyes of others.

Sociology, in all this, has found itself drawn into an appreciation of the importance of 'culture' for understanding how deeply rooted are surveillance and sanctions within the lifeworld. And rather than leave the topic of culture to others, sociology has embarked on an ever closer study of everyday institu-tions and practices – especially where these themselves are also grounded within the workings of establishments like hospitals or local councils. Surveillance in the workplace, for instance, includes colleagues, who may exercise power for instance by withholding affirmation of membership (Munro, 1999). In terms of opening up possibilities for the abuse of power, however, those in management positions can encourage those below to 'go for it' – without formally devolving *authority* down the 'relays' within a bureaucracy (cf Barnes, 1998); thus creating a threshold in which they can later apply their *discretion* to assess whether whatever happens constitutes 'delivery'.

At the heart of this renewed attention to the everyday is a re-habilitation of the vernacular and an over-turning of high culture that owes much to Raymond Williams. Just as the study of conversation and everyday speech, what structur-alists like Saussure (1983) called *parole*, is to be given an equal footing to *langue*, so too 'common culture' (Willis, 1990) is being brought alongside more priv-iledged ideas of aesthetics and morality – and can have no critic. Specifically, populism, the topic Ritchie Savage explores in Part 4 in a most helpful critique of Laclau, is shown to be integral to *developed* nations. The implication is that populism and the 'dumbing down' of society may go hand in hand. In this respect, if oddities in nuance and phrasing are no longer to be dismissed as ignorance, or attributed to idiosyncratic errors in grammer and wording, then syncretic and even seemingly unfounded 'attitudes' have to be listened to and given 'voice'. In the face of this, the position of the 'expert', as Kateřina Lišková in her paper on the discourse of sexual therapists demonstrates, has become more precarious as well as more embedded in heteronormative assumptions through perlocutionary speech acts.

Sociology, as a discipline, has had to become conscious that its grander narratives have no priority as claims to knowledge; and no more valency for governing the lifeworld than do, say, the competing claims of economics and psychology. Sociology has certainly thought itself to be in the vanguard of 'rubbishing' the establishment – the complicity of institutions and elites discussed earlier. But all this, in turn, surely entails a commensurate 'transparency', in which sociology has to be seen to contribute towards its own demystification? If what is sauce for the goose is sauce for the gander, then an interrogation of our own specialist languages, and the ideas and divisions that they naturalize, may be an inexorable part of that price.

In the wake of the rise of new 'governing' institutions – accounting, managerialism and public safety – all disciplines are finding it harder to justify holding onto their own 'analytical' terms without being accused of obscurantist jargon and this is the 'levelling' effect that also stems from academics having to treat theory as one form of narrative among others. It is also, arguably, a vindication of those who have sought to bring together their analysis of everyday conversation into the examination of institutional discourse. While institutional forms of discourse may appear to dominate, and surveillance and sanctions are key to 'governmentality' (Foucault, 1991), it remains the case that any structural stability of discourse still has to be accomplished daily through the exercising and iteration of particular constitutive phrases and meanings.

Social movement and organization

If much has been made of the 'politics of identity' in recent years, it is with the more general notion of social movement that the political, in all its ramifications, is being made most explicit. What social movements bring to the surface are aspects of domination; asymmetries of resources and privilege against which groups form, like the 'Small Island States' that are the focus of Zoë Irving's study in Part 5, seeking to alter how things are run and being done – and pressing for change over who benefits from things as they are.

Culture and change in all this appear to form their own antimony. Although many (eg Crossley, 2002) have sought to combine the two, for the most part the one trope still tends to take in what the other leaves out. Whereas Durkheim and Weber, for instance, are often taken to be explaining the status quo, offering both mimetic and rational understandings of social and cultural dominance, Marx's more economic analysis is pointed sharply towards change. As capitalists attempt to squeeze ever-greater amounts of surplus value from the factory system, revolt becomes inevitable. The rallying cry is change: an end to oppression and exploitation.

Consequently, sociological study veers towards those movements that arise out of dissent, opposition and contention (Tilly, 2004). Current contenders include a variety of anti-market, anti-money and anti-war movements, as well as environmentalists who rail against the waste and destruction created in the name of progress. We must though guard against any easy conflation of protest with left-wing politics, inasmuch as there are plenty of social movements today that garner against what they take to be the liberal mainstream – contenders here including the so-called Christian right who are in reaction against what they see to be the degenerate morals of contemporary life.

Yet, as Marx understood more than most, revolution also has to be *organized*. A crucial part of Marx's analysis is that labour is granted the potential to organize itself as a consequence of the capitalist system bringing people together in crowded conditions. Unlike the peasantry in France who were geographically isolated in the 19th century (or cottage workers in a 'putting-out' system), factories provide the conditions of possibility for the proletariat to form unions that are organized as well as oppositional. And organized, as illustrated in the paper by Isis Sánchez Estellés in Part 5 on the anti-war movement in Spain, not only to mobilize collective resources, but also in ways that create opportunities to accumulate and deploy further resources. As Tarrow (1998) points out, the interaction of opportunities and mobilization is dynamic: if opportunities can create mobilization, then mobilization can also in turn create opportunities.

For all this, the mores of organization can suck the lifeblood out of revolutionary zeal and leave a movement more concerned with its own perpetuation than with its transformational aims (cf Mann, 1986). Even for social movments formed with protest or rebellion in mind, the analysis of collectivities often ends up stressing their static qualities (Michels, 1915). The manacles of mimesis and the rust of routine are not just to be associated with the perennial problem of passivity, say, in respect of the readiness for the peasantry or the proletariat to live with their lot (a state more likely to be affronted by talk of false consciousness than swayed by it). It is a feature of the very forms that organizing takes that these generally tend to inhibit, if not divert, any momentum for change.

While the point about organization being inhibiting is not lost on anarchists, it has to be said that their fallback on charismatic leadership contains its own limits. So, too, the more contemporary 'cellular' form of organization, arguably adopted by many terrorist groups, also harbours its own forms of conservatism – inasmuch as action can become uncoordinated and degenerate, losing its oppositional function. All too easily the means becomes an end in itself, with disruption valorized as radical and terror reproduced for terror's sake.

Possibly for this reason, it is the seemingly *spontaneous* movement that attracts much attention in sociology. Developing Smelser's (1962) emphasis on 'initiating events', researchers have sought to identify the rallying points for dissent, or the defining moments from which resistance can grow – such as the Civil Rights movement in the US exploding with Rosa Parks riding the bus in the whites-only section. Here Tarrow's (1998) analysis of 'cultural frames' has been helpful in pinpointing some of the conditions under which injustice is magnified; and so resonates through a population.

If Canetti's (1962) seminal work on crowds and power suggests movements that seem spontaneous might also be orchestrated (as was probably the case with Rosa Parks), the search for a strong causal narrative can still have us looking in the wrong direction, overlooking the extent to which it is movements that change society, rather than society which causes change. Here serendipity has to be given a place on the operating table of history and analysis today looks not just inward to the 'logic of practice' within the movement itself (cf Crossley, 2002), but outwards to the alliances and *alignments* that are already latent in the form of 'networks'.

Under the influence of constructivism more generally, conceptions of organization have moved on from the 'hi-story' of the fixed and the formal to encompass the labyrinth in which the ephemeral and the transient cross over and connect up in radically different ways (Jones and Munro, 2006). It is in their very lack of definiton and structure that networks have the potential not only to let actors change horses, so to speak, but also to facilitate social movements. Indeed, it is precisely this indefiniteness that Micheal Janoschka refers to in his discussion of how dispossessed British homeowners in Spain claim European identity, thus demonstrating their recourse to a 'borrowed' organization.

Credence can also be given here to the more ineffable and intangible forms of relations – moments encapsulated say in Durkheim's notion of effervesence. Shilling and Mellor (2011) for example suggest how religious movements gather pace through ritually mediated intoxication – in ways that carry a more general valency. Additionally, the idea of *affect* has been growing in importance (Thrift, 2004), suggesting more attention should be paid to the very (human) way in which the animal in us can be 'turned over' rather than just 'turned around' (Munro and Belova, 2008). Too strong a reliance on continuities, in effect, can reinforce the locus for studies of mobility when, as has been argued elsewhere, it is motility (Latimer and Munro, 2006), the sudden and seemingly spontaneous reshaping of 'worlds' that would also repay study.

Discussion: opening sociological routes and recognizing political roots

As we hope is clear, it is possible to see many links between the various routes sociologists adopt. Discourse analysis has been used for instance to deconstruct the borders between medicine and quackery and between psychiatry and psychobabble. And questions can be asked as to what are the borders that really differentiate, for instance, a science of criminology from the study of a social movement that predicates itself on a revulsion against punitive forms of punishment? Or indeed, as Kuhn and Barnes have indicated, we can ask why 'hard' scientists like physicists should not be treated as belonging to a community like any other group? For example Thrift (2005) opens up the conventionally anodyne analysis of complexity science by placing the founders of the movement back to back in Sante Fe with all the flakey therapies of the day.

Yet, even so, knowing what can be said from what cannot, still creates material which separates off all sorts of 'insiders' from 'outsiders'. In my ethnographic work, for example, I have found it helpful to see 'management' as a social movement that got much of its start by inciting fellow adherents to be *against* the previously fashionable idea of 'administration'. Since then management has accomplished its rise and rise – and eventual domination throughout all forms of society – in part through a double-movement: evolving its discourse of strategic thinking around the art of policy-making on the one hand, while blending its own 'practices' of delegating decision-taking with a surveillance through the more rational mores of bookkeeping on the other. While many managers thus learn to absent themselves from the action and operate instead as a kind of zero – empty signifiers in themselves but placeholders around which everything else is defined – this effect is only made possible by those at home in management puff fencing themselves off from those who profess other forms of control and dismissing them as 'glorified supervisors' (Munro, 1998).

It is also possible though to link this opening up of sociological routes, at least in part, to a radical shift in perspective, what has been characterized elsewhere as the 'consumption view' (cf Edgell *et al.*, 1996). Whereas the *production* of sociology as a discipline centred previously on the 'building' of general theories – in a process of 'abstracting' the groundwater of social life – sociology today might be better characterised in terms of its attempts to chart the eddies and currents of the everyday. This may mean, among other things, attempting to follow how artefacts and other materials of the lifeworld, as Benson does in this volume, are used or deployed to make *relations* either present or absent (Munro, 1996). For many sociologists, the question is no longer about what appears to be being produced, issues of community and solidarity and so forth, but what is consumed on its way, the stuff in everday circulation (Lee and Munro, 2001). This might be seen just as a turn from the normative to the descriptive, but more is at stake.

In privileging consumption over production, the everyday over our own theories, researchers can first help to trace *how* things are made to matter, say by a union foregrounding poor timber props as the reason for going on strike, or by a therapist, as Lišková explicates, pronouncing what are normal sexual relations. To be sure saying 'how' things happen, rather than attempting to say 'why', has often been a recipe for eliding the political and marking a quick return to functionalism. But then any question, unless powered by curiosity, is surely bound to fail? And, conversely, in the absence of pressing the question of 'how', the risk is that of entering 'explanation' all too soon when more analysis is needed. The result is to keep generic, stereotypical reasons in circulation that barely scratch the surface of what the devil the actors are themselves up to (Geertz, 1973).

To keep themselves curious, researchers can go beyond the 'how' and also notice *when* things are put in place. And when they are removed, say by someone treating you as a friend and making absent your obligations to them as a boss. This typically involves attention to moments in which something latent like the construct of 'dependence' is made particularly problematic, as Weicht in his piece picks out. It is just this sensitivity to timing that allows the *analysis* of ostension by others to draw from the minutiae of everyday interaction. For instance, Tony Blair's constant use of advisors within Number 10 was an inte-

15

gral part of his attempt to make 'policy' in ways that by-passed parliament as the main decision-making body. Parliament was made present when he needed it, as with the ratification of his wish to go to war in Iraq, but was made absent otherwise in much of the daily crafting of policies and initiatives.

Researchers in the field learn not to rush to judgement and to *defer* explanation. Ultimately 'description' in a good ethnography is tantamount to explanation. What Goffman and Garfinkel bring to the party – the careful and persistant analysis of 'how' and 'when' – is not specifically a stress on conformity to tradition – although an emphasis on routine and custom is integral to both sets of writings. They do focus on aggregate effects brought about through an inevitable conformity to precedent and convention, the habitus if you like. But to stress only this is to overlook how each, in their very different ways, also illuminates how power works through endless processes of *division*. In what Giddens (1984) has re-termed 'strategic conduct', Goffman shows how mundane institutions, from queues to interviews, can be manipulated and bent to work for purposes of self-presentation; or, dare one say it, figuration? So, too, Garfinkel's breaching experiments show how easy it is to make someone feel 'outside'; that they just don't know what is happening or going on.

Analysis changes when it is observed that power arises not simply from that which is durable, but also – as Schillmeier and Pohler set out to show in the opening paper of this volume – from momentary fusions which may be motile and transitory. What is kept apart requires organization; organization that in turn creates fissures through which other things are possible. In this way sociologists can move away from the more customary questions of *what?* and *why?* – questions that return us respectively to the lure of essentialism and the lore of explanation. In their place we are set free to explore *how* things coalesce and *when* they act in concert. So that it becomes possible for sociologists to identify 'associations' that bring the human and inhuman together; and hence, instead of aiming to pick out single and originary causes, we can go on from this to trace their combinative effects.

Concluding comments

This collection of research papers came out of *The Sociological Review*'s 100th Conference *Imagining the Political/The Politics of Imagination*, held in June 2009. As is the way with conferences, a good number of the papers presented were directed at issues beyond those outlined in conference themes and, in publishing this monograph, we wanted to bring papers together that reflect the diversity of sociological routes by which key political issues are addressed.

All the papers in this volume reflect a growing consciousness of how much there is to explore in the overlaps between politics and the social. What is notable is how many of the papers, having been allocated into headings that seemed appropriate for this monograph, could have been grouped instead under several of the other headings. This illustrates that much of the vibrancy of contemporary work lies not so much with a disregard of disciplinary 'borders' but in a readiness by authors to 'leap the fence'. A willingness to investigate overlaps in topics that can be seen for instance in the papers of Ritchie, Sánchez Estellés and Weicht, who are all concerned with the thematics of both discourse and social movement.

A first 'route' opened up in all this is to acknowledge the extent to which power is no longer assumed to be 'held' in the centre – the tendency to ascribe leaders with omniscient powers of decision-making; or to attribute force to the seat of Empire as in Rome. As Robbins signals when contrasting Bourdieu's work with Lyotard's interventions over knowledge, power 'circulates' in the form of a distribution of artefacts, the sedimentation of discourse, the privileging of practices and the introduction of technologies. As much as current work is brought together through a recognition of the leakiness of one set of relations into another, 'porosity' as Pascale calls it in her piece, we need to be increasingly on our guard in these times of austerity as to *when* walls are being erected and notice for *whom* mobility no longer operates.

A second route concerns the unpacking of the social. As much as Durkheim's arguments over 'social facts' continue to hold sway, we no longer see these in totalizing terms. This has allowed authors, as do the participants in Forero and Smith's study, to exercise a much greater flexibility and interpretability over what passes for custom and practice. As with discussions of 'neo-liberalism' to be found elsewhere, for instance, the economic is being rediscovered as intricately tied up in the reshaping of social and moral relations, rather than being that which is assumed to have direct and immediate political consequences.

A third, if more troubled, route in research comes from taking up the concept of identity, already ubiquitous within sociological studies. As Janoschka and Benson bring out, identity is a moveable feast, something to be articulated as needs must and as borrowable organizations allow. Despite attempts to restrict its meaning to collective forms, or make its analytical use taboo (e.g. Brubaker and Cooper, 2000), discussion of identity continues to occupy sociological debate – to the extent that it is hard to deny that its currency, however devalued, has made it as major a trope within sociology as that of institution.

A fourth and still relatively unexplored route takes us beyond the possiblities that flowed from viewing organization as the 'production of its members' (Bittner, 1970) and stretches conceptions of *relations* to include 'partial connections' (Strathern, 1991). Although many continue to frame 'interaction' in terms of human co-presence, meanings of the social have gradually broken away from the constraint of 'dyadic' one-to-one relationships. What matters is that, as Adamczyk and Grüning bring out over matters of 'exclusion', relations can cross time as well as space, depending on just what is being made present and what is being made absent.

If the fifth and overarching route in all this has been the turn to the everyday, there has been an equally dramatic shift in focus over 'material' and the *parts* different forms of material play in offering us agency. Garfinkel's edict to 'follow the animal' in field studies might now be interpreted much more broadly, with actors not only becoming cybernetic (Haraway, 1986; Suchman, 2007), but also embedded in materials that are designed to affect or talk to each other *at a distance*. The possible emergence of a new edict to 'follow the material', rather than the actors, raises new and different questions about borders. There are even possibilities of backtracking through these in order to root out some of the more hidden issues of belonging, as is discussed by Law and Lin.

Yet conceptions of what is social have still to trace fully the 'heterogeneity' of materials in play for purposes of inscription (Latour, 1987), as well as take account of more transient and serendipitous forms of 'translation'. This is not only a case of waking up to the extent to which the human sciences have been delineating 'a world of actors devoid of things' (Joerges, 1988: 220); it is also a case of keeping a symmetry in focus between the human and the inorganic. There are deep moral issues in play in all our distinctions. What we can see in the meanderings of the Danube in Schillmeier and Pohler's paper though is the importance of being able to register effects being generated from any source. Which brings us back to the expansion of field studies, and an over-reliance on the taperecorded interview, since often it is in the here and now that different forms of relations making up 'associations' and 'networks' can be noted and documented.

In all we have said, we give most emphasis to links between the social and the political. What gives sociological work its body, as we have indicated, is this turning and returning to our 'political roots'. Belonging, and even identity, for sociologists do not necessarily arise from sharing theory; or even from sharing methodologies, important as these aspects may be for developing research programmes. There is also a commitment within sociology, sometimes unsaid, to developing a *moral* sensibility. What can also create feelings of membership and collectivity, is holding to a critical view that nothing is quite what it seems; and that, if we want to pursue questions such as 'Who benefits?', we surely also have to ask more about the political roots out of which issues entangle themselves and potential conflict grows.

References

Agamben, G., (1998), *Homo Sacer: Sovereign Power and Bare Life*, Stanford, CA: Stanford University Press.

Barnes, B., (1974), *Scientific Knowledge and Sociological Theory*, London: Routledge & Kegan Paul.

Barnes, B., (1998), *The Nature of Power*, Cambridge: Polity Press.

Barthes, R., (1967), *Writing Degree Zero*, trans. Lavers, A. and C. Smith, London: Cape.

Bauman, Z., (1989), *Modernity and the Holocaust*, Cambridge: Polity Press.

Becker, H., B. Geer, E.C. Hughes and A. Strauss, (1961), *Boys in White: Student Culture in Medical School*, Chicago: University of Chicago Press.

Bell, C. and H. Newby, (1971), *Community Studies*, London: Unwin.

Berger, P. and T. Luckmann, (1967), *The Social Construction of Reality: A Treatise in the Sociology of Knowledge*, Harmondsworth: Penguin.

Bittner, E., (1970), The Concept of Organization, in Salaman, G. and K. Thomson, (eds), *People and Organizations*, London: Longman.

Bloor, D., (1976), *Knowledge and Social Imagery*, London: Routledge.

Brubaker, R. and F. Cooper, (2000), 'Beyond "identity"', *Theory and Society*, 29: 1–47.

Callon, M., (1986), 'Some elements of a sociology of translation: domestication of the scallops and the fishermen of St Brieuc Bay', in Law, J., (ed.), *A Sociology of Monsters: essays on power, technology and domination*, Sociological Review Monograph, London: Routledge.

Callon, M., (1998), *The Laws of the Markets.*, Sociological Review Monograph, Oxford: Blackwell.

Canetti, E., (1962), *Crowds and Power*, London: Gollancz.

Clarke, J. and J. Newman, (1997), *The Managerial State*, London: Sage.

Cohen, A., (ed.), (1982), *Belonging: Identity and Social Organization in British Rural Cultures*, Manchester: Manchester University Press.

Cohen, A., (1985), *The Symbolic Construction of Community*, London: Tavistock.

Cohen, A., (1987), *Whalsay: Symbol, segment and boundary in a Shetland Island community*, Manchester: Manchester University Press.

Collins, R. and R. Munro, (2010), Exploring the sociological re-imagining of politics: a conversation, *The Sociological Review*, 58 (4): 548–562.

Crossley, N., (2002), *Making Sense of Social Movements*, Buckingham: Open University Press.

Dalton, M., (1959), *Men Who Manage*, New York: John Wiley & Son.

de Saussure, F., (1983), *Course in General Linguistics*, trans. Harris, R., London: Duckworth.

Derrida, J., (1982), *Margins of Philosophy*, trans. Bass, A. Hemel Hempstead: Harvester Wheatsheaf.

Derrida, J., (2000), *Of Hospitality*, Stanford, CA: Stanford University Press.

Edgell, S., K. Hetherington and A. Warde, (eds), (1996), *Consumption Matters, Sociological Review Monograph*. Oxford: Blackwell.

Foucault, M., (1970), *The Order of Things: An Archaeology of the Human Sciences*, trans. Sheridan Smith, A., London: Tavistock.

Foucault, M., (1973), *The Birth of the Clinic*, trans. Sheridan Smith, A., London; Tavistock.

Foucault, M., (1991), Governmentality, trans. Rosi Braidotti and revised by Colin Gordon. In G. Burchell, C. Gordon and P. Miller (eds), *The Foucault Effect: Studies in Governmentality*: 87–104, Chicage, IL: University of Chicago Press.

Frankenberg, R., (1966), *Communities in Britain*, Harmondsworth: Penguin.

Fuller, S., (2006) Intelligent Design Theory: a site for contemporary sociology of knowledge, *Canadian Journal of Sociology*, 31: 277–89.

Garfinkel, H., (1967), *Studies in Ethnomethodology*, Englewood Cliffs, NJ: Prentice Hall.

Geertz, C., (1973), *Interpretation of Cultures*, New York: Basic Books.

Giddens, A., (1968), 'Power' in the recent writings of Talcott Parsons', *Sociology*, 2 (2): 257–272.

Giddens, A., (1984), *The Constitution of Society*, Cambridge: Polity.

Goffman, E., (1959), *The Presentation of Self in Everyday Life*, New York: Doubleday.

Goffman, E., (1961), *Asylums: Essays on the Social Situation of Mental Patients and Other Inmates*, New York, Doubleday.

Goffman, E., (1964), The Neglected Situation, *American Anthropologist*, New Series, 66 (6): 133–36.

Gouldner, A., (1955), The Three Patterns of Bureaucracy, Chapter XII in *Patterns of Industrial Bureaucracy*, London: Routledge, Kegan & Paul.

Heidegger, M., (1962), *Being and Time*, translated by Macquarrie, J. and E. Robinson. Oxford: Basil Blackwell.

Hoskin, K., (1996), 'The Awful Idea of Accountability: inscribing people into the measurement of objects', in Munro, R. and J. Mouritsen, (eds), *Accountability: Power, Ethos and the Technologies of Managing*, London: Thompson International Press.

Jeffery, R., (1979), 'Normal rubbish: deviant patients in casualty departments', *Sociology of Health & Illness*, 1 (1): 90–107.

Joerges, B., (1988), Technology in Everyday Life: conceptual queries. *Journal for the Theory of Social Behaviour*, 18 (2): 219–37.

Jones, C. and R. Munro, (eds), (1996), *Contemporary Organisation Theory, Sociological Review Monograph*. Oxford: Blackwell.

Jones, C. and R. Munro, (2006), (eds), *Contemporary Organization Theory*, Oxford: Wiley-Blackwell.

Kilminster, R., (2011), 'A review of Gerald Delanty's', *The Cosmopolitan Imagination: The Renewal of Critical Social Theory The Sociological Review*, 59 (1).

Knights, D. and G. Morgan, (1991), 'Corporate strategy, organizations and subjectivity: a critique', *Organization Studies*, 12: 251–73.

Kuhn, T.S., (1970), *The Structure of Scientific Revolutions*, 2nd edn. Chicago, Il: University of Chicago Press.

Latour, B., (1987), *Science in Action: how to follow scientists and engineers through society*, Milton Keynes: Open University Press.

Latour, B. and S. Woolgar, (1979), *Laboratory Life: the social construction of scientific facts*, London: Sage.

Latimer, J. and R. Munro, (2006), 'Driving the Social', in Bohm, S., C. Jones, C. Land and M. Patterson, (eds), *Against Automobility*, Sociological Review Monograph. Oxford: Blackwell.

Lee, N. and R. Munro, (eds), (2001), *The Consumption of Mass*, Sociological Review Monograph, Oxford: Blackwell.

Luhmann, N., (1982), *The Differentiation of Society*, trans. Holmes, S. and C. Larmore. New York: Columbia University Press.

Lyotard, J-F., (1984), *The Postmodern Condition: A Report on Knowledge,* trans. Bennington, G. and B. Massumi, Minneapolis: Minnesota Press.

Mann, M., (1986), *The Sources of Social Power: A History of Power From the Beginning to A.D. 1760* (Vol. 1), New York: Cambridge University Press.

Michels, R., (1915), *Political Parties: A Sociological Study of the Oligarchical Tendencies of Modern Democracy*, trans. Paul, E. and C. Paul, New York: Free Press.

Mills, C.W., (1956), *The Power Elite*, Oxford: Oxford University Press.

Mills, C.W., (1964), *The Power Elite*, Oxford: Oxford University Press.

Munro, R., (1996), The Consumption View of Self, in Edgell, S., K. Hetherington and A. Warde, (eds), (1996), *Consumption Motters, Sociological Review* Monograph. Oxford: Blackwell.

Munro, R., (1998), 'Belonging on the Move: market rhetoric and the future as obligatory passage', *The Sociological Review*, 46 (2): 208–43.

Munro, R., (1999), 'Power and Discretion: Membership work in the time of technology', *Organization*, 6, 3: 429–50.

Munro, R., (2001), 'Calling for Accounts: numbers, monsters and membership', *The Sociological Review*, 46, 4: 473–93.

Munro, R., (2004a), 'Punctualizing identity: time and the demanding relation', *Sociology*, 38 (2): 293–311.

Munro, R., (2004b), 'The remains of the say: zero, double-crossing and the landscaping of language', *Journal for Cultural Research*, 8, 2: 183–200.

Munro, R. and O. Belova, (2008), 'Body in Time: Affect and the "interruption" of narrative', in Latimer, J. and M. Schillmeier, (eds), *Un/knowing Bodies*, Sociological Review Monograph, Oxford: Wiley-Blackwell: 87–99.

Rabinow, P., (1996), *Making PCR: A Story of Biotechnology*, Chicago: University of Chicago Press.

Runciman, W.G., (2008), 'Forgetting the Founders', *The Sociological Review*, 56 (3): 358–69.

Saussure, F. de, (1983), *Course in General Linguistics*, trans. Harris, R., Ch. Bally and A. Sechehaye (eds), La Salle, IL: Open Court.

Savage, M., G. Bagnall and B. Longhurst, (2005), *Globalization and Belonging*, London: Sage.

Schmitt, C., (1996), *The Concept of the Political*, Chicago: University of Chicago Press.

Schutz, A., (1967), *The Phenomenology of the Social World*, Evanston, Il: Northwestern University Press.

Shilling, C. and P.A. Mellor, (2011), 'Retheorising Emile Durkheim on society and religion: embodiment, intonication and collective life,' *The Sociological Review*, 59 (1): 17–42.

Simmel, G., (1972), *On Individuality and Social Forms*, edited (with an introduction) by Levine, D., Chicago: University of Chicago Press.

Skeggs, B., (2004), *Class, Self, Culture*, London: Routledge.

Smelser, N.J., (1962), *Theory of Collective Behavior*, New York: Free Press.

Spencer, L. and R. Pahl, (2006), *Re-Thinking Friendship: Hidden Solidarities Today*, Princeton: Princeton University Press.

Strathern, M., (1991), *Partial Connections*, Maryland: Rowman & Little.

Strathern, M., (1995), *The Relation: Issues in Complexity and Scale*, Cambridge: Prickly Pear Pamphlet No. 6.

Suchman, L., (2007), *Human-Machine Reconfigurations: Plans and Situated Actions (2nd edition)*, Cambridge University Press.

Tarrow, S., (1998), *Power in Movement: Social Movements and Contentious Politics*, Cambridge: Cambridge University Press.

Taussig, M., (1993), *Mimesis and Alterity: a particular history of the senses*. New York: Routledge.

Thrift, N., (2004), 'Intensities of feeling: towards a spatial politics of affect', *Geografiska Annaler*, 86 B(1): 57–8.

Thrift, N., (2005), 'The Place of Complexity', in *Knowing Capitalism*, London: Sage: 51–74.

Tilly, C., (2004), *Social Movements, 1768–2004*, Boulder, Colorado, USA: Paradigm Publishers.

Turner, B.S., (2007), 'The Enclave Society: towards a theory of immobility', *European Journal of Social Theory*, 10 (2): 287–303.

Wacquant, L., (1987), 'Reviewed work(s): *The Ethnomethodologists* by Wes Sharrock and Bob Anderson', *Acta Sociologica*, 30 (1): 111–14.

Whyte, W.F., (1949), *Street Corner Society: Social Structure of an Italian Slum*, Chicago: University of Chicago Press.

Willis, P., (1990), *Common Culture*, Milton Keynes: Open University Press.

Part 1
Borders

The Danube and ways of imagining Europe

Michael Schillmeier and Wiebke Pohler[1]

Abstract: This paper is concerned with the River Danube as a European object that articulates forms of relations which, by linking human and non-humans in highly specific ways, create actor-networks that dispute common societal divisions and (b)orders. By discussing the *contested social relevance* of the River Danube, this paper visualizes different ways of imagining Europe. Following some of the controversies concerning the River Danube, we outline a process oriented, transnational research agenda for a specific European object with the conceptual explication of human and non-human relations at its core.

Researching natures/cultures

In recent years the process of *Europeanization* has become the topic of numerous publications and discussions, especially in social sciences (see eg Beck and Grande, 2007; Delanty and Rumford, 2005; Delanty, 2006; Kramsch and Hooper, 2004; Graziano and Vink, 2008). Like globalization, Europeanization is thought to question and alter the borders of social relations, offering new forms of social frameworks that transgress and/or reconfigure traditional structures of societal action. It is argued that current European social change significantly disputes the concept of a 'national container' (Beck and Grande, 2007) as the primary agent of social change. Rather, new social, cultural, political or economic relations occur that reach far beyond national configurations. Europeanization, then, calls attention to alternative dynamics of de- and re(b)ordering practices that reassemble traditional (b)orders of Europe (Albrow, 1996; Deger and Hettlage, 2007; Delanty and Rumford, 2005; Delanty, 2006; Eder, 2006; Rumford, 2006). Europeanization links cultural, political, and economic issues that are locally, regionally and nationally highly specific with global concerns that cannot be grasped with a merely territorial focus. In effect, new *(b)ordering actors* appear, unravelling, disputing and configuring local, regional, national, transnational and global programmes of action as a mode of doing and imaging Europe (among others the European Union, European enterprises, the European Monetary Union, the European Science Community, European Media

Companies, NGOs, single issue movements etc.). This process of challenging and reconfiguring the existing political, social, cultural and economic spaces that transgress local, national *and* European coordinates, we like to call cosmo-politics (compare Schillmeier, 2008).

Cosmo-politics

By analysing the cosmo-politics of the Danube, we try to shift the focus of contemporary European studies, which predominantly understand Europeani-zation as the process of inter-cultural relations or as conflicts of *symbolic* (b)orderings and not as a conflict between 'naturally' given territories and differences. This concentration on 'culture' and 'the symbolic' is very much part of a central Europe idea that differentiates between non-human objects and how they are observed by humans. This difference describes the very European idea of bifurcating 'nature' and 'culture' into two separate realities and becomes constitutive for the self-image of European Modernity and its institutional arrangements. It includes the differentiation between 'hard' and 'soft' sciences. This is why social sciences focus primarily on the symbolic and socio-cultural construction of nature and not on 'nature' itself. Following theories of social change, the process of Europeanization is part of modernization as a complete culturalization of nature with all its well-known positive and negative side effects. Most interestingly, however, it is precisely the effects of a 'successful' bifurcation of nature that is currently questioning the very European imagine of social change. This is evident in current discussions on global climate change, practices of and debates on genetic/reproductive technologies, in scientific and bio-philosophical questions of everyday life, in discourses on the body, in medical practices, in disability studies and gender discourse (Law and Mol, 2004; Latimer and Schillmeier, 2009; Mol, 2003; Schillmeier, 2007a,b; Schillmeier and Pohler, 2006). All these discourses constantly configure and recon-figure the (b)orders of the relations of nature and culture and highlight the questionability of the modern imagination that was meant to create a clear, distinctive division between 'nature' and 'culture'. Hence, a European research agenda must concentrate not only on the social and symbolic construction of transnational de- and re-(b)orderings but also on the contestation of nature/culture relations that highlight social change (Latour, 1993, 2004a, 2005a; Schillmeier, 2008, 2009).

As we show, the River Danube is an excellent object for sociological research on re-imaging Europe and Europeanization as it addresses the social issues that contest common exclusive forms of territorial (eg local vs. national vs. global) and conceptual (nature vs. culture) (b)orderings. The controversies concerning the River Danube embody precisely the cosmo-political dimension of imagining and doing Europe by a) enacting trans-local, transnational dynamics, and by b) visualizing the contested relations that dispute a clear *a priori* difference between nature and culture. To draw upon changing nature/culture relations not only questions the 'bifurcation of nature' (Whitehead, 2000 [1920]: ch.2) by

European thought but also brings highly unusual objects of concern onto the sociological agenda. Objects that have been commonly seen as part of nature, like rivers, flora and fauna, global warming, etc. become main actors in the ways of re-imagining Europe. It is the flow of a European river like the Danube that re-imagines Europe and Europeanization as a 'fluid space' (Bauman, 2000) enacting multiple, heterogeneous and highly disputed spaces of natures/cultures (Latour, 2005a & b).

Actor-networks

In the following we offer a brief sketch into the relations which emerge from the very natures/cultures of the River Danube by using the concept of the 'actor-network' (see Callon, 1986, 1998; Latour, 2005a; Law and Callon, 2004; Law and Hassard, 1999; Schillmeier, 2007a,b, 2008, 2009; Schillmeier and Pohler, 2006). Actor-networks try to highlight that entities can be reduced neither to the relationships of fixed spatial scales (local, national, global), nor to the relationship of given and enduring substances – cultural and natural alike. Rather, by relating different entities (human and non-human), actors and scales, relationships come into being and the entities associated may change as well. Actor-networks gain societal relevance whenever they generate and stabilize, or question and alter, societal modes of (b)ordering – human and non-human alike. This means that what we understand as 'culture', 'society' or 'nature' is an effect of contingent relations of human and non-human relations and cannot be explained away by 'culture', 'society' or 'nature" as realities on their own. The Danube never becomes socially relevant as an exclusive form of pure and unaffected 'nature', nor as a 'culture' solely produced by humans. Rather, it is always and at the same time a cultural *and* a natural object. Neither does the river's nature exist outside of societal reach, nor can we imagine the cultural meaning of the River Danube without its non-human configurations.

Thus, natures/cultures of the Danube cannot be explained (away) by the social realm; but the social (b)orderings remain to be explained instead by the very contested natures/cultures. The social (b)orderings become either stabilized or *cosmo-politicized*, that is disrupted, questioned and altered, by the emerging natures/cultures. Accordingly, the actor-networks of the Danube make up plural spaces by which the river appears at the same time as a rigid border, such as a national demarcation-line, and as a de- and re(b)ordering actor offering transnational scopes of action. No *a priori* judgements can be made about what the social meaning of the river is, but it is up to the concrete actor-networks that manufacture the societal, cultural and symbolic relevance of the river. Thus the Danube's realities frequently change and multiply: being an unbending natural border, performing the connecting line between East and West, exemplifying the cultural line of separation of political bulkheads, as well as functioning as a symbol of a unified 'green corridor' of an economically vital and sustainable Europe.

Hence, to explain nature by culture or culture by nature is an effect of changing actor-networks and not a fixed explanatory power given by society, culture or nature. With this in mind, the concept of the 'actor-network' is methodologically most instructive for re-imagining Europe, precisely because it undermines the heredity of a most successful European thought: the bifurcation of nature. As an actor-network the bifurcation of nature is questioned, becomes controversial. Following the flow of the River Danube we are able to name some of these controversies. Additionally, the natures/cultures of the river multiplies possible actors and questions the actor-status itself. An endangered animal or flower can become a significant actor that equivalently plots political pressure and unravels specific forms of action. The political controversies over the natures/cultures of the River Danube involve *human and non-human* actors (Callon, 1986). It is precisely the controversies concerning the Danube that will bring to the fore the relevant actor-networks that make up processes of Europeanization.

The River Danube, conceptualized as controversial actor-networks, offers the possibility of imagining Europe beyond what Ulrich Beck calls the 'methodological nationalism' of sociological thought. In essence, the concept actor-network and the flow of the River Danube suggest a methodology of *societies in the making*, ie a fluid or processual methodology of social issues that refer to the controversies of social change. Moreover, these controversies make visible what we have called elsewhere 'cosmo-political events' (Schillmeier and Pohler, 2006; Schillmeier, 2008; Pohler, 2010). Cosmo-political events challenge the given b(orderings) of social practices and the way they are conceived by (social) scientists. With a river, floods may turn into a cosmo-political event, as we have seen in Pakistan most recently. Floods endanger human and non-human life, and disrupt social, political, economic and cultural organization etc.; at the same time, cosmo-political events make us re-imagine social natures/cultures.

The river multiple

Closely linking the human and non-human, the River Danube reveals a tremendously rich history of European social change (Fussenegger, 1983; Magris, 1988; Maier, 2001; Mészáros, 2006; Morath, 1995; Moser, 1991; Weithmann, 2000). Today the Danube – Europe's second longest river – connects ten nation states and serves as a food and drinking-water resource, an important energy resource, a major European line of transport, an object of tourism and recreation, and a habitat for human and non-human life. Thus, the *natures* of the River Danube make up a European object of *cultures* and *vice versa*. In that sense the natures/cultures of the River Danube create *collectives of experience*, which cannot be understood adequately as emerging from within fixed territorial spaces (such as nation states). Rather, they become visible by the common experience of transnational relations and the heterogeneous processes of natures/cultures enacted by the *flow of the river*.

Geopolitically, the Danube can be described as an object of bordering and un-bordering practices. For approximately 40 per cent of its length, the Danube embodies nation-state borders. Croatia, Bulgaria, Moldavia and the Ukraine only have access to one bank of the river. At the same time, however, the Danube as a shared life-source criss-crosses the nation-states and demands the neighbouring states' interaction for transnational dealings, responsibilities and coordination up and down the stream. Hence, the Danube delimits political competencies just as much as it demands transnational forms of political action.

Considering the dramatic ecological problems of the River Danube,[2] *shifts of institutional and national borders* can be observed, too. The river's European range relates and transforms regional into national and transnational competencies and responsibilities and *vice versa*. The WWF (World Wide Fund for Nature) project at the Danube Delta is just one of many examples for this. Due to its ecological variety (biodiversity), the Danube Delta is important to transnational actors like WWF or UNESCO (United Nations Educational, Scientific and Cultural Organization) since the Delta region is considered a 'world heritage of culture and nature'. Accordingly, the economically driven European Action Programme for the Promotion of Inland Waterway Transport (NAIADES) reads like a green pamphlet. WWF and UNESCO, however, still depend on the national governments of Romania, Bulgaria, Moldavia and the Ukraine to accomplish their ecological attempts to maintain the river's bio-diversity. These national institutions, again, have influence on more local levels, as fields, pastureland and fish farms have to be converted back into natural floodplains.

Obviously, local practice gains importance, since it no longer exclusively refers to local-level decisions and practices but is reconfigured and shaped by its enmeshment with trans-local responsibilities, interests and programmes of action. Here, the localities of the natures/cultures of the River Danube are directly linked to and responsible for the Danube being a 'world heritage' site; local institutions and associations of the river's natures/cultures (national politics, local citizens' groups, communal authorities) and global/translocal policy-making institutions (international environmental organizations, the European Community) are all interwoven. These direct links between local and global concerns enact new 'extitutional' (Serres, 2005; Schillmeier, 2009) European actors, like the transnational network 'Danube Environmental Forum' (DEF), which cut across traditional and institutionalized forms of action. This transnational platform of European citizens and politically independent non-profit-organizations from the Danube countries goes beyond trying to gain direct influence over local, national and international policies. For that reason the traditional fields of politics (state governments, local governments, ministries) are pluralized, involving non-governmental organizations (WWF, DEF, the German 'Bund Naturschutz') which all raise their specific voices within those multiple and highly contested disputes.

The specific effects of the River Danube's natures/cultures raise *public attention*, which brings about an increase in the sub- and supranational influence of non-governmental organizations and public alliances that give highly different entities – human and non-human – a voice. Many of these *public ecologies* contest the established dominance of national politics and propose new forms that not only undermine national framings but directly link local with global concerns, human with non-human concerns, and political with cultural, economical, scientific, aesthetic and ecological concerns.

In this process, the difference between *experts* and *laymen* becomes doubtful, too (see Nowotny, Scott and Gibbons, 2001). Experts (eg on the environmental compatibility of dam-constructions) no longer exclusively ask for governmental institutions to affirm their decision-making but can also be called in to strengthen non-governmental counter-arguments. Subsequently, singular and clear estimations and shared evaluations on matters of concern about the river become multiplied and question any one-sided attitude proposing a 'single nature' of the concerning issues. The debates on the river's ecology produce highly 'politicized' public controversies that reflect the heterogeneous conceptions, interests and requirements that occur and magnify along and around the flow of the natures/cultures of the Danube.

These 'assemblages' (Latour, 2005a) also undermine the distinction between *private* and *public* spheres. As there are not only governmental ministries that make decisions affecting the river's landscapes but also numerous pressure groups (eg the working groups for the protection of the Wachau,[3] or several protests against former cultivations of the river's course), the river represents not only a *public* resource (eg for the production of energy or to transport goods) but also the *private* sphere of its abutters.

River controversies

In the following, we discuss three different controversies, i.e. 'matters of concern' (Latour, 2005a), that allow us to start with a systematic research into the emerging actor-networks of the Danube and the related cosmo-politics of natures/cultures: floods, renaturation projects, and the disputes about the Danube Delta. These concerns bring to the fore not only the multiplicity of the River Danube as a political object which questions social (b)orderings, but also the way these different controversies articulate multiple, contested futures of the Danube. To address these relations we endorse a process-oriented[4] and multi-sited approach.[5]

Floods

The history of the River Danube has always been connected with floods and people living on its banks have always faced the risk of flooding. The WWF counts more than 20 floodings in the years 2000 to 2006 along the course of the river. Despite all efforts to prevent or reduce floods by installing dams and banks, the frequency and scales of floods have increased demonstrably in the last decades. Environmental activists and organizations associate contemporary floods with the lack of alluvial soils along the course of the river. In case of a possible flood castastrophe alluvial soil could be flooded to reduce the water level as well as the stream velocity. The progressive cultivation of the riverbanks, the increased installation of barrages and storage reservoirs, and river regulations, prevent a natural stream course following self-contained directions. Even in areas where water protection measures are already installed, the risk of floods has only been relocated to other areas, up- or downstream. If the river is dammed up, the water is concentrated upstream and menaces regions against the streaming of the river; if the river is regulated and the stream course is narrowed, regions downstream are affected with possible flooding.

This shows very strikingly that the 'global' sustainability of a river system like the Danube is a matter of constant fabrication, synchronization and execution of local natures/cultures. Still, for an adequate description, the significance of the dimension of changing natures/cultures is not confined to what seem to be merely local practices. These practices are very much enacted by dynamics that 'overflow' territorial localness: they are incxtricably enmeshed with trans-local practices and consequences that refer to regional cultures, knowledge and practices, national policies and institutional settings, as well as the effects of and on global processes and structures e.g. climate change.

Floods on the River Danube make national borders highly irrelevant. Floods can be characterized by their fluid spatial effects (Law and Mol, 2001), which ignore the socio-cultural importance of local, regional or national borders. Translocal and transnational cooperation are necessary, not only for flood control measures and flood protection. For these reasons the EU parliament calls for the foundation of an international flood-risk-management scheme, to address the risk of transnational floods. Following the course of the river, a variety of probable causes for floods appear: the 'flood of the century' in Rumania in 2002, for instance, was associated with the melting of the ice on the lower course of the river. The reasons for the flood damage in Bavaria (Germany) in 1999 were seen in the precipitation, which lasted for weeks. But the negative consequences of floods do not disappear with the decrease of the water levels. Significant socio-political tension and conflicts result from such catastrophes. Definitions of causes for floods are publicly demanded, whereas scientific expertise provides only one possible explanation among others, particularly because neither scientific prognoses nor scientific control measures have been able to prevent floods so far. Thus, it is essential:

- to describe the River Danube as a European and cosmo-political object transforming and transformed by *local, regional, national and global relations of natures/cultures.*
- to select, reconstruct and analyse empirically significant examples of *natures/cultures relations* that affect floods.
- to reconstruct and analyse the *key actor-networks* involved and to investigate their specific sets of practice.
- to construct *processes and practices of transnational crisis intervention.*

The main research questions of such an agenda will have to address a) the problems and chances of transnational risk management, b) the political impact and controversies of floods and possible political pragmatics (and their limits) for future flood protection, and c) the different local, national and transnational areas of conflicts that emerge from the public discussion of flood prevention.

In effect, such an agenda has to be future-oriented, inasmuch as it turns attention towards sustainable and transnational organized measures of flood prevention ('sensitive programmes' of environmental protection, eg the re-creation of natural alluvial soils). This includes the focus on *transnational collectives of experience*. The Danube collectives of natures/cultures make up *risk communities* facing the ambiguous realities of the River Danube – providing a common *chance* of European solidarity but also representing a global threatening *risk*. These collective experiences gain importance inasmuch as they transect local or national borders, loyalties, solidarities, belongings and responsibilities. This a) results in the merging of natures/cultures, and b) turns into alternative scopes and programmes for action that have a multi-scaled outlook of cooperation and networking. In general this means a thorough analysis of *public discourses* and associated regulatory procedures affected by the problems of floods. Of special interest are the construction, use and challenge of scientific facts by relevant actors and participants in such public discourse. Moreover, the cosmopolitics of the River Danube allows attention to be drawn to conflict situations, resulting in possible changes from functional, differentiated and disciplinary arranged argumentations to transdisciplinary forms of practice. The controversies concerning the EU NAIADES (European Action Programme for the Promotion of Inland Waterway Transport) action programme launched in 2006 as part of the TEN-T (TransEuropeanNetworks-Transport) initiative of the EU to produce 'Europe's green economy' (INE, 2009a, 2009b) would be an excellent area to visualize the controversies between local, regional, national, European and global perspectives, needs and interests. NAIADES is planning to build a 'transmodal' traffic-network reaching from the UK to the Black Sea; it is meant to be based on the 'green corridors' of waterways, in which the River Danube should play an important role. Waterways, from a greenish Euro-liberal stance, are promoted as a way of 'working with nature' to construct transport systems on and with 'smart rivers' with the aim of reducing the 'congestion, pollution, greenhouse gas emission,[6] danger, noise' (INE, 2009a) etc. that haunt contemporary societies depending predominantly on roads for lorries and cars. To analyse these controversies it is necessary to review knowledge of transdisciplinary *scientific* and *non-scientific* kinds, in order systematically to name the different rationalities involved. It also allows for special attention to be paid to the local experience and knowledge of the people living along the banks of the River Danube, knowledge that may challenge the national and European semantics, perspectives and interests.

Floods change the lives of the people who are affected by flooding; they influence or even destroy their existence. This means paying attention to the ways the river is discussed and perceived by the affected people and the values the river implies for their *everyday lives*, before and after a flooding has occurred, and especially how a flood experience has changed people's relation to the river itself. Obviously, it is of the utmost importance to focus on the different local practices and measures that are seen as best practices to prevent floods in the future. As already noted, these local measures may be challenged by – or are challenging – national actors, like the Austrian *viadona*, and transnational actors like the EU government. This hints at the cosmo-political impact of floods, which forms communities of people who share (conflicting or consensual) experiences of flooding. Hence, it is important to analyse the mediation between local and transnational scopes of and the responses to such experiences and how these different perspectives and their mediation illuminate and influence the different areas of conflicts. Tracing the Danube networks also includes working out a historical reconstruction of River Danube floods in order to extrapolate the different historical specificities of dealing with floods and how these practices have changed over the centuries. This offers the possibility of describing the relevant historical transformations of nature/culture-relations and enables us to carve out sedimented, ie *strong or robust*, knowledge that proves to be valid in coping with floods over time; or it may question the possibility that any such robust forms of knowledge exist.

Renaturation

The ecological problems of the River Danube are *fluid* ones, much as national borders are no boundaries for ecological catastrophes. The disastrous toxic accident in Baia Mare, Rumania, in 2002 illustrates dramatically the fluidity of such ecological dangers (Baia Mare Task Force, 2000). The breached levee of a storage reservoir generated a toxic wave, which contaminated small rivers, which discharged into the River Danube. As a result more than 1000 kilometres of the River Danube were contaminated. Not only are ecological catastrophes characterized as transnational phenomena, so are practices of environmental protection. Transnational actors like the WWF, UNESCO or the EU, viadonau and the International Commission for the Protection of the River Danube (ICPDR), the Danube Commission etc., are key actors in the protection of the Danube areas. Protection of these areas also means protection of a global ecosystem. In addition to their local manifestation, measures of renaturation always have a global dimension. Accordingly, the aims of re-imagining European research agendas are to analyse measures of renaturation, considering the coordinative relation of local and global conditions, and to describe the European and cosmo-political dimension of the ecological problems of the River Danube. In addition, this means emphasizing the impact of transnational ecological relations, which underline the need for measures of renaturation and how the effectiveness and sustainability of these practices notably transcend local and national interests but nevertheless influence them. It would necessitate investigating the formation and the practices of transnational environmental organizations enacted by the changing nature/culture-relations of the River Danube. Consequently, it demands the specification of the heterogeneous (human and non-human) actors regarding their political agency of cosmo-politicizing social (b)orderings. Obviously it is important, then, to evaluate systematically the spatial and material dimensions of measures of renaturation on the River Danube. Ecological problems no longer refer to a lack of knowledge or inevitable dangers but to the consequences of emerging multiple and heterogeneous actor-networks and their possible (often contradictory) agency. These networks involve different actors (navigation organizations, water and navigation administration, water management administrations, environmental agencies, citizen's initiatives and conservationists, endangered species, etc.) with different conceptions and interests concerning the 'nature of things' and their demands (Eden, Tunstall and Tapsell, 2000). Conflict-ridden discussions and discourse coalitions appear from these heterogeneous networks. Within these transdisciplinary networks, water frame directives and regional planning procedures are as important as the desire to protect a unique habitat and recreation area. Singular explanations and causations are no longer possible regarding the heterogeneity of such networks. These processes generate complex ways of forming transdisciplinary knowledge, which a) transcend the disciplinary boundaries between natural science and social science, b) intersect private and public spheres and c) blur the difference between expert and non-expert knowledge. Such a research agenda would have to exemplify systematically the specific strategies, processes and dynamics *of knowledge accumulation* on the basis of selected examples of renaturation measures, and would have to specify the different and often conflicting and contradictory actor-networks created by renaturation measures and their specific modes of operation.

The socio-cultural relevancies of the course of the river, as well as its ecological conditions, have changed significantly over the centuries. The historical importance of the river was given predominantly by its west-to-east direction through the Jurassic rocks. In modern times massive human interventions in the course of the river, especially for industrial use, had changed the characteristics of the river substantially. The River Danube is the result of processes of modernization, intended to increase economic outcomes (e.g. by cultivating areas for agricultural purposes, by improving navigation or by using the river for power supply more effectively). We have to be sensitive to the processes through which the consequences of modernization become societally relevant (e.g. through the problems of floods and endangered species), as non-intended side effects of the natures/cultures enacted by processes of modernization (e.g. Beck, 1992). These dynamics are more than important since their effects are undermining institutional standards and practices, as well as the economic interests that originally created these problems. They lead to conflicting publics which are redefining areas of decision-making, and related key actors (EU, WWF, UNESCO, NGOs, local and regional organizations) which put the European dimension of the nature/culture-relations of the River Danube in practice. It also brings to the fore how citizens' initiatives occur (e.g. the campaign against the regulation of the last natural river course between German towns of Straubing and Vilshofen, initiated by the 'Bund Naturschutz' a Bavarian Nature Conservancy Alliance). These initiatives draw attention to the urgency of measures of renaturation and their immediate political impact as an effect of specific conflicting nature/culture-relations. Again, measures of renaturation indicate a cosmo-political dimension of these practices and directly (re-)link human and non-human actors, local, regional, national, European and global dimensions. The historical specificities, continuities as well as discontinuities, about river regulation are important, as well as the specific nature/culture-relations that affect these measures.

Modernization predominantly meant cultivation of the river against the nature of the flow of the river. The negative effects of this cultivation (e.g. floods, endangered species) demand a change of the modern industrialized and exclusively human interest in looking at the nature/culture-relations of the Danube. Measures of renaturation can be read as cosmo-political practices that try to alter these specific one-sided nature/culture-relations. They try to give back the 'non-human' or 'nature' their own voice in order to create spaces of lived heterogeneity. It is more than important to specify these lived heterogeneities systematically. Obviously, this makes the cooperation with biologists, ecologists, and landscape conservationists among others necessary in order to gain adequate descriptions and counter-descriptions of the highly industrialized nature/culture-relations. This allows us to link old and new perspectives of river regulation measures to be studied in relation to both historical and present data and references.

The Danube Delta

Between and within the countries of Rumania, Moldavia and Ukraine, the River Danube expands to the Delta area, covering more than 5000 square kilometres, until it flows into the Black Sea. It still represents a *terra incognita* of and for European studies. About 15,000 multi-ethnic people live in this area. For these people the River Danube is a lifeline. It is also the habitat of a unique variety of rare animal and plant species, so much so that UNESCO declared this area one of its World Heritage Sites and large areas of the Danube Delta became a biosphere reserve. In the year 2000 Rumania, Bulgaria, Moldavia and Ukraine finally agreed on implementing measures of renaturation and on conserving the lower stretches of the river (more than 1000 km). The protection of this habitat can be described as the biggest European, transnational, border-crossing environmental programme. Thus it is more than important to analyse the specific nature/culture configurations of the Danube Delta and how they unravel trans-border matters of concern. Again, it is essential to follow the relations between local, national and transnational actors, interests and modes of operations and how the measures of renaturation contribute to processes of European cosmo-politics.

The disastrous environmental, economic and social conditions of the Delta region resulted mainly from particular national interests. The political era of Ceausescu had particular negative effects on the Rumanian part of the Delta: the government's economic plan intended to transform the region into a unitary agricultural area. For instance, large areas of reed were uprooted (mostly by political prisoners) and were used for the production of cellulose, textiles, animal feed and pharmaceuticals. The West has heavily sponsored these industries. In effect, the uprooting of the reeds started a vicious circle that contemporary measures of renaturation have been dealing with since and that transcend local and national decision-making and responsibilities. Reeds need wetland to flourish; uprooting them destroyed the basis of the wetland's existence. Another result is that the former rather windless region is now dried up by heavy winds coming in from the coasts. The dry ground also accelerates the extinction of the reeds. This also means a lack of food for resident animals and fish, endangering animal hatcheries. With the breakdown of the political system, illegal fishing has been increasing in the Delta area, endangering another life resource especially important for numerous birds. Besides these ecological problems of the Delta, the Ukrainian government is working on the so-called 'Bystroye Canal' project, i.e. the construction of a canal along the Bystroye arm of the Danube to the Black Sea in order to boost the economy of the region. Environmental campaigns in Rumania, the EU and UNO criticize this project sharply, especially for its ecological menace to the unique species and habitats of the Delta, which is protected under the UNESCO Man and Biosphere Programme (see WWF 2009).

Hence, local, regional and national decision-making processes evoke – as *non-intended side effects* – delocalized political reaction. New key actors emerge, questioning and altering the traditional boundaries of the natures/cultures of the Delta. What can we learn from this? The uprooting of the reeds not only initiated environmental conflicts but also became part of a transnational political agenda. Actors of different species and on different levels – human and non-human, municipal, regional, national, transnational – are *mobilized* to make the Delta region multiply as publicly contested, i.e. politicized matters of concern. Accordingly, the nature/culture-relations of the River Danube ignite political conflicts, which generate political pressure on different levels and subsequently enact trans-disciplinary processes of political communication.

The ecological problems of the Delta region cannot be ascribed just to local misinterpretations and faults but are significantly associated with pollutants in the river. These pollutants multiply and reach the Delta in much higher concentration and the Delta region is enacted as Europe's ecological 'filter system' that has to deal with transnational environmental pollution. The very natures/cultures of Delta habitat do not depend only on Moldavian, Ukrainian or Rumanian institutions but also on decision-making in Germany, Austria, Slovakia and Hungary. The River Danube, transcending local and national environmental standards, enters a field of European decision-making incorporating ten nation-states. Thus an object-centred European project intends to reconstruct and analyse, systematically, the multiple actor-networks of human and non-human actors and how they generate processes of action beyond national and disciplinary boundaries. It describes the initiation of transnational political or judicial measures of regulation caused by the specificities of the nature/culture-problems of the Delta area. It has to focus on the influence and effects of these nature/culture-problems for the people living in this area, how they are affected, live with and (re-)create the Delta.

Methodological possibilities

In general, this paper proposed a 'multi-sited' approach not in order to verify some abstract hypotheses with our data but to generate a framework for cosmo-political data that is able to re-imagine processes of Europeanization. To do so, the conceptual and methodological openness of ethnography offers special methodological advantages for such a primarily process-orientated research project of objects. Obviously, the connecting and disconnecting flow of the River Danube is a challenging object of research. Our methodological guidelines are enacted by the very flowing natures/cultures of the River Danube itself. According to the methodological imperative of Actor-Network-Theory to 'follow the actors' (Latour, 2005a), such a research agenda retraces the societal relevance of the river in a trans-local way. In effect, a newly conceptualized multi-sited method involves methodological possibilities to acknowledge and 'tame' such an open, fluid, and boundary-questioning research object as the River Danube. The difficulties in handling the emergent nature/culture-relations of the River Danube concern the methodological control of 'local' and 'global' conditions that may change with the flow of the river. Such an empirical project is most difficult to operationalize, since one has to take into consideration that the controversies of river Danube stretch in time and space. This means, geo-politically, that ideally all actors of all the countries involved, as well as the concerned non-governmental organizations, should be part of such a European research project. Moreover it needs comparison in time as well, in order to address the processual dynamics. At the moment we are not able to draw on experiences of any such project. Thus the following methodological possibilities refer to what Thomas Kuhn called a 'thought experiment'. For our concerns it offers the possibilities of imagining ways a European object like the Danube may be understood beyond the bifurcation of nature.

With the help of trans-local or multi-sited ethnography (Falzon, 2009; Lauser, 2005) we are able to avoid methodologically the very ontological separation between 'the local' and 'the global'. Trans-local ethnography focuses on the local practices and how these diverse practices enact the specificities of spatial and temporal relations (Appadurai, 2001; Held and McGrew, 2007; Marcus, 1998, 2005). Accordingly, the global can no longer be investigated in abstraction from the local and *vica versa*. Rather it unfolds the very localization of the global as a set of highly complex practices of heterogeneous actors that in turn question the commonalities of the fixed local (Schillmeier and Pohler, 2006; Schlehe, 2005). The local and the global don't represent static and independent times and spaces but create heterogeneous time-spaces, enacted/ing (by) the multiplicity and complexities of emerging natures/cultures (compare with Bird, Curtis, Putnam and Robertson, 1996). With such a trans-local perspective, the selectivity of singular localities can be avoided, bringing to the fore the multiplicities of conflicting localities that transcend the local/global divide. To cope with these 'trans-scaling' realities we need – beyond mere case studies – to retrace the multiple existences of the Danube over space and time and to follow how these connections between different localities are achieved, maintained and/or altered. Hence, the River Danube is a very challenging litmus test for multi-sited ethnography, due to the enormous variety of actor-networks involved, which constantly changes with the flow of the river.

Dealing with the highly incalculable and fluid practices of the river's natures/ cultures, an object-centred methodological framework cannot exclusively contain linguistic methods that inevitably refer to forms of functional clarity and communicational strictness. In order to go with the flow of events we look out for methodological techniques that flexibly retrace the various courses of the networks' actors. Multi-sited video-ethnography offers the possibility of covering trans-local realities systematically, beyond the scope of linguistic limits (compare Ballhaus and Engelbrecht, 1995). In that sense we expect, from an object-centred research, the methodological improvement given by video-ethnography that associates the visual presences/realities of the flow of the Danube's natures/cultures. Its methodological constraints are seen rather in questions of visibility and its selective screenings but can be partly avoided by using more than one camera, making 'trans-local recordings'. In this way video-ethnography offers the chance of maintaining the methodological openness and process-related flexibility required by 'flowing objects' like the Danube. Video-ethnographic material may also create new data when presented to the different people affected/ing the issues and controversies concerning the Danube. Video-ethnographic material may address – quite differently from a written text or a mere discussion – the similarities and differences of experiences, affectedness and attachments, as well as the different histories, presences and related conflicts and solidarities etc. that may arise from a flowing object like the Danube.

Ethnography in general offers a research method which allows integrating different types of data of the field of research (Geertz, 1977; Kaschuba, 2003; Marcus, 1998, 2005; Poehls and Vonderau, 2007). It also brings social scientists close to the object of research and resonates very much with ANT's research strategy of 'following the actors'. This obviously requires a symmetrical approach in order to retrace the networks of human and non-human actors alike (Latour, 2005a,b). 'Focus groups' (Glense, 2005; Krueger, 1994; Litosseliti, 2004; Merton, Fiske and Kendall, 1990; Morgan, 1988; Morgan and Krueger, 1998; Stewart, Shamdasani and Rook, 2007) also open space for transnational, transdisciplinary and transformative actor-network constellations, which may include – as in our case – members of citizen alliances; representatives of tourism, merchant shipping and fishing; abutters; victims of flood disasters; governmental and non-governmental organizations like the nature conservancy alliance, the WWF, the Institute for the Danube region and Central Europe (IDM), the UNESCO, the Union of the Danube states (ARGE Donau), the Danube Environmental Forum (DEF), the Delta National Institute (DDNI) as well as the International Commission for the Protection of the River Danube (ICPDR) etc. These organizational agents generate and articulate experiences, interests, perspectives as well as different, often conflict-ridden, relevancies and characteristics of the Danube natures/cultures – human and non-human alike. They articulate the different relevancies and controversies concerning the nature/culture-relations of the River Danube and the heterogeneous actors involved. The methodological aim is to unravel how different 'perspectives' are translated into moments of consent or how they unfold dissent (Morgan, 1988).

Concluding comments

We presented an unusual object for social research, the River Danube, which appeared to be a highly complex 'flowing object' that drew our attention to the different politics of imagining Europe. Due to its trans(b)ordering dimensions, such politics of imagining Europe cannot be restricted either to territorial (e.g. national) spaces and practices or to methodologies of bifurcating nature as the core explanatory frames of reference. Rather, the River Danube can be characterized as a flowing boundary object, emerging as the contingent effect of multiple and heterogeneous actor-networks that stabilize or transgress common social (b)orders.

Following the flow of the Danube, we find multi-sited politics that engage in the different ways we are living and how we want to live in the future. Consequently, an object-centred research agenda has to elaborate a multi-sited and process-oriented methodology of natures/cultures that intends to reconstruct the politics of imagining Europe in the past, present and future. This brings to the fore that the European idea of bifurcating nature into a human and non-human or social and non-social realm is constantly questioned by the very politics of imaging Europe itself, which constantly renders the (b)orderings of 'the social', 'the cultural', and 'the natural' controversial and conflicting. Consequently, such a research project tries to establish a transdisciplinary research programme connecting research agendas of social and natural sciences as well as humanities, instead of methodologically separating them. Following from that, we suggest that the emerging natures/cultures enact a common but highly diverse and politicized space of heterogeneous actors and differing discourses that also put the practices and limits of social research agenda in question.

Understood in this way, an object-centred, social research project places itself within these public contestations of the very natures/cultures involved. Social sciences would then take part in cosmo-politicizing the commonality of societal (b)orderings and may thus contribute to the visualization of the complexities of imaging Europe by re-linking what has been separated by the very process of Europeanization: the human and non-human.

By shifting the conceptual focus from a traditional methodology of bifurcating nature towards a methodology of natures/cultures of objects, the proposed research agenda not only proposes a comprehensive re-reading of social scientific methodology, it also offers new ways of imagining Europe. In this way, an object-centred research agenda is interested in making 'things' public in quite novel ways. Centring the research agenda around trans-national and trans-social objects like the River Danube, we have outlined a possible approach that generates 'political' data in order to question any form of methodological nationalism, globalism, sociologism or anthropocentrism. As such, we hope that this form of data will contribute to debate and feed into public contestation by giving a voice to multiple actor-networks, their presences and futures.

Notes

1 We would like to thank Florian Teufelhart for his work in making this project real.
2 Currently the Danube faces a new disaster due to toxic heavy metals stemming from rusting Soviet industry plants. See, eg http://www.guardian.co.uk/world/2010/oct/12/danube-toxic-soviet-hungary-sludge
3 The working groups for the protection of the Austrian region Wachau were formed in 1972. The group intends to restore the area of the Wachau to its original form. For further information see http://www.arbeitskreis-wachau.at/
4 See Latour's kajaking method in his Spinoza lectures, (Latour, 2008).
5 See, eg Falzon (2009).
6 In order to fulfil the Kyoto protocol, the reduction of CO_2 emission played a crucial role for the associated Austrian governmental organization *viadanube* (Austrian Society for Waterways). Currently, though, it seems that Austria remains the only European country unable to reduce their emissions according to the Kyoto protocol. On the contrary, Austrian emissions have increased significantly.

References

Ahrens, D., (2001), *Grenzen der Enträumlichung. Weltstädte, Cyberspace und transnationale Räume in der globalisierten Moderne* [*The Limits of De-Spatialization. World Cities, Cyberspace and Transnational Spaces in Globalized Modernity*], Opladen: Leske+Budrich.
Albrow, M., (1996), *The Global Age: State and Society Beyond Modernity*, Stanford: Stanford University Press.
Appadurai, A., (2001), 'Grassroots Globalization and the Research Imagination', in Appadurai, A. (ed.): *Globalization*, Durham: Duke University Press, 1–21.
Baia Mare Task Force, (2000), Report of the International Task Force for Assessing the Baia Mare Accident. Available at: http://www.reliefweb.int/library/documents/eubaiamare.pdf [last accessed: 20.08.2010]
Ballhaus, E. and B. Engelbrecht, (eds), (1995), *Der ethnographische Film. Einführung in Methoden und Praxis* [*The Ethnographic Film. Introduction to Method and Practice*], Berlin: Reimer.

Bauman, Z., (2000), *Liquid Modernity*, Cambridge: Polity Press.

Beck, U., (1992), *Risk Society. Towards a New Modernity*, London/Thousand Oaks: Sage.

Beck, U. and E. Grande, (2007), *Cosmopolitan Europe*, Cambridge: Polity.

Bird, J., B. Curtis, T. Putnam and G. Robertson, (eds), (1996), *Mapping the Futures. Local Cultures, Global Change*, London: Routledge.

Callon, M., (1986), Some Elements of a Sociology of Translation: Domestication of the Scallops and the Fishermen of St. Brieuc Bay, in Law, J., (ed.), *Power, Action and Belief: A New Sociology of Knowledge?*, London: Routledge, 196–233.

Callon, M., (1998), An Essay on Framing and Overflowing: Economic Externalities Revisited by Sociology, in Callon, M., (ed.), *The laws of the markets*, Oxford: Blackwell Publishers: 244–69.

Castree, N. and B. Braun, (eds), (2001), *Social Nature: Theory, Practice and Politics*, Oxford: Blackwell.

Castree, N., (2005), *Nature (Key Ideas in Geography)*, London: Routledge.

Daschkeid, A. and W. Schröder, (1999), *Umweltforschung quergedacht. Perspektiven integrativer Umweltforschung und –lehre* [*Lateral Thinking in Environmental Studies. Integrative Perspectives in Environmental Studies and Education*], Berlin: Springer Verlag.

Deger, P. and R. Hettlage, (eds), (2007), *Der europäische Raum. Die Konstruktion europäischer Grenzen* [*The European Space. The Construction of European Borders*], Wiesbaden: VS Verlag für Sozialwissenschaften.

Delanty, G. and C. Rumford, (2005), *Rethinking Europe*, London: Taylor & Francis.

Delanty, G., (2006), Borders in a Changing Europe: Dynamics of Openness and Closure, *Comparative European Politics* 4: 183–202.

Dewey, J., (1989), *The Public and Its Problems*, Athens, OH: Ohio University Press.

Dewey, J., (2000), *Experience and Nature*, enlarged and revised edition, New York: Dover Publications.

Donahue, J.M. and B.R. Johnston, (eds), (1998), *Water, Culture, and Power. Local Struggles in a Global Context*, Washington: Island Press.

Eden, S., S.M. Tunstall and S.M. Tapsell, (2000): Translating Nature: River Restoration as Nature-Culture, *Environment and Planning, Society and Space* 18: 257–273.

Eder, K., (2006), Europe's Borders. The Narrative Construction of the Boundaries of Europe, *European Journal of Social Theory* 9: 255–271.

Falzon, M.-A., (ed.), (2009), *Multi-sited Ethnography. Theory, Praxis and Locality in Contemporary Research*, Farnham: Ashgate.

Foucault, M., (1972), *The Archaeology of Knowledge*, London: Routledge.

Fussenegger, G., (1983), *Eines langen Stromes Reise. Die Donau, Linie, Räume, Knotenpunkte* [*The Long Journey of a River. The Danube, Route, Spaces, Intersections*], Stuttgart: Deutsche Verlags-Anstalt.

Geertz, C., (1977), *The Interpretation Of Cultures*, New York: Basic Books.

Giddens, A., (1995), *Die Konstitution der Gesellschaft. Grundzüge einer Theorie der Strukturierung*, Frankfurt / New York: Campus.

Glense, C., (2005), *Becoming Qualitative Researchers: An Introduction*, Boston: Allyn & Bacon.

Graziano, P. and M.P. Vink, (eds), (2008), *Europeanization. New Research Agendas*, Houndmills/ New York: Palgrave.

Held, D. and A. McGrew, (eds), (2007), *Globalization Theory: Approaches and Controversies*, Cambridge: Polity Press.

INE (Inland Navigation Europe) (2009a): Just Add Water, in: http://www.inlandnavigation. org/documents/Waternews/Publications/Brochures/INE_Just_add_water.pdf [last accessed: 20.08.2010]

INE (Inland Navigation Europe)(2009b): A Changing World, in: http://www.inlandnavigation. org/documents/Waternews/Publications/Brochures/INE_A_changing_world.pdf [last access: 20.08.2010]

Kaschuba, W., (2003), *Einführung in die Europäische Ethnologie* [*Introduction to European Ethnology*], München: Beck.

Kramsch, O. and B. Hooper, (eds), (2004), *Cross-border Governance in the European Union*, London: Routledge.

Krueger, R., (1994), *Focus Groups. A Practical Guide for Applied Research*, London: Sage Publications.

Latimer, J. and M. Schillmeier, (eds), (2009), *Un/knowing Bodies*, Oxford: Wiley-Blackwell.

Latour, B., (1988), *Science in Action: How to Follow Scientists and Engineers Through Society*, Cambridge: Harvard University Press.

Latour, B., (1993), *We Have Never Been Modern*, Cambridge, MA: Harvard University Press.

Latour, B., (2004a), *Politics of Nature: How to Bring the Sciences into Democracy*, Cambridge, MA: Harvard University Press.

Latour, B., (2004b), Whose Cosmos, Which Politics? Comments on the Peace Terms of Ulrich Beck, *Common Knowledge* 10: 450–462.

Latour, B., (2005a), *Reassembling the Social*, Oxford: Oxford University Press.

Latour, B., (2005b), What is the style of matters of concern? Two lectures in empirical philosophy, in: http://www.ensmp.fr/~latour/articles/article/97-STYLE-MATTERS-CONCERN.*pdf* [last accessed: 23.04.07].

Latour, B., (2008), *What Is the Style of Matters of Concern? Two Lectures in Empirical Philosophy*, Assen: Van Gorcum.

Lauser, A., (2005), Translokale Ethnographie [Translocal Ethnography]. Forum Qualitative Sozialforschung [Online Journal], *6*(3), available at: http://www.qualitative-research.net/fqs-texte/3–05/05–3–7-d.htm [last accessed: 20.01.2007].

Law, J. and M. Callon, (2004), Absence-Presence, Circulation and Encountering in Complex Space, I, *Society and Space* 22: 3–11.

Law, J. and J. Hassard, (1999), *Actor Network Theory and After, Sociological Review* Monographs, Oxford: Blackwell.

Law, J. and A. Mol, (2001), Situating Technoscience: An Inquiry into Spatialities, Environment and Planning D, *Society and Space* 19: 609–621.

Law, J. and A. Mol, (2004), Regions, Networks and Fluids: Anaemia and Social Topology, *Social Studies of Science* 24: 641–671.

Litosseliti, L., (2004), *Using Focus Groups in Research*, London: Continuum International.

Luhmann, N., (1998), *Observations on Modernity*. Stanford: Stanford University Press.

Magris, C., (1988), *Donau. Biographie eines Flusses* [*Danube. Biography of a River*], München/Wien: Carl Hanser.

Maier, D. (2001), *Die Donau. Natur, Kultur, Land und Leute* [*The Danube. Nature, Culture, Land and People*], Eggolsheim: Nebel.

Marcus, G.E., (1998), Ethnography in/of the World System: The Emergence of Multi-Sited Ethnography, in Marcus, G.E., (ed.), *Ethnography through Thick/Thin*, Princeton: Princeton University Press.

Marcus, G.E., (2005), The Refashioning of Ethnography, *Soziale Welt*, Sonderband 16: 387–396.

Mészáros, L., (2006), *Die Donau* [*The Danube*], München: Christian.

Merton, R.K., M. Fiske, and P.L. Kendall, (1990), *The Focused Interview. A Manual of Problems and Procedures*, New York: Free Press.

Michael, M., (2000), Reconnecting Culture, Technology and Nature: From Society to Heterogeneity, London: Routledge.

Mol, A., (2003), *The Body Multiple: Ontology in Medical Practice*, Durham: Duke University Press.

Morath, I., (1995), *Donau* [*Danube*], Salzburg/Wien: Otto Müller.

Morgan, D.L., (1988), *Focus Groups as Qualitative Research*, Newbury Park: Sage Publications.

Morgan, D. and R. Krueger, (1998), *The Focus Group Kit*, London: Sage Publications.

Moser, D.-R., (1991), Literatur am Strom. Eine literarische Donaureise von der Quelle bis nach Wien [Literature on the Stream. A Journey in Literature from the Origin to Vienna], *Literatur in Bayern* 26: 2–14.

Nordquist, M., (2009), 'A Cosmopoltical Proposal: Towards the Democratic Composition and Participation of Environments'. Department of Political Science, University of Minnesota: 1–34. Mimeo.

Nowotny, H., P. Scott and M. Gibbons, (2001), *Re-Thinking Science. Knowledge and the Public in an Age of Uncertainty*, Cambridge: Polity Press.

Poehls, K. and A. Vonderau, (eds), (2007), *Turn to Europe*. Kulturanthropologische Europaforschungen, Münster: Lit.

Pohler, W., (2010), SARS – Ein globales Risikoereignis [SARS- A global risk event], in Holzinger, M., S. May and W. Pohler, (eds), (2010), *Weltrisikogesellschaft als Ausnahmezustand*, Weilerwirst: Velbrück: 121–151.

Robertson, G., L. Tickner, J. Bird, B. Curtis and T. Putnam, (eds), (1996), *FutureNatural. Nature, Science, Culture*, London/New York: Routledge.

Rumford, C., (2006), Introduction. Theorizing Borders, *European Journal of Social Theory* 9: 155–169.

Schillmeier, M. and W. Pohler, (2006), Kosmo-politische Ereignisse, *Soziale Welt* 57: 331–349.

Schillmeier, M., (2007a), Dis/abling Spaces of Calculation – Blindness and Money In Everyday Life, *Environment and Planning D: Society & Space* 25(4): 594–609.

Schillmeier, M., (2007b), 'Zur Politik des Behindert-Werdens – Behinderung als Erfahrung und Ereignis', in Schneider, W. and Waldschmidt, A. (eds), *Soziologie der Behinderung und disability studies. Kultursoziologische Grenzgänge*. Bielefeld, transcript.

Schillmeier, M., (2008), Globalizing Risks – The Cosmo-Politics of SARS and its Impact on Globalizing Sociology, in *Mobilities* 3: 179–199.

Schillmeier, M., (2009), The Social, Cosmopolitanism and Beyond, *History of Human Sciences* 22(2): 87–109.

Schillmeier, M., (2010), *Rethinking Disability: Bodies, Senses, and Things*. London/ New York: Routledge.

Schlehe, J., (2005), *Transkulturalität in der Ethnologie: Neue Forschungsbeziehungen [Transculture in Ehtnology. New Research Relations]*, Projekt 'Zeichen der Herrschaft', Altertumswissenschaftl iches Kolleg Heidelberg, in http://www.akh.uni-d.de/texte/schlehe 240605.pdf [last accessed: 3.2.2006].

Serres, M., (1995), *The Natural Contract*, Michigan: University of Michigan.

Serres, M., (2005), *Atlas*. Merve: Berlin.

Stengers, I., (2005), The Cosmopolitical Proposal, in Latour, B. and Weibel, P., (eds), *Making Things Public. Atmospheres of Democracy*, Karlsruhe: ZKM: 994–1003.

Stewart, D., P.N. Shamdasani and D.W. Rook, (2007), Focus Groups: Theory and Practice. *Applied Social Research Methods* Volume 20, London: Sage Publications.

Strathern, M., (2004), *Partial Connections* (updated edition), Lanham: AltaMira Press.

Urry, J., (2002), *Global Complexity*, Oxford: Polity Press.

Weber, M., (1973), Die 'Objektivität' sozialwissenschaftlicher Erkenntnis [Objectivity in Social Sciences], in Winkelmann, J., (ed.), *Soziologie. Universalgeschichtliche Analysen*, Stuttgart: Kröner: 186–262.

Weber, M., (2002), Schriften 1894–1922 [Writings]. *Ausgewählt und herausgegeben von Dirk Kaesler*, Stuttgart: Kröner.

Weithmann, M.W., (2000), *Die Donau. Ein europäischer Fluss und seine 3000-jährige Geschichte [The Danube. A European River and its 3000 Years of History]*, Regensburg: Pustet.

Whitehead, A.N., (2000 [1920]), *Concept of Nature*, Cambridge: Cambridge University Press.

WWF (World Wide Fund for Nature), (2009), *Information document: along the Bystroye arm of the Danube*, available at http://assets.panda.org/downloads/infodoc_bystroye_01dec2009.pdf [last accessed: 20.08.2010]

The art of narrating and the question of cultural acknowledgment: the case of *Die Kinder von Golzow* and a reunified Germany

Barbara Grüning

Abstract: Some twenty years since the reunification of Germany, the cultural and interpersonal communication between eastern and western Germans remains problematic – complicated by oversimplified media representations of the GDR-past that induce an attitude of mistrust towards eastern Germans as well as making them feel unacknowledged. This paper explores the question of German integration post-1989 through an analysis of the documentary series *Die Kinder von Golzow* (Winfried and Winfried, 1961–2005). The aim is to show how the series, even if marginal in the public memory, offers a cultural meeting ground by narrating the recent past from the perspective of everyday-life. The paper argues that the construction of a political community is not only the result of institutional politics, but also of everyday praxis. In other words, it is necessary to distinguish between two levels of integration in the case of the reunification of Germany: on the one hand the acceptance of institutions of the Federal Republic; and on the other the exchange of historical (collective and individual) experiences, since these form the basis of a cultural and mutual acknowledgment of identity and difference among eastern and western Germans.

Introduction

Twenty years after the fall of the Berlin wall the reunification of Germany is still incomplete. One of the central questions relating to this concerns the construction of a 'German collective identity'. In political, scientific and media discourses the main issue has been the integration of eastern Germans into the democratic and liberal system of the Federal Republic; as currently framed, this depends on their capability to adhere to the cultural and social rules of western German society. From this perspective, the integration of East and West Germany is considered to have been ineffective for the reasons outlined below.

Firstly, after the reunification eastern Germans constructed an 'East German identity' that paradoxically did not exist before. This 'invented' identity was based on their shared experiences in the German Democratic Republic (Cooke, 2005). Thus eastern Germans tend to express nostalgia (the so called *Ostalgia* phenomena) for GDR society, with the GDR regarded as the lost *Heimat* (homeland). Secondly, their considerations of themselves as German rest upon an idea of 'German identity' based on traditional German cultural heritage. Their sense of belonging is therefore related to the 'outdated' image of *Heimat*. In contrast western Germans are oriented towards a post-national identity based on post-materialist values that have a positive influence in asserting democratic principles (eg Trommsdorf, 1994; Gabriel, Falter and Rattinger, 2005). It is this latter sense of identity that has become dominant within the political discourse of integrating East and West Germany.

In essence the process of integration has been problematic, particularly when considered in relation to the academic literature on the establishment of political communities and shared identities. Habermas (2006), for example, has argued that such processes should mutually acknowledge the different historical and cultural experiences characteristic of the various social groups within a newly instituted society. The perceived problem – the absence of a shared political and cultural community – therefore does not depend just on the difficulty eastern Germans have in adapting to the new Germany but rather on the lack of a mutual recognition. By exchanging narratives a collective identity could be developed which would have an open and dialectical character and be historically grounded. The main difficulty in achieving this sense of recognition is the way in which the mainstream media constructs the public memory of the GDR-past.

Specifically, the mainstream media present simplified representations of East Germany in one of two ways. On the one hand the GDR state is characterized by the Stasi (the secret police of East Germany), the wall, the doping and the Stalinist ideology (eg Grüning, 2010; Ahbe, 2005; Cooke, 2005). On the other the mainstream media exoticize life in East Germany (as was the case with the 'Ostalgie-shows' broadcasted in 2003) by presenting it 'as a world with a curious material culture' (Cooke, 2005: 159) – with the result that 'eastern experiences remain peripheral to the west' (Cooke, 2005: 156). In this respect 'counter-narratives' (Bhabha, 1990) could highlight aspects of the GDR-society ignored by dominant master narratives and, in this way, offer different perspectives on the ways of living, the feelings and the memories of eastern Germans. In this context such counter-narratives have a particular relevance because they offer deeper insights into the cosmology and life worlds of eastern Germans.

The second problematic point is the fact that the counter-narratives (or counter-memories) of eastern Germans are often considered as 'nostalgic' in a negative way. Indeed, in most of the public discourses, nostalgia is regarded as either a 'restorative nostalgia' that expresses the longing to reconstruct the lost *nostos* (Boym, 2001), or a 'romanticist nostalgia' that conveys a rose-tinted view of the life in the GDR-society that leads one to ignore the oppressive character of the GDR-state (Cooke, 2005). However, as the analysis of Cooke (2005) and Berdahl (2010) show, *Ostalgia* has multiple meanings. Ostalgic narratives or practices, for this reason, can have a productive use, either to normalize the exoticized everyday life of East Germany or to criticize the politics of re-unification. Thus the expression of nostalgia is not always a symptom of the incapacity to adapt to reality but – as the expression 'reflexive nostalgia' suggests – it can be doubly helpful (Boym, 2001). On the one hand it allows one to elaborate and communicate individual or collective experiences so as to share them with a larger community. On the other, in the case of Germany, it offers a different perspective with which to examine problems and issues that concern both eastern and western Germans.

Finally, a further barrier to integration for many eastern Germans lies within their understanding of *Heimat* – which, in itself, expresses a feeling of collective belonging and plays a central role in eastern Germans' considerations of what it means to be German. From an historical perspective, the concept of *Heimat* is problematic in German culture for two main reasons. First, during the Nazi-period and the GDR-Dictatorship it coincided with that of *Vaterland* and thus was associated with an antidemocratic political culture. Second, *Heimat* suggests a traditional way of life and a traditional system of values that are considered antithetical to the post-materialist values of western societies. *Heimat*, however, when used to suggest a feeling of belonging often associated with nostalgia, can assume various meanings depending on the way it is 'narrated'. Thus, depending on the way it is interpreted, the concept of *Heimat* contrasts with the idea of a 'post-national German identity'.

In order to explore and elucidate the problems of integrating eastern Germans into a 'post-nationals German identity', and also investigate the possibilities of constructing a shared German identity through the mutual recognition and acknowledgement of the eastern and western German conceptions of what it means to be German, I analyse the documentary *Die Kinder von Golzow* (The Children of Golzow). This documentary was shot between 1961 and 2006 in Golzow, a small village in the Brandenburg. This series of documentaries followed the lives of about twenty 'children' born in Golzow from the point where they started school into adulthood. The most relevant aspect of the documentary is that it talks about both the GDR-society and the new German society by narrating the life-stories of eastern Germans before and after the fall of the wall. Thus the series of documentaries presents a 'counter-narrative' to the dominant master-narratives that represent eastern Germans both during the GDR-society and today and abstract them from the context of their everyday lives (see also Grüning, 2010a). Nevertheless, as I discuss below, the series poses two ambivalent problems.

With respect to the period before the fall of the wall, first impressions of *Die Kinder von Golzow* are that the early documentaries seem to propagandize the official political culture of the GDR-state. Such an impression arises from the fact that the genre 'documentary' was often used in the German Democratic Republic as a propaganda instrument. Moreover the rural setting, which typifies the *Heimat*, was typically deployed to create a sense of belonging to the socialist *Vaterland* (fatherland). However, the focus of these documentaries is on the everyday life experiences of the 'children of Golzow' and not on the ideological aspects of the GDR-political culture.

With respect to the period after the fall of the wall, the later documentaries seem to express a romanticized nostalgia towards the past, particularly by their still focusing on a small village community. However two important aspects of these later documentaries tone down this impression. By illustrating the transformations in eastern Germany and proposing images and stories cut because of censorship, the filmmakers perform memory-work by helping to remember the political and economical difficulties that were faced in the GDR. Furthermore, by following the destiny of the *Children of Golzow* in the 'new' Germany, the authors make constant reference to western Germans, without passing firm judgement on the reunification. Instead they depict individual and collective stories that are normally difficult to hear, allowing the audience to observe at the same time how over time the protagonists negotiated their identities by meeting western Germans and western culture.

As I elucidate below, by interweaving the various stories of a small province of East Germany over forty years, this series of documentaries offers new understandings of the concept of *Heimat* in reunified Germany. It therefore enables us to reflect further upon the role that *Heimat* played in the historical construction of the German state and national identity. Indeed, in the documentaries the *Heimat* does not correspond simply to a physical space or to an ideological category but to a series of narratives that take place over time, both 'before' and 'after' the fall of the wall. In this respect, the documentaries lay bare different ways of expressing this feeling of belonging. However, such feelings of belonging should not be associated automatically with '*restorative* nostalgia', with its implicit desire to reconstruct the lost *nostos*. Rather the documentaries express a sense of '*reflexive* nostalgia', one that awakens consciousness to the different levels and complexities of everyday life (eg Boym, 2001). In this second case, images of collectivity do not have an essential character, but result from the 'meeting' of subjective narratives.

In the next section I illustrate the main narratives of the German Democratic Republic in order to highlight how they can contribute to increasing the distance and the distrust of eastern Germans. Then I analyse the series of documentaries *Die Kinder von Golzow*, by considering the series not only as a witness to GDR-society but also as a cultural text that offers eastern and western Germans a meeting ground between their different perspectives. Finally, on the basis of this analysis, I go on to propose a new way of considering the category of *Heimat* by focusing on the relations that link *Heimat*, memory and narrative.

The German reunification in media narratives

The problem of achieving political and cultural reunification – and so of constructing a shared national identity – is strictly connected with the problem of coming to terms with the past of the GDR and with wider German history. It is in this respect that the mainstream media play an important role. The dominant discourses that appear in the media were clearly illustrated in 2009, when

Germany commemorated the 20-year anniversary of the fall of the Berlin wall – the event that started the reunification process – and the sixty years since the establishment of the Federal Republic.[1] At that time, the most controversial question about East Germany's past in the mainstream media concerned the juridical-political nature of the GDR-State. This was after the Prime Minister of Mecklemburg-Vorpommern, Erwin Sellering, declared he considered the GDR a dictatorship, but added that he did not think that it had been an *Unrechtstaat* (a state not founded on the rule of the law). Although the media criticized this declaration heavily, they never dealt with his question in juridical terms; specifically, they never established the difference between the concepts of dictatorship and *Unrechtstaat*.[2]

The legal status of the GDR was discussed in the political sphere after 1989 and resonated in media debates. The main proponents of the *Unrechtstaat* thesis were East German dissidents and members of the citizen movement, as well as West German anticommunists. In 1992 the *Bundestag* (the German Parliament) set up an Enquiry Commission with the aim of investigating the role of institutions within the GDR. The findings of the final parliamentary report underlined the notion that the GDR was an *Unrechtstaat* and thus a totalitarian system rather than a socialist dictatorship. According to Cooke, the central thrust of the report was 'the de-legitimization of the GDR regime. Along with this de-legitimization comes a concomitant legitimization of the FRG' (2005: 39). Furthermore by constructing a totalitarian image of the GDR, a historical narrative was built 'in which guilt can be unambiguously apportioned, heroes identified, and unification painted as a redemptive moment for German people' (ibid: 43). This historical narrative predominated in media representations of the GDR past, in the German reunification process and, as a consequence, in the popular imagination (see for example Grüning, 2010).

It seems evident that the media debates in 2009 about the legal status of the GDR reinforced the totalitarian image of the GDR-society, focusing on its brutal character and its ideological nature, while ignoring the complexities of everyday life in the GDR.

The examination of how the media dealt with the two anniversaries highlights that the founding of the nation-state was recognized as the main event, while the fall of the Berlin wall was relegated as an event belonging to East German history, and not common to all Germany. Indeed, while 1989 has been remembered through historical and episodical narratives, the 'Sixty years of the Federal Republic' is recognized in commemorative narratives, assigning a symbolic meaning to this event that is significant for the new political community. Celebrating 'Sixty years of the Federal Republic' allowed for a wider and continuous narrative in comparison to an event whose meaning has been absorbed by the dynamics of the reunification process that followed. Furthermore, the focus of these media representations was on political events and institutional figures. In particular the documentary 'Bonner Republic' (The Republic of Bonn) is built on the actions, decisions and speeches of the Federal Chancellors.

In the last part of 'Bonner Republic' the history of the Federal Republic is summed up symbolically as proceeding from the Chancellor of the 'economic miracle' (Adenauer) to the Chancellor of the reunification (Kohl). In the media context, the GDR appears to have no more relevance to the German nation-state than any other foreign state. The paradox is that despite an original exclusion of the East German stories from the federal collective narrative, a symbolic inclusion follows, thanks to the fictive continuity promoted by the sixty-year history of the republic, an inclusion that plays down East German history.

Two conjoined questions follow from this. Do such representations of collective identity – as regularly appear in the media and are promoted more widely – mainly mirror western German perspectives? And do they allow eastern Germans either to feel themselves as 'German first of all', or to identify with the institutions of the Federal Republic?

Sociological and political studies

Sociological and political studies of German reunification mainly adopt the interpretation of a halted or slow modernization in eastern Germany. While in the course of the years an improvement in economic integration has been recorded since reunification, the question of political, social and cultural modernization remains open.

The first empirical studies identified the lack of integration as being due to the influence of socialization on East Germans' personalities (*Beeinflußungsthese*). According to these theories, the internalization of the norms and rules of the past regime led to a spirit of subjugation (Hanke, 1991; Maaz, 1992), to passivity (Güsten, 1990; Maaz, 1992), to lethargy (Berentzen, 1990), to apathy (Hanke, 1991), to infantilism (Maaz, 1992), to dependence on the authorities (Spittmann, 1991), to a 'welfare state-mentality' (Güsten, 1990; Hanke, 1991; Maaz, 1992; Köcher, 1991), to a sense of impotence (Winiarski, 1991) and to a blocked personality (Berentzen, 1990; Maaz, 1992). In brief these studies depicted the GDR society as a totalitarian state and the former GDR-citizens as psychologically unable to integrate into the new system. In contrast other authors have argued that the GDR was a 'Niche-Society' (*Nischengesellschaft*) and that the factors affecting integration negatively were to be found in the new context created by the transformations brought about by reunification.

From the mid-1990s, new empirical studies highlighted how eastern Germans had accepted the rules and the principles of the liberal-democratic system. Furthermore, the image of the GDR changed, revealing how since the 1970s the values and lifestyles of East and West Germans had become similar (Trommsdorf, 1994; Gensicke, 1998, 2000). However, there was a continued interest in exploring why East Germans had problems in identifying with federal institutions. As I outline below, three propositions have been put forward.

1. Although eastern and western Germans share the same values, they give them different meanings (Trommsdorf, 1994).
2. The transformation of individual behaviours concerns the private sphere, while the relationship between the citizens and the state is still influenced by paternalistic socialization. The latter results in mistrust of modern federal institutions.
3. Though eastern Germans have the potential to complete the integration process, when confronted with the strategies of differentiation adopted by western Germans they build their own collective identity. This is framed by a collective memory, not shared with the western Germans, of the GDR era.[3] Integration into the Federal Republic is therefore further delayed or hindered by a sense of political nostalgia (which Neller, 2006, has argued to be regressive in character).

Interpretations thus focus on the criteria of inclusion and exclusion among eastern and western Germans respectively, the role of memory in the construction of German identity, and the model of a normative collective identity. As we have seen, there are fundamental differences between how eastern and western Germans conceptualize German identity, which relates back to different cultural orientations, with the eastern Germans focussing on material values while the western Germans expound post-material values.[4] From a functionalist perspective eastern Germans can adapt to the new system only by abandoning the traditional cultural frame and conforming to the modernization processes.

Memory, and the role it plays in the construction of a German identity seems particularly significant in the case of the east Germans. Memory is not merely a process of reflection upon the past – nostalgia – but a means of overcoming the habits and values acquired in the GDR that could affect integration into the Federal Republic. Nostalgia is explained either as a consequence of the previous socialization of the eastern Germans or as reaction to the negative representations proposed by the western Germans. As mentioned earlier, individual and collective memories about the everyday-life in the GDR-Society are mostly considered to be expressions of a *restorative* or *romanticized* nostalgia.

In many ways, the eastern German rendering of German identity is considered to be antithetical to the normative collective identity promoting identification with the institutions, norms and values developed during the sixty years of the Federal Republic. By evoking the GDR's past, eastern Germans appear to ascribe to a collective identity that contradicts this post-national collective identity. The eastern German identity has thus been considered as a 'negative identification of Eastern as non-western' (Glaeser, 2000: 150).

This raises further questions about the qualities of the post-national identity promoted by the Federal Republic, questions which particularly concern the alleged character of post-national identities. Firstly, despite the reflexive character of post-national identity, there is an expectation that the eastern Germans will identify with the identity promoted by the Federal Republic without questioning or criticizing it. Beyond this, their identification as 'eastern German', as already noted, is considered deviant and falsely based on a feeling of 'restorative' or 'romanticist' nostalgia towards GDR society. Finally, it seems that the admission of eastern Germans into the new German collectivity, and thus their acceptance, and even acknowledgement, by western Germans, is seen as an act of goodwill (on the part of the Federal government) that can thus be given or not (Emcke, 2000). What is overlooked in this interpretation is the fragility of the relationship *between* subjects, and the continuous process by which this relationship is rendered. As the term 'between' indicates, both unification and differentiation are implicit in this process (compare Ricoeur, 2004). It is paradoxically a process that encourages integration while maintaining the autonomy of the groups involved (compare Sennett, 2003). So rather than 'acknowledgement' resulting in the construction of a homogeneous and reified identity, it helps maintain and renew the relationship *between* subjects, consolidating differences between these as social groups.

How then might a collective identity meaningful to both eastern and western Germans be achieved? As I demonstrate in the next section, the series of documentaries *Die Kinder von Golzow*, which through life-stories make visible the complex processes involved in the experience of individual and collective identities in the GDR and reunified Germany, give some insights into the possibility of such a collective identity. In particular, I consider *Heimat* – as a physical and utopic place – and its role in how people construct a sense of belonging as it appears in this documentary. I trace how various narratives and meanings of *Heimat* emerge over time, from the building of the Berlin Wall to reunification. As I argue, by making public the polyphonic narratives, these documentaries can be considered as constructing a form of *Heimat* wherein both eastern and western Germans can find their place.

Die Kinder von Golzow

In GDR political culture the socialist *Heimat* had an exclusive character not only with respect to the national socialist *Vaterland* but also with respect to the romantic representation of the nature and the idea of *Heimat* as the product of a subjective relation with place. Specifically the feeling of nostalgia (*Heimweh*) was antithetical to the socialist *Heimat* because it built a surrogate-image of the *Heimat* as idyllic (Lange, 1975). In the socialist image the *Heimat* is not the landscape but the cultivated fields and the factories (Kretzschmar, 2003). Finally, from a temporal point of view *Heimat* was intended to imply a future, with its meaning related to the socialist utopia.

A starting point is to consider to what extent *Die Kinder von Glozow* expresses this understanding of *Heimat*. These documentaries contain various socialist elements, with the narrator openly expressing socialist rhetoric in the earlier films.[5] For example in the first episode *Wenn ich erst zur Schule geh* ('When I finally go to school', 1961), the children learning the alphabet are not just doing their work; in the words of the narrator 'they teach something to us about our

German Democratic Republic'. The generation born in the GDR – and destined to grow separated by a wall – are the basis of the new society. The themes of the 'productive work' and of the agricultural cooperatives (LPG)[6] – features particular to the socialist regime – frequently recur in the narrative, representing respectively the ideal of progress and the passage from an individualist to a socialist society. A further element of the political culture of the GDR that we find in the documentaries, and one that helped the GDR-citizens to feel German, is the positive bourgeois heritage.[7] Indeed the documentaries mention the figure of Fontane, who was judged positively because of his criticism of the II Reich (Strzeleczyk, 1999).

This said, I argue that the documentaries allude to other understandings of *Heimat*; the longitudinal aspect of the filming allows for non-socialist under- standings to emerge, particularly in those documentaries filmed in the GDR- phase. The choice to film in Golzow, rather than resulting in the depiction of a socialist utopia, reveals a more heterogeneous, non-linear and even incoherent account of life in the GDR. The images of childhood portrayed in *Lebensläufe* ('Resume – the story of the children of Golzow in separate portraits') filmed from 1980 to 1981, present insights into individual stories and lives, as the 'children' – now adult – retrospectively narrate the images of their everyday lives filmed when they were younger. Nine of these individuals comment on the different images of their childhood and early adulthood: for example, Bernd showing his record collection in his student-room in Schwedt, Jürgen watching the football-match on the TV in his living room in Golzow, Bernd going to work by bike with his future wife and Jürgen feeding his son. They then recon- struct the period after the end of the school, when their lives went in separate directions: the choices at work or at the university, the family problems and successes, the hobbies and the political activities, the new house and the new town, the fairs and the official ceremonies. The film ends with views of the Oder River and village (the culture centre, the Konsum,[8] the bakery and the rectory), and emblematic images of progress such as the tractor,[9] the aeroplane and the official discourse at the opening of the new school year. Finally the narrator poses the question 'Why Golzow? And why not?'

The filmmakers respond to this question in the following film *Die Zeiten 1* (The Times, Part 1, 1992) in the episode *Also Golzow und wie es begann* ('Then Golzow and how it began') shot in 1983, but never broadcast. In the latter the stories of the *Kinder* are entangled with the individual experiences of the docu- mentary-makers and of the wider production process. The film opens with an interview with the documentary-maker, who explains how, in the summer of 1961, when he finished shooting a separate documentary on the construction of the wall he decided to do something 'more relaxing' and work with children. He chose to follow a group of children throughout their lives to see how they would affirm themselves in socialist society. The location for this was a farm damaged by the war, which, he believed 'would develop in time'. Following the interview with the documentary-maker, the film shifts to display scenes of 'backstage-work' on the production of the film. From this point onwards similar images and scenes are embedded in the film, telling the stories of the documentary-makers depicting their work, relationships with the child protagonists of the documentary, political censure and economic problems involved in the production, and the fear of overstepping the boundaries of the private sphere. Most importantly they reveal the lack of an initial well-defined project or plan.

The choice of Golzow was therefore rather haphazard; it was not chosen as a filming location because it was a model socialist community, but was rather chosen because it fulfilled different criteria. Instead of reproducing the propaganda about socialist society, it advances hesitantly, following the life-stories of its protagonists. In this manner it reveals the nuances involved in reconciling the desire for a socialist society with the permanence of the *Biedermeier* culture. The focus on the private and public life of the children, and the documentary-makers' participation in the everyday life of the village, make the narratives presented particularly emotive and implicitly reveals features of life in the GDR which could not be narrated openly at that time.

Golzow as *Heimat* is not only the place of birth of the protagonists or the place of the socialist utopia. It is rather an entanglement of the various stories of the children, oscillating between the private and the public sphere, socialist and family education, between the desire to conform to the GDR-society or to village life and the desire to develop an individual personality, between the attempt to abandon Golzow forever and the appeal of settling down in the place where they grew up. The documentaries therefore reveal the complexity of GDR society and culture as experienced by the people who were part of it. They depict the complex relationship between the private and public spheres otherwise not witnessed by the media, and lay bare the socialization process in which individual identities are influenced by official discourses and other cultural factors mediated by personal experience.

Rivers, borders and change

The issue of *Heimat* also depends on the issue of defining its physical, cultural, symbolic and, last but not least, temporal boundaries. The village of Golzow lies in the Oderbruch, separated from Poland by the river Oder which gives the name to the area. In the documentaries images of this river open and close most of the films. The river is presented as a romantic idyllic place. It is the place of everyday life activities where people fish or children play.[10] It is also depicted as a melancholic place, with the *Kinder von Golzow* as adults, crossing the river by ferryboat to their original *Heimat* to spend a day together. Beyond these representations, and drawing on the examples presented below, I highlight two further meanings attributed to the river: as signifying change and as a border.

In film shot in 1966, the teacher asks the children what a Greek philosopher (Heraclitus) meant by saying that 'No-one can cross the same river twice because neither the person nor the river are the same.' The children listen fascinated and then try to give an answer, but eventually the teacher gives no interpretation. Then, in the episode *Ich sprach mit einem Mädchen* (I spoke to a girl, 1975) the narrator returns to this reference from Heraclitus. Marie-Luise, one of the *Kinder*, is now twenty and lives in Berlin, where she is an apprentice. She is in a delicate phase of her life with no concrete plans for her future. She is not satisfied with her job, but at the same time she does not want to go back to Golzow because it is too small and she would like to try something new. Also she does not want to have a baby (while most of her friends are mothers already, as was common in the GDR) since she feels she is still too young. The narrator participates, gives advice and remembers with her, how she was different from the other children because she had no fear of expressing her opinions. When faced by her fear of being disappointed by the future, the narrator, talking to a larger audience, gives his interpretation of the words of Heraclitus: we change continuously in time, we change our opinion and we make new experiences that transform who we were and what we thought and felt. The river is thus a symbol of the continual changes in the individual's life and, as a consequence, it makes visible the constructed character of individual identity, negotiated, formed and elaborated day by day through interactions and everyday experiences. When applied to the concept of *Heimat*, the river as changing reminds us that boundaries of belonging can change and shift over time.

The river as symbolic of borders emerges through the discussion of Fontane. The episode *Neue Zeiten* (New Times), was shot on location in Letschin (also in Oderbruch) five days before the official date of the reunification. The authors quote Fontane, who studied there as a pharmacist: 'Here I observed a province for the first time' ('*Hier habe ich erstmals eine Provinz beobachtet*'). The link between Fontane and the authors of the documentaries is not so much due to his critical position toward the II Reich but more related to his role as storyteller and author. His volume *Das Oderland* is dedicated to the Oderbruch. In the text he refers to himself as a traveller without a destination, who wanders (*wandern*) to discover the land and the people. This gives his stories a unique flavour derived from his observations and conversations with local inhabitants, who described their everyday life and told him the history and myths of the place that formed an integral part of its identity.

Die Kinder von Golzow, as a result of the filming methods used, has a similar flavour to that found in Fontane's work. Through interviewing and filming it similarly collected the stories and myths of the place as told by its inhabitants: the German colonization of the *Wende*, a Slavic population, who lived in the Oderbruch; the reclamation of this area thanks to Friedrich II; the destruction of 55 per cent of the land after the Second World War and the new-beginning in Golzow. Such stories reveal that while the river may symbolically mark a border, it can be crossed by individuals and populations who find on the other side of the river a temporary or permanent destination, a place to stay or a place to abandon either for a short time or forever. In any case they always leave behind the traces of their physical or temporal crossing.

By linking all these traces it becomes clear that 'unofficial' narratives penetrate the historical narrative: the documentaries talk not only about the children of Golzow but, we can argue, about the whole of Germany. As the authors indeed said in the film *Anmut sparet nicht noch Mühe* ('Neither charm nor toil is spared', 1979) by narrating the 'ground zero' of Golzow, 'the documentary tells their (the inhabitants of Golzow) stories'. The time represented here is thus not the time conceptualized in historical materialism, but the human time of generations that follow one another, of people that meet each other somewhere at some time, leaving traces in the nature and stories that continually form the place. It is a narrative time that also makes it possible to overcome the physical, cultural and symbolical boundaries of Golzow. Thus Golzow is not only a small village of East Germany with a GDR-past, but, through the documentaries, it becomes a narrative and utopic place, a repository of stories and memories made available even to those who never lived there.

After the fall of the wall

In the films shot after the fall of the wall we find another river that plays a relevant role in the documentaries: the Elbe, a symbol of the German division. The film *Die Zeiten 1* opens with a display of fireworks over the Elbe in Hamburg on the day of the reunification. The spectators are 'Germans', 'western and eastern Germans tied by the word of the year: absurd (*Wahnsinn*)'. They celebrate 'the end of the other state, the freedom of the press and our film' that in Hamburg received greater visibility. This celebration in Hamburg also features one of the last times we see the protagonists of *Die Kinder von Golzow* together. After this the series tends to focus on individual stories.

These later episodes, focussing on individual 'children', cut between old and new images and interviews, showing the various breakpoints and connections, adding parts that were cut during the GDR-regime (due to censorship concerns). They narrate the feelings and the opinions of the protagonists of *Die Kinder von Golzow* in the present and the different ways they organized their lives: some of them stayed in Golzow and could not find their way, some found new opportunities, some adapted to the circumstances and some waited years to get a job. In this way the authors also illustrate the interruptions and continuities in the social life of Golzow, what changed (the closing of the cultural centre and the opening of a western supermarket) and what continued as before (the country fairs and the new school-year opening, even if without political speeches). Thanks to this complex narrative time, the different ways of connecting past, present and future, the film-makers also make visible the 'time of reflection upon the past' (the time of remembering) – how the *Kinder* reflect on their lives in Golzow and in the GDR under particular political, social and cultural conditions and reconcile their past experiences with those of the present-day.

The narrative presented is not linear because of the way that the film has been edited; it switches from past to present and back again. The narrative is also not cyclic, since there is no repetition: it turns back on itself in the form of reflection, giving a new meaning to the past experiences of the *Kinder von Golzow*, of the narrator and of the different audiences catered for over time. The narrative is thus not imprisoned in the past but is opened up to those who did not share the same experiences.

Thus we can also claim that the *Heimat* represented in the documentaries does not correspond just to a physical place or to an idealized place of nostalgia. Rather the *Heimat* is the tangle of stories collected over time both in and beyond Golzow. The documentaries therefore have an epic character (Benjamin, 1991: 453), adding everyday life stories to the stories of the histories and myths of Golzow, thus enlarging and transforming *Heimat* and the sense of belonging, giving new social actors (the new generation born in eastern Germany and the western Germans) the opportunity to understand, to participate and to recognize themselves in this collective and polyphonic narrative.

Concluding remarks: Heimat, memory and narrative

Master-narratives in the public spaces interpret the question of German re-unification exclusively as a problem of integration of eastern Germans into the Federal German system. In particular, these master-narratives foster the thesis that eastern Germans have difficulties in understanding the democratic and liberal values of the Federal Republic because of (1) their socialization under the totalitarian state of the GDR and (2) their allegiance to a traditional German identity constructed around the concept of *Heimat*. While the idea of *Heimat* was politically exploited by the GDR Dictatorship, as well as during National Socialism, these master-narrative also tend to treat *Heimat* as referring to a local community with a homogeneous and exclusive character – a rendering that reflects a way of life and system of values considered antithetical to those of a post-national state.

With regard to these master narratives, the documentary series *Die Kinder von Golzow* offers an alternative perspective for reflecting upon the sociocultural difficulties of German reunification and the persisting question of German identity. Throughout the series the issue of a single 'bounded' notion of *Heimat* is challenged by the experiences of the child protagonists of the films, with the result that more complex understandings emerge that previously lay hidden. The documentaries can therefore be read as proposing a new way of understanding the experience of life within the GDR and, furthermore, the continuing socio-cultural problems involved in the reunification of Germany.

At first glance the early documentaries appear to present the propagandistic image of the socialist *Heimat* alongside an idyllic view of *Heimat* as related to traditional local communities. My argument, however, is that the interweaving of different life-stories shows how other cultural traditions, not incorporated into these distinct notions of *Heimat*, influenced the everyday lives and understandings of the people living in the GDR. Insights into the private lives of the 'children' reveal the persistent influence of Protestant and Catholic cultures, the Biedermeier culture, and not least the influences of Western culture: as teenagers the boys wore long hair, the girls wore miniskirts, they were followers of popular music (as Bernd's record collection reminds us) and went to parties at the disco. These were images of life that the GDR chose to suppress in their propaganda. Everyday life in Golzow, and by extension more generally in the GDR, was always a complex and heterogeneous matter undergoing transformation. Reflections on reunification, together with memories of life in the GDR, once again challenge homogeneous representations of eastern Germans. While the masternarratives stress the nostalgia towards GDR society – a representation considered as antithetical to post-national collective identity – my point is that the documentaries shed light on how the protagonists try to reconcile the past with the present and construct continuity within their individual biographies. Such reflections are facilitated both by the longitudinal nature of the documentaries and, inherent to the production of their filming, the relaxation in censorship over the years. Furthermore, later re-editing of the film material enables the documentaries to be viewed in light of the new political and cultural context.

Critically, nuances in the meaning of *Heimat* are revealed through the interweaving of the life-stories of the 'children', following them to the different places they travelled through or lived, in paying attention to their hopes and desires for the present and future. In this way we can observe how the meaning of *Heimat* changes continually, incorporating different spatial, social and cultural dimensions. This is writ large following reunification, as western Germans also become part of the narrative. Furthermore, the documentaries demonstrate different ideas of *Heimat* can coexist, that there are different ways of belonging that go well beyond those of feeling 'at home' or those of people thinking about their 'homeland'.

The documentaries do not present a fixed image of the *Heimat*, but offer a dynamic repository of stories and memories. From this perspective it becomes possible to create a new understanding of *Heimat* out of the tension between the past and the present, between a 'no more' and a 'still not'; a space perhaps wherein past identities in the form of experiences can co-exist with future identities in the form of desires or hopes. In this interpretation *Heimat* becomes a utopic place, taking form by passing from the condition of being bound to the place and the other (*sich binden*) to the condition of heading to the place and the other (*sich ausrichten*). Whereas the second condition frames the possibility of creating new experiences over time, the first condition postulates the time of 'resting on the way-to' (*Unterwegs-im-Ruhen*) –corresponding to the time frame of narrating the various kinds of estrangement experienced far from the home. Thus the time frame of narrating makes it possible to acknowledge oneself, helped in turn by the acknowledgement of those who participate in the narrative (Joisten, 2003). In this sense *Heimat*, as a place to construct feelings of belonging, becomes the narrative itself (Jedlowski, 2009).

To conclude, by collating the past and present experiences of eastern Germans, giving them a place and a visibility, and by showing how they are also interlaced with those of western Germans, the documentaries I have discussed offer the possibility of greater cultural and mutual acknowledgment. They open up possibilities for sharing the same story, even if it is a story marked by contrasts and incomprehension.

Notes

1 For example, the issue has been dealt with in *Der Spiegel-Geschichte* 'Eine deutsches Wunder. Sechzig Jahre Bundesrepublik' (II vol., 2009) and in the television documentary 'Bonner Republik' (ARD, 22.04.09, 29.04.09).
2 I refer in particular to the interview with the political scientist Schroeder in *Der Spiegel* 18/09 and to the debate in the talk-show 'Anne Will' (ARD, 26.04.09).
3 According to Gensicke (1998) it is possible to reach the hoped identification through an institutional political education.
4 Most of the empirical researches adopt the distinction of Inglehart (1977).
5 The series is made up of 16 DVD. Each DVD can include one to three films. Each film can contain six to twenty episodes.
6 Landwirtschaftliche Produktionsgenossenschaft.
7 W. Ulbricht, 'Unser guter Weg zur sozialistischen Menschengemeinschaft', in 'Neues Deutschland', 23th March 1969. The official memory of the GDR was based on three elements: the antifascist memory, which constitutes the nucleus and the symbolic legitimization of the GDR-State; the memory of the worker and communist movements; the classical cultural heritage, which handed down the 'progressive humanist values' of peace and solidarity (see for example Grüning, 2010).
8 A supermarket chain in the GDR.
9 The tractor symbolized the end of the Junker-era.
10 In these two examples the river is the 'Alter Oder'.

References

Ahbe, T., (2005), *Ostalgie. Zum Umgang mit der DDR Vergangenheit in der 1990er Jahren*, Erfurt: Länderzentralen für politische Bildung.
Bhabha, H.K., (1990), *DissemiNation: time, narrative and the margins of the modern Nation*, in H. K. Bhabha, (ed.), *Nation and Narration*, London – New York: Routledge.
Benjamin, W., (1991), *Gesammelte Schriften*, Vol. 2, Frankfurt/M.: Suhrkamp.
Berdahl, D., (2010), *On the Social Life of Postsocialism*, Bloomington: Indiana University Press.
Berentzen, D., (1990), 'Der autoritäre Charakter – Made in DDR', in *Psychologie heute*, 4: 32–35.
Boym, S., (2001), *The Future of Nostalgia*, New York: Basic Books.
Cooke, P., (2005), *Representing East Germany since Unification. From Colonization to Nostalgia*, Oxford-New York: Berg.
Emcke, C., (2000), *Kollektive Identitäten*, Frankfurt/M. – New York: Campus.
Fontane, T., (2005), *Das Oderland. Wanderungen durch die Mark Brandenburg*, Berlin: Aufbau Taschenbuch Verlag.
Gabriel, O.W., Falter, J.W., and Rattinger, H. (eds) (2005), *Wächst zusammen, was zusammen gehört?*, Baden-Baden, Nomos.

Gensicke, T., (1998), *Die Neuen Bundesbürger. Eine Transformation ohne Integration*, Opladen: Westdeutscher Verlag.

Gensicke, T., (2000), *Deutschland im Übergang. Lebensgefühl, Wertorientierungen, Bürgerengagement*, Speyer: Speyerer Forschungsberichte 204.

Glaeser, A., (2000), *Divided in unity*, Chicago: Chicago University Press.

Grüning, B., (2010), *Diritto, norma e memoria. La Germania dell'est nel processo di transizione*, Macerata: Eum.

Grüning, B., (2010a), *Luoghi della memoria e identità collettive. Rielaborazione del passato tedesco orientale*, Roma: Carocci.

Güsten, S., (1990), 'Kulturschock lähmt die ex-DDR. Wie die Menschen ihre neue soziale Realität verarbeiten', in *Frankfurter Rundschau*, 31.12.1990: 29.

Habermas, J., (2006), *Lotta di riconoscimento nello stato democratico di diritto*, in J. Habermas and C. Taylor, *Multiculturalismo. Lotte per il riconoscimento*, Milano: Feltrinelli: 63–110.

Hanke, I., (1991), *Die Ungleiche Nation*, in B. Muszynski (ed.) *Deutsche Vereinigung. Probleme der Integration und der Identifikation*, Opladen: Westdeutscher Verlag: 45–60.

Inglehart, R., (1977), *The Silent Revolution. Changing Values and Political Styles Among Western Publics*, Princeton: Princeton University Press.

Jedlowski, P., (2009), *Il racconto come dimora. Heimat e le memorie d'Europa*, Torino: Bollati Boringhieri.

Joisten, K., (2003), *Philosophie der Heimat – Heimat der Philosophie*, Berlin: Akademie Verlag.

Köcher, R., (1991), 'Viel Zündstoff in der Verfassungsdebatte', in *Frankfurter Allgemeiner Zeitung*, 4.12.1991:5.

Kretzschmar, J., (2003), *Sein Vaterland in Film – Die DDR-Reportagen*, in T. Prase and J. Kretzschmar (eds.), *Propagandist und Heimatfilmer. Die Dokumentarfilme des Karl-Eduard von Schnitzler*, Leipzig: Leipziger Univesitätsverlag: 83–174.

Lange, G., (1975), *Heimat. Realität und Aufgabe*, Berlin: Akademie Verlag.

Luhmann, N., (2006), *Beobachtungen der Moderne*, Wiesbaden: Verlag für Sozialwissenschaften.

Maaz, H-J., (1992), *Der Gefühlsstau. Ein Psychogramm der DDR*, München: Vollständige Taschenbuchausgabe.

Neller, K., (2006), *DDR-Nostalgie. Dimensionen der Orientierungen der Ostdeutschen gegenüber der ehemaligen DDR, ihre Ursache und politischen Konnotationen*, Wiesbaden: Verlag für politischen Wissenschaften.

Ricoeur, P., (2004), *Parcours de reconnaissance*, Paris: Éditions Stock.

Sennett, R., (2003), *Respect in a World of Inequality*, London: Penguin.

Spittmann, I., (1991), 'Wir und die da drüben', *Deutschland Archiv*, 24/1: 1–4.

Strzeleczyk, F., (1999), *Un-heimliche Heimat. Reibungsflächen zwischen Kultur und Nation*, München: Iudicium Verlag.

Trommsdorf, G., (1994), *Psychologische Probleme bei den Transformationsprozessen in Ostdeutschland*, in Id. (ed.), *Psychologische Aspekte des sozio-politischen Wandels in Ostdeutschland*, Berlin-New York: De Gruyter: 19–42.

Winiarski, R., (1991), 'Vom Buckel zum Ellenbogen', in *Report Psychologie*, 45/5–6: 12–13.

Part 2
Belonging

Landscape, imagination and experience: processes of emplacement among the British in rural France

Michaela Benson

Abstract: This paper traces the process by which the British residents of the Lot, a department in rural France, develop a deeper understanding of their new surroundings. While their initial perceptions of the landscape as providing a beautiful view and a backdrop to their everyday lives prompted their migration, once they are living in the French countryside these perceptions subtly change in response to their experiences of life there. As I argue, it is not simply the case that their initial impressions are replaced with the knowledge gained from their embodied experiences. Indeed, it becomes clear that their idealizations of rural living continue to frame, partially, their understandings of how *really* to live in rural France; through valorization and imitation of the lives and practices of their French neighbours my respondents lay claim to local belonging. The paper thus demonstrates the ways that imaginings and experience coalesce in the production of a continually renewed understanding of their new location.

Introduction

This paper argues that in order to understand the relationships my respondents, British lifestyle migrants living in rural France, have to their new physical surroundings, it is necessary to account for the process by which they come to develop a deeper understanding of their new environment. As the ethnography presented in this paper demonstrates, this is a process characterized by complex negotiations between imagination and lived experience. I argue here that it is necessary not only to account for the role of the migrants' direct engagements with the landscape, but also to recognize the continued role played by their idealized preconceptions of rural living and explore how these intersect with their understandings and interpretations of life within the destination.

Previous research on the British in rural France has demonstrated the extent to which culturally-specific imaginings of landscape and location are central to the decision to migrate. The seminal work in this field by Buller and Hoggart (1994a) argued that, in the absence of available housing in the British countryside, the French countryside has come to represent the rural idyll, a British middle class idealization, influencing both decisions to migrate and property selection. This is an argument that has remained unquestioned within the literature, reinforced and confirmed by subsequent research including my own (see for example Barou and Prado, 1995; Gervaise-Aguer, 2004, 2006; Benson, 2011).

This paper supplements Buller and Hoggart's argument by exploring the role that such imaginings play in life following migration, particularly in the migrants' emerging relationships with the landscape. It builds on the idea that the landscape is in continual process (see for example Bender, 1998), presenting the migrants' relationships to their new surroundings as also in process, subject to change as they gain increasing knowledge and experience of their surroundings. Furthermore, it focuses on the complementary and contradictory roles of imagination and experience in developing these relationships. Following authors such as Massey (2006) and Bender (1998) the paper therefore recognizes that both practice and representation are intrinsically intertwined in the construction of the landscape.

The insights into the migrants' relationships with the landscape thus provide a lens through which to understand the process by which they become emplaced in their new surroundings and gradually acquire embodied knowledge of how to live in the Lot. As the ethnography presented here demonstrates, culturally-framed interpretations of the landscape were important to my respondents – they were one way in which the migrants were (post-hoc) able to justify and rationalize the decision to migrate – but these existed alongside and in tension with subjective experiences of their new surroundings, at times confirming, while at other times contradicting preconceived ideals about their new surroundings.

I argue that the migrants' complex relationship with their new surroundings can best be understood through reference to Bourdieu's (1977, 1990) logic of practice; their experiences of and responses to the Lotoise landscape mediated through their bodies. As they worked in their gardens, fields and vineyards, feeling the soil beneath their nails, they repeatedly subjected their bodies to the materiality and physicality of landscape. Such embodied experiences of the landscape subtly changed their relationship to it. In this respect, the process of getting to know the landscape was one through which the embodiment of their knowledge became more visceral, changing my respondents' understandings of their new lives. Nevertheless, such engagements were justified through reference, once again, to rural France as the rural idyll. In this respect, the focus on the migrants' relationships with the landscape reflects the way in which imagination and subjective experience are mediated through the body.

'Locating' the research

The research presented in this paper is part of a larger piece of ethnographic research carried out between 2003 and 2005 into the lives of the British living in the Lot, a rural inland department in southwest France. This consisted of extensive participant observation and unstructured interviews with members of the British population living permanently in the Lot. My respondents had moved to the Lot within the last twenty years, and while some had been there for a long time, others had only moved the previous year. While there were many retirees among them, typical of this more lifestyle-oriented migration, they ranged in age upwards from young children, some of whom had been born in France. The timing and context of their migration, both in terms of their arrival in the Lot and their stage in the life course were also diverse (Benson, 2009, 2010). Importantly, the migrants' homes in the Lot were their primary residences, and they stayed there year round, perhaps leaving to visit friends and family back in Britain once or twice a year, or going on holiday.

The Lot is a particularly apt place to explore the relationships of these lifestyle migrants to their surroundings because of the way that it has been represented both as a tourist destination and as a place to live. In particular, the Lot is renowned for its rurality, and the sense of ruggedness that the landscape exudes (Martin, 2008). It offers awesome limestone cliffs as a backdrop to everyday life, medieval French villages, alongside the tranquillity of its natural beauty, and emptiness (it is one of the least populated departments in France).

In the last fifty or sixty years, the Lot has attracted British migrants of all ages. Many of these migrants have been lured by the promise of rurality (a stark opposition to their cynical and fatalistic presentations of life in Britain) that they perceive the French countryside to offer, with initial preconceptions of the landscape encouraging migration and property selection (see also Barou and Prado, 1995; Buller and Hoggart, 1994a & b; Depierre and Guitard, 2006; Gervais-Aguer, 2004, 2006). On one level, this can be understood as a romantic valorization of the countryside. However, only a more sustained examination of post-migration lives can reveal the true extent to which these imaginings shape the migrants' expectations of their lives within the rural idyll. In what follows I therefore reveal how culturally-specific imaginings intersect with everyday practices and understandings of post-migration lives.

Imagining and enacting a better way of life

When I first met many of my respondents in the Lot, I often asked them to recall the initial decision to migrate and explain to me why they had chosen the Lot, or indeed, their individual properties. As they reminisced, the unique scenery had been an important factor in property selection, an aspect of the area that had made a distinct impression on them during their first visits to the Lot. Some of them had visited the Lot on their summer holidays, while others only discovered the department once they started to search for a home in rural France. For most, though, the first experience of the area was remembered in terms of an aesthetic appreciation, even admiration, of the Lotoise landscape, with a particular value placed on the beautiful backdrop.

> He [the estate agent] brought us, we had lunch in Saint-Cirq and then he brought us along the fantastic road from Saint-Cirq to this village. At that stage I think we would have bought the shed because it was, it was just so colossal, the view along the edge. To think that we were going to be living 3 km away from that was just something else. (Robert and Justine Grange)[1]

> The view is wonderful from here. That's what made us buy it. (Trish Greenham)

Their accounts thus reflected the common desire for a scenic view found among lifestyle migrants (King, Warnes, and Williams, 2000; O'Reilly, 2000; Waldren, 1996). Such a scenic backdrop is desirable, as Hirsch (1995) argued, because of the promise of what life might be like, or, as Urry (2002) has argued in the case of the tourist gaze, because of a sense of escape central to the tourist gaze.

Beyond the natural beauty of the Lot, its British residents focussed on how the landscape was emblematic of a better and different way of life, and packaged as the rural idyll (cf Buller and Hoggart, 1994a; Barou and Prado, 1995), with its natural and holistic way of living. This was a way of life that they wanted to be a part of, their actions within their new surroundings providing testament to their efforts in this direction. In this respect, the landscape represented the possibility of a distinct break from their lives before migration, a space where they would have opportunities to live their lives the way they felt they wanted. The ethnography presented below demonstrates that over time, and through their embodied experiences of the landscape, they develop a relationship with their surroundings that is as much influenced by their own experiences of life in the Lot as it is by wider collective imaginings.

As my ethnographic enquiries reveal, by repeatedly evoking images of the rural idyll, my respondents stress their own search for social harmony, continuity, stability, and order (cf Selwyn, 1996), aspects of rurality predicated on community (Strathern, 1982; Rapport, 1993). They emphasize their desires for a localized, bounded, 'traditional rural community' based on mechanical solidarity (Rapport, 1993: 33) and valuing the 'immediate family and friendship ties, local community solidarity and supportiveness' (Perry, 1986: 22). In this respect, they demonstrate the centrality of imagination in how they understand and experience their new surroundings. They measure their post-migration lives against their idyllic representation(s) of the French countryside, particularly focussing on the ways in which the local population commune with one another and their surroundings. Importantly, from an early stage, their experiences taught them that the sense of community that they had been seeking existed in the Lot, as they revealed in their discussions of their neighbours:

> Everyone knows everyone. Everyday dealings are based more on community, sharing things. (Pat and Jean Porter)

> There is a big sense of community here. (Vivian St-John)

> The local community, it's just like family. (Trevor and Susan Sparrow)

> They have more value for time and people. (Kay Morris)

The desire to become part of the local community is common among lifestyle migrants. However, as O'Reilly (2000) has argued in the case of the British in Spain, there is often a discrepancy between rhetoric and action when it comes to the discussion of integration; while they stress that they want to become part of the local community, their actions instead seem to be directed towards the creation of a parallel community, normally made up of their compatriots. In such circumstances, claims to integration are often exaggerated.

Among my respondents in the Lot, claims that they were becoming part of the local community were, however, more than just rhetoric; they visibly worked towards creating meaningful relationships with members of the local community, even though their efforts were not always successful. The contexts in which they developed these relationships often reinforced their imaginings of the rural idyll, as they attended the *chasse* (hunt) dinner, the local fête or market, and had the opportunity to meet and get to know local social actors. They witnessed first hand the close-knit community of the Lot. Through commensality they gained opportunities to get to know local social actors, and over time, started to develop relationships with them. This was, as many of my respondents stressed, a slow and often frustrating process.

How my respondents related to the landscape was, however, more complex than this image presents. Their actions were informed not only by understandings about what life in rural France might afford them, but also by their wider imaginings and aspirations for life following migration. The context of life before migration was crucial in understanding how this was framed, with the changes in working status, the opposition between work and leisure, and position in the life course often featuring highly within it. In this respect the better way of life that the migrants sought through migration was often characterized, in part, by increased time for leisure activities such as walking, reading and playing golf. Once again, this reflects a wider discourse about the need to re-evaluate work-life balance in order to achieve a more wholesome and fulfilling way of life. For my respondents in the Lot the paramount emblem of such leisurely lives were the swimming pools that adorned their back gardens, set within locations chosen to make the most of the view. In this respect, it became clear that the migrants' various engagements were shaped by their preconceptions about what life following migration might afford.

Nevertheless, it was often the case that such different understandings of the landscape and how it should be used did not sit alongside one another comfortably. This became clear through the example of a swimming pool that was highly visible from one of the area's viewpoints. My respondents often described this particular pool as an eyesore, deemed to be out of keeping with the 'natural' surroundings. Built in the garden of a British resident, it stood out because of its unusual figure-of-eight shape and bright green pool liner. As the migrants explained how they had chosen the location of their own swimming pools to complement the local scenery, or hidden it from view, they drew attention to the tensions that existed between their representations of the Lot as the French rural idyll, the possibilities for leisure that their new surroundings afforded, and its visual-aesthetic value. Nevertheless, these efforts to enact wider cultural repertoires – the rural idyll, self-improvement, and the drive for a better way of life – demonstrate the role that imagination plays within the production of post-migration lives.

In many ways, the centrality of such imaginings both in the decision to migrate, and in life following migration is reminiscent of the *imagination as a social practice*, proposed by Arjun Appadurai. In this rendering, 'the imagination has become an organized field of social practices, a form of work (in the sense of both labour and culturally organized practice), and a form of negotiation between sites of agency (individuals) and globally defined fields of possibility' (Appadurai, 1996: 31). In this understanding, in the globalized world imagination is the property of the individual and underlies the multiple ways in which their everyday practices and activities are constantly 'at work' in how people understand and enact their lives.

As Appadurai (1996) explicitly argues, imagination inspires migration; in privileging the individual migrant, he stresses that imagination is what helps them to make sense of the possibilities around them and choose a particular route. However, Ong (1999) emphasises that there is a need to contemplate the structural conditions, and perhaps constraints, that shape the ability to act upon such an imagining. Indeed, as I highlight elsewhere, British migration to rural France is not only the result of the romantic idealization of the French countryside presented here, but is also made possible by the relative affluence of the migrants, and structural conditions such as the freedom of movement within Europe and ease of travel (Benson, 2011).

Beyond the structural context that allows migration, the examples also draw attention to the role of structure – in this case articulated as culture – in shaping the possibilities for their future lives that the migrants will consider as well as the way that they narrate these. In this respect, I argue that while it is important to understand the role of individual agency in bringing about migration, it is clear that the choice of destination and the framing of post-migration life is in part inspired by wider, collectively held imaginings. It is these that explain how my respondents in the Lot make sense of (1) their migration to rural France specifically – they were acting upon an understanding of rurality that could be recognized by their peers – and (2) their new surroundings – with their experiences interpreted through the lens of their imaginations. This understanding draws attention to the way in which what appear to be individual actions were justified through the recourse to collective imaginings. In this manner, understanding the relationship between imagination and migration also highlights the structural roots of the migrants' routes from Britain to the Lot.

Experiencing and embodying post-migration life

While it is clear that imaginings of the rural idyll shape both expectations and experiences of life in the Lot, it is also the case that through their own engagements with the landscape, my respondents gain subjective experiences of their new surroundings. These, in turn, inform their broader rhetoric of life in the Lot alongside their imaginings. In particular, working the land is perceived as an entrée into the landscape. As my respondents explain, through their various gardening and horticultural projects, they achieve a deeper knowledge of their new environments. In this respect, their accounts reflect an understanding of their relationship to the landscape premised on engagement; as they present it, in order to understand their surroundings, they have to feel the dirt beneath their fingernails (cf Theodossopoulos, 2003; Tilley, 1994, 2006a & b (in relation to gardens)).

For example, Connie and Harry Earl have a large vegetable garden, which requires a lot of care and attention. From ploughing and preparing the ground for planting, to weeding, nurturing, watering, tending, protecting, and eventually harvesting, this vegetable garden is a year-round undertaking, requiring work each day irrespective of the season. In the summer months, when most vegetables are ready to harvest, Harry and Connie could be out in the garden working for four or five hours a day. Early in the morning, before it becomes too hot, they harvest whatever is ready or needed for the day's food, as well as weeding. In the evening, they spend at least one and half hours watering the patch. As they explain, they grow their own vegetables because they taste good. I remain unsure whether they mean that they taste better than other vegetables or whether they taste better because of all the work that they have put into producing them. But there is more to it than that.

As another of my respondents, James Harvey-Browne explains, 'you probably tend to grow your own vegetables more because you're that bit further away from the main town', implying that in some sense, growing your own vegetables is part of rural living. This correlation is also central to the account of Martin and Sarah Johnstone, who run a *chambre d'hôte* (Bed and Breakfast) up on the *causse* (limestone plateau). They too grow many of their own vegetables and raise chickens. In the evenings, they provide their guests with a hearty rustic meal, made using home-grown vegetables, while breakfast include freshly laid eggs.

Another way that my respondents feel that they have developed a deeper understanding of their surroundings is through walking. Most villages have a rambling club, and by joining in with such activities the migrants are able to explore their surroundings alongside their neighbours, whose knowledge of the landscape has often been formed over a lifetime of living within it.

> We belong to a walking club and stuff and we don't get out there much but it's nice when you do go because you get to see all the places that you wouldn't know with locals and it's a good way to see things (Jon and Kay Morris).

> Surprising sometimes, you go out for walks and you think you know all the houses in the area, and all of a sudden, you come across a little house in the middle of nowhere . . . Jacques, the man who leads us, has got all sorts of plans of the old part of the commune, and he is working out various different routes to find things that are interesting, so we can learn a bit more about the history of the area (Martin and Sarah Johnstone).

The migrants then incorporate this newly-found knowledge into their own narratives about life in the Lot. They often make short observations about the flora and fauna, for example, pointing out the strange holes in the freshly ploughed fields, stressing that this is evidence of the wild boar searching for roots to eat, or identifying the calls of the local birds. In this manner, my respondents become engaged in the landscape, imitating the 'authentically' local knowledge of these social actors. Furthermore, through their shared participation in the rambling club, my respondents are able to develop relationships with local French actors, which extend into their everyday lives. It seems that through walking, the migrants establish an intimate relationship with their new surroundings, characterized by a distinctive understanding, with their routes intersecting those of other inhabitants of the landscape (Lee and Ingold, 2006; Ingold and Lee Vergunst, 2008).

Through practices such as gardening and walking the migrants believed that they were able to develop a personal, interactive relationship, becoming part of the local landscape. This highlights the privileging of engagement in the migrants' accounts of their relationship with their new surroundings, and their efforts to emplace themselves within the locality. In this respect, it is clear that their accounts aimed to produce a sense – reminiscent of that proposed by Ingold (1993, 1995) that they were dwelling within the landscape. As Ingold argues (1993, 1995), through dwelling social actors become an integral part of their surroundings, building up relationships with other people, animals, and objects and gaining an intimate understanding of the landscape. In other words, a connection to the landscape through engagement results in a sense of rootedness, of localness.

Furthermore, it became clear that these activities set the stage for my respondents to become part of the local social landscape, interacting with their local French neighbours. Indeed, Martin and Sarah had stuck certificates from the village association to the fridge door, attesting to the quality of their produce; they had come first and second at the village competition for their home-grown vegetables. Their efforts in the vegetable garden evidently give them an intimate knowledge of the physical landscape, but have also resulted in their paths crossing those of other local users.

This seamless image of integration into the local landscape through engagement overlooks the persistence of imagination in shaping how the migrants understand their surroundings; in other words, it is not the case that the migrants exchange their preconceived ideals for personal experience. For example, focusing on the role of engagement in the development of a relationship with the landscape overlooks the complexity of this relationship, which often contains an element of detachment – the landscape viewed from a distance and often shape by imagination.

This contradicts Ingold's (1993, 1995) model for understanding the landscape, through which he stresses that engagement with the landscape and detachment from it are mutually exclusive. Nevertheless, it is clear that for my respondents in the Lot, both engagement and detachment characterize their relationships with the new environment, as is the case for many modern actors. Indeed, as Carrier (2003) implies, modern social actors often hold contradictory understandings of the environment that simultaneously privilege both engagement with and detachment from the landscape. Furthermore, the privileging of engagement as practice undermines the extent to which preconceived understandings of the landscape shape the very practices that evolve. In sum, the dwelling perspective privileges practice and activity over representation and a coherence in perceptions of the landscape which cannot fully account for the lived experience of my respondents (see Carrier, 2003; Cloke and Jones, 2001; Massey, 2006 for more developed critiques of Ingold's perspective).

Indeed, the migrants' actions had a history and context behind them that is frequently overlooked by the dwelling perspective. The landscape of the Lot is not a blank canvas for the migrants, and their practices and activities remain framed by their early representations of the rural French landscape. For example, examining the migrants' accounts of gardening more carefully reveals that they often conflate their efforts to engage with the landscape with those of local farmers. It was thus common to find that migrants would explain how, like their French neighbours, they had an intuitive understanding of the landscape, or they would claim that they imitated these local actors, watching how, when, and what they planted.

Although their French neighbours cultivate the land out of economic necessity, the migrants nevertheless believe they imitate the local French. Their actions, therefore, suggest a mimicry, which serves as a way of claiming a particular type of belonging. In the case of less privileged actors mimicry has been identified as a tool of the colonizers (Taussig, 1993; Bhabha, 2002) or as a way of claiming an overarching supranational identity (Ferguson, 2002). In contrast, for my respondents in the Lot, mimicry serves uniquely as a way of claiming membership of a particular locale. This clearly maps on to their ambitions for life in the Lot, which include, as Justine Grange explained, the desire 'to be part of the village'.

As the following section demonstrates, the migrants' activities within the landscape continue to be shaped by wider cultural repertoires, even if they also account for practice. In this respect, as Cloke and Jones (2001) argue, it is necessary to account for the dynamism and interpenetrativeness of the con-temporary landscape that is not permitted by Ingold's dwelling perspective. Furthermore, there is a need to examine the (messy) process through which embodied knowledge is developed, focussing particularly on the interrelationships between vicarious knowledge and social practice.

A more complex picture

The examples presented so far have extracted, on the one hand, the culturally-specific imaginings that promoted migration to rural France and the role that these continue to play in shaping the migrants' perceptions of their new surroundings. On the other hand, the ethnography demonstrates the extent to which the migrants privilege engagement with the landscape as a way of developing an intimate knowledge of their surroundings. However, closer examination of their narratives reveals a more complex picture of how they use, interpret, and relate to their new surroundings. In this respect, a model needs to be developed that broadly accounts for how culturally-specific imaginings of the rural idyll, embodied knowledge and individual experiences coalesce in the development of a relationship with the landscape.

It was clear that despite their experiences of life in the Lot, their imaginings of this place and their lives within it continued to influence their understandings of it. This was evident in the way that they talked about their lives in the Lot; as the examples in this paper have shown, they often referred to the virtues of the rural idyll and reflected on how these were a central part of their lives. However, it was also the case that they continued to value the visual beauty of their surroundings. Indeed, they recalled how this often caused them to step back from their daily lives and survey their surroundings just as they had done on their first visits to the Lot.

> The view across the Vers (a local valley) is absolutely stunning . . . why are we here? Because it's beautiful. (David Lomax)

> It's a beautiful area. There's no doubt about it. We still pinch ourselves when we're driving round doing work. (Jon and Kay Morris)

The complexity in the ways that my respondents experienced the landscape became clear as they recalled how their imaginings of rural life had been modified by their experiences. For example, Susan Sparrow had imagined that she would be able to make jam from her home-grown produce, but when she had returned home with her fruit trees, her neighbour had informed her that the tree would not grow in the local soil and would, therefore, not produce any fruit. While Susan, by her own admission, had stubbornly refused to accept her neighbour's advice, it soon became clear that her new trees were not faring very well. Through this experience she realized that the locals, 'know far more than we do about living here', in the process gaining her own embodied knowledge of how to live in the Lot. This was an experience that many of my respondents held in common with Susan. As Vic Wilson recalled, many people thought that they could grow anything in the Lot; importing their seeds from Britain, they were often surprised when they did not grow. As he explained, he had learned very quickly that the seeds that you could buy locally would produce the best results, as they were specifically cultivated to match local conditions.

It seemed that through their experiences, the migrants were able to graft their imaginings onto their new surroundings, invoking local knowledge to make the environment meaningful in their own terms. Undeniably, their sense of what constituted local knowledge was itself the product of both their romantic imaginings of rural life and their direct experiences and was often highly selective. This demonstrates the extent to which imagination and experience are inextricably intertwined.

However, it was also the case that the migrants' imaginings of the landscape could be not only in tension with one another – as outlined earlier – but also with their everyday practices. In other words, they did not always act upon their imaginings, nor was it the case that their actions reflected their accumulated embodied knowledge of how to live in the Lot. For example, despite having learned that certain vegetables that he would have grown in Britain would not grow in the Lot, and despite his previously thwarted attempts to produce a close-cut, luscious green lawn, Harry Earl persisted in striving to create the perfect lawn. Similarly, the idea of being close to nature that was part of their dreams about living in the countryside was very much at odds with other migrants' efforts to build fences that would keep the local wildlife away from their vegetable gardens.

These examples demonstrate the contradictions and complexity in the ways that the migrants imagine and perform their relationship with the landscape. The migrants' various engagements with their new surroundings reflect the three ways that people relate to the landscape as outlined by Barbara Bender (1998: 6): palimpsest, structure of feeling, and through embodiment. Bender's perspective thus allows for a landscape that undergoes continual change while maintaining the residues of past use; a landscape that has a particular learned significance for individuals, a meaning embedded in their habitus; but finally, this is also a landscape that is learned through practice and activity, as individuals, metaphorically, get their hands dirty. These different perceptions have a combined influence on the way that people relate to landscape at any particular point in time Bender (1993, 1998), with the landscape in continual process (Bender, 1993, 1998; Hirsch, 1995; Massey, 2006).

These more dynamic perspectives on understanding the landscape place both representation and practice at their centre, recognizing that these are thoroughly entangled (Bender, 1998; Cloke and Jones, 2001; Massey, 2006). In other words, perceptions of the appropriate practices and activities to carry out in the landscape may be influenced by representations and these, in turn, may be affected by lived experience. By recognizing the complex and multiple perceptions of the landscape held by individuals, it is possible to reveal the continuing co-dependence of practice and representation, engagements and detachments that are foundational to the landscape-making process. These conceptualizations of how people understand the landscape, provides a framework for exploring the migrants' relationships to their new surroundings, presenting a position that recognizes the thorough and inextricable intertwining of representation and practice, gazing and dwelling, detachment and engagement.

Concluding comments

While previous scholars have stressed that British migrants understand the French rural landscape in terms of popular cultural representations of rurality, depicted through the lens of a tourist gaze, the ethnography presented in this paper has demonstrated that following migration, such migrants have a dynamic relationship with their new surroundings that is premised, not only on their imaginings of their new surroundings, but also their everyday experiences. In this respect, over time it is clear that my respondents develop more nuanced understandings of the landscape as they strive to develop embodied knowledge of life in the Lot.

The focus on the landscape presented here reveals the way that imaginings are a central feature, not only of the decision to migrate, but also in shaping and framing experiences of life following migration. While the myth of the rural idyll has been the predominant explanation for why British people migrate to rural France, the decision to migrate, as this paper has shown, is also influenced by other imaginings that relate not only to understandings of place, but also to hopes and dreams for life following migration. In particular, imaginings of a more leisurely life and scenic representations of the landscape exist alongside the imagery of the coherent rural community. In this respect, it has become clear that the landscape may, simultaneously have multiple significance for the migrants, with these understandings of the landscape influencing and shaping their relationships and uses of their new surroundings.

Beyond this, however, there is a need to recognize the messy entanglement of experience and imagining. Neither of these alone can explain the relationship that the migrants have to their new surroundings. It is rather the case that their multi-layered understandings of the landscape emerge out of the negotiation between imagination and experience. As the examples presented in this paper have demonstrated, through this negotiation, imagination may persist unchanged, or be modified or appropriated to be made meaningful in the terms of the individual migrant. Experience may contradict imagination, creating a tension between the two, a continuing source of ambivalence in the migrants' lives.

The negotiation between imaginings and experiences, as the migrants seek to gain embodied knowledge of life in the Lot, demonstrates that relationships with the landscape continually undergo change. They are a process in which representations and practices are thoroughly intertwined (Bender, 1998; Massey, 2006). In the case of British migrants in the Lot, they are also a site for recognizing that the process of settling into life in new surroundings draws upon both imaginings and experiences, and is influenced by structural preconditions, culturally-specific imaginings, but also by subjective interpretations and experiences. Following Bourdieu's logic of practice, this is a process of embodying knowledge about how to live within a new environment, of incorporating such knowledge into the emergent and emerging embodied experience of living in the Lot. The examples presented here demonstrate the extent to which the migrants continue to reflect upon this process; it appears that life in the Lot has not yet become second nature.

It is thus the case that, over time, the migrants' accounts of life in the Lot continue to be framed around an expressed desire to become part of this landscape. Yet understandings of this landscape are themselves a moveable feast, gradually being altered by a more nuanced understanding of its history and its effect on other users; and perhaps most by the toil necessary to emplace themselves within it.

While there are times when the migrants' practices directly correspond to their representations, on closer examination, it appears that they may simultaneously represent and practise the landscape in contradictory ways. As the ethnographic examples demonstrates, they may expound the virtues of relating to the landscape through an engagement premised upon their understandings of the Lot as a rural idyll, but their accounts also tell of their regular relapses when they reduce their surroundings to its aesthetic and hedonistic qualities. It is thus the case that their perceptions of the landscape are not coherent; they change from one moment to the next, and are, in reality, continually negotiated.

Nevertheless, the contradictory perceptions that the migrants hold are not mutually exclusive: they inform and affect one another. Over time, the nuanced understanding of the landscape that the migrants gain through their own embodied experience becomes the guiding inspiration that shapes their perceptions. This reflects their belief that they have moved from being incomers to locals, making their hands dirty by working the land. However, the contradictions between their practices and representations and those of other 'locals' demonstrate an underlying ambiguity in their lives. In many respects, this ambiguity reflects their position as global social actors who want to become local, *without* completely abandoning their previous idealized perceptions of rurality. It can therefore be concluded that the British migrants living in the Lot hold, 'different landscapes in tension' (Bender, 1993: 2), often adopting confused criteria for judging their surroundings.

Note

All names appearing in the text are pseudonyms.

References

Appadurai, A., (1996), *Modernity at Large: Cultural Dimension of Globalization*, Minneapolis: University of Minneapolis Press.
Barou, J. and P. Prado, (1995), *Les Anglais dans Nos Campagnes*, Paris: L'Harmattan.
Bender, B., (1993), 'Introduction: Landscape – Meaning and Action', in Bender, B., (ed.), *Landscape: Politics and Perspectives*, Oxford: Berg:1–18.
Bender, B., (1998), *Stonehenge: Making Space*, Oxford: Berg.
Benson, M., (2009), 'A Desire for Difference: British Lifestyle Migration to Southwest France', in Benson, M. and K. O'Reilly (eds), *Lifestyle Migration: Expectations, Aspirations and Experiences*, Aldershot: Ashgate.
Benson, M., (2010), 'The Context and Trajectory of Lifestyle Migration: the Case of the British Residents of Southwest France', *European Societies Forum.* Availabel online at: http://myblogs. informa.com/europeansocieties/2010/01/25/the-context/.

Benson, M., (2011), *The British in Rural France: Lifestyle Migration and the Ongoing Quest for a Better Way of Life*, Manchester: Manchester University Press.

Bhabha, H., (2002), 'Of Mimicry and Man: The Ambivalence of Colonial Discourse', in Essed, P. and D.T. Goldberg, (eds), *Race Critical Theories: Text and Context*, Oxford: Blackwell: 113–22.

Bourdieu, P., (1977), *Outline of a Theory of Practice*, Cambridge: Cambridge University Press, (R. Nice trans).

Bourdieu, P., (1990), *The Logic of Practice*, Cambridge: Polity (R. Nice trans).

Buller, H. and K. Hoggart, (1994a), *International Counterurbanization*, Aldershot: Avebury.

Buller, H. and K. Hoggart, (1994b), *British Home Owners in Rural France: Property Selection and Characteristics*, King's College London Department of Geography Occasional Paper, #40.

Carrier, J., (2003), 'Mind, Gaze and Engagement: Understanding the Environment', *Journal of Material Culture*, 8: 5–23.

Cloke, P. and O. Jones, (2001), 'Dwelling, Place, and Landscape: an Orchard in Somerset', *Environment and Planning A*, 33: 649–66.

Depierre, F. and F. Guitard, (2006), *L'accueil et L'installation des Nord-Europeens en Limousin, L'exemple des Britanniques: Quel Poids, Quels Effets, Quelles Perspectives?* Rapport de stage, Conseil regional du Limousin et Université de Limoges.

Ferguson, J., (2002), 'Of Mimicry and Membership: Africans and the "New World Society"', *Cultural Anthropology*,17(4): 551–69.

Gervaise-Aguer, M.-M., (2004), *Les Fondements de L'attractivité Territoriale Résidentielle: les Enseignements d'une Recherché Portant sur les Résidents Britanniques en Aquitaine (France)*. Cahiers du GRES, 2004–25.

Gervaise-Aguer, M.-M., (2006), *Prospective Analysis, Residential Choice and Territorial Attractiveness*, Cahiers du GRES, 2006–30.

Hirsch, E., (1995), 'Introduction. Landscape: Between Place and Space', in Hirsch, E. and M. O'Hanlon, (eds), *The Anthropology of Landscape*, Oxford: Clarendon Press: 1–30.

Ingold, T., (1993), 'The Temporality of Landscape', *World Archaeology*, 25(2): 152–74.

Ingold, T., (1995), 'Building, Dwelling, Living: How Animals and People Make Themselves at Home in the World', in Strathern, M., (ed.), *Shifting Contexts: Transformations in Anthropological Knowledge*, London and New York: Routledge: 57–80.

Ingold, T. and J.L. Vergunst, (2008), *Ways of Walking: Anthropology and Practice on Foot*, Aldershot: Ashgate.

King, R., A. Warnes and A. Williams, (2000), *Sunset Lives: British Retirement Migration to the Mediterranean*, Oxford: Berg.

Lee, J. and T. Ingold, (2006), 'Fieldwork on Foot: Perceiving, Routing, Socialising', in Coleman, S. and P. Collins, (eds), *Locating the Field: Space, Place and Context in Anthropology*, Oxford: Berg Publishers.

Martin, H., (2008), *Lot: Travels through a Limestone Landscape in Southwest France*, Wiltshire: Moho Books.

Massey, D., (2006), 'Landscape as a Provocation: Reflections on Moving Mountains', *Journal of Material Culture*, 11: 33–48.

Ong, A., *Flexible Citizenship: The Cultural Logres of Transnationalism*, Durham and London: Duke Univeristy Press.

O'Reilly, K., (2000), *The British on the Costa del Sol: Transnational Identities and Local Communities*, London: Routledge.

Perry, R., (1986), *Counterurbanisation: International Case Studies of Socio-Economic Change in the Rural Areas.*, Norwich: Geo Books.

Rapport, N., (1993), *Diverse World-Views in an English village*, Edinburgh: Edinburgh University Press.

Selwyn, T., (1996), 'Introduction', in Selwyn, T., (ed.), *The Tourist Image: Myths and Myth Making in Tourism*, Chichester: John Wiley and Sons: 1–32.

Strathern, M., (1982), 'The Village as an Idea: Constructs of Village-ness in Elmdon, Essex', in Cohen, A., (ed.), *Belonging, Identity and Social Organisation in British Rural Cultures*, Manchester: Manchester University Press: 247–77.

Taussig, M., (1993), *Mimesis and Alterity: a Particular Study of the Senses*, London: Routledge.

Theodossopoulos, D., (2003), *Troubles with Turtles*, Oxford: Berghahn.

Tilley, C., (1994), *A Phenomenology of Landscape: Places, Paths and Monuments*, Oxford: Berg.

Tilley, C., (2006a), 'Introduction: Identity, Place, Landscape and Heritage', *Journal of Material Culture*, 11: 7–32.

Tilley, C., (2006b), 'The Sensory Dimensions of Gardening', *The Senses and Society*, 1(3): 311–30.

Urry, J., (2002), (2nd edn.) *The Tourist Gaze: Leisure and Travel in Contemporary Societies*, London: Sage.

Waldren, J., (1996), *Insiders and Outsiders: Paradise and Reality in Mallorca*, Oxford: Berghahn Books.

The reproduction of 'cultural taste' amongst the Ukrainian Diaspora in Bradford, England

Oscar Forero and Graham Smith

Abstract: This paper refers to research with Ukrainian families in Bradford that was conducted in an attempt to investigate the transmission of values, with particular reference to food. Here we report on how this research led us towards a better understanding of how cultural 'taste' evolves between generations. The paper thus draws upon three studies undertaken in the 1980s, 1990s and more recently between 2005 and 2008 with those who identify themselves with the Ukrainian communities in the city. The first two studies used oral history to collect life stories, while the more recent research used a range of anthropological methods. We have sought to draw in particular on, and combine theoretical insights from, Bourdieu and Passeron's work on 'habitus' (1979) and Mannheim's concept of 'generational style' (1997). By combining the earlier testimonies with more recent data, we conclude that each generation has developed its own distinctive projects and styles as it has negotiated its historical times. In arriving at this conclusion we want to suggest that while the influences of technology and media are influential in transforming 'taste', and foodways in particular, the generational projects and their food ideologies were the main determinant factor shaping the foodways of the Ukrainian diaspora.

Introduction

While 'taste', as a sense, allows individuals to differentiate gustatory qualities of foods, differentiation is meaningless without a frame of reference. It is 'symbolic schemes of edibility' (Sahlins, 1990) which allow the basic distinction of edible versus inedible foods. All societies create, transform and reproduce the cultural representations of foods that make them distinctive from other societies. Or, as Falk (1994) puts it: 'members of the same culture eat the same kind of food'; and it is in this sense that taste is always cultural.

To understand better how 'taste' evolves between generations, the research informing this paper interrogated the notion of transmission of values, with particular reference to food, amongst Ukrainian families in Bradford.[1] In considering the evidence of social reproduction and transformation of a distinctive 'cultural taste' we revisited Bourdieu's concepts of 'cultural capital' and 'habitus'. We were especially interested in explaining how material conditions and family membership influence the choices made by individuals (Bourdieu and Passeron, 1973; Bourdieu, 1984), including in diet and eating patterns.

Bourdieu (1984) used the concept of habitus to refer to the collective schemata of experience and perceptions within which individuals make decisions. Although habitus was not proposed as an absolute determinant of individuals' cultural practices it served to explain 'dispositions'; that is those processes that make individuals more likely to choose certain ways of doing and practising. Using the case study of evolving foodways, that is the procurement, preparation, and consumption of food, of Ukrainian post-war émigré people in Britain, we aim to illustrate how habitus provided individuals and generations with a framework for making sense of their social experiences.

The studies of Lupton (1996), Tivadar and Luther (2005), Warde and Martens (2000) seem to confirm that income and education continue to influence individuals' food preferences. But what would be the impact of the dynamics of habitus on eating amongst a diasporic community? How would individual histories and their experience of war and displacement affect their food choices? How would these experiences influence the reproduction of values associated with food and the foodways of successive generations born in the host country? This paper surmises how our investigations advanced in addressing these questions.

The schemata that helps the individual to discern what is edible and to consider the convenience and appropriateness of food practices is not automatically 'transmitted' from one generation to the next. Food preferences are adapted, adopted, transformed or generated in the practices of everyday life. The personal and social memories that influence preferences regarding edibility are in turn shaped by broader socio-political changes. The result is that 'cultural taste' is constantly disputed. It is through considering the preferences of other social actors within the same community that an individual's judgment of taste is constructed. In the words of Bourdieu (1977), 'there is always interested or competitive conduct within the symbolic system'.

Bourdieu and Passeron (1979) defined cultural capital as forms of knowledge; skill; education; or any advantages a person has which gives them a higher status in society, including high expectations. In particular, they suggested that parenting provided children with the attitudes and knowledge that allowed them to navigate more or less successfully through their generational time. Mannheim (1997) proposed that the social position of a generation depended on how a particular cohort navigated the historical period they lived through, with this confluence creating a 'community of location'. He also noticed that members of a single generation within a community of location seemed to believe that they shared a 'common destiny' and in doing so developed distinctive 'generational styles'.

Following this approach in our study of a particular Ukrainian diasporic community we will identify and describe the unique settings in which each generation has exercised differing cultural practices. We were fortunate to be able to draw upon three projects conducted within the same community in which participants made reference to food. In re-examining the narratives of three generations of family members in Bradford who considered that they were Ukrainian or with Ukrainian heritage, it was revealed that food was a key marker in how they sustained a collective diasporic identity. Similar processes have been made evident in previous studies (i.e. Bak, 1997; Mintz, 2008; Threadgold, 2000) but we believe our study achieved something else by characterizing how this marker changes over time.

Before examining these styles in some detail we would refer briefly to our sources and the general background to this study. Since the mid-1980s a number of projects have been conducted with members of the Ukrainian communities in and around Bradford. The first of these projects by the Bradford Heritage Recording Unit (BHRU) collected oral histories with those who arrived in Britain during the late 1940s (Perks, 1986; Smith, Perks *et al.*, 1998). Life history interviews were also conducted as part of the East European Migration to Bradford projects in the 1990s as well. In addition interviews were carried out in this second study with the children and grandchildren of the 'primary settlers' as the researchers on the second study called those who arrived in the late 1940s (Smith *et al.*, 1998).

A third study, ours, was conducted in 2006–2007. The research aims included investigating whether there were distinctive cultural practices among the diaspora and if so, how such practices effected changes in the food habits of successive generations. We documented the reproduction of rituals that bring stability in the communication exchange between generations. But we also documented inter-generational tension, made obvious when divergent projects or differences in style were discussed (narratives) or performed (in every day cooking or at festive occasions).

References to the narratives recorded during the most recent fieldwork (2006–2007) have been coded beginning with PS and references to narratives recorded prior to this research have been coded beginning with SS. The data generated through our project comes from the categorization of ethnographic notes and recorded interviews.[2] The same categories and codes were then used when reviewing the archived material generated by the earlier projects.[3] In this way we were able to contrast 'cultural practices' against the narratives in which they are embedded.[4]

Ukrainians in Britain

The histories of Ukrainians in Britain have been explored in some depth (Cesarani, 2001; Smith *et al.*, 1998). Before the Second World War there was little Ukrainian presence in Britain and within a little more than five post-war years migration was complete. Ukraine after the war had become a part of the USSR and the 'iron curtain' dividing Europe meant that contact and travel to and from Ukraine was extremely difficult. By 1951 there were around 34,000 Ukrainians in Britain who found themselves cut off from friends and family in Ukraine. Until the 1990s Ukrainian communities in Britain were isolated from the motherland in a way that was unusual even in comparison with other eastern European émigrés, there was, for example, more contact amongst Polish communities in Britain and Poland in this period. The Soviet regime effectively prevented subsequent migration from the homeland to Britain. As a consequence along with the isolation the profile of the initial migrants would in turn produce sharply defined generational cohorts within the Ukrainian communities.

Ukrainian communities in Britain were also distinct in composition in relation to other Ukrainian communities. For example, the settlements in North America were not only longer established, but also socially, religiously and politically heterogeneous, and included members of the political left who had escaped Tsarist terror before the First World War. In contrast the largest number of activists in Britain belonged to the Organization of Ukrainian Nationalists (OUN). These were split between Banderists (OUN/B) and a smaller grouping who were the followers of Andriy Melnyk (OUN/M). Most originated from rural Galicia, western Ukraine, were practising Ukrainian Greek Catholics, and formed the Association of Ukrainians in Great Britain (AUGB). There was a small minority from the east, who tended to be Eastern Orthodox and who thought of themselves as better educated and more urbane and were more likely to belong to the rival Federation of Ukrainians in Great Britain.

Just over a quarter of the men who arrived had been members of the Ukrainian-SS Galician Division of the German Army before surrendering to the British. Controversially, in 1948 they were brought to Britain and released (Smith *et al.*, 1998; Cesarani, 2001; Hrycyszyn, 2002). However, the majority of the men and almost all of the women had served as forced labour in Germany. Some formed good relationships with the Germans they worked for, especially on farms (PS: M), but others were ordered into munitions production and experienced harsh conditions (SS: B0042). After a period at the end of the war as 'Displaced Persons', they volunteered to join one of the European Volunteer Worker (EVW) schemes that brought them to textile towns in Britain (Smith *et al.*, 1998; Hrycyszyn, 2002). The majority of these migrants were not fluent in English and had little education (PS: M, WG; SS: B0005, B0016, B0133).

Referring to the 'imagined community' of Ukrainians in Bradford, Smith and Jackson (1999) called attention to the negotiation processes that take place within a diaspora whilst 'narrating the nation'. Narrating the nation is always contextualized. The individuals' re-creation of events is influenced by numerous factors, including age, gender, class, status, kinship, education, ethnic or religious affiliation, geographical location, and health. And the formation of 'national identity' for a diasporic community is further complicated by the migrant 'experience of being from one place and of another'. In this way, Anthias argued, 'diaspora' is both a condition and a societal process (1998: 565).

Accurate statistics for post-1990 Ukrainian emigration are notoriously difficult to obtain as often Ukrainians are grouped together in official counts with other so-called 'eastern Europeans'. In addition temporary, seasonal and irregular migration adds to a confused picture both nationally and globally. The World Bank (2006; 2007) calculated that some 7 million people have been annually exiting Ukraine (including seasonal workers) with Britain attracting a very small number, perhaps around 12,000.

The imagined cuisine of an imagined Ukraine

Almost all those who were interviewed in the 1980s, 1990s and in the most recent study agreed that for the oldest generation Ukrainians who settled in Britain, marriage and the creation of family and home were as important as the acquisition or construction of churches, both Ukrainian Catholic and Orthodox, for the service of the 'community'.[5] Families were not only created through marriage, but also through establishing fictive kin networks, most obviously through children's godparents and the making of 'uncles' and 'aunts' (SS:EMB 21, 07, 05, 03, 13, 15, 18).

Their ambiguous status of having residency and work permits, but no passports or voting rights was of little concern to the settlers of the late 1940s, given that most believed that their stay in Britain was temporary and that they would return to an independent Ukraine freed from Soviet influences in the foreseeable future (PS:WGI; SS: B0018). Above all else their efforts were directed towards influencing 'international politics' and preparing their families for the return to the 'fatherland' or 'father's country' (SS: B003, B0008, B0016). They were to develop the infrastructures that their social and political projects required. In Bradford as early as 1961 the AUGB premises, 'the club', began to develop offices, a kitchen and dining hall, a bar, an auditorium, a school and a library. A church was also purchased in a nearby location. (PS: WGI, M, D, S, Ach, AB; Smith et al., 1998).

In respect to the handling of foods, the cooking practices and eating patterns were all influenced by post-war shortages, the housing conditions, transport infrastructure and social institutions of post-war urban life. First and second generation Ukrainians in Britain remember that food was often stored in the cellars of their homes (PS: TAI, WGI, ACh); few if any would have had refrigerators (PS: WGI, D, S, Ach). Food tended to be purchased from two large markets in Bradford with the main shopping taking place during weekends. There were many corner shops, a few bakeries, one of them selling 'Ukrainian' bread. A tiny number of Polish and Ukrainian migrants opened delicatessen shops where 'home ingredients' were purchased for the cooking of traditional dishes on special occasions, particularly during Christmas and Easter (PS: WGI, M, D, S, Ach, AB, JK; SS: B0059).

Members of the oldest generation interviewed during the most recent research repeated narratives similar to those collected in the earlier studies with respect to the value they attached to food (eg PS: TO, M, AB; SS: B0016). An important factor emphasized is experienced and imagined food scarcities; the primary settlers portrayed pleasant childhoods interrupted by the war. In such narratives Ukrainians are invariably portrayed as victims reacting against irrational or evil external forces who deprived them of human security, including food. Food has a greater meaning in these stories than recalled individual hunger. After all, these are recollections of childhoods that were spent in communities in which farming and food processing were important determinants of peasant identity.

Performing traditional food at home and in public

Before looking at the changing meanings of food between generations in more detail, we need to say a little more about our use of theory in understanding that change. An early critique of structuralism was that researchers who were interested in cultural practices as signifiers or codes tended to overlook the influence of material conditions in cultural practices. Bourdieu proposed habitus as an alternative way of considering the problem; thus, whilst acknowledging that 'cultural practices' represent and need to be understood as signifiers within a larger framework, he brought back Marxism's interest in how 'material conditions' actually influenced cultural practices as well. In following this approach, we provide an account of material conditions and their influence in habitus settings, but we also signal how the apparent changes in generational style, particularly the use of foodways as artefacts and tokens (described later in this article) by successive generations actually sustains the identity of the diaspora as a perceived collective.

According to Lévi-Strauss (1965), 'endo-cuisine' involves the consumption of food within a small closed group, such as the family. This is contrasted with 'exo-cuisine', which is food intended to be offered for more public consumption. Lévi-Strauss's earlier attempt was to generalize, linking particular cooking methods as indicative of either endo- or exo- cuisine, with boiling associated with endo-cuisine and roasting with exo-cuisine. Other researchers have been more cautious in making this type of generalization but retained the conceptual distinction (see for example Ulrich Tolksdorf, 1976). Following such a route, one could refer to endo-cuisine as the daily consumption of meals in the domestic sphere and to exo-cuisine as food prepared for special occasions or consumed after its public display, including in restaurants. For some, including Phillip Kleinfelder (2004), building on the earlier work of Klaus Roth (2001), this distinction can also offer a way of thinking about how new 'foreign' cuisines can be introduced. Thus, it is argued, new and exotic dishes are usually first encountered in the 'exo-cuisine', although in the long term they can be adopted into the 'endo-cuisine' following the adaptation and performance made to suit 'local' tastes. We will return to these ideas later when discussing the ways in which different generations have related to exo- and endo- culinary practices and their overall effect as cultural practices.

The model or ideal traditional meal as recalled by participants in the most recent research, regardless of their age, was: *borsht* (beetroot soup) *pyrohy* or *vareneky* (dumplings filled with potatoes or cheese) accompanied with fried onion sauce or mushroom sauce and *holubtsi* (cabbage rolls) which could be filled with corned beef, or rice and pork.[6] During Christmas an additional dish called *kutia* was prepared, containing a mixture of poppy seeds, wheat, nuts and honey. At this time some families ate *oseledets* (pickled herring) served on their own or with beetroot salad. Occasionally cakes or a sweet version of *vareneky* (cheese with strawberry or cherry sauce) accompanied the meal. During Easter each family arranged food in a basket to be blessed by the priest on the day before Easter breakfast. The baskets observed in the most recent study contained *kovbasa* or *sosysky* (sausages and other pork meats), *paska* (rich sweet bread) or *babka* (sweet bread with dried fruit), boiled eggs and *pysanka* (decorated eastern eggs), horseradish, some pickles and *kvashena kapusta* (sauerkraut). For the blessing, the baskets were placed in a line, covered with embroidered cloths with traditional designs.

As Fishkin (2005) has noted, one extensively investigated aspect in the literature of foodways is the question of authenticity in cuisine and its relation to a group's identity. In the case of the diasporic community we observed that claims of 'authenticity' were strongly associated with 'traditional' foods. On closer examination Ukrainian cookery has borrowed ingredients and dishes from a range of culinary traditions, including Russian, Polish and German. There is little that makes the dishes prepared by Ukrainians in Britain distinctively Ukrainian. However, through family and social rituals that the oldest generation of the diaspora pursued so emphatically, these dishes became a powerful symbol of the lost nation. In reference to 'traditional food practices' it has been documented in the past 'that people often feel it necessary to supply that identity with a past, even if much of that past was specially created for the purpose' (MacClancy, 2004: 68). As Murcott (1996) suggested, once imagined, these cuisines become a concrete expression of national-ethnic identities. In this case, the imagined cuisine of the diaspora became an integral part of the creative process of nationhood.

Older Ukrainian women who had worked on family farms as children and who later were forced to labour for the Germans during the war had to learn their cooking on the march, with scant regard to the quality of ingredients or fidelity to family recipes. The priority was to provide nutrition and survive but inadvertently they were creating the 'lost nation's cuisine'. After settling in England, these women would cook and serve 'Ukrainian food' as well as instruct their daughters in 'Ukrainian traditional cooking' (PS: WGI). For the primary settlers the Ukrainian food tasted (and still tastes) better than any other food and for good reason: it tastes of the nation. This is an important marker of a distinctive food ideology: the oldest generation of the diaspora ate what they ate, and ate in the ways that they did, because they pursued the diasporic interest of an imagined national Ukraine.

The recipients of this well crafted symbolism surrounding the 'national cuisine', the children of the primary settlers, reinterpreted and relocated their food experiences. They questioned their parents' generational project, reconsidered the aesthetics and values attached to traditional foods and set to develop a new lifestyle that could distinguish them from their parents.

When they were young many of the children were sent to Ukrainian school on Saturdays and to church on Sundays, with vacation time programmed into the club activities as well. Second generation Ukrainians have consistently complained that they had little time for mixing with non-Ukrainian friends (PS: WGI, D, S; SS: B0007, B0008) and began to rebel and search for what they conceived to be the English experience. (PS: WGI, D, S, JK, SM; SS: BOO8; Smith *et al.*, 1998).

Although some of them permanently broke off contact with all things they considered to be Ukrainian, the AUGB and other community activities are run today by those who were raised as Ukrainians in Britain. There are those who have consistently remained involved with political and social activities and there are others who have more recently returned to assist with the various organizations, often after starting a family of their own. They work together with a small number of new post-1990 immigrants who, although they do not share the experiences of the diaspora, are willing to work with the AUGB and the Association of Ukrainian Schools. And in doing so, they aim to protect and develop the diasporic models of traditional Ukrainian community and family life (PS: WGI, D, St, T). This is reflected in the caution exercised by members of the Bradford AUGB and the Ukrainian School in accepting volunteers. As the president of AUGB Women's group in Bradford explained to us this caution includes a certain amount of scepticism about recent migrants who express an interest in affiliating to AUGB activities (WGI).

It is noticeable that members of the younger generation refer to themselves as British-Ukrainians and to Ukrainian food as part of their heritage rather than a signifier of national identity (PS: JK, S, D, WGI; SS: B0005, B0007, B0007). Within this reconstruction of identity Ukrainian foodways have been re-contextualized. British-Ukrainians' recollections of school dinners are little different from those of any British child or teenager (PS: D, S. WGI). Indeed, their narratives demonstrate that their food practices reflect broader changes in British culture, particularly available in the restaurants of Bradford. So, for instance, they are not only critical of their parents' lack of appetite for foods of 'other ethnicities', and an understanding of the significance of exo-cuisine, but they also consider themselves – and are perceived in turn by their own children – as more adventurous with food than the primary settlers (PS: D, S, WGI, TAI, JK, St, Dy, Mt, P). Unlike the oldest generation of Ukrainians, they like to try different foods and enjoy the experience of eating out (PS: WGI, D, S, TAI, TO, St, Dy, Mt, P).

There are some similarities in these findings to those of Tivadar and Luthar (2005) in their research into food traditions in Slovenia. They differentiated between traditionalists and post-traditionalists regarding the group's capacity to accept other food cultures. Traditionalists' rejection of 'foreign food, among other distinctions (the main one being a preference for meat) reflects, Tivadar and Luthar suggest, an inability to accept diversity, while post-traditionalists are attracted to ethnic cuisines and other people's food cultures. Not surprisingly, then, in our study, the oldest generation Ukrainians reject foreign foods even when these are presented outside the home. Their conservatism is matched in their political and religious beliefs, whilst in contrast their children are more likely to accept cultural diversity and political liberalism as well as the value of religious plurality. They also have an appetite for foreign foods to the extent that the cuisines of others are not only consumed in public but are now prepared and eaten at home. Here we see a movement between generations in what constitutes exo- and endo-cuisines, although, as we will show below, less of a change in distinction in practice between the two than might be supposed.

A number of researchers have previously made the point that 'traditional foodways' in post-modern society have been eroded by economic and technological developments (eg Fishler, 1988; Crouch and O'Neill, 2000). It could then be construed that socialization amongst families, peers, and within home and community settings is less influential than broader social influences, including the media (old and new), the rise of the supermarket and the demise of the corner shop and street market, in promoting significant changes in our foodways. Project participants, however, considered such changes less significant in the transformation of food habits and values. What these findings suggest is that claims of 'authenticity', and indeed of 'erosion', of 'traditional food' are narrated or staged with the intention of communicating particular food ideologies rather than as a reflection or record of historical change.

Finch (2007) has suggested that changes in displaying and doing family reflect evolving features of the relationships within and around the family. However it should be acknowledged that such changes are at least in part the result of the changes in material conditions in which such relationships are located. The men and women of this incipient diaspora had limited material resources. 'Displaying' and 'doing family' in the public sphere was mainly restricted to Church, shopping at the centre market and in the social activities of the club and school. While the primary settlers' public activities were somewhat limited this was not the case amongst their children, who had more income than their parents and also new ways of spending. The children of the primary settlers were often fluent in at least two languages; some became professionals and most bettered their socio-economic position in comparison to their parents. Changes in the city infrastructure, such as new roads, supermarkets, restaurants, theatres and music venues opened a whole range of new possibilities for displaying family; and second generation Ukrainians made use of these opportunities.

As British-Ukrainians, though, they retained traditional rituals that continued to spell out a degree of distinction between endo- and exo- cuisines. The most prominent example of this occurs during Easter. Whilst the blessing of food baskets is done in public at church or at the club, with food displays to be appreciated by all those who wish to attend, the breaking of the fast happens at home within the family. After enjoying this intimate moment, families head towards Church for Mass. There then follows organized community activities (dancing and singing). During these ritual celebrations, foods to be consumed within the family (endo-) and foods to be offered or shared (exo-) are differentiated. As instructed by the oldest generation, all participants follow traditional proceedings in displaying family and community.

The foodways of British-Ukrainians are said by many of those we interviewed to have become similar to or undistinguishable from those they perceived as archetypically 'British'. However, significantly, a new distinction has appeared in the narratives of food between the foodways of the diaspora and those that could be found (or imagined to be found) in independent Ukraine (PS: D, S, SM, T). In making this distinction, members of this generation discursively located themselves as outsiders. In the narratives of the British-Ukrainians (the children of the primary settlers) the distinction between traditional food and day-to-day food is usually made in order to emphasize that food practices are important for the cohesion of the family. Again the differentiation of endo- and exo-cuisine is instrumental in claims of authenticity, doing family and sustaining identity. In order to fulfil what they perceived as a common destiny, British-Ukrainians effectively use the foodways of the diaspora as a cultural artefact of integration; a 'cultural artefact' that represents the synthesis of performance and narrative.

Ukes' food in multicultural Bradford

Evidence from the three studies that have been conducted between the 1980s and 2007 suggests that the Ukrainian family ideal has remained that of heterosexual couples willing to submit their children to instruction in Ukrainian and of the traditional values held by the diasporic community. The requirement continues to be that children and teenagers should attend church and Saturday school, and participate in the youth association activities including the celebrations surrounding Ukrainian's Independence Day.

Our most recent study included exploring the attitudes towards food amongst a third younger generation of Ukrainians in Britain. We asked the teenagers about their food interests, including whether they were concerned about diet. We also asked about food practices at home, at school and among the diaspora, whom they refer to as 'Ukes'. In doing so we became aware that implicit in the narratives of the youngest there was a distinction between their own food interests and the interests they identified as belonging to former generations of AUGB and Ukrainian Saturday School authorities.[7] For instance, they were conscious of recent concerns about 'healthy eating' and food habits in relation to gender that their parents and grandparents had not experienced:

Interviewer: In many of the interviews that followed the photographic food journey all of you said that many younger children are eating crap.
A, B, C, D: Yes, they are.

Interviewer: So, how could this problem be solved effectively?
A: By teaching about healthy eating.
B: But the problem is that if they have option they would not eat better, you would have to get rid of the choice of eating crap food.
C: Yes I agree, like say the school meals, if you have options of vegetables and fruits instead of chips and other crap food . . .
B: like in a Communist regime? (laughs).
A: The other reason kids choose [crap foods] is the advertisement of these foods, sweets and everything, they know about it and where to get it . . .
B: Well you would have to have that choice of food but as special treat, not always.
C: Yes, once you get used to it you take it for granted
Interviewer: Do you think there is a difference between girls' and boys' approach to foods?
D: Yes, [Be]cause as girls get older they worry about their weight and stuff, they go into diets, whilst boys don't care as much.
B: But they should just do more exercise.
C: That is the problem I think boys exercise more than girls.
D: That is not true, girls exercise as well.
Interviewer to D: Have you felt that pressure yourself or felt some of your friends have been pressured in that way?
D: Yes [I have] sometimes [experienced that pressure].
Interviewer: At school have you received information about problems with eating habits or healthy eating?
B, C: We have.
D: In our school they really don't talk about it but [have] decided on changes.
A: Yes that is right they have gone all healthy eating.
Interviewer: So you are aware of where to get help if you feel anxious about food or if you think someone needs help?
B: No I would not go as far as saying that there is.
Interviewer: There is not that kind of worry then.
C: Well someone can be called a fatso and then they need to do something to get fit.
D: Girls do worry about this and they say mean things. [. . .]
C: In our school there is a good canteen offering healthy food, but all around there are many fish and chips shops, curry foods, there is sweets shop and there are two bakeries, which mostly sell junk food.
A: Come on! You cannot say the bakeries sell junk food.
B: The healthier there is sandwiches.
C: You can advise but not impose.
A: That is what I was trying to say.
D: You cannot stop someone from eating junk food [. . .]

Another significant generational difference they highlighted when interviewed individually and in a group was that their awareness of Ukes' food made them more adventurous with foreign foods in general:

Interviewer: What is the Ukrainian word for 'taste'?
D: 'cmak' is used to refer about the taste of something.

Interviewer: So is there such thing as 'good taste'?
A, B: Yes there is.
Interviewer: Thus you can say that X or Y has good taste?
C: Not really, that is individual.
D [Answering interviewer]: No I would not say that.
B: Well you can say some people had good taste in music or clothes but it relates to what you like, so it is your personal taste [. . .]
Interviewer: How do you think that the way you have been brought up has influenced your food habits?
D: Because you are aware of particular things, for example the use of cabbage and carrots in certain ways. . . things like that.
Interviewer: It makes you more adventurous [with food?]
D: Yes definitely.
C: Look, if you are from an ethnic minority you identify with others that are from minorities.
A: That is right, you would not reject some food because it is different, on the contrary it makes you want to try it.
B: Yes. [. . .]
Interviewer: Is there any special value in Ukrainian food?
A, B, C, D: There is.
B: It is delicious (gestures – laughs) We have our traditional food pirohy, borsh,. . .
C: It is best, but it is for special occasions.
B: Yes it is like, people is used to have turkey for Christmas, and it has a special value then, but you can have it occasionally in other times. The same with Ukes' food.
Interviewer: Would you like to pass on these values?
C: I would like to, [. . .] I want to have this skill of making traditional food.
A: Although sometimes I take it to school and a few of my friends show interest but others don't, some of them hear of potato dumplings and they go 'wack', don't want it, keep it there . . .
D: You could not have it all the time anyway.
C: You have to build up to it. [. . .]
[D and C last statements are referring to the richness of the food (oily carbohydrates)]
D: There is also the decorations and arrangements of the baskets [during Easter], that is nice . . . [. . .]

The teenagers pointed out that it is precisely the fact that they know of the particularities of Ukrainian traditional foods that enables them to appreciate other culinary traditions. Such appreciation, as a marker of generational change, relates to the process of 'foreign' foods making their way from exo-cuisine to endo-cuisine. For instance, as described above, while the sons and daughters of primary settlers would initially eat out as families in 'Chinese' and 'Indian' restaurants as an occasion, the consumption of such food has in more recent years not only become more frequent, but is now consumed and even in some cases prepared in the home.

The space provided for teenagers to express current preferences regarding organization of community activities, including dinners and other festivities is limited. The generational project of their parents, grandparents and great grandparents has influenced the settings in which this new generation negotiate their preferences; however, an important part of such settings is the institutional organization of Ukrainian organizations in Britain. Since their foundation, the AUGB, the Youth Association and the Ukrainian Schools have retained formal committee structures. Membership of these committees is voluntary although participation is limited. In addition to the formal rules, there are informal systems of control and checks. These can be seen during functions, or even fortuitous encounters, pub gatherings or at extended family and friends gatherings. Often these involve the consumption of food: dinners, barbeques, Wednesday lunches at the club, charity or fund raising diners.[8] This implies that although teenagers can be innovative, the changes in social practices they propose or perform need to be perceived as non-threatening to the reproduction of the models of Ukrainian family and community, as overseen by School authorities and UUGB committees.

Although the food practices of the latest generation seem undistinguishable from those of other British teenagers, they could and sometimes deliberately exhibit their knowledge of traditional foods not simply to distinguish themselves from others, but also as a socialization tool. For instance, teenagers attending Ukrainian school volunteered to organize the serving of traditional food in 2007 Christmas celebrations at the Club; they also invited 'non-Uke' friends to the fundraising event organized by the women's group (in 2007) and were observed explaining their culinary traditions to those who showed interest. Some of those who attend Ukrainian school on Saturday often participate in state school activities designed to promote cultural diversity. On special occasions, such as 'Ukrainian-day', some of them dress in traditional costumes and take part in traditional Ukrainian dancing or singing. The mere fact that most of them showed interest in our research, took time to address our questions, allowed us to accompany them, or participated in photographic food journey research activities, demonstrates that they are interested in making new social uses of the skills and performance of traditional foods.

The latest generation showed genuine appreciation for the particular taste of traditional foods, but when they were asked individually if 'Ukes' food' tasted better, they said that they did not consider that traditional Ukrainian food was tastier or healthier than any other 'ethnic' or 'traditional' food. However as demonstrated in the recorded discussions they did highlight that having this food heritage as a part of their identity gave them a willingness to try and taste a diversity of foods. The knowledge practices of traditional Ukrainian food are performed and displayed not only in intra-community activities, but sometimes amongst friends and (non- Ukrainian) school peers as well (PS: P, D, St, Pt, B, TGI).

Perhaps one way of thinking about what the teenagers are doing is through the concept of 'cultural tokenism'. Cultural tokenism is sometimes referred to as the inauthentic display of cultural identity – the token as poor replacement for the real. Such a perception is found in the humanities (Niemann, 2002), art studies (Wallace, 1997), sociolinguistics (Lamy, 1974; Balutansky, 1995; Cox,

1998) and criminology (Rutherford, 1975). But here and in reference to the narratives and behaviour of the teenagers that participated in this project we refer to a positive value of 'tokenism' that is perhaps similar to that described by Wyman (2004) in her study of Yup'ik peoples. That is as a shared method of making and marking group identity.

These youngsters (and this includes those observed as well as those who took a more active part in the project) were seen assisting in serving food, arranging tables and taking part in the ceremonies and rituals in which traditional Ukrainian food is reified. Such disposition shows concern on their part about their role within family and community. It has been highlighted in previous studies that the provision of food and the sharing of meals symbolise, among other things, the provision of care and some sense of being a family (Holdsworth and Morgan, 2005). We would not argue that teenagers taking an active part in ceremonial meals signify an endorsement of the food ideologies of their parents and grandparents, but we believe it gives expression to a sense of belonging to a distinctive community.

The teenagers' tokenism is enacted by displaying knowledge of traditional practices, (including cooking practices), by narrating the myths that accompany food festivities and by performing food manners with competence during traditional festivities (table manners may be accompanied by praying or singing in Ukrainian, or by dressing in traditional costumes and dancing in a distinctive Cossack style). The token works as a networking medium in a multicultural society, and is a valuable symbol of a distinctive heritage as well. It is in this sense that the latest cohort of the Ukrainian diaspora is currently using 'Ukrainian food', its practices, rituals and associated ideologies as a cultural token.

Concluding comments

By drawing on two earlier oral history projects and supplementing these with a third study that had a distinctive ethnographic component, we have attempted to offer a way of understanding how a particular community has changed from 1948 to the present. We have used the lens of food to explore the ways in which successive generations of an Ukrainian diasporic community in Bradford imagined, adapted and reified narratives and rituals to suit the particular projects they felt destined to pursue in amalgamation with changing life styles.

By combining the theoretical insights of Bourdieu and Passeron (1979) and Mannheim (1997) in particular, we were able to examine changing ideas of edibility across generational and historical time. Significant here were Mannheim's concept of 'generational style' and Bourdieu's 'habitus' in our attempts to understand how individuals responded to broader historical changes. In undertaking our study we have therefore analysed how each generation has negotiated their historical time and in doing so how different generational styles have developed.

We wanted to appreciate better how taste evolves over generations. We aimed to do this by studying a community in which a core group had stated objectives and developed structures intended to ensure the continuation of cultural tastes over generational time. It was particularly useful to our study that the founders of this particular community, the primary settlers, were drawing on, as a key part of their constructed collective identities, recalled foodways of a homeland that they were isolated from. They could also express with clarity what they wanted to transmit to their children in terms of cultural values and practices, including those transmitted through foodways.

It could be safely said that the Ukrainians who arrived in Britain as a generation in the late 1940s established the settings within which family and community would narrate and perform food and feeding. This was part of a larger political project that they thought would prepare their return to an imagined Ukraine. Their children subsequently developed their own project and thus transformed their food practices in ways that they figured would sustain Ukrainianness while mainly serving their interests in settling in Britain.

Although members of this community, regardless of age, continue to narrate and perform 'Ukrainian' food traditions at home and in the community space, effectively reproducing the foodways of the diaspora, two distinctive projects were identified, corresponding to two generations developing their own style and food practices that in turn reflect different ways of conceiving food: what it means to them as individuals, to their families and to the larger community. The oldest generation of the diaspora ate what they ate in the way they did with a distinctive Ukrainian nationalistic purpose. They thought and laboured hard in constructing the settings for reproducing nationhood among successive generations. They associated, bought buildings for religious observance, formed a club, constructed a school, organized and funded youth centre activities. They carried out food festivals and performed rituals in which claims of authenticity were constructed so as to assert the ubiquitous presence of Ukrainian culinary traditions. However the food ideology of the second generation was quite different. They remained loyal to the central idea of Ukrainianness but they ate what they ate in different ways from that of their parents. Unlike first generation Ukrainians they developed a taste for other peoples' foods and through their food practices they considered cultural diversity. Such variance reflects the changes in both the material conditions and the food practices of the two generations.

Those who settled in Britain in the late 1940s viewed food as symbolic expression of their identities. In contrast food had a different significance for their children, who were also more likely to consume the foods from other cultural traditions. However distinctions continued to be made by the children of primary settlers in terms of food consumed in public celebrations (exo-cuisine) and in everyday life (endo-cuisine). What had changed was an increased consumption of the food from other cultures in both the domestic sphere and in eating out with non-Ukrainian friends or immediate family. What emerges is that the foodways of the diaspora are displayed as marking British-Ukrainianness in a multicultural society.

There is some evidence that the youngest generation, the grandchildren of the primary settlers, have taken this development further. They see British-Ukrainian cuisine as one of a myriad of cuisines in Britain that offers them a way of participating in what they see as multiculturalism. We believe that 'Ukrainian food' is used as a cultural token by the youth in their social practices. Thus while distinctions are maintained, we suspect a transformation is taking place, as these distinctions are becoming a marker of group identity, whilst at the same time allowing individuals to reaffirm their belonging to the wider world.

Reflecting upon shifts in habitus over time we have demonstrated that for making choice in foodways, the objective material circumstances together with the cultural practices have been instrumental to both individuals and generations. The food practices relating to the home cooking and endo-cuisine as well as exo-cuisine and the preparation of foods for festivities reifying Ukrainian traditions are evidence of effective use of material and social settings to promote transmission (adoption and adaptation) of food values. It could then be concluded that it is within these settings that generations discuss differential food ideologies as they provide individuals with the socio-cultural space where they can express their food choices.

It would be of value to know if current teenagers develop, as their parents and grandparents did, a generational project of their own and continue reproducing 'Ukrainianness'. They currently participate, narrate and display traditional foods to interact and network with other youngsters who have in turn their own distinctive foodways. In this way they are already making use of the knowledge practices of traditional foods as a positive cultural token.

Previous studies have suggested that in general, traditional foodways in post-modern society have been eroded by economic and technological developments. Without denying the influence of technological change and the media in transforming foodways, the illustration provided by our case study demonstrates that claims of authenticity or of erosion of 'traditional food' are narrated and performed with the intention of communicating (or attempting to pass on) particular food ideologies. As highlighted throughout this article we found that the generational projects were by far the main determinant factor shaping the foodways of the Ukrainian diaspora.

Notes

1 This article is informed by the data generated through the research project 'Socio-historical reproduction of food and dietary values', which was part of the 'Changing Families Changing Food' programme funded by the Leverhulme Trust.
2 Most of the activities observed took place in the Ukrainian Club (which includes a pub and a large dining hall where meals are served every Wednesday and during community events) and

the Ukrainian School run by the Bradford branch of the Association of Ukrainians in Britain. We also followed the families into Church and attended family meals at home. All semi-structured recorded interviews were conducted in three sections. The first part focused on family experiences with food, food habits, cooking and eating. The second focussed on investigating provisioning and budgeting. In the third part interviewees were encouraged to assess the significance of food in culture, including perceptions about food security and (un-) healthy food. The interview schedule was adapted from Conevey (2004: 292).

3 In the second study ('East European Migration to Bradford) conducted in the 1990s, researchers interviewed children of primary settlers who no longer considered themselves to be Ukrainian or even with an ongoing attachment to the community they were raised in. Although during the third study (2006–7) we considered these interviews and coded them, we failed in our attempts to re-contact individuals who had left the diasporic community. It was the case that some participants who were interviewed in the most recent project recognized that their children, relatives or former friends have been lost to the community through either a conscious decision to reject or a disinterest in their Ukrainian heritage and/or the activities of the community (PS: ThO, WGI).

4 Two of the group interviews were filmed, one with four members of the women's group of the Bradford branch of the Ukrainian Association (WGI) and one with a group of teenagers who were attending Saturday Ukrainian School in Bradford at the time of the study. Twelve interviews were also audio-recorded with eleven adults belonging to six different families. The participation of these families during Ukrainian community activities was then closely followed. We analysed hundreds of photographs, and a number of video recordings of community activities, cooking practices, art performances and religious ceremonies.

5 The connection between religion and politics, especially anti-Soviet activities, was closely intertwined, especially given the suppression of religion in Soviet Ukraine. Bandera himself was the son of a cleric. The diaspora tended to regard priests, bishops and the churches themselves as emblematic symbols of anti-Soviet resistance. For this reason many of the Ukrainian diaspora celebrations are intermixed with religious festivities. Participating in church-based activities is often read as a marker of belonging to the diasporic community more than a testament of faith. This is the reason why by following the activities of this community we ended up in religious celebrations or in Church, but this should not be read as indicative of us choosing to do research in Church based settings.

6 Referring to the ritual foodways of Ukrainians in Canada, Klymasz (1985) highlights that the traditional Christmas meal does not and 'must not' include meat and thus the cabbage rolls served during Christmas meals are filled with rice or buckwheat. In contrast, the 2006 meal served at the Christmas dinner of the Ukrainian Association in Bradford included cabbage rolls filled with corned beef. Although some research participants later signalled that during Christmas one was supposed to abstain from eating meat, they acknowledged that corned-beef filling of *holubtsi* during Christmas had become common practice.

7 The teenagers were observed during Saturday activities, during the Youth Association annual meeting in Weston on Trent (July 2006) and other numerous activities they engaged with during year 2006–07. Some of the more active participants of our research agreed to make photographic 'food journeys', after which they were interviewed individually. We then filmed a group interview with four of them, three boys (A, B, C) and a girl (D). The quotations of this section of the paper are taken from this filmed group interview.

8 Lunch is offered in the AUGB premises every Wednesday and many of the so-called 'first generation' Ukrainians attend. Wednesday's lunch as an intergenerational form of communication is discussed elsewhere (Forero, Ellis *et al.*, 2009).

Acknowledgements

This article was presented during the 100-year anniversary conference of *The Sociological Review* (June 2009). The authors are grateful to fellow conference participants for valuable comments and critique and to the journal's two anonymous reviewers for their very helpful comments.

References

Anthias, F., (1998), 'Evaluating "Diaspora" Beyond Ethnicity?' *Sociology* (32): 557–80.

Bak, S., (1997), 'McDonald's in Seul: Food Choices Identity and Nationalism' in Watson, J.L., (ed.), *Golden Arches East*, Stanford: Stanford University Press:136–60.

Balutansky, K.M., (1995), 'Surviving Tokenism', *Concerns: Women's Caucus for Modern Languages*, 25 (2): 41–46.

Bourdieu, P. and J.C. Passeron, (1973), 'Cultural Reproduction and Social Reproduction' in Brown, R., (ed.), *Knowledge, Education and Social Change*, London: Tavistock: 71–112.

Bourdieu, P. and J.C. Passeron, (1979), *The Inheritors: French Students and Their Relation to Culture*, Chicago: University of Chicago Press.

Bourdieu, P., (1977), *An Outline of a Theory of Practice*, Cambridge: Cambridge University Press.

Bourdieu, P., (1984), *Distinction: a social critique of the judgement of taste*, Nice, R, trans, Routledge: London.

Cesarani, D., (2001), *Justice Delayed: How Britain became a refuge for Nazi war criminals*, (revised 2nd edn), London: Phoenix Press.

Conevey, J., (2004), 'A qualitative study exploring socio-economic differences in parental lay knowledge of food and health: implications for public health nutrition', *Public Health Nutrition*, 8: 290–97.

Cox, R.A.V., (1998), 'Tokensim in Gaelic: the language of appeasement', *Scottish Language* 17: 70–81.

Crouch, M. and G. O'Neill, (2000), 'Sustaining Identities?' Prolegomena for inquiry into contemporary foodways, *Social Science Information*, 39 (1): 181–92.

Falk, P., (1994), *The Consuming Body*, London: Sage Publications (Theory, Culture and Society series).

Finch, J., (2007), 'Displaying Families', *Sociology*, 41: 65–81.

Fishkin, S.F., (2005), 'Crossroads of Cultures: The Transnational Turn in American Studies', Presidential Address to the American Studies Association, November 12, 2004, *American Quarterly* 57,1: 17–57.

Fishler, C., (1988), 'Food, Self and Identity', *Social Science Information*, 27: 275–92.

Forero, O., K. Ellis, A. Metcalfe and R. Brown, (2009), 'Institutional Dining Rooms: Food Ideologies and the Making of a Person', in Jackson, P., (ed.), *Changing Families, Changing Foods*, Hampshire:Palgrave Macmillan: 226–45.

Holdsworth, D. and C. Morgan, (2005), *Transitions in Context: Leaving Home, Independence and Adulthood*, Buckingham: Open University Press.

Hrycyszyn, M., (2002), *God Save Me From My Friends: A Ukrainian Memoir*, Cambridge: Vanguard Press.

Kleinfelder, P., (2004), 'American Influence on Filipino Food Culture-A Case Study'. MA Thesis, LMU, Munich.

Klymasz, R.B., (1985), 'Male and female principles as structure in the ritual foodways of Ukrainians in Canada', *Journal of Ukrainian Studies*, 10,1: 15–27.

Lamy, P., (1974), 'Bilingualizing a Civil Service: Politics, Policies, and Objectives in Canada', *Journal of Comparative Sociology*, 2: 53–70.

Lévi-Strauss, C., (1965), 'Le triangle culinaire', *L'Arc*, 26: 19–29.

Lupton, D., (1996), *Food, the body and the self*, London: Sage.

MacClancy, J., (2004), 'Food, Identity, Identification' in *Researching Food Habits Methods and Problems*, Macbeth, H. and MacClancy, J. (eds), Vol 5 of The Anthropology of Food and Nutrition series. Washington, London: Berghahn Books,.

Mannheim, K., (1997), 'The Problem of Generations', in *Studying Aging and Social Change: Conceptual and Methodological Issues*, M.A. Hardy, (ed.), London: Sage Publications: 22–65.

Markova, E. and R. Black, (2007), East European immigration and community cohesion. York: Joseph Rowntree Foundation.

Mintz, S., (2008), 'Food and Diaspora'. *Food, Culture and Society: An International Journal of Multidisciplinary Research*, 11,4: 509–23.

Murcott, A., (1996), 'Food as an expression of identity', in *The Future of the Nation State: Essays on Cultural Pluralism and Political Integration*, Gustafsson, S. and Lewin, L. (eds), Stockholm: Nerenious & Santerus: 49–77.

Niemann Flores, Y., (2002), 'The Making of a Token: A Case Study of Stereotype Threat, Stigma, Racism and Tokenism in Academe' in Flores, Y.N., S.H. Armitage, P. Hart and K. Weathermon, (eds), *Chicana Leadership: The Frontiers Reader*, Lincoln, NE: University of Nebraska: 280–314.

Perks, R., (1986), ' "Everyone has a story to tell": The Bradford Heritage Recording Unit and the value of oral history', *The Bradford Antiquary*; 3rd Series, 2: 18–27.

Roth, K., (2001), 'Turkentrank, Gulyas, Joghurt, Doner: Stereotypen in der europaischen Esskultur' in Heuberg, V. (ed.), *Vom Schwarzwald bis zum Schwarzen Meer*, Frankfurt: Lang.

Rutherford, A., (1975), 'Taylor House: an example of penal tokenism', *Howard Journal of Criminal Justice*, 14:46–9.

Sahlins, M., (1990), 'Food as Symbolic Code', in Alexander, J.C. and S. Seidman, (eds), *Culture and Society: Contemporary Debates*, Cambridge: Cambridge University Press: 94–101.

Smith, G. and Jackson, P., (1999), 'Narrating the nation: the 'imagined community' of Ukrainians in Bradford', *Journal of Historical Geography*, 25: 367–87.

Smith T., R. Perks and G. Smith, (1998), *Ukraine's Forbidden History*, Manchester: Hushion House.

Threadgold, T., (2000), 'When home is always a foreign place: Diaspora, dialogue, translations' *Communal/Plural*, 8, 2: 193–217.

Tivadar, B. and B. Luthar, (2005), 'Food, ethics and aesthetics', *Apetite*, 45: 215–33.

Tolksdorf, U., (1976), 'Strukturalistische Nahrungsforschung', *Ethnologia Europea*, 9: 64–85.

UNHCR (2004) *2003 UNHCR Statistical Yearbook*, New York: UNHCR.

Wallace, M., (1997), 'Black Female Spectatorship and the Dilemma of Tokenism'. in *Generation: Academic Feminists in Dialogue,* Devoney, L., and E.A. Kaplan, (eds), Minneapolis, MN: University of Minnesota: 88–102.

Warde, A. and L. Martens, (2000), *Eating Out*, Cambridge: Cambridge University Press.

World Bank, (2006), *World Development Report,* Washington: World Bank.

World Bank, (2007), *Migration and remittances. Eastern Europe and the former Soviet Union*, Washington: World Bank.

Wyman, L., (2004), Language Shift, Youth Culture, and Ideology: A Yup'ik Example, PhD dissertation, Education, Stanford University.

Forum for the Ugly People – study of an imagined community

Maria Adamczyk

Abstract: This paper asks how sickness, aesthetics and politics intervene when it comes to labelling oneself ugly. My study of an online community named 'Forum for the Ugly People' on the biggest Internet portal in Poland, *Gazeta Wyborcza* (www.gazeta.pl) raises two key questions. What are the self-ascribing criteria for being ugly? Is ugliness treated as a disease, or as a personal fault of the stigma bearer? Treating ugliness as Douglasian 'dirt' – matter out of place – an anomaly that must be separated and dealt with accordingly, I explore the everyday politics of defining ugliness. The analysis details the various ways in which ugliness is held to handicap everyday experience and outlines three modes of 'treatment' that are discussed frequently by the Forum members. Critically, the paper not only demonstrates how users of this Internet Forum derive comfort and a sense of belonging from participating in their 'imagined community' – a solidarity comprised of those who similarly self-ascribe themselves as ugly – but also how they exercise their own forms of inclusion and exclusion.

Introduction

The *Forum for the Ugly People* was founded by <antonel>, a woman in her thirties, over three years ago on the portal of *Gazeta Wyborcza*, the biggest daily Polish paper. I came across it last winter. First I thought it was a joke, only later to realize that it was not, and that to self-ascribe as ugly (either real or imagined), as well as to be ascribed as ugly by others were grave issues for its members. Themes discussed by the members vary, but roughly concentrate on eight distinctive spheres where beauty, or rather the *right* looks, really do matter. Interestingly, in the first months of the forum's existence, equal numbers of men and women contributed towards discussions, but in time female voices became more prominent with the same few female users most often voicing their concerns and mourning their life-situation, although a small number of men remain involved. <antonel>, the founder of the forum, says (sarcastically) that as she has a great deal of experience (over 30 years) of being ugly, she is well qualified to preside over this community.

The *Forum for the Ugly People* was created to serve as a safe niche from the hostile outside word; a safe place where those who feel they are ugly can take a break from the endless feeling of being excluded from society and, instead, find comfort among those who understand their sense of 'stigma'. As the founder says: 'I wanted to create a safe place for people who feel ugly, unattractive and suffer for that reason. It should be a place where they could finally talk with others who are like them, exchange (similar) experiences, make new friends.' A sample post suggests this aim has been accomplished: <4_bree>: 'I am happy that there is a place where I can honestly reveal that I am the ugly and unattractive one without being forced to listen to revelations about how this is probably not true and how this is just a delusion I have due to low self-esteem.'

Ugliness is a stigma that is both discreditable and discredited. Yet, for some, ugliness can be covered. There is seemingly a plethora of ways to hide one's unwanted attributes and such ways are commonly discussed. Such questions arise as 'how do you hide your ugliness? <reenis>' However, the *Forum for the Ugly People* is a place where ugliness can stand free in the open, a space for social affiliation where someone can be true to their self-perception of being ugly and where this ugliness (imagined or real) marks people as members of the forum's community.

The *Forum for the Ugly People* takes place in the virtual space of the Internet, but at the same time is rooted in the contemporary Polish socio-cultural context. *The ugly* (as I refer hereafter to those designating themselves as such in this Forum) watch the same television shows, read the same news in the press, gossip about Polish celebrities and politicians, and exchange childhood experiences and traumas of school parties. So what specific socio-cultural factors could facilitate or foster the creation of this virtual community? According to Giza-Poleszczuk, a respected sociologist: 'Only four per cent of Polish women describe themselves as attractive. In other countries that were researched 13 percent of women on average described themselves as attractive'. Giza-Poleszczuk also says: 'This might be an outcome of the cultural pressure to blend in, to fit in with everybody else. We (Polish people) live in the culture of judgment; we have a feeling that everybody judges and evaluates us, that we are constantly being watched by the others. In Polish culture it is not popular to give compliments, to smile to strangers or to have small talk' (Wysokie Obcasy, 06.11.2006).

According to a popular Polish saying: 'there are no ugly women, just sometimes not enough wine'. Contemporary media such as *Polsat Café* (a Polish television channel whose watchers are mostly women, a sort of English Club) currently specialize in reality TV shows where an unattractive, plain Jane has a makeover to become more attractive through the use of new fashionable clothes, make up and a stylish hairdo (*Metamorfozy Polsat Café, W Obiektywie Justyny Steczkowkiej* etc). Such shows expound an official, politically appropriate approach that demonstrates the constructed nature of attractiveness: there are no ugly women, just women who cannot take proper care of themselves. However, *the ugly* disagree. They say that ugliness is a material fact (only a few claim that ugliness is socially constructed). To them it is a fact one must face and live with accordingly, having his or her fate and life chances determined by this physical attribute. How *the ugly* deal with the felt stigma of ugliness is discussed in a later part of this paper. Nevertheless, as the narratives presented in this paper demonstrate, the sense that ugliness is a cultural construction is not totally displaced; my respondents' ambivalence about ugliness therefore remains implicit in their discussions and strategies for dealing with their ugliness.

Web and virtual communities

The Internet has had a profound role in altering the foundations that traditional communities were thought to rely on. First of all, a virtual community is not territorial and spatial; people from any corner of the globe can be a part of it as long as they understand the language used/deployed in the communication process and, as such, it offers a valuable alternative in the age of a decline of public *agora*. Secondly, the corporeality of its users is of lesser importance, which may eliminate the common inclination or tendency to hierarchize, marginalize and exclude members on the basis of visual cues. Therefore, virtual communities are commonly thought of as being less hierarchical, more loosely structured and more volitional than traditional communities – their membership is voluntary and not based on arbitrary and accidental fundaments of geographic proximity, shared ethnic identity or common descent (Bruckman, 1998; Wellman and Gulia, 1999).

Online communities are also perceived, mistakenly in certain cases, as less oppressive to its members. Unlike in the real world, members of virtual communities are able to choose and focus on what they personally find most important from the plethora of virtual possibilities, changing their identities aptly and quitting the interaction when they feel like it. However critics of the Internet argue that its anonymity is detrimental to the feeling of personal responsibility, to the duties of a citizen and to the social trust that are all associated with traditional communities. Avatars, for instance, are commonplace in the virtual space of the Internet and, unlike in the real world, false identities are free from bearing the usual consequences of fraud.

How do these issues apply to my research? In his work *The Rise of the Network Society* Manuel Castells (2007: 186–187) notes several relevant features concerning Internet use, such as depression, social isolation and Internet addiction, which could lead people into joining such a forum as this. So membership of an Internet forum can, on occasion, be transitory and possibly spurious. Equally though, Sherry Turkle (1995), in one of the first studies on the psychology of the Internet, has shown that even though users of the Internet did play roles and created virtual identities online, a feeling of togetherness arose and even if engagement in sites like mine was just temporary, it gave comfort to people who were searching for communication and self-expression. People who live their second life on the computer screen are still bound with the desires and pain of their real selves (Turkle, 1995: 267).

The advantage of using the Internet is that it enables you to create multiple loose social ties with others that in the offline situation would not have been created, or were restricted due to members' social characteristics and attributes. A more egalitarian pattern of interaction emerges, since bodiless interaction is more open and less risky. Online communication facilitates more unrestrained discussion even if one of its consequences is also a high rate of online friendship mortality when one of the interaction partners decides to cut off the communication.

Castells (2007) wonders whether virtual communities are still communities. He claims that virtual communities are in some respects different from physical communities and specifically that they do not obey rules or communication and interaction patterns that apply in physical and traditional communities. Nevertheless he accepts that they are still communities and that they are, in certain senses, still 'real'. Virtual communities are made up of interpersonal social networks, mostly with multiple weak ties that are diversified and specialized but are able to generate support and mutuality due to the dynamics of interaction (Castells, 2007: 365).

Ethical considerations also apply. Some social researchers take the view that Internet space is really a public, open space, a sphere which everyone has access to and can make use of (Denzin, 1999). In their opinion, data coming from Internet chats and forums forms a part of public discourse and, as such, does not require authors' consent prior to its reproduction. This, however, seems to be a controversial issue and this controversy arises from the fact that the status of Internet public space is ambiguous, especially since the classic division between public and private seems obsolete and a clear distinction of what is public and what is private is not possible here. Denis Waskul argues that Internet discourse has a special character, it is privately-public or publicly-private, since people discuss private affairs in public space (Waskul, 2005). While many participants are probably unaware of the fact that they may be the subject of someone's research, informing them may in turn affect and distort the results of the research. Knowing that they are part of research that is being conducted may lead to a Hawthorne effect, in which research subjects may alter their communication, for example by beginning to control their opinions and viewpoints, or by becoming more or less hostile and even stopping communication altogether.

In line with these discussions, I had quite a few qualms and second thoughts about doing research on the Internet. I felt as if I was walking in a fog. My subjects were invisible. Only a few (circa 5 per cent) posted their pictures; most of them remained hidden behind their nicknames and with the following reservations I chose to believe their narratives. First of all, as other researchers of the Internet have pointed out, it is not possible to verify which of the authors of the posts are serious. Some might be just pranksters doing a social experiment and checking how the idea of 'too ugly to live' resonates within this Internet society. Secondly, it is impossible to tell whether their ugliness is imaginary or a material fact (ugly as in the abnormal body, where normal is the form that fits contemporary aesthetics; or a part of the body that is on the verge of the grotesque; or a body made ugly as the result of a physical disease). For this reason I decided to depend on their subjective self-ascriptions as *the ugly*. Also it is important to emphasize that I was interested mainly in the consequences of such self-ascription and wanted here to explore how *the ugly* themselves deploy this stigma in order to make sense of their everyday social reality.

Possible groupings in the study

Many of the members of the *Forum for the Ugly People* are in their late teens and twenties which, according to Eric Erikson and many others, is a formative time for the construction of one's identity (Erikson, 2000). A few are middle-aged but still not reconciled to their lack of beauty. Roughly over three hundred people take an active part (i.e. post their opinions) but apparently many more read it. A majority of participants are women, which supports feminist claims about the entangled and sometimes frustrating relationship that women have with their bodies and I discuss this in more detail later. Still, a few of the registered members are men and they voice their concerns regularly.

Drawing on their contributions, people participating on the Forum *(the ugly)* can be roughly divided into five different groups:

A. Average looking (occasionally even good looking) people with issues: very low-self-esteem or presumably suffering from some body dysmorphic disorder. They seek reassurance in order that they may feel better about themselves when comparing themselves with those that have serious defects.

B. People that have one significant flaw, such as a big nose, acne, a scar, or extra weight. These try to fit into the beauty matrix but this particular thing stands in their way. They are aware that they are prettier than the really ugly ones. They also tend to be quite bitter since this one flaw prevents them from feeling normal and socially adequate.

C. The really ugly ones. After reaching a certain age these tend to be optimistic because they know they will never be (have zero chance to be) attractive or perceived as such by the other. They are reconciled with their looks and often seek alternative goals and values in life.

D. Missionaries, preachers who say: 'It is all in your head, you have a low self esteem and lack in confidence and that is what makes you feel and appear unattractive. Change your attitude then your looks will change too eg <margie>'. Missionaries are pretty much hated by *the ugly* and are often ridiculed by other members of the Forum.

E. Peeping Toms – far more people may read the forum than actively participate. Some may do it out of sheer curiosity, some may identify at times with the dilemmas and hardships faced by its members. Others may do it because it they find the whole idea of the forum very amusing.

In my research I never took an active part in online discussions, I did not post anything, I did not provoke any themes, I just observed it day by day. In this respect, I must admit somewhat shamefully that I was a peeping Tom, a member of the fifth group.

Let us face it, most people are not beautiful (not as beautiful as the ones portrayed in the media) and feel unattractive at times or in some situations. Being not beautiful is of course a much wider category than being ugly. What is essential to emphasize is that being ugly becomes the prime identifier for *the ugly*, a central part of their identity. Ugliness gains a master status and becomes a pair of lenses through which to see and interpret everyday experiences (as well as to reinterpret the past).

Whether real or imaginary, ugliness is an obvious Goffmanian stigma, meaning a particular trait that is deemed not only different but deviant. Physical ugliness leads to rejection and avoidance by the others. The felt stigma of ugliness may result in feelings of shame, inadequacy, anxiety, worthlessness, depression and lowered self-esteem. Self-ascribed or not, it can have a profound influence on people's lives and their relationships with others. It is also something they have to try to deal with, or rationalize, from moment to moment as well as reconcile themselves with, or seek to change, over their lifespan.

Self-ascribed deviant status also works as a self-fulfilling prophecy. A physically unattractive woman learns to perform the role of an unattractive woman. Even if she has not been labeled as a social deviant, she will become one in the end. In a classic experiment men were handed photographs of either attractive or unattractive women (women's attractiveness was judged in a pilot test by independent evaluators) (Snyder, Tanke and Berscheid, 1977). Later men had a phone conversation with a person they thought was the woman from the photo, but in reality it was another woman. The results showed that men were more cordial and pleasant towards women they previously found attractive in the photographs, and women were also more cordial in return. Another experiment showed that women informed, prior to an encounter, that they were considered attractive were scored by independent evaluators as more attractive than ones that were told the opposite (Tseelon, 1995). When we believe that others perceive us as attractive, we act as though we are attractive; when it is the opposite, we can lack the necessary confidence and appear less alluring.

Spheres for the circulation of ideas of ugliness

In planning the analysis for this project I identified eight questions or issues pertinent to ugliness relevant to the online forum: 1) what is ugly in essence, 2) what is construed as ugliness, 3) ugliness in the public sphere, 4) ugliness in the media, 5) ugliness as a problem that needs a solution, 6) being an ugly woman or an ugly man, 7) friendships and romantic relationships, 8) comparisons with pretty people.

Posts written by the members of the forum oscillate around these eight issues. Nonetheless those with the greatest number of responses have to do with one's exposure to public humiliation, with embarrassing moments in a romantic context, with ways to hide the felt stigma of ugliness, and with questions about how to deal with one's otherness on a daily basis.

The ugly body is the Other. It is the Douglasian anomaly of being 'matter out of place'; and as anomaly must be treated in particular ways so that it does not endanger the social order. For Douglas (2007) these include: elimination, avoidance, being classified as dangerous, and being utilized as a powerful source of social symbolism. How then is the 'dirt' of ugliness dealt with? First of all, *the ugly* complain in their posts that they are avoided, that people do not approach them, that members of the opposite sex do not want to have anything to do with them. Crucially, even during 'instrumental' or 'formal' conversations, *the ugly* claim that others keep physical distance and avoid eye contact. Second, talk of ugliness seems to be a social taboo. Even if someone is thought of or tagged as ugly, no one either tells him, or compliments her about their looks. Here silence is read by *the ugly* as very meaningful.

Anomaly and ambiguity

Ugliness-Beauty is not a 0–1 choice, but rather it has gradients, it is a scale, a spectrum. In some instances ugly may even be considered good looking, while in others the good looking ones may feel ugly. But what if not belonging turns out to be more threatening than belonging? One of the members of the forum, <panna lee>, says: 'I have been thinking that our lovely humankind has a tendency to treat as important things that really are nothing else but an outcome of a few random factors (facial features, proneness to diseases). Ugly people are "the Others" necessary for our society to keep the ball rolling (to keep hierarchy going)'.

These 'Others' obviously engage in a lot of Othering as well. For *the ugly* the beautiful people are the Others; in their perception attractive people constitute an internally homogenous group which *the ugly* look up to, despise and envy at the same time. As well as *the ugly* never understanding them, *the ugly* feel they never will be understood by them. Their worlds diverge. They also fear them and distrust them. If a pretty girl wants to befriend an ugly one, she is likely to be imputed as having some reason for it other than pure affection. 'Do attractive people like to hang out with you? <not.a.love.song>' 'Do you have beautiful girlfriends? <cora-lina>' 'Do you hate the pretty ones as much as I do? <verfluchte>' These are all popular discussion topics.

Social constructions of ugliness and their simulation

What I found particularly interesting in my analysis was the basis of all this Othering or self-discrimination. This involved more than asking what kinds of people consider themselves to be part of this Internet community. In attempting to unpick what criteria are at stake, I was looking for the boundaries and borders of ugliness that might tie up with, say, Bourdieu's sense of being in the right place or being out of place; for a sense of 'placement' within a certain territory. Where exactly does being *ugly* start and where does it end? Perhaps it is impossible to answer these questions but I tried to come up with the definition of the feeling of being at home and being in one's place. What determines ugliness and who decides?

First of all, the feeling of being ugly is always the outcome of social interactions. Others' opinions and statements about one's physical looks are crucial to the formation of one's self-perception as being a member of *the ugly*. Identity is an outcome of social interactions. Self emerges as a result of communication with others. In my analysis I therefore drew on Charles Cooley's symbolic interactionist concept of the mirror-self. How others perceive us gives us a major hint as to what we are like; our identity (me) is a product of society. To make matters more clear: it matters if we feel rejected by peers and love-objects on the basis of our looks, or are brought up to think that there are more important things in life than beauty; or, again, it matters that we learn that it's the inside that counts, if say we stood by the wall during high school dances. Our personality, our social self, is a product of social interactions with other people. Both our subjective-self (meaning our self esteem, self-concept, a set of our subjective images about ourselves that are highly dependent on the social environment we were raised in) and reflective-self (how others perceive us, a sphere for social control and coercion) are formed as an outcome of our interactions in the social world.

Another factor that I must mention is the media and its influence upon ideals of physical beauty. I do not wish to enter into discussions here over how standards of beauty have changed over time but we are all aware that, to a degree, these are socially constructed and vary from one epoch to another. Modern standards of beauty are promoted through the air-brushed, and computer-altered virtual bodies of 'adolescent adults' of both sexes. They are a simulacrum according to Baudrillard's (2005) concept, only a 'copy' with no actual reference to reality. The ideal body matrix is a simulacrum to which we all should aspire, mould and shape our bodies accordingly. The diversity praised in the media is welcome only in Dove commercials and in Michael Jackson's utopian music hits.

Simulacra are copies in the oddest of ways. They are models of reality, which seek to be more perfect than the original which they stand for. Separate therefore from reality, but still also affecting it. Baudrillard writes: 'territory does not precede the map or does not last longer than the map. Now the map precedes the territory' (2005:6).

This simulacrum leaves approximately 95 per cent women feeling inadequate with their looks. In reality such an omnipresent model communicates that 'there is one way or the high way'. What I found striking was its seeming tyranny over most of the members of the Forum. For *the ugly* seem to have internalized and accepted the media discourse unconditionally. In this case, the dominant ideology, the myth, is thought of as natural (culture is converted into nature). It is made transparent.

Interestingly, in their definition of their lack of beauty *the ugly* resort to dominant ideology. The women say they are asymmetrical, they have wrong facial features (small eyes, narrow lips, big nose – certainly not the baby face desirable worldwide), that they have acne, oily skin, thinning hair, or a lack of waist. They supposedly lack the features claimed by sociobiology, and by evolutionary psychology, that certify the worth of female youth, the virtues of good health and fertility (having good genes). *The ugly* claim that they are doomed to become extinct, to perish (and here it appears that it is about nature not culture). Thus they readily justify their own rejection on the part of society.

If we insist that ugliness and beauty are socially constructed, then we are able to discern a symbolic violence behind sociobiology that is deployed as a myth to justify the oppression and marginalization of *the ugly*. Yet few of the members of the forum share this viewpoint, or tend to revolt against discriminating standards of beauty. Most either conform or disassociate and search for an imagined community of their own; they look for the place where they will feel at home. And *Forum for the Ugly People* is one reasonable option.

An additional factor to be considered in any discussion of the social construction of ugliness is how most of us have experienced situations in which we felt ugly. What is crucial for *the ugly* though, is that being ugly becomes their prime identifier; it forms a central part of their identity. As a prism or a filter through which *the ugly* see the world, it seems to be something *the ugly* first think of, something that most quickly comes to mind in defining who they are. In the forum at least, they first identify themselves as ugly and only later as Polish citizens, students, vegans, believers and so on. This felt stigma has certain consequences. The feeling of shame, as already discussed, is certainly one of them, especially in a romantic context. Many members of the forum claim never to have had an intimate relationship, even of a casual nature. Their deeply inherent shame paralyses them from engaging in any close relationship. They describe a feeling of looking grotesque, of being a freak whose nudity and exposure might scare the partner away or grossly disgust him or her. Ugly, for *the ugly,* means revolting, nauseating, repulsive. Women who on average are more critical of their bodies in the topic concerning intimate situations openly reveal their self-disgust and self-hatred. Importantly, for any analysis, they self-stigmatize their bodies and thereby justify their rejection.

Before proceeding further with the analysis though I want to pause briefly to consider this opposite question: what is beauty?

A pause to reflect on beauty

According to *the ugly*, beauty is symmetry, slenderness, youthfulness. Beauty is about how we look, what impression we give. It is not what we are, or how we act – contrary to the results of findings by Dove Report (conducted in the US in 2004, www.prawdziwpiekno.pl). It is about having the right face, figure, weight, height, and proportions. Seen in these terms, evolutionary psychology becomes a banalized metanarration. It justifies the pitiful situation of *the ugly*. And they use it as a rationalization of their failures and social rejection.

I understand metanarrative as a myth, something that changes history (culture) into nature (Barthes, 1957: 181–233). Something that changes what is arbitrary into something that is real. *The ugly* are often very detailed, meticulous about their ugliness. They specify the body traits and parts they find ugly. They enumerate things that keep them from transgressing, trespassing beyond the borders of ugliness and entering the world of the attractive *others*. For most of *the ugly* it is all about fitting in, about the criteria, about the ideal bodily matrix, and they feel that the forum for the ugly people is their right place to be.

It has been written that the right body is a form of cultural capital for a woman, since her worth is equated with her physical attractiveness and her outer beauty (which is a form of currency). In Lucyna Kopciewicz's empirical qualitative research in Poland about what meanings are ascribed to femininity, good looks are the first that came to respondents' mind. Forty-two percent of them answered that femininity means physical beauty (2003: 121–123). Beauty is thought to be a passport to all the good things in life (Suchańska, 2000). We are our own masters, we are in control of our fate, our body and of our beauty. Beauty can be acquired, it can be bought if we have the right means (economical resources) and consequently it can buy us more colourful, satisfying and exciting lives (Buczkowski, 2005). The ugly women say they have it harder.

Women, body image and patriarchal gaze

John Berger (1997: 47) wrote that men act and women appear (ie make a spectacle of themselves). The female body is to be looked at; it is the object of the male gaze. Pierre Bourdieu says in *Male Dominance*: 'Women exist only for and through the gaze, therefore they are an object: available, eye-catching, ready to use. Society expects of them to be feminine, meaning: smiling, subordinated, watchful, discrete and withdrawn' (Bourdieu, 2003: 82, my translation). (Cryptically I might add that the male authors are somewhat flattering their gender here, overlooking the extent to which it is women who provide most of the surveillance over other women).

A feminist psychoanalyst, Ellyn Kaschack writes:

> It is thought that every aspect of woman's body says something about her overall value. In patriarchy, she simply is her body and her face. What is being judged though is not her strength, health or ability to act but her looks. It is not the body's speed or skillfulness that is being evaluated but its shape and size or how well it fits the masculine standard of femininity. If her looks get accepted this means that she is attractive and she will be treated according to her looks. If her looks are not considered desirable such a woman is unworthy of attention. She might even become a target for laughs and jokes – it is her fault after all. The hidden presumption is that lack of attractiveness is a conscious move on the part of a woman and it is okay to treat her badly if she is not attractive (1996: 96, my translation).

In the age of plastic surgery, with the human body perceived as culturally plastic (Bauman, 1995; Bordo, 1993) ugliness comes to be considered as the personal fault of the ugly person, an outcome of not using proper disciplining techniques. Ugly women are held responsible for their ugliness and negative vices are projected on them. 'What is better: being a cripple (having disability) or being ugly? <ryba8888>' This topic gained much popularity among *the ugly* and many members said they would prefer to be disabled and not be blamed for their disfigurement, since they are commonly blamed for their unattractiveness. Many of the forum users perceive their flawed physicality as a form of impairment. <liveonjapanesetv> writes: 'I feel the same. Ugliness is a form of disability, it affects us in a similar way, makes socializing harder, it isolates us'.

The ugly body forms a Kristevian abject (2007), something that evokes abomination and disgust, something that signals the approaching of classification boundary (Douglas, 2007). An ostracized and marginalized ugly body makes the previously invisible and hidden normalization and neutralization practices apparent. The reaction (fear and disgust) to the abnormality (ugliness) defines the (external) boundaries of the accepted female figure; it reveals the beauty norm.

According to Foucault (1998), in modernity, the unmarked norm is the reference point. Those who depart from the normative standard are most subordinated. Foucault's 'Eye of Power' claims, 'There is no need for arms, physical violence, material constraints, just a gaze. An inspecting gaze, a gaze which each individual, under its weight will end by interiorizing to the point that he is his own overseer, each individual thus exercising this surveillance over, and against himself' (1980: 155; cf Driscoll, 2002). Wonder Diets, slimming pills, gym equipment, light substitutes for 'dangerous' fattening products, all belong to the same disciplinary spectrum of the corporeal self. We are told beauty is within our reach if only we try our best. If we only work harder, run faster, or eat less. And, if we make enough money, we can buy beauty piece by piece.

According to Rosemarie Garland Thomson 'In a society where appearance is the primary index of value for women, beautification practices normalize the female body (perceived a priori as deviant – from the male norm) while disabilities (stigma such as ugliness) abnormalize it – they further deviance it' (1998: 23).

Where good looks are the expected norm, ugliness is a social deviation, a stigma that makes you overly visible in some contexts and invisible in others. Being stared at, ridiculed in public, being invisible from a sexual point of view, being evaluated as unattractive means being not looked at, being omitted and being ignored. Female members of *the ugly* report a feeling of transparency in mixed-gender situations. Since ugliness can be discreditable, there is a question of revealing the stigma – by say wearing or not wearing make-up. Wearing make-up is seen by some of *the ugly* as putting on a façade in order to mask their true identity. On the Forum there has been a heated debate about make-up and why women use it. 'Make-up gives confidence, it serves as a shield in a hostile world,' says <noc listopadowa>.

Self-objectivization is a key concept in the studies on female body. According to Ellyn Kaschack, contemporary women are never alone. They always have a feeling of being watched by an anonymous male observer. This leads to the common experience that you look at your body from the outside and examine how well it fits the heterosexual standards of sexual attractiveness (Głębocka, in print). A typical female problem is the disparity between how your body looks and how it should look, leading to a feeling of shame, guilt and anxiety deeply inherent and familiar to many women.

Rejected social wisdom

When referring to popular adages, most users of the forum repeatedly reject the well-known sayings about beauty and love. They treat them as popular myths, as false stories deployed to give hope in an otherwise hopeless situation. While most parents tell their children to not judge the book by its cover – however right this may sound – it does not apply in the case of the ugly women, since the cover is what is most important, according to those who supposedly lack the right one.

1. Beauty is in the eye of the beholder.

Members of forum argue that there is objective beauty and objective ugliness. Let me cite a post by <antonel>, the founder:

> Ugliness is a fact, it does exist, I do not understand all these denials, since beauty exists, ugliness does too. Even though it is such a terrible stigma that a normal person would never dare to call anyone ugly hence all these no-nos. Apparently I am the only ugly girl left, even though when I take good care of myself I still look bad. Anyway, what does it really mean to take good care of oneself? Today I was walking through the forests and fields. I was sweaty, dirty, messy and it felt great. I don't like taking care of myself. I like being ugly, scaring people, I am fine with that.

In the second part of her post <antonel> mentions societal discrimination of ugly people:

> I would like to start fighting with the stereotypes about the ugly people, especially with stereotypes about ugly women. I don't have to be nice, smart and neat (well-groomed) in order to be treated like a human being. I would send to a psychiatrist all these guys who to feel better about themselves, must put other people down. I do not think it is ugly people's fault that others treat them in a nasty way. If I followed this path of reasoning I could have argued that if only black people painted themselves white, there would be no racism. I feel that [when] somebody denies my ugliness, I feel like suffocating, so please don't torture me anymore.

2. It is what's inside that counts

All of *the ugly* claim that physical beauty helps, and what they would like most of all, is to be attractive. Since physical beauty has a halo effect it simply makes your life easier and more fun. You are more likeable, more desirable; you are simply more everything. What is the body for? The aim of having the right body is having *this* body on display; those who cannot reveal/display their bodies feel discriminated and left out (Buczkowski, 2005). Plastic surgery is an acceptable way (if not the most accessible way) to transgress the limits of living the life of the ugly. An instrumental approach to the body pervades much of the discussion in the forum. *The ugly* dream of using the body as a tool to get more out of life, to have more control over their fate. *The ugly* live by Naomi Wolf's *beauty myth* – women of the Forum see the social world as a race and they perceive beauty as the source of competition and envy among all women. 'Do you also hate the pretty women as much as I do' <verfluchte >? As mentioned before, this is one of the more popular topics on the forum.

3. For every Jack there is a Jill

Among the most popular themes discussed by the community are relationships, especially romantic ones. Themes concern sexual experiences, number of relationships, rejections, cheating on one's partner. For instance, one of the discussions focuses on whether is it possible to have a good-looking partner when you yourself are unattractive? There is a presumption shared by most members that they should expect less since they are worse. 'The ugly ones should only date the ugly' (<marianna>).

4. It is all up to you

Is it all up to you? No it is not. On the contrary, most members of this forum appear to believe in some form of determinism, if not 'predestination'. To exaggerate this: they feel doomed to extinction. *The ugly* argue and seem to believe that with bad looks you cannot get much in life: you should expect less and be happy with whatever you get; you are not able to get far in the workforce since you need the right looks for that too; you cannot get an alpha-male boyfriend since you do not have much to offer in exchange, or not much to keep his interest going. *The ugly* marginalize themselves, attributing their life chances to a factor they say they have no control over. As social psychologists claim, the most long-lasting and satisfying relationships are between people whose level of attractiveness is pretty much the same (Aronson *et al.*, 1997). For example romantic relationships are seen as a form of exchange and *the ugly* do not see themselves as having much currency (meaning right looks). 'A stud – not for an ugly Betty' <gatto-kot> has been a hot topic on the forum.

Among *the ugly* there is a pervasive feeling of one's placement in the social order: is he attainable, is he available for me, is this for me? The notion of boundaries (Bourdieu, 2003) imparts a strong sense of borders that cannot be crossed. What am I entitled to expect, how far can I get, who can I get? 'Finally I am in the right place', as one of the members (<panna lee>), has said about finding the forum.

A feeling of being at home is a theme that pervades the forum. Doxa is a sense of one's place and one's sense of belonging, which is closely connected with the idea that 'this is not for us' (ce n'est pas pour nous). All in all, this imagined community (Anderson, 2006) serves as a social support centre and social network for *the ugly*; it facilitates a sense of belonging to the same enclave and a feeling of togetherness.

Strategies deployed in dealing with felt stigma

Physical attractiveness is a highly valued concept in our culture. So what if one lacks it? What can one do about it? How can one attain this capital? Discussion on the *Forum for the Ugly People* elicits three main ways to approach these issues.

According to the members, the best cure or the simplest way of dealing with one's bad appearance is either to cover it or to camouflage it (they discuss in great depth their ways of hiding or minimizing the flaws or body features which they consider repulsive). It is about *conforming* to the norm. Mostly by wearing the right make up, right clothes, right shoes, right hairdo and avoiding possibly embarrassing and stressful situations such as a swimming pool, or the beach, wearing skimpy clothes in front of other people, or being seen naked. Being well-groomed, neat or dressed-up makes *the ugly* feel attractive but they complain that the pretty ones always look pretty, and on the contrary, that *the ugly* need to spend a lot of time in order to look good or even to look decent. They dream of getting rid of their flaws (the idea of having plastic surgery is fiercely supported by members of the forum). So it is not about changing your set of values or your priorities in life, or coming to terms with your lack of beauty, since such an idea has been scorned and rejected by the *ugly*. It is about changing the corporeal self to fit in, not about changing the dominant ideology. From hairdos and wonder diets to breast lifts and tummy tucks, there is a spectrum of corporeal disciplinary practices that make the body become more like the accepted norm. Ugliness is therefore a deviation that must be straightened out, an anomaly that must be assigned to either of the two categories, a label that must be either hidden or erased.

Secondly, *the ugly* mention psychotherapy just to deal better on a daily basis with the felt rejection and scorn, which they say is quite common. This is a form of *reconciliation* with your lack of beauty. But it is a far less popular solution. *The ugly* see their bad looks, and the social consequences they produce, mostly as a personal hindrance, their personal flaw, their own vice. They do not perceive their uneasiness and social angst as a result of class or gender oppression (they tend not to see the bodily standard itself as a social construction created to serve interest of a particular group, to discipline and control). Such a standpoint on the issue of ugliness illustrates Foucault's argument: that the displacement of spectacular punishment by discipline practices produces observation as a dominant mode of exercising power, one that does not straightforwardly distinguish between the subject and object of that power (Foucault, 1998: 191–220; Driscoll, 2002).

Finally, the last way to approach one's imagined or literal ugliness is to *revolt* against the ideal itself and question its right to judge people on the basis of something they cannot really control. 'We should be called beautiful in our own way' says <antonel> (the founder) playfully; 'be ugly and proud' comments <ashton>. *The ugly* try to change the perception of the others by emphasizing the social, arbitrary and particular construction of ugliness in modern society. The aim here would be the creation of a 'new quality'; rupturing 'ugliness' from its physical referent and releasing corporeality from any anomalous status (Douglas, 2007: 81). For the moment, though, this is the least popular answer to the issue of ugliness. The majority of *the ugly* blame themselves for their personal misfortune, and so withdraw and suffer.

Concluding comments

In this paper I have tried to illuminate how the social construction of ugliness is an outcome of three factors. It is a triangulated relationship between social interactions, media influence, and individual processing. We all have our ugly moments, but for *the ugly,* the people who inhabit the forum, self-ascription as ugly serves as a prime identifier. It becomes their master status.

As I have discussed, if ugliness is a stigma (which to some extent can be manipulated), it is also an anomaly, something that is out of place: dirt that must be dealt with accordingly, allocated and separated. Yet *the ugly* are not only classified, they also classify themselves. In such cases ugliness can serve as a tag that prevents those who feel themselves to be ugly from taking risks in life and living life more fully. Being 'ugly' becomes a safe option, or at least something to put blame on in cases of personal failures and misfortunes. Some members critically point this out:

> What truly limits your life <Rybo> (a forum member) is your mind. Actually you are fine with your situation. You feel safe when you tag yourself as the ugly girl. You don't need to make any effort in your life, since you, the ugly one, are not going to make it anyway. Every failure is due to your ugliness. You are doing it to yourself, you are caging yourself in, you restrict yourself and you feel comfortable with it and most of all you feel safe (<Langera>).

Such opinions are very unpopular, since ugliness is perceived by the majority of the members of the forum as a problem that needs coping with. *The ugly* are the bearers of Goffmanian stigma; ugliness for them is a social hindrance, something that stops them from living their lives fully, something that makes them feel shameful, unconfident and bitter. In short, it spoils their identity (Goffman, 2003) and is often perceived as a form of disability that handicaps their everyday experience. *The ugly* stigmatize themselves, many of them adopting the dominant ideology and lowering their ambitions. Many withdraw and disassociate.

The Others are also seen to do the Othering. For *the ugly* the Others – who they compare themselves to – are the beautiful people whom *the ugly* see, with envy and distrust, as an internally homogenous group. Analysis of discussion on the forum suggests there are three main ways participants deal with this: most *conform,* using the whole range of disciplining practices that are available from make-up to tummy tuck; some *reconcile* after years of psychotherapy; while a few *revolt* against the whole social construction of ugliness altogether and try to change the dominant optics. For the most part, though, the boundaries are created and maintained.

The boundaries of this virtual community are marked by the 'othering' practices carried out by members of the forum. Those who they view as beautiful, their enemies, serve as stereotypes against which they define themselves – and by their shared sense of themselves – as *the ugly.* They have their heroes (ugly actors and actresses they admire) and the monster Buka, who serve as emblems of their identity. Critically, claiming ugliness in itself is not enough to maintain membership.

As a group, members of the forum tend to rebuke and expel 'missionaries' or people they find to be 'out of place' (the ones that are too attractive), demonstrating that a certain way of dealing with ugliness is also necessary in order to achieve belonging. In these respects, the forum acts as a space where those who figure themselves as 'ugly' can foster a sense of community; an 'imagined community' that has already evolved its own categories of inclusion and exclusion, which are in turn rigorously upheld. As I have shown, the *Forum for the Ugly People* not only allows people to openly discuss what it means to them to self-ascribe as 'ugly', it provides a virtual space where individuals who feel misplaced and misunderstood by the wider society can experience togetherness and comradeship.

References

Anderson, B., (2006), *Imagined Communities,* London, New York: Verso.

Aronson, E., T. Wilson and R. Akert R., (1997), *Psychologia społeczna,* Warszawa: Zysk I Ska.

Barthes, R., (1957), *Mythologies,* Paris: Editons du Seuil.

Baudrillard, J., (2005), *Symulakry i symulacja,* Warszawa: PWN.

Bauman, Z., (1995), *Ciało i przemoc w obliczu ponowoczesności.* Toruń: Uniwersytet Mikołaja Kopernika w Toruniu.

Berger, J., (1997), *Sposoby widzenia,* Poznań: Wydawnictwo Rebis.

Bordo, S., (1993), *Unbearable Weight. Feminism, Western Culture and the Body.* Berkley: University of California Press.

Bourdieu, P., (1985), *The Forms of Capital,* in J.G. Richardson (ed.), *Handbook of Theory and Research for the Sociology of Education.* New York: Greenwood.

Bourdieu, P., (2003), *Męska dominacja,* Warszawa: PWN.

Bruckman, A., (1998), Finding one's own in cyberspace, in Holeton, R., (ed.), *Composing Cyberspace: Identity, Community and Knowledge in the Electronic Age,* Boston: McGraw Hill.

Buczkowski, A., (2005), *Społeczne tworzenie ciała. Płeć kulturowa i płeć biologiczna,* Kraków: Universitas.

Castells, M., (2007), *Społeczeństwo sieci,* Warszawa: PWN.

Cooley, Ch. N., (1902), *Human Nature and Social Order,* New York: Holt.

Denzin, Norman K., (1999), Cybertalk and Method of Instances. in S. Jones (ed.), *Doing Internet Research*. London: Sage, pp. 107–125.

Driscoll, C., (2002), *Girls*, New York: Columbia University Press.

Douglas, M., (2007), *Czystość i zmaza*, Warszawa: Państwowy Instytut Wydawniczy.

Erikson, E., (2000), *Dzieciństwo i społeczeństwo*, Poznań: Rebis.

Foucault, M., (1980), *Power/Knowledge: Selected Interviews and Other Writings*. New York: Pantheon.

Foucault, M., (1998), *Nadzorować i karać*, Warszawa: Wydawnictwo KR.

Garland Thomson, R.A., (1998), *Extraordinary Bodies, Images of Disability in American Culture and Literature*, New York: Columbia.

Garner, D.M., (1997), Body Image Survey Results, *Psychology Today*, n.1–2, pp. 30–55.

Głębocka, A., (in print), *Treści związane z wizerunkiem ciała w przekazach prasowych na przykładzie miesięczników „Playboy" i „Twój Styl"*.

Głębocka, A. and W. Kubalt, (eds), (2005), *Wizerunek ciała. Portret kobiet*, Opole: Uniwersytet Opolski.

Goffman, E., (2003), *Piętno. Rozważania nad zranioną tożsamością*, Gdańsk: GWP.

Heatherton, T.F. *et al.*, (2007), *Społeczna psychologia piętna*, Warszawa: PWN.

Kaschack, E., (1996), *Nowa psychologia kobiety. Perspektywa feministyczna*, Gdańsk: GWP.

Kopciewicz, L., (2003), *Polityka kobiecości jako pedagogika różnic*, Kraków: Impuls.

Kopciewicz, L., (2004), *Kobiecość, męskość i przemoc symboliczna*, Kraków: WUJ.

Kristeva, J., (2007), *Potęga obrzydzenia. Esej o wstręcie*, Kraków: WUJ.

Melosik, Z., (2010), *Ciało, tożsamość i władza w kulturze instant*, Kraków: Impuls.

Snyder, M.L., E.D. Tanke and E. Berscheid, (1977), Social perception and interpersonal behavior: From social perception to social reality. *Journal of Personality and Social Psychology*, 35, pp. 656–666.

Suchańska, A., (ed), (2000), *Podmiotowe i społeczno-kulturowe uwarunkowania anoreksji nervosy, Wybrane zagadnienia*, Poznań: Wydawnictwo Fundacji Humaniora.

Tseelon, E., (1995), *The Masque of Femininity. The Presentation of Woman in Everyday Life*, London: SAGE Publications.

Turkle, S., (1995), *Identity in the Age of the Screen. Identity in the Age of the Internet*, New York: Simon and Schuster.

Waskul, D., (2005), *Ethics of Online Research.: Considerations for the Study of Computer Mediated Forms of Interaction* http://venus.soci.niu.edu/-jthomas/ethics/tis/go.dennis

Wellman, B. and M. Gulia, (1999), Virtual Communities as communities: net surfers don't ride alone, in Wellman, B., *Networks in the Global Village: Life in Contemporary Communities*. Boulder: Westview.

Wolf, N., (1991), *The Beauty Myth. How Images of Beauty are Used against Women*, New York: Anchor Books Doubleday.

Internet sources:

www.nottingham.ac.uk/. . ./Purity_and_Danger_book_review_by_Ana_Zimmermann.Pdf

www.wysokieobcasy.pl/wysokie-obcasy/1,96856,3715398.html, nr 06.11.2006,

http://www.wysokieobcasy.pl/wysokie-obcasy/1,96856,3715398.html

www.gazeta.pl

www.prawdziwepiekno.pl

Part 3
Theory

Sociological analysis and socio-political change: juxtaposing elements of the work of Bourdieu, Passeron and Lyotard[1]

Derek Robbins

Abstract: The paper considers the relationship between sociological analysis and political action by subjecting the work of Bourdieu to scrutiny, especially in relation to the work of some of his contemporaries – Raymond Aron, Jean-Claude Passeron, and Jean-François Lyotard. The first part of the discussion focuses on educational research carried out collaboratively by Bourdieu and Passeron in the 1960s and considers the shared assumptions that underpin their projects. The paper discusses their philosophical divergence after the beginning of the 1970s, suggesting that Bourdieu's development was essentially in the Durkheimian tradition whereas Passeron's was more sympathetic to the legacy of Weber. Bourdieu's inclination to regard objective science as the product of subjective disposition meant his social science became inseparable from his socio-political mission, whereas Passeron distanced himself from Bourdieu's phenomenological or ontological reflexivity.

The second part of the paper suggests Bourdieu is trying to practise phenomenological sociology within a historical social situation that, after 1979, was rapidly transforming into the postmodern condition, the diagnosis of which Lyotard had provided as an extension of his own reading of Husserl. The paper goes on to argue that, while *La distinction* sought to reconcile modernist sociology with postmodernism, Bourdieu could not relinquish what Aron regarded as the totalizing orientation of 'sociologism'. Although Lyotard, in contrast, pursued the implications of his own insights in a philosophical exegesis of Kant, the paper explores how there may yet be scope for some more fruitful view of the contemporary relationship between sociology and politics in mass democracy, particularly if we advocate socio-analytic reflexivity in association with a recognition of the 'différend'.

Introduction

In June, 2003, I organized a conference at my university which was entitled: 'Social Science Beyond Bourdieu'. This, of course, was only just over a year after Bourdieu's death. The guest of honour at the conference was Jean-Claude Passeron. I remember that he began his keynote address by reflecting on the title of the conference, asking himself whether he should consider himself as 'before', 'after', 'alongside' or 'beyond' Bourdieu. He had only shortly before published his obituary of Bourdieu, which he called 'Mort d'un ami, disparition d'un penseur' [death of a friend, disappearance of a thinker] (Passeron, 2002).

The clear implication was that Passeron considered that the passing of Bourdieu signified the passing of the mode of thinking which Bourdieu represented. His death marked the end of the totalizing sociologism which Raymond Aron had associated with the legacy of Durkheim and had castigated – in favour, instead, of the tradition established by Weber. Passeron was, therefore, making two kinds of associated judgement. He was suggesting that the historical moment of Bourdieu's project had now passed and, secondly, that sociology should accept its position as one of the social sciences rather than as *the* social science, a meta-narrative capable of explaining cultural, economic, political or educational behaviour. To subject this view to scrutiny, I want to examine the development of Bourdieu's thinking in its historical context. Of course, by taking this historical approach I am tacitly myself taking a position on the status of social scientific explanation which can be situated with reference to the conflicting positions of Bourdieu and Passeron.

In the process, I shall also attempt to advance a position which benefits from the philosophical insights in the work of Jean-François Lyotard. I shall suggest that Bourdieu responded to the critiques of sociology current at the time of the 'May events' of 1968, particularly those of Althusser and his followers, that the discipline was an instrument of bourgeois political domination, by adapting his 'objective' social anthropological analyses of Algerian social organization so that they might become the bases for participative, subjective, socio-political action. Thereafter, Bourdieu's sociological analyses were integrally related to his socio-political intentions, and his work became vulnerable to the kind of criticism made during his lifetime by Jeannine Verdès-Leroux in her *Le savant et la politique. Essai sur le terrorisme sociologique de Pierre Bourdieu* [The scientist and politics. Essay on the sociological terrorism of Pierre Bourdieu] (Verdès-Leroux, 1998).

The nature of the integral relationship between Bourdieu's sociological research and his socialist politics was fundamentally Durkheimian, an attempt to revive the social function of social science that had been assumed in the political development of the 3rd Republic. By contrast, Passeron was more inclined to sympathize with the position outlined by the mentor whom Bourdieu and Passeron shared – Raymond Aron. It was in 1959, shortly before he had appointed Passeron to be his research assistant at the Sorbonne and Bourdieu to be the secretary of his research group, the Centre de Sociologie Européenne, that Aron published, with a long introduction, the first French translations of Weber's famous essays on 'Science as a vocation' and 'Politics as a vocation' in *Le savant et le politique* [the scientist and the politician] (Weber, int. Aron, 1959). Aron insisted that social science should impinge on political practice, but only on condition that science develops in apolitical independence within an autonomous academic context. Passeron's subsequent attempt to define sociolinguistically the boundaries between explanatory discourses in the disciplines of social science was an endeavour which was politically committed in a Weberian manner and, consequently, in opposition to Bourdieu's inclination to reduce intellectual to social distinction.

I suggest that Bourdieu's emphases of agency as an explanatory tool for understanding interactions between people in society and, reflexively, for understanding the social effects of his own analytic labour, were both related to an underlying desire maieutically[2] to bring about the creation of an egalitarian, participative social democracy. There was, in other words, a hidden political agenda which was in control of his social and sociological dialogism. Philosophically, perhaps, this was a manifestation of the early influence of Leibniz which enabled him to see apparently random encounters as contributory to the final actualization of an originally pre-defined teleology. Through the inter-generational operation of the 'habitus', however, the teleology appeared to be a historical 'grand narrative'. I argue, therefore, that although Bourdieu's emphasis of 'inter-subjectivity' in his advocacy of 'socio-analytic encounter' was phenomenological, it was linked, in theory and practice, to a traditional, modernist attachment to the transformative political prospects of social movements.

Contemporaneously, Jean-François Lyotard explored the implications of the Husserlian legacy in a way which rejected historical grand narratives and provided a philosophical underpinning for his recognition that 'information' was replacing 'knowledge' and that, consequently, there was a crisis of legitimation which was affecting institutions such as families, universities, and nation-states. Apart from writing 'fables', Lyotard chose to pursue the consequences of his insights in the field of philosophy where they became esoteric contributions to academic debate rather more than politically engaged actions. To avoid heading in a similar direction, I ground the general arguments that follow within the institutions specifically affecting education, both in terms of Bourdieu's writings and in respect of the crisis to which Lyotard refers.

My concluding contention is that many of Lyotard's observations have proved to be accurate or to be predictions which have been fulfilled. With Bourdieu, we find ourselves trying to practise social science within a political sphere which has currently made its conceptual apparatus moribund. We have to guard against making allegiance to Bourdieu's reflexivity subliminally into a device for restoring the structuralist straitjacket from which he could not escape. Rather we have to use Bourdieu's reflexive method to sociologize Lyotard's 'différend' so as to establish a socially interactive sociological consciousness as the basis for a dialogistic politics.

The work of Bourdieu and Passeron in the 1960s

Most of the research of Bourdieu which is normally considered to contribute to the 'sociology of education' was undertaken in the 1960s. I am thinking, of course, of the research undertaken in collaboration with Jean-Claude Passeron which led to the publication of *Les Héritiers* in 1964 (Bourdieu and Passeron, 1964, 1979) and of *La Reproduction. Eléments pour une théorie du système d'enseignement* in 1970 (Bourdieu and Passeron, 1970, 1977), but also of articles such as 'Langage et rapport au langage dans la situation pédagogique' (Bourdieu and Passeron, 1965, 1994), 'Les étudiants et la langue d'enseignement' (Bourdieu, Passeron and de Saint Martin, 1965, 1994), 'L'école conservatrice, les inégalités devant l'école et devant la culture' (Bourdieu, 1966, 1974), 'La comparabilité des systèmes d'enseignement' (Bourdieu and Passeron, 1967), 'Systèmes d'enseignement et systèmes de pensée' (Bourdieu, 1967, 1971), 'L'examen d'une illusion' (Bourdieu and Passeron, 1968) and 'Reproduction culturelle et reproduction sociale' (Bourdieu, 1971, 1973). It is pertinent to my argument to emphasize that the two main texts were published in English translation in 1979 and 1977 (Bourdieu and Passeron, 1979; and Bourdieu and Passeron, 1977); the first two articles were assembled late in the day in English translation in *Academic Discourse*, published by Polity Press in 1994 (Bourdieu, Passeron and de Saint Martin, 1994); while the others were all published in English in the 1970s, in collections associated with the 'new directions for the sociology of education' movement initiated by M.F.D. Young's collection of essays published as *Knowledge and Control* (Young, (ed.), 1971), with the exception of 'La comparabilité des systèmes d'enseignement' and 'L'examen d'une illusion', which have never been translated.

We can say that the researches of Bourdieu and his colleagues in this period were essentially structuralist, even though Bourdieu had contributed an article to a special number of *Les Temps Modernes* of 1966 devoted to 'The problems of structuralism' in which he began to formulate the idea that structures are constructed by agents ('Champ intellectuel et projet créateur', Bourdieu, 1966, 1971). They were structuralist in the sense that the researchers contended that they were disclosing what was *really* happening in education irrespective of the perceptions of the participants. This disclosure was happening at two levels. In the first place, educational procedures operated as if curriculum content were culturally neutral, as if the absolute competence or intelligence of students could be measured in terms of their capacity to understand or reproduce the knowledge transmitted to them without reference to the differentiated extents to which they had previously been provided with the necessary conceptual apparatus by their prior social and cultural backgrounds. This *méconnaissance* operating in classrooms and lecture theatres was only the immediate instrument of the systemic *méconnaissance* disclosed by Bourdieu and Passeron in their researches. Not only did they expose pedagogical self-deceit but they also argued that the educational system colluded in the self-deception of the state in that it perpetuated social privilege whilst pretending to found life opportunities on the recognition of culturally neutral merit.

I want to elaborate further on some of the assumptions or mind-sets on which the educational researches of Bourdieu and Passeron seem to have been predicated in the 1960s, and I shall then explore the ways in which their work diverged after 1972.

Underlying assumptions of the work of Bourdieu and Passeron in the 1960s

Bourdieu and Passeron were in agreement ideologically in opposing two features of the socio-political situation in France in the mid-1960s. Although Passeron was only associated a little with the research which led to the publications of *Un art moyen, essai sur les usages sociaux de la photographie* in 1965 (Bourdieu, Boltanski, Castel and Chamboredon, 1965, 1990) and *L'amour de l'art, les musées d'art et leur public* in 1966 (Bourdieu, Darbel and Schnapper, 1966, 1990), he would have been supportive of the attempt to deploy sociological research to challenge the cultural policies of Général de Gaulle's Minister of Cultural Affairs, André Malraux. Whilst in office in the second half of the 1960s, Malraux inaugurated Maisons de la Culture which were designed to bring a national high culture to the whole population and in so doing, as he said when opening the fifth Maison in Amiens in 1966, to eradicate 'the hideous word Province' (quoted in Kedward, 2005: 408). In as much as Malraux's innovations were an attempt to secure the *rassemblement* of the French people culturally in formal imitation of the attempts of the Third Republic to standardize the French population educationally through the imposition of a centrally controlled curriculum, Bourdieu and Passeron were united in opposing state centrism and recommending provincial values.

They were equally united in opposing enthusiasm for the perceived benefits of an emerging mass culture or mass media culture. In 1963, they co-authored a scathing critique of 'massmediologues' entitled 'Sociologues des mythologies et mythologies de sociologues' (Bourdieu and Passeron, 1963), targeting, in particular, Edgar Morin's *L'Esprit du Temps* (Morin, 1962), arguing that mass media discourse advanced a myth of a new age and of a transformed humanity. In one of their less vituperative sentences, for instance, Bourdieu and Passeron said of mass media discourse that

> . . . installed in the order of mythic reason it is able to announce that "the time has come" and that, precedent-less mutation, *homo-loquens* is transforming himself into *homo-videns*. (Bourdieu and Passeron, 1963: 1015).

In short, Bourdieu and Passeron were both, instinctively, defenders of the indigenous cultures of their provincial origins – Bourdieu of the Béarn near to the French/Spanish border and Passeron of the Alpes-Maritimes, inland from Nice – against both state and mass culture.

Bourdieu and Passeron were both concerned philosophically about the status of their sociological findings, afraid that they were betraying their indigenous cultures by adopting a research methodology which might be thought to be an instrument of state control. Whilst the educational research of the early 1960s was generating the sequence of books and articles I have described, they collaborated with Jean-Claude Chamboredon in producing *Le métier de sociologue* (Bourdieu, Chamboredon and Passeron, 1968, 1991), and, together, wrote an article, published in English and not in French, entitled 'Sociology and

Philosophy in France since 1945: Death and Resurrection of a Philosophy without Subject' (Bourdieu and Passeron, 1967b). *Le métier de sociologue* was sub-titled: 'préambules épistémologiques' [epistemological preliminaries]. Bourdieu and Passeron argued that the legacy of the 19th century was that there were two competing philosophies of social science. One, derived from positivism, sought to impose the model of the natural sciences on the social sciences, while the other, reflected in the predominantly Germanic reaction to positivism, sought to emphasize that the social sciences have to acknowledge that they are dealing with participating people rather than inert physical objects and are, therefore, necessarily humanistic, involving hermeneutics. Bourdieu and Passeron contended that it must be possible to develop an epistemology of the social sciences *sui generis* which is neither scientistic by false analogy with the natural sciences nor humanistic, after the fashion of *Geistesgeschichte* or *Kulturgeschichte*. The jointly authored article of 1967 attempted to clarify the nature of the proposed middle way by reference to an account of the tensions in contemporary French social science between, on the one hand, the neo-positivist revival in American sociology as exemplified by Lazarsfeld and, on the other, the humanist, libertarian revival which followed from the affinity between existentialism and resistance politics.

I can summarize briefly some of the other assumptions of the joint research undertaken by Bourdieu and Passeron in the 1960s.

Firstly, there was a deep-seated philosophical attachment to Husserl's phenomenology, probably mediated most of all by the influence of the work of Merleau-Ponty. In Bourdieu's case, the legacy of Husserl was modified by his love/hate relationship with the thought of Heidegger, emphasizing ontology. The consequence of this phenomenological influence was that the work of Bourdieu and Passeron showed little interest in the referential content of the curriculum. They analysed the processes of pedagogic transmission without showing any interest in the truth claims of the knowledge that was transmitted educationally. Although Husserl's phenomenology was rooted in realism through his concept of 'intentionality', Bourdieu and Passeron's work seemed to have an affinity with social constructivism. This seemed to be most apparent in the emphasis in *La reproduction* on 'arbitrariness', in other words on the way in which the curriculum is historically contingent rather than a reflection of absolute scientific truths. This was compounded by the fact that the interviews and questionnaires on which *Les héritiers* and *La reproduction* were based were issued to students of Philosophy and Sociology. In the Centre de Sociologie Européenne at the time Claude Grignon carried out research on technology students, but the concentration of Bourdieu and Passeron on subjects in the humanities and social sciences meant that their socio-centric findings were a function of their choice of objects of enquiry.

Secondly, the methodology adopted by Bourdieu and Passeron presupposed a social structure in which family allegiances remained dominant. Simultaneously, Bourdieu's 'Célibat et condition paysanne' of 1962 (Bourdieu, 1962, republished in Bourdieu, 2002, 2006), in which he analysed his own native Béarn, borrowed substantially from the legacy of Le Play's studies of the family, and his early anthropological studies of the social structure of Algerian tribes deployed Lévi-Strauss's structural analysis of genealogies in order to analyse matrimonial exchanges. The assumption of the research for *Les héritiers* was that the identity of students, confronted by an imposed curriculum, could be established through scrutiny of their family backgrounds. The emphasis of the *habitus* was that it was the internalized disposition derived from formation within a traditional nuclear family.

Thirdly, and relatedly, the methodology of the formative educational researches of the 1960s presupposed existing gender relations. Alongside 'Les étudiants et leurs études' (Bourdieu and Passeron, 1964a) on which *Les Héritiers* was based, Passeron did write a research report on 'Les étudiantes' [women students] (Passeron, 1963), but the questionnaires for the surveys for *Les Héritiers* only asked about the occupations of fathers and grandfathers. The discussion of their findings contained within *Les Héritiers* emphasized the social psychological differences between male and female students, positing the notion that women students were more passive and acquiescent than their male counterparts.

A further factor in the early educational research was that it was essentially dualist. Bourdieu has written that he commenced a study of de Saussure's linguistics. He discarded it and was subsequently embarrassed by it. He quickly rejected the notion that our *parole* is a reflection of a pre-existent *langue*. It went along with his phenomenological orientation to reject the notion that thoughts or actions are the enactment of *a priori* dispositions and this was precisely why he attacked Chomsky's theory of generative grammar as fundamentally Cartesian. Nevertheless, the concept of *habitus* was formulated within a dualist framework. Our actions are softly predetermined by our inherited dispositions. Our strategic actions are the modifications of a structured set of predispositions. Although Bourdieu denied that these dispositions were *a priori* because they were socially constructed rather than psychologically absolute, nevertheless the form of his conceptualization appeared to be dualist. This sense was reinforced by the formative dualism of the relationship between metropolitan French social anthropology and the indigenous cultures of observed Algerian tribes. Colonialism seemed to have imposed a dualism. Even the famous 'three modes of theoretical knowledge' formulated between *Esquisse d'une théorie de la pratique* and *Outline of a Theory of Practice* in the 1970s, in which Bourdieu advocated an epistemological break between primary experiential knowledge and objectivist scientific knowledge was predicated on a functional dualism in which agency and explanation might enter into a creative encounter. Bourdieu never denied that his post-structuralism was dependent on structuralism.[3]

Finally, Bourdieu and Passeron shared an interest in, and an uncertainty about, the logical status of social scientific explanation. In *La reproduction*, they tried to generate 'propositions' as if these might be regarded as universally valid conceptual tools rather than as themselves contingent interventions in contingent

Derek Robbins

circumstances. This was to be a major source of opposition between Bourdieu and Passeron.

Divergence in the work of Bourdieu and Passeron from the 1970s

After the publication of *Le métier de sociologue*, which also coincided with the events of May 1968, Bourdieu and Passeron began to go their separate ways in developing their views of the way in which the middle way should be secured. As we all know, Bourdieu first articulated what could be called his 'post-structuralist' position in an article in English – 'The Three Forms of Theoretical Knowledge' (Bourdieu, 1973) – which anticipated the transition from the anti-structuralist presentation of *Esquisse d'une théorie de la pratique* (Bourdieu, 1972) to the post-structuralist presentation of its 'translation' as *Outline of a Theory of Practice* (Bourdieu, 1977). Bourdieu sought to reconcile an acknowledgement that social behaviour is the product of the agency of individuals with an acknowledgement also that it can be the object of scientistic observation, by making a differentiation between 'primary', 'experiential' knowledge and 'constructed' 'objective' knowledge. To become 'science', knowledge has to objectify experience in accordance with the discreet rules of different sciences, but, equally, we have to accept that these rules are themselves social constructs rather than categorally autonomous and *a priori* modes of knowing. By subjecting scientific objectifications to sociological analysis, as a result of a second 'epistemogical break', we become aware of the extent to which social science is grounded in 'life-world' experience and is in an equal dialectical relationship with other discursive practices within the 'life-world'.

In short, in spite of the hostility towards existentialist humanism expressed by Bourdieu and Passeron in 'Sociology and Philosophy in France since 1945' (Bourdieu and Passeron, 1967b), Bourdieu was prepared to deploy neo-positivist social science discourse as a scientistic device to liberate humanistic agency, or, at the least, to insist that the language of scientific explanation has no privileged truth claim but is just one amongst competing language games – one which derives its power and influence only from the social recognition bestowed on it rather than from its intrinsic value. My use of the expression 'life-world' has been deliberate. One way to re-state what I have just been saying is to suggest that Bourdieu's work was influenced by Husserl's phenomenology. Bourdieu shared the anti-psychologist orientation of Husserl's early *Logical Investigations* (Husserl, 1900–1, 1970) and he came under the influence both of Heidegger's ontology and of the work of the late Husserl, which was itself influenced by Heidegger. Hence we can say that Bourdieu's use of scientific logic was a means to the end of disclosing ontological reality. Bourdieu articulated a scientific theory of the relationship between agency and structure in culture and society but, more importantly, he situated that scientific theory as itself a kind of agency. His theory *of* society also constituted a theory of his theoretical engagement *within* society. Science offered functional rather than intrinsic objectivity. Scientific action and scientific authority were as much dependent on *méconnaissance* as were the pedagogic action and authority analysed in *La reproduction*.

Passeron sought a different kind of resolution. Right from the early years of their collaboration when both Bourdieu and Passeron carried out research on the implications of the spread of photography as a popular cultural form, Passeron had been interested sociologically in the distribution of emergent photographic discourses – ones which, relative to social class, developed the capacity to autonomize visual judgements which could be said to be aesthetic rather than moral. By contrast, Bourdieu was more interested in the extent to which the aestheticization of photographic criticism was a direct reflection of the position-taking of social agents – their motivations to join photographic clubs and to distinguish their practice from everyday photographic activity. Bourdieu tried to acknowledge the importance of linguistic formulations by describing his approach as (hyphenated) 'socio-logical' rather than merely 'sociological', but his approach was more inclined towards the analysis of ontological adjustments whereas Passeron's sociology was sociolinguistic, concerned with the logic of social scientific explanation. Passeron resisted any suggestion that his logical orientation was necessarily idealist and, for instance, deliberately sub-titled his subsequent book *Le raisonnement sociologique,* with a directly oppositional reference to Popper's *The Logic of Scientific Discovery*, emphasizing instead the need for a 'non-Popperian space of natural reasoning' (Passeron, 1991) or, as he changed it in the revised edition, for 'a non-Popperian space for argument' (Passeron, 2006). Passeron was as ideologically committed as Bourdieu to resisting the cultural domination of the socially dominant and, similarly, as committed to the view that social science is practised within society rather than in some spatial and conceptual detachment from it, but his was a linguistic reflexivity that did not logically impinge upon his personal social trajectory whereas Bourdieu's was an ontological reflexivity which meant that his intellectual and social trajectories were inextricably connected or, perhaps, existentially integrated. Bourdieu's social mobility was the objective correlative of his concepts of 'habitus' and 'field'. His life-trajectory generated the concepts which explained it. There was a self-fulfilling circularity between his *Bildung*, his personality formation, and the theory of pedagogic communication which was predicated on the humanistic assumption that the acquisition of transmitted knowledge modifies the self, or, to put this in Bourdieusian terms, that the habitus acts as a conduit which collapses the dualistic separations of mind and body, subjective and objective.

Bourdieu's work became inseparable from his social mission. Passeron's work remained autonomously distinct, to be deployed in pursuit of a comparable mission. During the latter part of the 1970s, Passeron wrote a doctoral thesis which was based on his teaching activities with doctoral students at the University of Nantes where, a decade earlier, he had established the Department of Sociology. The thesis, entitled *Les mots de la sociologie*, published in 1980 (Passeron, 1980), had little currency, so little that Passeron included several chapters from it in his

Le raisonnement sociologique (Passeron, 1991). In *Le métier de sociologue*, Bourdieu and Passeron had agreed, as we have seen, that it should be possible to define an epistemology of the social sciences without resorting either to imitation of positivism or hermeneutics. Following Bachelard, they were agreed that the new scientific spirit which had emerged at the time of Einstein's theory of relativity entailed the development of an epistemology based upon constantly changing scientific practice rather than on the evaluation of the static correspondence of scientific theories with reality. As a consequence, Bourdieu and Passeron (and Chamboredon) had been able to agree that the way forward would be 'to subject scientific practice to a reflection which, unlike the classical philosophy of knowledge, is applied not to science that has been done – *true* science, for which one has to establish the conditions of possibility and coherence or the claims to legitimacy – but to science in progress'. (Bourdieu, Chamboredon and Passeron, 1991: 8). The unarticulated disagreement – which meant that the proposed succeeding volumes of *Le métier de sociologue* were never written – related to the way in which this reflection was effected with a view to providing a handbook for research students in the social sciences in the Ecole des Hautes Etudes en Sciences Sociales. The first half of the book offered an account of Bachelard's formula whereby, in all sciences, 'the scientific fact is won, constructed, and confirmed' (Bourdieu, Chamboredon and Passeron, 1991: 11). The second half of the book provided extracts from the work of some of the founding fathers of sociology, notably of Durkheim and Weber, which were designed to demonstrate that the practice of these researchers illustrated Bachelard's formula in action and showed that the achievement of scientific rigour in sociology was dependent on the exercise of a common methodological procedure and independent of ideological difference. In effect, *Le métier de sociologue* sought to offer Bachelard's formula as an up-to-date equivalent of the 'primary philosophy' of Comte, who had supposed that all phenomena would be explicable scientifically by becoming amenable to the same positivistic analysis.

Bourdieu, Passeron and Lyotard, 1979–80. The challenge to sociology of postmodernism

So far I have been concentrating on some of the assumptions underlying the work of the 1960s for which Bourdieu is most famous. I want to jump to about 1979/80 to revisit some of these assumptions. I choose these dates because it was in 1979 that Bourdieu published *La distinction* (Bourdieu, 1979, 1986) and Lyotard published *La condition postmoderne* (Lyotard, 1979, 1985). In 1980, Passeron produced his *Les mots de la sociologie*.

My argument is that, philosophically, Bourdieu and Lyotard had much in common as a result of their common interest in the work of Husserl as well as their common view that their experience of the Algerian war of independence had discredited the Marxist explanation of social change. Lyotard's *La Phénoménologie* was published in 1954 (Lyotard, 1954, 1991) in the same paperback series of Presses Universitaires de France – Que Sais-je – as was Bourdieu's *Sociologie de l'Algérie* of 1958 (Bourdieu, 1958, 1962). Lyotard's text was reprinted nearly 20 times during the second half of the 20th century and has remained a standard short introduction to phenomenology. Lyotard argued that discussion of the historical meaning of phenomenology could be pursued indefinitely since it is not definable once for all but is constantly in movement. The second part of his text was a consideration of phenomenology and the human sciences, in which he discussed in separate chapters its relation to psychology, sociology and history. Lyotard taught in the philosophy department at the experimental University of Paris 8 during the 1970s when Passeron was head of the department of sociology there.

It was explicitly as a philosopher that he wrote his report on knowledge. The report was presented to the Conseil des Universités of the government of Quebec and it was dedicated to the Institut Polytechnique de Philosophie of the Université de Paris VIII at, as Lyotard put it, 'this very postmodern moment that finds the University nearing what may be its end, while the Institute may just be beginning'. (Lyotard, 1985: xxv). The source of Lyotard's conception of the postmodern condition was a phenomenological skepticism about the referentiality of knowledge and, hence, a recognition that information exchange has destroyed the traditional assumption that the transmission of knowledge potentially performs a moral and humanist function. Philosophically, Lyotard had also added an interest in the work of Wittgenstein to his phenomenological orientation. As we all know, the consequence was that Lyotard felt able to describe a new condition of society in which there were in operation competing language games and in which the idea of grand explanatory narratives had collapsed. He described the 'mercantilization of knowledge' and the implications which this would have for the authority of the state in legitimizing knowledge.

I don't want to go into further detail about Lyotard's analysis of the postmodern condition. My point in referring to Lyotard is to suggest that *La condition postmoderne* set Bourdieu a problem. I have no evidence whether Bourdieu engaged intellectually with Lyotard's book. I have not encountered any references in Bourdieu's work to Lyotard's writings, but I think it is useful to regard *La distinction* either as a response to *La condition postmoderne* or as Bourdieu's attempt to conceptualize differently the situation portrayed by Lyotard. Briefly, I think the difficulty for Bourdieu was that Lyotard's diagnosis of the time followed logically from philosophical positions which he shared with him. However, Lyotard's account of postmodernity legitimated philosophically the modish acceptance of mass media discourse which Bourdieu and Passeron had attacked in 1964. Lyotard's *Discours, figure* of 1971 (Lyotard, 1971, 2010) also seemed to legitimate philosophically the independence of visual expression from cognition which, again, had been heralded by the 'massmedialogues'.

As Bourdieu often stated, he was an 'oblate', someone who was emotionally loyal to the system within which he had been educated in spite of his awareness of its shortcomings. He needed a conceptual system which would enable him to sustain his loyalty to the social process of his own formation and yet acknowledge the notion of rootless contingency to which he had been intellectually driven by that formation. *La distinction* is a text which sought to reconcile modernism with postmodernism by positing a confrontation between a modernist *habitus* and contingent, postmodern 'fields'. It is significant that it was in 1979 that Bourdieu revisited the concept of 'cultural capital', writing 'Les trois états du capital culturel' (Bourdieu, 1979) in which he attempted to differentiate between three forms of cultural capital, which he called the 'incorporated', the 'objectivated' and the 'institutionalized' states. The first of these seemed to be indistinguishable from the habitus and, hence, intrinsically modernist; the second seemed to be a fluid state in which cultural goods acquired value in an exchange market and, hence, postmodernist; and the third seemed to anticipate a post-postmodernity in which market values would be consolidated through institutionalization.

It was at this period, I think, that Bourdieu found himself trying to work with the conceptual framework which had brought him a reputation and, incidentally, appointment to the Chair of Sociology at the Collège de France, whilst becoming increasingly aware that Lyotard's account of the postmodern condition was rapidly becoming actualized. He became increasingly aware that changes in society were necessarily challenging the conceptualizations which he had developed in the status quo ante. Briefly to recapitulate in relation to his earlier assumptions, it was, for instance, becoming clear that the institution of the family was in collapse and, equally, that there had been a revolution in gender relations. The structural/agency dualism no longer seemed viable nor the dualistic relationship between the scientific observer and the observed. The premises of the research of the 1960s no longer applied but, nevertheless, the concepts which had been generated by that research were still current in the market of ideas and had become a part of the apparatus of sociological enquiry.

Responses to the postmodern challenge

Bourdieu reacted to this crisis in slightly contradictory ways. On the one hand, he increasingly situated himself as agent within his conceptualization of the world. In other words, he developed a theory of practice which reflected his personal attempt to reconcile his indigenous culture with his acquired intellectual culture and then he situated himself within his own construct, presenting himself as one social agent amongst a population of agents rather than as the detached scientific observer of the agency of others. His social mission and his conceptualizations became mutually supportive and mutually constitutive. He embraced the contingency of his social participation.

As his texts became available internationally in translation, particularly in English, through the efforts of Polity Press from 1984 onwards, Bourdieu struggled to keep control of his own 'griffe', his label or logo, desperately wanting to retain the integral relationship between his actions and his concepts; but, increasingly, he found that his work was subject to misinterpretation and misunderstanding. He was fighting for modernist meaning in a postmodern market of intellectual exchange which was indifferent to any referential meaning and only interested in commodifying and exploiting his concepts. Hence his turn towards direct action and direct communication through his own publishing label, Raisons d'Agir, in the last decade of his life. On the other hand, however, Bourdieu was always tempted to insist on the universal validity of the concepts which had been developed contingently. Rather unconvincingly, he attempted to justify, in the opening pages of *La Noblesse d'état* (Bourdieu, 1989, 1996), his use of old research findings and data. It was not that he believed that his findings had a-temporal, *a priori* universality. Rather, his view of his mission as a social agent was, in a rather Kantian way, that the transmission of his particularity would contribute to the universification of values through the reflexivity of socio-analytic encounter between citizens of society and of the world. His conceptual endeavour was, therefore, inextricably linked with his socio-political vision, which involved the institutionalization of society on the basis of social relations rather than on the basis of political, legal or economic regulation. As he wrote, 'tout est social' (Bourdieu, 1992), 'everything is social,' and his ideal society was one that resurrected what he believed he had witnessed in the gentilitial democracy of traditional Kabyle social organization. It was always the case, therefore, that pedagogical communication was, for Bourdieu, an instrument for the achievement of social harmony rather than for the transmission of knowledge, a mechanism by which members of states might constitute the systems within which they lived.

In the terms outlined by Aron in respect of Durkheim, Bourdieu turned out to be a totalizing intellectual, committed to an all-embracing sociologism rather than to the pursuit of a circumscribed sociology with limited explanatory boundaries. He was not interested in the sociology of education as such but only in as much as educational institutions constituted one mechanism for the transmission of values within society, which had to be analysed in totality.

Passeron had always disagreed with the way in which Bourdieu appropriated the meaning of their jointly authored *La reproduction*. The original French text of 1970 was sub-titled: Eléments pour une théorie du système d'enseignement [elements for a theory of the educational system], but Bourdieu rapidly produced an article entitled 'Reproduction culturelle et reproduction sociale' [social and cultural reproduction] (Bourdieu, 1971, 1973) which imposed the idea that the original text was establishing that cultural reproduction had no autonomy but was only the concealed manifestation of social position-taking. Passeron had always argued that cultural reproduction could be analysed sociologically without insisting that the one form of reproduction was 'reducible' to the other. It followed that Passeron had no sympathy for the way in which Bourdieu proceeded to live the correlation between his intellectual and social trajectories. In *Les mots de la sociologie* (Passeron, 1980), Passeron sought to analyse sociologically the language used by sociologists, and he subjected the use he and Bourdieu had made of the concepts of cultural capital and habitus to scrutiny. Similarly, with Claude Grignon, Passeron published several times during the 1980s a debate of 1982, finally published in 1989 under the title of *Le savant et le populaire* (Passeron and Grignon, 1989) in which he tacitly argued that Bourdieu had inappropriately transferred concepts developed in a colonial situation to metropolitan France without adequately reflecting on the differences between 'outsider' and 'insider' research. Passeron constantly argued that the rules of different disciplines in the human sciences are constituted contingently and can only be understood through the analysis of their research practices rather than by seeking to formulate idealist logics of scientific discovery, but he has also refused to allow sociological research to become identical with missionary social action.[4]

Of course, it was part of Bourdieu's totalizing sociological argument that philosophical discourse possessed no intrinsic autonomy. It is not always sufficiently realized that Lyotard struggled philosophically to develop an intellectual and ethical position which would respond adequately to the postmodern condition which he had identified. In *Au juste* (1979, 1985), in his contribution to *La Faculté de Juger* (1982–1985, Derrida, Descombes, Kortion, Lacoue-Labarthe and Nancy, 1985) and in *Le différend* (1983, 1988) he attempted to formulate the basis for legitimation in the recognition of difference rather than through the imposition of pre-existing dominant narratives. Much of his discussion followed from a close consideration of Kant's *Critiques*, particularly *The Critique of Judgement*. Again, it is significant that Bourdieu included a section on Kant's *Critique of Judgement* within *La distinction* and that, indeed, the sub-title of *La distinction* deliberately connotes Kant's text: *Critique sociale du jugement*. Lyotard had argued in *La phénoménologie* that, logically, phenomenology had constantly to recognize the grounds of its own existence in the 'life-world', but he chose, nevertheless, to articulate a blueprint for social dialogue within postmodernity from within the field of philosophy. Lyotard equally argued that the implication of phenomenological thinking was that sociology should also constantly maintain a relation with the experiential base of its conceptualizations. Bourdieu tried to do this by advocating a reflexive sociology and, by this means, he did in effect seek to operationalize Lyotard's 'différend' sociologically rather than philosophically.[5]

Concluding comments

I think it is clear that Lyotard's postmodern condition has been actualized in many of the aspects of contemporary society. In particular, for instance, the internet has actualized the contemporary dominance of information exchange over knowledge transmission. Everywhere we have indications of the collapse of legitimation as government policy-makers are in debate with scientific advisors and where committees of enquiry constantly question the validity of previous committees of enquiry.

In my analysis I have tried to consider some of the relations between the thinking of Bourdieu, Passeron and Lyotard. Specifically, I have suggested that the sociology of education that was attributed to Bourdieu and Passeron developed in a historical context which quickly became a world which had been lost by the 1980s and is certainly a world which is no longer that of the generations born since 1980. In going on to describe how Bourdieu attempted to identify his subsequent sociological research with his socio-political mission, I have detailed how Passeron reacted to the changing circumstances by continuing to develop an epistemology of the practice undertaken in discrete disciplines within the social sciences – thus rejecting Bourdieu's attempt to transform sociology into a meta-narrative capable of explaining all aspects of social reality. Finally, I have commented on the ambivalence of the putative relationship between the thought of Bourdieu and Lyotard, suggesting that Bourdieu's work might now stimulate a response to the collapse of legitimation by enabling a sociological implementation of the philosophical ideas contained in *Le différend*. This would free Bourdieu's notion of agency from the incubus of the totalizing Durkheimian legacy, allowing sociology to inform small narratives, shaking off its association with the 19th century desire to generate a grand narrative of society.

To move 'beyond Bourdieu' might, therefore, involve us in continuing Bourdieu's own attempt to revise his work of the 1960s to accommodate the tangible social changes occurring from the 1980s. The choice before us is stark and is inevitably connected with our perception of the choice before sociology as a discipline. We can choose to follow the modernist Bourdieu and deploy his conceptual apparatus in a way which, in appearance, uses Bourdieu counter-culturally, but, in reality, only offers that critique from within academic institutions subservient to government funding and to the managerial intentions of dominant politicians. This, perhaps, is to follow the line taken by Passeron – disengaging 'Bourdieusian' sociological analysis from the reflexivity of Bourdieu's personal project. Or we can accept the loss of legitimacy of academic sociology and of academic institutions by seeking to adapt Bourdieu's philosophical sociology to make a contribution to the ways in which contemporary social issues present themselves, embracing the forms of individualization characteristic of western democracies, such as the personalization agenda in social policy.

The choice can, perhaps, be stated politically and, of course, it is part of the contemporary debate whether discourse on these issues is 'political' or 'social'. Bourdieu tried to hang on to the grand narrative of French republican socialism, fighting against the incursions of neo-liberalism. I remember him warning me as early as 1997 that Tony Blair was the most dangerous man in the world. Realpolitik seems to suggest that a form of postmodern neo-liberalism is, however, now triumphant and that institutions within which instrumental sociology is now taught are themselves trapped in the concomitant market of intellectual distinction, removed from practical social function. To go beyond

Bourdieu in a way that does not betray his vision, we have to try to find ways to encourage in the whole population opportunities for socio-analytic encounter which emphasize the social democratic possibilities of the exchange of small narratives without treating these as subordinate to the pre-defined agenda of any prior grand narrative.

Notes

1 This is a revised version of a paper given as 'Habitus, Capital and Education' to a conference entitled 'Beyond Bourdieu – Habitus, Capital & Social Stratification', organized by the Department of Sociology, University of Copenhagen, Dec. 1–2, 2009. It also benefits from research on 'The work of Jean-Claude Passeron, 1960-present: a case-study analysis of the development of a philosophy of social science' supported by the ESRC (Ref: RES-000–22–2494).
2 to use the word which Bourdieu used to describe his intention in writing *La Misère du Monde* (Bourdieu *et al.*, 1993, 1999).
3 For more discussion of this point, see Robbins, D.M. (2008).
4 For further discussion of Passeron's position, see my introduction to Passeron (forthcoming, 2011/12).
5 For further elaboration of this argument, see my conclusion to Robbins, D.M., (forthcoming, 2011).

References

Bourdieu, P., (1958), *Sociologie de l'algérie*, Paris: PUF.
Bourdieu, P., trans of 2nd edition of 1961, (1962), *The Algerians*, Boston: Beacon Press.
Bourdieu, P., (1962), 'Célibat et condition paysanne', *Etudes rurales*, 5–6, April–September: 32–136.
Bourdieu, P., (1966), 'L'école conservatrice, les inégalités devant l'école et devant la culture', *Revue française de sociologie*, VII, 3, July–September: 325–347.
Bourdieu, P., (1966), 'Champ intellectuel et projet créateur', *Les temps modernes*, 246, November: 865–906.
Bourdieu, P., (1967), 'Systèmes d'enseignement et systèmes de pensée, *Revue internationale des sciences sociales*, XIX, 3: 367–388.
Bourdieu, P., (1971), 'Systems of education and systems of thought', in Young, M.F.D., (ed.), (1971).
Bourdieu, P., (1971), 'Intellectual field and creative project', in Young, M.F.D., (ed.), (1971).
Bourdieu, P., (1971), 'Reproduction culturelle et reproduction sociale', *Information sur les sciences sociales*, X, 2: 45–99.
Bourdieu, P., (1972), *Esquisse d'une théorie de la pratique*, Geneva: Droz.
Bourdieu, P., (1973), 'Cultural Reproduction and Social Reproduction', in Brown, R., (ed.), (1973).
Bourdieu, P., (1973), 'The three forms of theoretical knowledge', *Social Science Information*, XII, 1: 53–80.
Bourdieu, P., (1974), 'The school as a conservative force: scholastic and cultural inequalities', in Eggleston, J., (ed.), (1974).
Bourdieu, P., (1977), *Outline of a Theory of Practice*, Cambridge: Cambridge University Press.
Bourdieu, P., (1979), 'Les trois états du capital culturel', *Actes de la recherche en sciences sociales*: 30, 3–6.

Bourdieu, P., (1979), *La distinction. Critique sociale du jugement*, Paris: Ed de Minuit.

Bourdieu, P., (1986), *Distinction. A Social Critique of the Judgement of Taste*, London and New York: Routledge and Kegan Paul.

Bourdieu, P., (1989), *La noblesse d'état. Grandes écoles et esprit de corps*, Paris, Ed. de Minuit.

Bourdieu, P., (1992), 'Tout est social', *Magazine littéraire*, 303: 104–111.

Bourdieu, P., (1996), *The State Nobility. Elite Schools in the Field of Power*, Cambridge: Polity Press.

Bourdieu, P., (2002), *Le bal des célibataires*, Paris: Seuil.

Bourdieu, P., (2006), *The Bachelors' Ball*, Cambridge: Polity Press.

Bourdieu, P., *et al.*, (1993), *La misère du monde*, Paris: Seuil.

Bourdieu, P., *et al.*, (1999), *The Weight of the World*, Cambridge: Polity Press.

Bourdieu, P., L. Boltanski, R. Castel and J.-C. Chamboredon, (1965), *Un art moyen, essai sur les usages sociaux de la photographie*, Paris: Ed. de Minuit.

Bourdieu, P., L. Boltanski, R. Castel and J.-C. Chamboredon, (1990), *Photography. A Middle-Brow Art*, Cambridge: Polity Press.

Bourdieu, P., J.-C. Chamboredon and J.-C. Passeron, (1968), *Le métier de sociologue*, Paris: Mouton-Bordas.

Bourdieu, P., J.-C. Chamboredon and J.-C. Passeron, (1991), *The Craft of Sociology*, New York: Walter de Gruyter.

Bourdieu, P., A. Darbel and D. Schnapper, (1966), *L'amour de l'art*, Paris, Ed de Minuit.

Bourdieu, P., A. Darbel and D. Schnapper, (1990), *The Love of Art*, Cambridge: Polity Press.

Bourdieu, P. and J.-C. Passeron, (1963), 'Sociologies des mythologies et mythologies de sociologues', *Les temps modernes*, 211, December: 998–1021.

Bourdieu, P. and J.-C. Passeron, (1964), *Les étudiants et leurs études*, Paris/The Hague, Mouton.

Bourdieu, P. and J.-C. Passeron, (1964), *Les héritiers, les étudiants et la culture*, Paris: Ed de Minuit.

Bourdieu, P. and J.-C. Passeron, (1965), 'Langage et rapport au langage dans la situation pédagogique' in Bourdieu, P., Passeron, J.-C. and M. de Saint Martin, (eds), (1965).

Bourdieu, P. and J.-C., Passeron, (1967), 'La comparabilité des systèmes d'enseignement', in Castel, R. and J.-C. Passeron, (eds), (1967).

Bourdieu, P. and J.-C., Passeron, (1967), 'Sociology and Philosophy in France since 1945: Death and Resurrection of a Philosophy without a subject', *Social Research*, XXXIV, 1: 162–212.

Bourdieu, P. and J.-C. Passeron, (1970), *La Reproduction. Eléments pour une théorie du système d'enseignement*, Paris: Ed de Minuit.

Bourdieu, P. and J.-C. Passeron, (1977), *Reproduction in Education, Society and Culture*, London-Beverley Hills: Sage Publications.

Bourdieu, P. and J.-C. Passeron, (1979), *The Inheritors, French Students and Their Relation to Culture*, Chicago-London: University of Chicago Press.

Bourdieu, P. and J.-C. Passeron, (1994), 'Introduction: Language and Relationship to Language in the Teaching Situation' in Bourdieu, P., Passeron, J-C. and de M. Saint Martin, (eds), (1994).

Bourdieu, P., J-C. Passeron and M. de Saint Martin, (1965), 'Les étudiants et la langue d'enseignement', in Bourdieu, P., J.-C. Passeron and M. de Saint Martin, (eds), (1965).

Bourdieu, P., J-C. Passeron and M. de Saint Martin, (eds), (1965), *Rapport pédagogique et communication*, Paris/The Hague: Mouton.

Bourdieu, P. and J.-C. Passeron, (1968), 'L'examen d'une illusion', *Revue française de sociologie*, IX: 227–253.

Bourdieu, P., J-C. Passeron and M. de Saint Martin, (1994) 'Students and the Language of Teaching' in Bourdieu, P., J-C. Passeron and M. de Saint Martin, (eds), (1994).

Bourdieu, P., J-C. Passeron and M. de Saint Martin, (eds), (1994), *Academic Discourse*, Cambridge: Polity Press.

Brown, R., (ed.), (1973), *Knowledge, Education, and Cultural Change*, London: Tavistock.

Castel, R. and J.-C. Passeron, (1967), *Education, développement et démocratie*, Paris/the Hague: Mouton.

Derrida, J. *et al.*, (1985), *La faculté de juger*, Paris: Galilée.

Eggleston, J., (ed.), (1974), *Contemporary Research in the Sociology of Education*, London: Methuen.

Husserl, E., *Logische Untersuchungen*, (1900–1), first edition, 2 vols, Halle: Max Niemeyer.

Husserl, E., (1970), [trans. of 2nd edition of 1913], *Logical Investigations*, London: Routledge and Kegan Paul.

Kedward, R., (2005), *La Vie en bleu. France and the French since 1900*, London: Allen Lane, Penguin Books.

Lyotard, J.-F., (1954), *La phénoménologie*, Paris, P.U.F.

Lyotard, J.-F., (1971), *Discours, figure,* Collection d'esthetique, 7, Paris: Klincksieck.

Lyotard, J.-F., (1979), *La condition postmoderne: rapport sur le savoir*, Collection 'Critique', Paris: Minuit.

Lyotard, J.-F., (1979), *Au juste: conversations*, Paris: Bourgois.

Lyotard, J.-F., (1983), *Le différend, Collection 'Critique'*, Paris: Minuit.

Lyotard, J.-F., (1985), *The Postmodern Condition*, Manchester: Manchester University Press.

Lyotard, J.-F., (1985), *Just Gaming*, Manchester: Manchester University Press.

Lyotard, J.-F., (1985), 'Judicieux dans le différend' in Derrida *et al.*, 1985.

Lyotard, J.-F., (1988), *The differend: phrases in dispute*, Manchester: Manchester University Press.

Lyotard, J-F., (1991), [trans. of 10th edition of 1986], *Phenomenology*, Albany: State University of New York Press.

Lyotard, J.-F., (2010), *Discourse, Figure*, Minnesota: University of Minnesota Press.

Morin, E., (1962), *L'esprit du temps*, Paris: Grasset.

Passeron, J.-C., (1963), 'Les étudiantes', Paris, Working Papers of the Centre de Sociologie Européenne.

Passeron, J.-C., (1980), *Les mots de la sociologie*, Nantes: The University of Nantes.

Passeron, J.-C., (1991), *Le raisonnement sociologique*,Paris: Nathan.

Passeron, J.-C., (2006), *Le raisonnement sociologique*, 2nd edition, Paris,: Albin Michel.

Passeron, J.-C., forthcoming, trans of 2nd edition, (2011/12), *Sociological Reasoning*, Oxford: Bardwell Press.

Passeron, J.-C., (2002), 'Mort d'un ami, disparition d'un penseur', *Revue européenne des sciences sociales*, 124: 77–125.

Passeron, J.-C. and C. Grignon, (1989), *Le savant et le populaire: misérabilisme et populisme en sociologie et en littérature*, Paris: Seuil/Gallimard.

Robbins, D.M., (2008), 'Indigene Kultur und Symbolische Gewalt' (Indigenous Culture and Symbolic Violence), in Schmidt, R. and V. Woltersdorff, (eds), (2008). (English text available from author).

Robbins, D.M., forthcoming, (2011), *French Post War Social Theory: International Knowledge Transfer*, London/ Thousand Oaks/ New Delhi: Sage Publications.

Schmidt, R. and V. Woltersdorff, (eds), (2008), *Symbolische Gewalt. Herrschaftsanalyse nach Pierre Bourdieu*, Konstanz, UVK Verlagsgesellschaft mbH.

Verdès-Leroux, J., (1998), *Le savant et la politique. Essai sur le terrorisme sociologique de Pierre Bourdieu*, Paris: Grasset.

Weber, M., int. Aron, R., (1959), *Le savant et le politique*, Paris: Plon.

Young, M.F.D., (ed.), (1971), *Knowledge and Control. New Directions for the Sociology of Education*, London: Collier-Macmillan.

Cultivating disconcertment[1]

John Law and Wen-yuan Lin

Abstract: In this paper we explore a moment of intersection between 'Western' and Taiwanese social science knowledge that took place in a Taiwanese seminar in 2009. Our interest is post-colonial: we treat this as an encounter between dominant and subordinate knowledge systems, and follow Helen Verran by conceiving of the bodily disconcertment experienced by the participants as an expression of metaphysical difference. We then provide three contexts for that disconcertment: one, the post-1949 story of Taiwanese economic development; two, the syncretism of Taiwanese street Daoism; and three, the history of philosophy where we draw on contrasts between Western and Chinese traditions. We suggest that each of these contexts is embedded in and informs the disconcertment experienced in the exchange. We then argue that rendering the origins of this disconcertment discursively accountable is performative. Our conclusion is that the cultivation and articulation of disconcertment is a crucial tool for interrogating and moving beyond the metaphysics, the subjectivities, and the institutional organisational forms that together help to reproduce hegemonic Western knowledge traditions.

The problem

What happens when dominant and subaltern knowledge traditions encounter one another? How do they interact? The postcolonial literatures remind us that much is at stake. The Western Enlightenment tradition may be in its death throes, but as scholars such as Dipesh Chakrabarty and Arturo Escobar have shown, it also powerfully conditions the possibilities for subaltern scholarship[2]. And subaltern politics[3]. How is it possible to know, know well, and know differently, in contexts conditioned for so long by relations of dominance?

Since subaltern worlds are many and varied, there can be no one answer to this question. But then again, the Western legacy carries its own somewhat stable baggage. So what does this look like? Any putative list is long, and since 'the West' is not itself consistent and coherent, caution is needed. Even so, any attempt to characterize what this stands for needs minimally to simultaneously attend to *metaphysics*, to *institutions*, and to *subjectivities*.

- The dominant Western knowledge traditions carry and reproduce a *metaphysics* that seeks to distinguish the world on the one hand from knowledge of that world on the other. To say it grandly, much too quickly, and to ignore innumerable variations and exceptions, in the Western scheme of things it is generally taken for granted that there is a world out there, a cosmos, that is ordered and structured. It is also assumed that it is possible to gather knowledge about that world, to represent it, to debate the merits of different putative representations, and to arrive at provisional conclusions about its structure. In short dominant western knowledge traditions exhibit what philosophers Ames and Hall characterise as a 'second order' problematic[4].
- Second, Western knowledge traditions rest in and reproduce specific *institutional* arrangements. These take many forms, and have changed profoundly since pre-Socratic Greece (where some of these structures were first laid down). They are clearly undergoing major transformations in the contemporary world, not least because the links between the academy and academic knowledge on the one hand, and other institutions (including the 'technoscience' of private capital, the law, and politics) appear to be metamorphosing[5]. Even so, for certain purposes the distinction between truth and power is sustained at least in rhetorical form, and this division is embedded in institutions (academic and otherwise) that reproduce and are reproduced by specific but hegemonic truth practices and their metaphysics, career structures, statuses, and systems for circulating knowledge.
- Third, the Western tradition and its institutional arrangements also imply particular *subjectivities*. Though breaches are legion, the normative expert is often taken to be a rational and intellectual subject who expresses truths about the world in symbolic form. In the case of the empirical sciences, this subject is also committed to experimental, observational, or historical inquiry. Competent subjects are thus those that reliably find out about and represent the world. They reproduce and embody both the representational metaphysics and the institutional structures mentioned above. And, though this is a matter for debate and disagreement, as a part of this, in the normative case, the 'personal' emotions and bodily states of such subjects are Othered to the subordinate (and often gendered or racialised) category of 'private life'. In the first instance, the assumption is that messy bodies get in the way of clean thinking.

This is obviously a caricature. More obeyed in the breach than the observance, it has also been persuasively argued that the Western legacy precisely works by artfully combining observances of its normativities with systematic breaches thereof[6]. However, whatever the subtleties, as a scheme it nonetheless retains its power. Indeed, it is surely the partial *intersection* between the components of this unholy trinity that makes it so difficult to think alternatives well. This is because any attempt to rethink knowledge traditions needs to be able to treat all three simultaneously. It needs to be able to rethink the character of the *real*, re-order the workings of *institutions*, and enact alternative knowing *subjectivities* all at the same time. The problem is that if these are individually well-embedded, then taken together they are just extraordinarily well-entrenched. Small wonder that despite the efforts of post-colonial scholars, the chronic internal crises of the Enlightenment tradition laid bare in disciplines such as STS (Science, Technology and Society), cultural studies, and anthropology, and the changing relations between the academy and its environment, overall it is pretty much business as usual in high status Western – and, as we will see, Eastern – knowledge traditions.

In what follows we join the long list of those seeking to chip away at the grip of this hegemonic trio. Our approach, which draws on chosen STS and postcolonial literatures, is empirical and specific. We work by exploring a particular exchange that occurred during a seminar series in Taiwan in the spring of 2009. But before moving to this we want to make two brief explanatory methodological points.

First, our approach is intensive rather than extensive. That is, we work on the assumption that large issues can be detected in specific practices. Leibniz famously wrote that:

> 'Every portion of matter can be thought of as a garden full of plants, or as a pond full of fish. But every branch of the plant, every part of the animal, and every drop of its vital fluids, is another such garden, or another such pond.' (Leibniz, 1998: 277)

Analogous sensibilities inform the work of many more recent writers – Walter Benjamin being a notable example. Thus, though we cannot argue the point here, this means our approach is 'baroque' in the specifically methodological sense of the term[7]. The whole can be found within. This is our assumption: if we can teach ourselves the appropriate skills then the whole world can be found in a small seminar interchange. And in particular, we take it that if we examine these in the right way then large post-colonial knowledge predicaments can be found at work within specific interactions.

Second, however, this means that we also run up against the inconvenience of dealing with subjectivities. Though we've just said we need to handle metaphysics, institutions *and* subjectivities altogether, the problem with subjectivities (as again we've noted) is that within western metaphysics important components of these are coded up as 'personal'. Outside the psy-disciplines (which turn these into an object of study in their own right), their appearance in academic writing is taken to be a diversion (or light relief) at best and a sign of self-indulgence at worst. In this way of thinking what is properly interesting is the *world* rather than those describing it. Perhaps unsurprisingly, it also turns out that the intellectual tools for thinking subjectivities-and-knowledge-together are poorly developed. Foregrounding subjectivities simply doesn't fit with the scheme being reproduced in the hegemonic trio. However, in what follows we need to breach this convention. In particular, we need to follow Helen Verran by suggesting that bodily *disconcertment* may be understood as an expression of metaphysical disjuncture. To put this slightly differently, we are making a methodological proposal: that discomfited and 'personal' bodily states are crucial potential *detectors of difference*. But this means that we need to talk about subjectivities, including our own. Unease, as Dipesh Chakrabarty also implies, is a place to go looking for difference[8].

In what follows we first briefly outline the circumstances of the 2009 Taiwanese seminars. Next we describe a particular moment of disconcertment. We then make three detours in order to provide a context for that disconcertment or – to use the terminology used above – to find the world that lies within it. The first takes us to the post-1949 story of Taiwanese economic development. In the second we describe features of Taiwanese street Daoism. And in the third we briefly touch on the history of philosophy to draw some contrasts between the Western and the Chinese traditions. Each of these, we contend, is *embedded* in the exchange. Each helps to *inform* the disconcertment. But, and in addition, we suggest that exploring the origins of the disconcertment in these ways and thereby rendering them discursively accountable, is also *performative*. Our conclusion is that the *cultivation of disconcertment* is a crucial tool or sensibility that will help us to move beyond the metaphysics, the subjectivities, and less directly the institutional organisational forms that reproduce the hegemonic Western knowledge traditions. Alterity beckons.

Seminar Disconcertment

In 2009 John Law was invited by Wen-yuan Lin to speak at a series of seminars and workshops for the opening of a STS centre in the cutting-edge technological National Chiao-Tung University (NCTU) in Hsinchu, Taiwan. The audiences for the seminars were heterogeneous. They included academic engineers interested in how 'the social' is implicated in the design and consumer purchase of technologies. Important, too, were scholars and students working in science, technology and medicine who (like the engineers) were interested in technological safety and failure [9]. The workshops attracted more specialist STS audiences but these too were heterogeneous. Some attending were interested in technological innovation or other forms of modernisation, some were intellectually and politically critical, and others had specific interests in post-foundational theories of science or knowledge. In each of the workshops Law first gave a presentation, and his talk was followed by comments from Taiwanese scholars and general discussion. The somewhat contradictory aim was to create a space for simultaneously learning about and challenging STS approaches, including those of actor-network theory and its successor projects with which Law is particularly associated.

In the last seminar of the series Law argued that the social world is non-coherent[10]. He used a case study to suggest that the smooth narratives common in social science (1) fail to catch what is going on, (2) are misleading because they make the world look more coherent than it actually is and (3) tend (though only partially) to *perform* it as coherent. As an alternative, Law argued in favour of methods for describing and enacting *non-coherence*. He argued, for instance, that there were good reasons for juxtaposing different narratives in ways that resist coherence and instead enact non-coherence or 'mess'. Finally, he suggested (in an argument consistent with much postcolonial writing, though he did not make this explicit) that representing and enacting non-coherence needs to be understood as a political act. This is because marginalised but desirable realities might be strengthened and made more real if social scientists no longer assumed (1) that there is a single and coherent reality and (2) that this reality is destiny.[11]

To state the obvious, an academic seminar is an institutionalised material and discursive knowledge location. It frames and bounds the actions and subjectivities legitimately available to participants. The character of that space has been endlessly debated, but is based in part on the assumption (touched on above and observed in the breach as much as in the rule) that truth can be divorced from status and power. As we have noted, truth depends on appropriately logical and coherent argument and, if the topic is empirical, it depends in addition on representational empirical adequacy. This reproduces the presupposition that what is being said appropriately describes something beyond itself. As we have noted, all of this has a long history within the truth practices of Western knowledge[12].

The audience listened attentively, but was not completely convinced by Law's position. For instance Dawei Fu asked whether there was not:

'. . . an issue of preference or of choice here? Whether we want to choose several worlds . . . , or whether we *really* want to understand the totality of it, . . .'. '[S]o . . . there is an issue here, and it has something to do with our political position and also something to do with . . . political negotiation.'[13]

Hsin-Hsing Chen pressed a related point by telling an empirical story. The day before the seminar, 29th March, was the last day of the major annual touring festival of the Goddess Mazu[14]. This Goddess is popular in Taiwan. She has 400 temples, she protects many people, and she has a huge following. Chen had taken his students to watch the largest religious event in Taiwan – Mazu's pilgrimage to her most important site, the Da-Jia Jenn Lann Temple in Taizung[15]. About a million other people had had the same idea. As a consequence, Mazu herself was caught up in the crush[16] and Chen and his students were able to get nowhere near either Mazu or her temple[17]. Chen told the seminar that:

'[T]he whole scene simply defies accurate description of any kind, because it is very fragmented'.

He talked about the performing troupes and groups – two or three hundred of them – that included martial arts, brass bands, classical Chinese bands, rock groups, and puppet theatres[18]. He used the Chinese phrase, 're nao', which translates into English as 'heat and noise':

'there were firecrackers, millions of them, exploding behind our ears. It was very difficult to keep a steady line of thought . . . at all.'

All in all the experience was overwhelming and difficult to put into words. But what it *meant* was similarly confused. One example: the students asked

Chen about the meaning of the little umbrellas being carried by a group of women with one of the bands. Chen didn't know, and when the students asked the participants they came back with five or six quite different answers. Pressed with other unanswerable questions, Chen eventually told the students: 'It is *like* this! There *is* no explanation!'

> [R]eligion' ('zong jiao') is a theoretical construct, but this isn't a religion. It is a ritual that 'doesn't have a name for itself. . . . It is just the way we live.' '[T]his [is a] massive event without a straight or coherent narrative for itself.

Then he added:

> 'I was particularly attuned to the messiness of the whole event yesterday, and from that observation I think I [want] to argue that messy method at this moment here in Taiwan, the struggle against grand narrative in general, is not that productive.'

This is the crucial moment of encounter, and lies at the origin of our inquiry. Taiwan, Chen was saying, does not need mess, let alone messy description. Instead it needs some kind of descriptive coherence. He – together with Fu – were reminding Law of an STS claim that he had apparently forgotten: that knowledges are situated, his own included.

What to make of this? First note that it is a reversal. This is not orientalism, a matter of 'black skin and white mask'[19]. Instead it is a set of *occidental* subjectivities and interior incoherences in the Western metaphysical and intellectual project that are being thrown into sharp relief (the subjectivities and metaphysics are nearly indistinguishable). Second, look at the moves. One, Law has said that the world, a single world, can be described. Two, it turns out that this world is messy. Three, this means that truths are locally situated. Four (this is the point where the rot sets in), he has implied that this is *generally* the case (for why else would he be talking about this in Taiwan?) At this point, then, he's talking in a way that reflects what Ribeiro and Escobar call 'metropolitan provincialism'[20]. Five, this is obviously self-contradictory. And six (here is the post-colonial twist) he has been told that this doesn't work in Taiwan which doesn't have, but desperately needs, coherence. What's interesting here is not so much the contradictions, real though they are, within the Western hegemonic project (these have been widely noted by those critical of relativism, and there are routine ways of handling this). What's more important is that they were being highlighted in a different *location*. The argument was not so much: 'you are contradicting yourself'. Rather it was: 'this does not work *here*.'

Now we can introduce the term we mentioned above. This, we want to argue, was *a moment of disconcertment*. We're going to say that it was disconcerting for Law, but perhaps more interestingly, that it was also disconcerting for members of his Taiwanese audience such as Wu and Chen. As we mentioned earlier, we borrow the term from Helen Verran:

> 'Aboriginal Australian peoples,' she writes, 'generally understand themselves as having a vast repertoire by which the world can be re-imagined, and in being re-imagined be re-made. In English this usually goes under the title of 'the dreaming'. I

think a more helpful name for this conceptual resource is 'the ontic/epistemic imaginary' of Aboriginal knowledge systems. It is this imaginary, celebrated, venerated and providing possibilities for rich intellectual exchange amongst all participants in Aboriginal community life, which in part enables the eternal struggle to reconcile the many local knowledges which constitute Aboriginal knowledge systems. Many Aboriginal communities know how to negotiate over ontic categories; they have the epistemic resources for devising a radical form of land title acknowledging disparate ways of knowing land.'[21]

Verran is telling us that imaginaries are sets of metaphors for *thinking* and *enacting* the world. At the same time they are embodied metaphysical sensibilities for choreographing experience[22]. Of course others have experienced disconcertment. Famously, Michel Foucault laughed out loud when he collided with the alternative metaphysics implied in Borges' list of entries from a Chinese encyclopaedia – and he went on to explore the modern Western episteme. Perhaps in doing the latter he was 'writing away' his disconcertment[23]. Verran's experience was similar but her response was different: she put the enactment of metaphysics and subjectivities together[24]. Indeed, Law's argument about mess is closely linked to Verran's position (both are insisting on the metaphysical performativity of practice), but Verran makes a crucial additional argument. She says that when radically different metaphysics intersect, their disjunction is experienced as *bodily disconcertment*[25]. She initially encountered this in a Nigerian classroom when students and pupil-teachers needed to find practical ways of handling incongruous differences between Western and Yoruba numbering. Here disconcertment took the form of belly laughter. There wasn't much belly laughter in the Taiwanese seminar, but there was certainly disconcertment. Law was disconcerted because he was being told: 'your contexted metaphysics don't work here'. And members of his audience were disconcerted because Law's talk played into chronic tensions in many Taiwanese metaphysics-subjectivities. But how to think about this? To explore this we make the first of the detours mentioned in the Introduction.

Modernization and its paradoxes

Most social scientists in Taiwan do their PhDs in the West returning with, for instance, empirical sociological skills, or with versions of critical theory such as feminism or Marxism. Some are exposed to 'post-theories': post-structuralism, post-colonialism, post-modernism or 'after actor-network theory'[26]. But why do they go abroad? The quick answer is that in the paradoxical world of universalism they want to study at the centre rather than the periphery. Perhaps the collective hope is that in due course the Taiwanese academy will become intellectually competitive.

This is a specific academic version of the stories of progress and modernization that have been important in Taiwan for several centuries. Colonialism can be traced to the sixteenth century with the arrival and colonisation of parts of the island by the Portuguese and especially the Dutch. Narratives of modernisation become powerful in the 19th century with the sustained encounter between Qing dynasty China and the imperialism of the British and especially the Japanese, who colonised the island in 1895.[27] With the military defeat of the Japanese in 1945, the Chinese civil war, the withdrawal of the Kuomintang to Taiwan in 1949, and the subsequent recognition of the Republic by the US, the narratives of modernisation intensified.

Currently these come in various forms. One powerful variant is economic. Taiwan has made astonishing strides since 1949. GDP has grown around 8% per annum over the last three decades, and per capita income in 2009 was around $17,000[28]. This economic narrative of progress is often interwoven with stories and practices that have to do with technological innovation. For instance, it is frequently said that Taiwan is adept at the rapid and highly efficient assembly of (for instance IT) technologies designed in the US, in Japan, or in Europe. At the same time it is also argued that it lags behind because it doesn't itself design state-of-the-art, world-conquering technological products[29].

The general story, then, is one of modernization and progress. As is obvious, this grand ordering narrative is set within and helps to enact a single space substantially defined by a competitive neo-liberal global economy and an analogously competitive global intellectual system. Differences between locations are treated as expressions of position in progressive time: countries are located as leaders or laggards[30]. And, on a smaller scale, this is happening in the university system where major Taiwanese universities are trying to improve their ratings in the various international-league tables.

What, then of Taiwanese students who do their PhDs at MIT or the LSE? Or the fact that scholars from the West are invited to visit Taiwanese universities? Both phenomena can also be understood as expressions of the narratives of modernisation. Here Taiwan is enacting itself as lying somewhat behind the Western cutting edge, but as hoping to learn and catch up[31]. And all this is a powerful imaginary. Whether it is uniquely Western we might debate, but it certainly 'hardens the categories' in the way described by Verran. This is because a single world is being assumed and enacted in which relevant differences have either been Othered as blind alleyways, or been transmuted into different positions on linear scales such as per capita GDP and, as we have seen on a smaller scale, the level of development of Taiwanese academic life and Taiwanese STS, where the latter becomes an expression of what Ribeiro and Escobar refer to as 'provincial cosmopolitanism'[32].

Put this on hold, and note that 'post-theorists' such as Law are struggling to refuse important parts of these Western narratives and their metaphysics. Is the world a single reality? Post-theory says 'no'. Is the world separable from its representations? Again the answer is 'no'. Are technoscience narratives especially privileged? Once more, the answer is 'no'. Are particular locations epistemically privileged? The answer is: not in any foundational way. Is knowledge located or situated? Yes, of course it is. Are knowledges power-saturated? Yes to this too. Such is the message.

But here come the paradoxes. For just as Taiwan starts to play the game of intellectual modernisation seriously it finds it's being told: 'Sorry, but we got this wrong: there *is* no general intellectual privilege.' The consequence is disconcertment, for as we've suggested, metaphysical difference and embodied confusion are the same thing here. And this is the initial importance of Chen's intervention. Law is disconcerted for the reason we mentioned above: he's being told that his argument doesn't work in Taiwan, and that grand narrative is needed in this location. But Chen and his colleagues are disconcerted too. This is because all the alternative histories that have been Othered in the narratives of progress are being released, and space is being granted to the unruly confusions of events such as Mazu's procession. It is also, however, and very importantly because Law's argument touches on and resonates with chronic tensions that are lived on a daily basis in Taiwan. To understand why his argument is so disconcerting we need, therefore, to say something about Taiwanese daily life.

Shopping for Gods

Just outside the gates of NCTU there's a small but busy temple. Tu-di Gong is the God of Land. He's a kindly old man with a white beard, but his powers have grown and now he helps students to pass their exams. They come to the temple, offer him a sweet drink, light incense, and pray to him[33]. Tu-di Gong is good at answering prayers and has become a popular unofficial NCTU icon.[34]

There's a transactional or market logic at work here. In Taiwan Gods that answer prayers become popular. Those that don't, lose their following. People *shop* for Gods. Here's an example. A young woman trying to get pregnant writes about the process in her blog[35]. She started by unsuccessfully trying intra-uterine insemination (IUI). Then she prayed to the different Gods and Goddesses at Da-Jia Jenn Lann temple, before concentrating on the Goddess of Children, Zhu-Sheng Niang-niang. The results were ambiguous (perhaps the Gods were jealous of one another, perhaps the temple was too crowded). Her sister told her that the Yu-Ji temple in Ping-dong had a good reputation, so she went there to pray to Heaven's Boy, Ten-tong[36]. His advice wasn't clear, so she moved on to the Boy God's temple (he's called San Taizhu). At first he was confusing too, but then he told her that her gifts were too mean. Once she'd put this right by being more generous, she described the technicalities of IUI and IVF (she was worried he might not understand, and explained these four times). His advice was still unclear. Her family thought he might be fed up with her, but she joked that if she harassed him enough he might help her simply to get rid of her. When she next went to petition him she teased him by asking him for his marbles (he's a small boy, remember) and (a common Taiwanese greeting) whether he'd eaten enough. After telling her he hadn't, he changed his mind, and she moved on to the IVF clinic where she decided to have three embryos implanted because the Boy God had given her three marbles.

These transactional stories about Gods illustrate the syncretism of Taiwanese popular Taoism. The logic is empirical and pragmatic: the guiding idea is that it is worth trying anything once. If it works, then good. If it doesn't you move on. The logic is one of *accretion*. Anything can be absorbed. New divinities can be added (most Taiwanese temples have multiple gods.) The list of Gods is an expandable resource. You ask them for help. You debate with them. You tease them. And if they don't deliver you walk away. But here's the important point. The search for practical success apart, there *is no overall ordering story*. The woman whose blog we've described is utterly pragmatic. Hi tech intervention? Fine. Intercession by the Gods? Fine too. If the latter are any good they will help with the IVF anyway[37].

This is a way of choreographing the real that does without any overall ordering story. It is simultaneously a contingent set of *institutional relations*, an assemblage of embodied but utterly tactical *subjectivities*, and a *metaphysics of ontic pragmatism*. Where does one go to get help? The institutions are there offering (or failing to offer) help. Temples are like supermarkets. One's being in the world as a person is contingent, tactical, and pragmatic. What there *is* in the world is more or less variable, conditional and syncretic. Indeed, whether there is 'a world' or a single reality at all is an open question. Certainly the nature of the real is vague, fluid and ambiguous. Nothing coheres except pragmatically. This is why it is so easy to add Gods, or to take them away again. Or, for that matter, to combine IVF and divine intervention. And, as we've seen, this is also the source of Chen's unease. 'It is *like* this!' we quoted him, 'there *is* no explanation!' There is no story.

This is important to our argument about disconcertment because Taiwanese scholars *live* in a syncretic world. This is a world of folk religion, but also a world of poorly observed town planning regulations, chaotic traffic management, and proliferating street market stalls. The logics in each of these contexts are specific, make pragmatic sense for those involved, but the overall effect does not add up to an order. 'Re nao', 'heat and noise', events as they unfold are more or less un-narratable. All of which, however, sits ill with the ordering and singular stories of natural science, social science, or town planning. Or with the hegemonic Western metaphysical assumption that there is an underpinning reality whose order can be uncovered if we look for it in the right way. Or the embodied sense that it is possible to live an orderly life. And this takes us back to disconcertment. It isn't just that the sceptics in Law's audience don't agree with him (though they don't). It's also that they recognise the place they live in to be an uneasy cohabitation of order and non-coherence. Every day the Taiwanese members in the seminar negotiate the tension between a *lived* metaphysics of syncretism on the one hand, and the promise of singularity and order held out by the grand narratives of epistemic authority, progress and modernization on the other. Law's talk interferes with this balance. He's undermining the promise of an ordered reality. And this is the second refraction. The history of Taiwan and its current tensions are located within – and expressed by – the seminar and its exchanges. But there is another layer to the disconcertment, and to explore this we make our third brief detour.

The singular and the multiple

We briefly mentioned Hall and Ames in the introduction. These are philosophers who have explored the distinction between classical Chinese and European philosophy[38]. Their argument is subtle and we cannot conceivably do it justice here. Indeed, and more deeply, there is no neutral way of comparing and contrasting two such different metaphysical traditions[39]. In practice we're caught within the metaphysics of one or the other. What follows, then, is Western version of the difference. However roughly speaking their argument runs so.

In the Western tradition an originary and potentially continuing chaos is treated as a threat to be repelled by *order*. Reality becomes a single cosmos, with a specific and coherent form, shape and motion, whilst the stuff of reality, ordered into shape and form, is inert or indeterminate in and of itself[40]. So what is an explanation? The answer is that it is the discovery and representation of that underpinning order[41]. To explain is to move away from what is described to the description itself. It is to *displace*, a characteristic of what Hall and Ames call 'second problematic' knowledge. Some other consequences follow. For instance, history is teleological, driven by underlying causes. Again, since the cosmos has a single pattern, explanatory consistency is not only possible: it's also important. Further, since explanation involves explicating underpinning principles, differences are often handled by appealing to explicit meta-level abstractions. The result is that in the Western tradition, clarity and definition are valued. They help to deepen understanding and resolve explanatory differences[42].

As Foucault discovered, the Chinese tradition is quite different. Classical Chinese philosophy imagines an 'acosmotic'[43] world with no foundational cosmogonic order. It makes few assumptions about coherence or unity, attending instead to uniqueness and specificity[44]. The world is taken to be multiple and the 'ten thousand things' of the world are taken to be mobile, transformative, specific and fluid. Change (or becoming) is privileged over rest (or being), and explanation is associative, analogical, correlative, specific, indeterminate, ambivalent, and never exhaustive.[45] Analogies and historical authorities are related together in dynamic but specific processes.[46] Explanatory images come in pairs that simultaneously include one another and are in tension[47], and it is assumed that alternative explanatory patterns arise elsewhere. Explanation is anthropomorphic with many perspectives and no claims to generality. At the same time there is little distinction between representation and what is represented. Both are simultaneously part of *and* express the disposition of things[48], and it is often inappropriate to distinguish means from ends[49]. History is non-teleological, and becomes an expression of particular multiple constellations. Finally, differences are handled aesthetically rather than analytically. It is the implicit that is valued rather than the explicit.[50]

So there is the contrast. Let's underscore the health warnings. The contrast is a 'second problematic' list. It may be useful but it certainly reproduces the hegemonic metaphysics of the Western tradition. Then again, the two traditions are much more heterogeneous than this way of talking about them makes them appear. Finally, a considerable difficulty, Taiwan is not China. It has its own distinctive historical, political, economic, and ethnic specificities. That said, it *is* also aligned to China in important respects. And it is this thought that leads us to the last part of our account of the seminar disconcertment, for these philosophical differences are *also* at work here too.

First, though the differences between street Daoism (or the activities of street vendors and builders) on the one hand, and classical Chinese philosophy on the other are huge, the lived syncretism of such activities described in the last section resonates in some measure with Chinese first order acosmotic metaphysics. Second, the mirror point, the narratives of progress and explanation embedded in the realities of economic growth and modernisation (and also in organisation of PhD training and the visits of Western scholars), reflect, resonate, and reproduce realities consistent with the cosmogonic metaphysics of Western philosophy. And then, third, the chronic and embodied tension between these two realities described above was amplified by Law's critique of order and his advocacy of non-coherence. We have already quoted Dawei Fu. Is there not, he asked:

'. . . an issue of preference or of choice here? Whether we want to choose several worlds . . . , or whether we *really* want to understand the totality of it, . . .'.

We've also cited Hsin-Hsing Chen's observation that the struggle against grand narrative is not productive in Taiwan. But Chen went on to add this potent further comment:

'Description of messiness is part of the story. I think that it has a lot to do with the cosmic view of the Chinese, Yin and Yang [are] always together, chaos and order, the multitude and the ruler, . . . [these are] always paired. So this fits with what . . . Law says: that some re-enactments will simply reinforce the powers that be. . . . But, then, what are we going to have to say? [Do] . . . we simply accept how people see these kinds of things, represent these kinds of things? [Or do] . . . we try to [find] another level of interpretation?'

Here he's rendered explicit the philosophical tension implicit in Fu's intervention. In Hall and Ames's terms his question is this. Should we be reproducing Chinese first order aesthetic metaphysics? Or should we rather be adopting a version of the Western analytical and explanatory second order system? Of course we already know his answer. In its present circumstances Taiwan is in need of the latter, not the former. And, as we have noted, what is lived is also metaphysical. And vice versa. Subjectivities, metaphysics and institutions are all involved. So Chen's disconcertment simply gave voice to what many were feeling. For Taiwanese academics – and engineers and managers and planners – are struggling, often against the odds, to enact a somewhat orderly cosmos. They struggle to create and reproduce a country, a modern economy, and a set of organisational forms ordered by some kind of coherent structure. They also struggle to produce *representations* of this reality. That is what they do in their daily lives and their places of work. It is not surprising that Law's post-foundational position was disconcerting.

Conclusion

Though we've talked of individuals – and of Law and Chen in particular – as we indicated in the introduction, our interest is analytical rather than personal or confessional. Building upon the work of Verran, our working hypothesis is that metaphysics, institutions and subjectivities are mixed together and mutually supportive of one another in the generation of knowledge spaces, hegemonic and otherwise. We've also suggested that disconcertment can be understood as an embodied response of the subject to metaphysical disruption. Carefully understood, disconcertment can thus be treated as a bodily indicator of metaphysical difference. Then, and more specifically, we've argued that the origins of Law's disconcertment in this seminar have to do with place. He's not so much being told that his position is self-contradictory (an argument that is an abstraction that can be played with), but that it is *located*. Perhaps it works in the UK, but it does not work in Taiwan. Paradoxically, this undoes the lived universalism and the 'metropolitan provincialism' of hegemonic social science[51]. Differently, we have suggested that Chen's disconcertment arises because Law's argument resonates with and threatens to unbalance the embodied metaphysical tension of being an academic (or a planner or an engineer) in Taiwan. In this reality the world needs to be ordered. It is important to *describe* that order. Yet this is difficult, for all around there is syncretism and incoherence. The balance is precarious and easily upset.

This leads us to a methodological suggestion. We've noted that while Western knowledge traditions may be insecure, they are also hegemonic. We have added the further post-colonial commonplace that though subaltern knowledge traditions vary (Ghana is not like Colombia and neither resemble Taiwan[52]), they have in common that they are in part conditioned by the ordering propensities of Western hegemony[53]. That said, however, it is also possible to tinker with the metaphysics of the latter (which is in any case less coherent than these quick suggestions make them sound). In particular, it is possible to work with the subjectivities and embodiments that resonate with and enact those metaphysics.

An outline of the argument runs so. The practices of academic institutions may be understood as *techniques for circumscribing disconcertment*. They work by seeking to discipline subjects and their responses to the world. There are endless complexities here, but as many feminists have noted, the intellectual subject in Western tradition is unmarked. It is pre-eminently cognitive, rational, discursive, and perhaps experimental or observational in particular and specific ways. It is also, and as a consequence, a subject that is substantially disembodied, devoid of sensations and emotions. The latter are Othered to the 'personal' of private life.

Now here is the tension. There is plenty of room for disagreement in this world, but the character of such disagreement is specific. It takes the form of debate or discussion of empirical findings. Hall and Ames point to the importance of clarification, articulation, and moves towards the meta. To put it differently, disagreement is common, but bodily disconcertment is to be avoided. The result is that if the choreography of subjects and institutions is effective then we are sealed into our metaphysics. The world is orderly and the disruptions simply get Othered. The implication, simultaneously methodological and political, is that it is important to attend to and cultivate the capacity for disconcertment. But how? And where? And when? How might a hegemonic project open itself to Otherness?

If we have learned anything it is that questions such as these are not susceptible to general answers. There is no way of avoiding specificities, and these will come in many forms. So, for instance, Fabian (he's talking of anthropologies) proposes that the latter might 'perhaps be envisioned as events or rallies more than as institutions or organizations'[54], a way of thinking and a mode of practice that perhaps describes aspects of the World Social Forum[55]. Differently, the stories we have told – and our experience in writing this paper – suggest the importance of dwelling on disconcertment. For as time has gone on Law has become more rather than less disconcerted about his exchange with Chen. But why? Our answer is analytical and methodological rather than personal. It is that the exercise of writing this paper can be understood as an exercise in *cultivating* disconcertment. Such has been the consequence of exploring the three narrative diversions. To contrast the narratives of progress and modernisation with the agglomerative syncretism of street Daoism, and context these with the metaphysics of classical philosophy has been to enact difference.

This, then, is our provisional conclusion. First, even if disconcertments are mostly Othered, there are also techniques for cultivating these within the Western tradition. Second, one powerful way of doing this is to trace stories that narrate and enact differences or seemingly improbable, impossible, or unreal worlds. Third this is not simply an intellectual project but is also a corporal matter of embodied subjectivities. This implies the cultivation of what one might think of as *bodily empiricism*. And then finally and perhaps surprisingly, as a part of this it turns out to be useful to return carefully and perhaps ironically to the large categories that STS scholars have done so much to undermine. Appropriate attention to 'cultural difference' may play a role in the cultivation of embodied disconcertment in quite specific material encounters.

Notes

1 We thank the participants in the seminars discussed in this paper, and in particular Hsin-Hsing Chen, Dawei Fu and Chan-yuan Wu. We are also deeply grateful to Helen Verran for long-term discussion about 'post-colonial' encounters and their disconcertments.

2 See Chakrabarty (2000) and Escobar (2008).

3 Consider the discussion in Ribeiro and Escobar (2006).

4 Hall and Ames (1995). We return to work of these authors below.

5 For two small anthropological examples of a very large genre, see Toussaint (2006) and Berglund (2006). For a more extended account of British sociology see Savage (2010).

6 As Bruno Latour artfully observes, 'we have never been modern'. See Latour (1993).

7 The point is monadological. For methodological discussion, Kwa (2002) and Law (2004b).

8 For discussion of representation and discomfiture, see Law (2002).

9 The second lecture was sponsored by the Science, Technology and Medicine centre at the National Cheng Kung University (NCKU), Tainan.

10 The date was 30th March 2009. Law was talking to an argument developed in (2004a).

11 On ontological politics see Mol (1999). For a book-length version of the argument about mess see Law (2004a).

12 The Western distinction between truth and power finds its roots in Greek philosophy, but as historians Shapin and Schaffer have shown, it was institutionalised in more or less modern form in post-Restoration England. What counts as adequate argument is ancient too, as is the distinction between the represented and representation. However, like the truth/power distinction, these were similarly institutionalised in roughly their contemporary scientific form in the spaces of witnessing created in post-Restoration England. See, for instance, studies on the laboratory (Shapin: 1984), (Shapin and Lawrence: 1998), (Lynch and Woolgar: 1990), the clinic (Atkinson: 1997; Foucault: 1972), the museum (Bennett: 1995), photography (Daston and Galison: 2007), and fieldwork (Goodwin: 1996; Latour: 2000; Law and Lynch: 1990).

13 From DVD of Workshop 3, 1:22–3.

14 Mazu was a fisherman's daughter or, in another version, the daughter of an official. The story is that she originally protected fishermen by standing at the harbour entrance holding a light up to guide vessels back to port. But now her protective powers have spread far beyond fishermen.

15 See http://www.dajiamazu.org.tw/.

16 By the time they finally caught the 9.00 pm train back to Taipei, Mazu was still two kilometres from her temple. Chen adds that they knew where she was because her sedan chair was wired with GPS and her position was being reported via cell phone.

17 They'd taken the train and arrived at noon, expecting to see the Goddess return to her home. (Mazu, like many of the other Goddesses and Gods, is carried on special occasions in a sedan chair from one temple to another.) She, the Goddess, was supposed to arrive back after her eight day procession at 3.00 pm so Chen and his students were in plenty of time.

18 His favourite, he adds, was a puppet of the Goddess dancing to the theme song of last year's Taiwanese blockbuster movie, 'Cape No.7'.

19 Fanon (1970). See also Said (1991).

20 Ribeiro and Escobar (2006, 13).

21 Verran (1998, 242).

22 Verran, personal communication.

23 Foucault (1972).

24 This is a *self-consciously performative* metaphysics. For both Verran, and the Cape York aboriginal people she is describing, the real and knowledge of the real are melded together. Epistemics and ontics cannot be prised apart. But here's her point. In the self-conscious world of aboriginal Australia this is self-evident. In Balanda (or 'white') worlds it is not, even though there are, of course, Western imaginaries. Like Australian aboriginal people Europeans and North Americans also have metaphors for thinking and enacting the world. We touched on this at the beginning of this piece. These are metaphors that treat the world as separate from practice. Reality is habitually taken to be pre-existing, unitary, solid, definite in form, and quite likely in need of discovery and description. And this is how Westerners *do* their world, in and beyond academic seminars, in a process that Verran characterises as a 'hardening of the categories'.

25 Verran (1999).

26 Lin who studied with Law is one of the latter.

27 The long story of the Western colonialist encounter with China goes back to the Portuguese arrival in the early years of the sixteenth century. For an account of this, and Sino-Japanese relations, see, for instance, Schirokauer (1991).

28 Directorate General of Budget Accounting and Statistics (2009).

29 Executive Yuan (2005).

30 On the significance of spatial difference as opposed to time see Massey (2005).

31 But this unpacks in other ways too. For instance, when PhD students return to Taiwan they find themselves back on the periphery. And because that periphery is oriented to the centre, the local academic space is also both marginal *and* fragmented. Quantitative sociologists are likely to work on some aspect of a globally-marginal albeit rather successful country, Taiwan. Critical theorists *may* get published back in the US, but there's a high probability that they won't be 'international' enough. ('International' usually means North American). 'Post-theorists' encounter the same predicament. STS is alive and kicking in Taiwan, where an East Asian-focused English-language STS journal has been established, the *East Asian Science, Technology and Society: an International Journal* but it lies on the margins of 'world STS'. See Fu (2007), the editor in chief of the journal, for reflections on this.

32 Ribeiro and Escobar (2006, 13).

33 The drink is called *shan-chao me*. They do this because a student once dreamed that he, the God, is too old to eat fruit but likes this jelly drink.

34 In 2008 the graduating students arranged for a company to manufacture a Land God USB stick.

35 http://blog.yam.com/missingwhy/article/15680333. Last visited on 7 May, 2009.

36 One of Ten-tong's officials (she writes) 'told me that there were some problems with my body. Then she mentioned my right ovary has a problem. But I remember that the doctor told me that it was the left one has a problem. Does it mean that both have problems?!'

37 One of the present authors describes the heterogeneous approach to therapy in a different medical context. See Lin (2005).

38 Hall and Ames (1995).

39 Any such list is fraught with difficulties. It finds an order, explains specificities by displacing them into that order, and works by finding consistency and coherence whilst eliding inconsistency and non-coherence. It is second problematic thinking applied to (a version of) itself. Hall and Ames appreciate both this and the incongruity of applying second problematic metaphysics to first problematic Chinese philosophy. The latter is predominantly practical rather than theoretical (Gernet (2002, 89–90)), and local or specific in intent.

40 The sources of second problematic thinking in Europe can be traced to the origin myths of classical antiquity which set a series of metaphysical parameters that have been surprisingly and consistently important for subsequent Western theological, philosophical, scientific and commonsense imaginaries. Indeed it is only in the last 150 years that there has been a sustained attempt to think outside these metaphysics in philosophy – and, of course, in the 'post-theories' mentioned above.

41 The latter, then, is loosely causal (it might be the hand of God, or the laws of physics).

42 This is one of the reasons why Western thinking often removes itself from the fluidities of common sense. Another reason is the primacy of rest, of stability in matter, of being, over becoming.

43 'The Chinese tradition is "acosmotic" in the sense that it does not depend on the belief that the totality of things constitutes a single-ordered world'. Hall and Ames (1995, 11–12).

44 Hall and Ames (1995, 184–5).

45 'Han thinking,' as Hall and Ames put it, 'depends upon the acceptance of "images" and "metaphors" as the primary means of expressing the becoming of things.' Hall and Ames (1995, 40).

46 Talking of 'shi', of the potential born of disposition, a term that crops up equally in war, calligraphy, politics and the propensities of nature, François Jullien characterises the Daoist

version of wisdom so: '. . . the very disposition of things results in a trend that never falters or deviates and can neither be "chosen" nor "taught." Things "tend" of themselves, infallibly, with no need for "effort"'. Jullien (1995, 39).
47 Hall and Ames (1995, 260).
48 For instance, in calligraphy 'the figure produced and the movement producing it are equivalent'. Jullien (1995, 76).
49 The general is not a hero. 'Efficacy proceeds from an objective determination or, more precisely, a dispositional determination, and success stems from this alone too; the more discreetly it does so, the more infallible it will be.' Jullien (1995, 61).
50 Hall and Ames (1995, 55).
51 Ribeiro and Escobar (2006, 13).
52 For a small sample of the possibilities see Kane (2003) on Muslim Nigeria, Hountondji on African philosophy, (1996), Benedict for a Western understanding of Japan (1989), Chakrabarty (2000) on subaltern Bengali histories, Huang (1989) on Chinese history and Escobar (2008) on the *redes* of post-colonial knowledge traditions in Pacific Colombia.
53 Rouse (1987).
54 Fabian (2006, 287).
55 For discussion, see de Sousa Santos (2004a; 2004b) Conway (2008).

References

Atkinson, Paul (1997), *The Clinical Experience: the Construction and Reconstruction of Medical Reality*, Brookfield, USA: Ashgate.
Benedict, Ruth Fulton (1989), *Chrysanthemum and the Sword: Patterns of Japanese Culture*: Houghton Mifflin.
Bennett, Tony (1995), *The Birth Of The Museum*, London and New York: Routledge.
Berglund, Eeva (2006), 'Generating Nontrivial Kowledge in Awkward Situations: Anthropology in the United Kingdom', pages 181–199 in Gustavo Lins Ribeiro and Arturo Escobar (eds), *World Anthropologies: Disciplinary Transformations within Systems of Power*, Oxford and New York: Berg.
Chakrabarty, Dipesh (2000), *Provincializing Europe: Postcolonial Thought and Historical Difference*, Princeton and Oxford: Princeton University Press.
Conway, Janet (2008), 'Decolonizing Knowledge/politics at the World Social Forum', paper delivered at the International Studies Association, San Francisco, 27 March 2008, also available at http://www.allacademic.com//meta/p_mla_apa_research_citation/2/5/1/4/1/pages251415/p251415-1.php (downloaded 23 July 2010).
Daston, Lorraine, and Peter Galison (2007), *Objectivity*, New York: Zone Books.
de Sousa Santos, Boaventura (2004a), 'The World Social Forum: Toward a Counter-Hegemonic Globalisation (Part I)', pages 235–245 in Jai Sen, Anita Anand, Arturo Escobar, and Peter Waterman (eds), *World Social Forum: Challenging Empires*, New Delhi: Viveka.
de Sousa Santos, Boaventura (2004b), 'The World Social Forum: Toward a Counter-Hegemonic Globalisation (Part II)', pages 336–343 in Jai Sen, Anita Anand, Arturo Escobar, and Peter Waterman (eds), *World Social Forum: Challenging Empires*, New Delhi: Viveka.
Directorate General of Budget Accounting and Statistics (2009), *Latest Indicators*, Taipei: Executive Yuan, also available at http://www.dgbas.gov.tw/ct.asp?xItem=14616&CtNode=3566 (accessed 22nd Deceber 2009).
Escobar, Arturo (2008), *Territories of Difference: Place, Movements, Life, Redes*, Durham and London: Duke University Press.
Executive Yuan, National Science Council (2005), *National Science and Technology Development Plan (2005 to 2008)*, Taipei: Executive Yuan, also available at https://nscnt07.nsc.gov.tw/tc/DOC/%E6%A0%B8%E5%AE%9A%E7%89%88_94_97E.PDF (downloaded 22 December 2009).

151

Fabian, Johannes (2006), 'World Anthropologies: Questions', pages 281–295 in Gustavo Lins Ribeiro and Arturo Escobar (eds), *World Anthropologies: Disciplinary Transformations within Systems of Power*, Oxford and New York: Berg.

Fanon, Frantz (1970), *Black Skin, White Masks*, London: Paladin.

Foucault, Michel (1972), *The Archaeology of Knowledge*, London: Tavistock.

Fu, Daiwie (2007), 'How Far Can East Asian STS Go?', *East Asian Science, Technology and Society: an International Journal*, 1: 1–14.

Gernet, Jacques (2002), *A History of Chinese Civilization*, translated by J.R.Foster and Charles Hartman, third edition, Cambridge: Cambridge University Press.

Goodwin, Charles (1996), 'Professional Vision', *American Anthropologist*, 96: 606–633.

Hall, David L., and Roger T. Ames (1995), *Anticipating China: Thinking Through the Narratives of Chinese and Western Culture*, Albany: State University of New York.

Hountondji, Paulin J., (1996), *African Philosophy: Myth and Reality*: Indiana University Press.

Huang, J-Y., (1989), *Essays on Chinese History by the Riverbank of Hudson* (in Chinese), Taipei, Taiwan: China Times Press.

Jullien, François (1995), *The Propensity of Things: Toward a History of Efficacy in China*, translated by Janet Lloyd, New York: Zone Books.

Kane, Ousmane (2003), *Muslim Modernity in Postcolonial Nigeria: A Study of the Society for the Removal of Innovation and Reinstatement of Tradition*, Leiden, Boston and Tokyo: Brill Academic Publishers.

Kwa, Chunglin (2002), 'Romantic and Baroque Conceptions of Complex Wholes in the Sciences', pages 23–52 in John Law and Annemarie Mol (eds), *Complexities: Social Studies of Knowledge Practices*, Durham, N.Ca and London: Duke University Press.

Latour, Bruno (1993), *We Have Never Been Modern*, Brighton: Harvester Wheatsheaf.

Latour, Bruno (2000), 'When Things Strike Back: a Possible Contribution of "Science Studies" to the Social Sciences', *British Journal of Sociology*, 51: 107–123, also available at http://www.ensmp.fr/~latour/articles/article/078.html.

Law, John (2002), *Aircraft Stories: Decentering the Object in Technoscience*, Durham, N.Ca.: Duke University Press.

Law, John (2004a), *After Method: Mess in Social Science Research*, London: Routledge.

Law, John (2004b), 'And if the Global Were Small and Non-Coherent? Method, Complexity and the Baroque', *Society and Space*, 22: 13–26, also available at http://www.lancaster.ac.uk/fass/sociology/papers/law-and-if-the-global-were-small.pdf.

Law, John, and Michael Lynch (1990), 'Lists, Field Guides, and the Descriptive Organization of Seeing: Birdwatching as an Exemplary Observational Activity', pages 267–300 in Michael Lynch and Steve Woolgar (eds), *Representation in Scientific Practice*: The MIT Press.

Leibniz, Gottfried Wilhelm (1998), *Philosophical Texts*, translated by R.S.Woodhouse and Richard Franks, Oxford and New York: Oxford.

Lin, Wen-yuan (2005), *Bodies in Action: Multivalent Agency in Haemodialysis Practices*, Thesis, Lancaster University, Lancaster.

Lynch, Michael, and Steve Woolgar (eds) (1990), *Representation in Scientific Practice*, Cambridge, Mass.: MIT Press.

Massey, Doreen (2005), *For Space*, London and Thousand Oaks: Sage.

Mol, Annemarie (1999), 'Ontological Politics: a Word and Some Questions', pages 74–89 in John Law and John Hassard (eds), *Actor Network Theory and After*, Oxford and Keele: Blackwell and *The Sociological Review*.

Ribeiro, Gustavo Lins, and Arturo Escobar (2006), 'World Anthropologies: Disciplinary Transformations within Systems of Power', pages 1–25 in Gustavo Lins Ribeiro and Arturo Escobar (eds), *World Anthropologies: Disciplinary Transformations within Systems of Power*, Oxford and New York: Berg.

Rouse, Joseph (1987), *Knowledge and Power: Toward a Political Philosophy of Science*, Ithaca and London: Cornell University Press.

Said, Edward W (1991), *Orientalism: Western Conceptions of the Orient*, London: Penguin.

Savage, Mike (2010), *Identities and Social Change in Britain since 1940: the Politics of Method*, Oxford: Oxford University Press.

Schirokauer, Conrad (1991), *A Brief History of Chinese Civilization*, San Diego: Harcourt Brace Gap College.

Shapin, Steven (1984), 'Pump and Circumstance: Robert Boyle's Literary Technology', *Social Studies of Science*, 14: 481–520.

Shapin, Steven, and Christopher Lawrence (1998), 'Introduction: The Body of Knowledge', pages 1–19 in Christopher Lawrence and Steven Shapin (eds), *Science incarnate: Historical Embodiments of Natural Knowledge*, Chicago: The University of Chicago Press, also available at STS: general.

Toussaint, Sandy (2006), 'A Time and Place beyond and of the Center: Australian Anthropologies in the Process of Becoming', pages 225–238 in Gustavo Lins Ribeiro and Arturo Escobar (eds), *World Anthropologies: Disciplinary Transformations within Systems of Power*, Oxford and New York: Berg.

Verran, Helen (1998), 'Re-Imagining Land Ownership in Australia', *Postcolonial Studies*, 1: (2): 237–254.

Verran, Helen (1999), 'Staying True to the Laughter in Nigerian Classrooms', pages 136–155 in *Actor Network and After*, Oxford and Keele: Blackwell and the Sociological Review.

Epistemology and the politics of knowledge

Celine-Marie Pascale

Abstract: If scholars accept that all knowledge is socially constructed, and historically situated, we must also understand social research methodologies as historically
produced social formations that circumscribe as well as produce culturally specific
forms of knowledge. In this article I examine some of the ways in which an underlying
19th century philosophy of science constrains the ability of contemporary researchers
to examine 21st century cultural complexities. In particular, I discuss how the notion
of evidence derived from the physical sciences prevents social sciences from examining
a range of phenomena such as routine relations of privilege and contemporary media.
Taking up the argument that *social* sciences need *social* epistemologies, I explore
sociological studies of language as one form of epistemic shift that would enable
researchers to apprehend the circulation of power as expressed in routine relations of
privilege, as well as apprehend the porous social relations introduced through media
old and new.

Introduction

Social sciences emerged as part of a modernist discourse of progress, concerned
with goals of value neutrality and an ever-increasing effort to generate insights
into social life that could stand as the equivalents of physical laws. With the
benefit of hindsight, social scientists in the 21st century frequently recognize
that science has been more than a search for objective knowledge. One does not
have to look hard to find scientific research that advanced various forms of
bigotry; today such studies clearly reveal more about cultural hierarchies of
power than about the people, places, and cultures that were studied. The 'ways
of knowing' that have been privileged by academics in dominant cultures continue to be a site of contention and resistance – particularly for those who have
been constructed as 'Other' in their discourses. Linda Tuhiwai Smith (2004: 1)
writes: '. . . the term "research" is inextricably linked to European imperialism
and colonialism. The word itself, "research," is probably one of the dirtiest
words in the indigenous world's vocabulary.'

The practical work of scientific research necessarily reproduces culturally specific assumptions among dominant groups regarding how the world exists and how it works. To the extent that social sciences developed alongside the nation-state, they are bound by national assumptions and experiences (della Porta and Keating, 2008). The epistemological ground of social research developed, in part, as a legitimated form of knowledge about 'the Other' produced by and for those in power. Social research is itself a relation of power that produces (and is produced by) 'domains of objects and rituals of truth' (Foucault, 1977: 194).

Long before Foucault, Bertrand Russell (1938: 10) described the fundamental concept in the social science as power – in the same sense in which energy is the fundamental concept in physics. Like energy, there are many expressions of power, and none of these can be necessarily regarded as subordinate to another; there is no single expression of power from which other forms derive, no stagnant expression of power and no expression of power that exists in isolation. The complex networks of power that infuse social life require specific and diverse methodologies and methods.

Despite many significant changes in social research paradigms, the discipline of sociology continues to rely upon epistemic foundations derived from the physical sciences, even in qualitative methods. For example, qualitative paradigms rely upon 'local contexts' for data. Such contexts are constructed to be congruent with a physical science model and then are made to appear in scientific discourse as if they are naturally occurring phenomena. Social sciences have no 'scientific' means for addressing the broader cultural conditions that shape these localized contexts. This is particularly significant since the *meaning* of any utterance or text exceeds localized contexts.

Sociologists can never fully examine the production of routine relations of power and privilege if we attend only to a localized context of interaction, regardless of whether we use qualitative or quantitative methods. In addition, sociological studies of media have yet to join mainstream sociological research in any substantial way largely because the methods best suited to apprehending media tend to fall outside the frame of 'scientific methods'. If it has been difficult to effectively study old media (such as film, television, and newspapers) with existing sociological methods, the narrow conceptions of evidence makes it all but impossible to study new media that have radically transformed all understandings of social interaction and social context.

The social sciences in general and sociology, in particular, can benefit from additional analytic strategies, which apprehend the complex networks of power that infuse the (re)production of culture and knowledge; yet our research methods successfully inhibit such innovation. In what follows I make the argument that *social* sciences need *social* epistemologies. I focus explicitly on qualitative research and suggest sociological studies of language as one form of epistemic shift that would enable researchers to apprehend the circulation of power as expressed in routine relations of privilege, as well as apprehend the porous social relations introduced through media – old and new.

Celine-Marie Pascale

The politics of knowledge

Auguste Comte (1798–1857) believed that authentic knowledge came from personal experience, rather than from metaphysical or theological foundations. He argued that by 'relying solely on observable facts and the relations that hold among observed phenomena, scientific inquiry could discover the "laws" governing empirical events' (Hawkesworth, 2007: 472). Comte's positivism articulated a search for laws of social life that could stand as equivalents to the natural laws of the physical sciences.[1] It is anchored to the same ontological premise of the natural sciences: the world exists as an objective entity and is (at least in principle) knowable in its entirety; epistemologically, the tasks of the researcher are first to describe the reality accurately and then to analyse the results (della Porta and Keating, 2008).

In this sense, positivism (and neo-positivism) mirrors the commonsense ontology of daily life in which things exist as they appear, unless one is dreaming or deceived. Positivist research is characterized by a quest for determinacy; its reductionist impulse is reflected in attempts to develop precise meanings and operational indicators. By embracing the ontological belief that a single reality exists and the epistemological claim that this reality can be known objectively, social scientists have argued that there was one, and only one, correct logic for scientific inquiry. Positivism served as *the* methodological foundation of the early social sciences.

Antonio Gramsci (1995) was an early critic of the desire to use the methods of the physical sciences as the basis for empirical research in the social sciences. He referred to it as 'science as fetish' and wrote: 'There do not exist sciences *par excellence* and there does not exist a method *par excellence*, "a method in itself"' (Gramsci, 1995: 282). At the time Gramsci was concerned with social science's inability to apprehend Italian politics. The same narrowness, however, makes it impossible to critique processes such as reification and hegemony through social science. Gramsci had argued that every process of inquiry must be congruent with its own particular purpose. Despite the prevalence and power of such critiques, the discourses of the physical sciences have been used to legitimate all forms of social research.[2] As scientific knowledge became idealized, its philosophical underpinnings largely faded from view.

For well over a century qualitative data has been limited to that which we can point to – that which we can see in a localized context. For those immersed in hegemonic scientific discourse, it is difficult to imagine why this could possibly be problematic or how it might be otherwise. Yet within the parameters of a localized context it is impossible to apprehend particular aspects of power, privilege, culture and knowledge, which always and inevitably exceed any immediate context. If we don't see '. . . the big picture, narrow empiricism provide[s] an ingenious smoke screen. It is a method perfectly tailored to an epistemology of ignorance. As the adage goes, we "look" but never "see".' (Steinberg, 2007: 11).

Generally ignorance is understood as a result of a bad or neglectful epistemic practice, not as a substantive epistemic practice in itself (Alcoff, 2007: 39). Yet ignorance is not simply 'not knowing' but an active misapprehension that systematically produces inaccurate information – *ignorance is an active social production*. An epistemology of ignorance exists when one uses socially acceptable but faulty systems of justification (Alcoff, 2007; Sullivan and Tuana, 2007).

Eugenics, for instance, can be understood as an epistemology of ignorance (Zuberi, 2001; Zuberi and Bonilla-Silva, 2008). The intrinsically scholarly framing of race discourse was not, in itself, enough to establish the scientific legitimacy of race research in general or eugenics in particular. Such studies gained prominence in particular times and places because they also have practical applications that resonate with perceptions held to be 'commonsense' by dominant groups in society. In this sense, academic research has provided what might be called facticity to racism: it appealed not to greed nor to spiritual passion, but to reason, albeit reason that is prefigured and operating in a particular mode.

Similarly, much of Freud's work is based on an epistemology of ignorance (Hoagland, 2007). Consider that although Freud initially believed the stories of women reporting rape, he subsequently chose to discredit their testimony in favour of a theory in which women and children fantasized about being raped, a theory which helped to silence women's voices and deny their experiences for decades. Misrepresentations of race and gender such as these found widespread scientific acceptance because they supported hegemonic worldviews in Europe and North America. Science validates itself, yet hegemonic culture provides structural validation for epistemologies of ignorance that reproduce existing social hierarchies. Science itself is a cultural activity, a kind of performance that enacts itself.

If we accept that all knowledge is socially constructed, and historically situated, we must also understand social research methodologies as historically produced social formations articulated through particular discourses and systems of signification. Any mature science needs to include a broad range of strategies and tools in order to be fully capable of responding to contemporary issues. From this perspective, it is possible to appreciate the importance of refusing to reify the analytical constructs of social research.

The most basic (and perhaps most powerful) level of critique directed at social science takes up the issue of 'evidence.' In all research methods, 'evidence' counts as evidence only if it is recognized in relation to a potential analysis (Gordon, 1997; Scott, 1991). Evidence is always the political effect of decisions regarding what constitutes valid and relevant knowledge as well as decisions that regard the conditions a researcher must fulfill to give her or his work value as science. The changing social landscapes of the 21st century mandate a shift in how social sciences conceptualize the nature of 'evidence.'

Power and privilege

A social scientist needs evidence – indeed a particular kind of evidence, something in a specific context to which one can point. Yet privilege does not leave a trail of evidence in the same way that oppression does. Once routinized, privi-

Celine-Marie Pascale

lege functions largely as an unmarked category. For example, white racial identities, as an *unmarked* category, leave little or no empirical evidence in daily interaction or in media, precisely because they pass without remark in dominant discourse. If researchers can prompt interviewees to talk about whiteness (cf Bonilla-Silva, 2003) analysing whiteness in interaction, in unprompted conversation, and in media, poses an arguably insurmountable challenge within the existing paradigms of science.

All *routine* relations of power and privilege pass without remark; this is the measure of how deeply embedded such relations are in a culture. Even though scholars appreciate the importance of whiteness, we lack effective social science tools for demonstrating how it functions. Social science is not prepared to enable scholars to examine the effects of what isn't expressed. On the one hand, a reader must ask, should it be? On the other hand, this problem directs us back to an analysis of the politics of knowledge production. If social research is not yet capable of fully accounting for human experience, there must be something in our assumptions that alienates research processes from aspects of human experiences.

What I am suggesting here is that the social sciences have been predicated on 'an epistemology of ignorance,' a state of 'unknowingness,' in relationship to routine relationships of power and privilege – indeed our identities as social researchers are forged through institutional processes that simultaneously construct and obfuscate our own privileged positions of power. We should not and cannot trust that research methodologies, created by the most privileged and during eras of great oppression, will serve as the basis of socially just research. It is not a matter of good methods applied to bad uses but, rather, academia's ignorance of its own processes of reproduction. Opacity seems to be built into our own formation as we construct 'others' who are knowable.

Media old and new

In the 21st century, daily life is mediated by technology in unprecedented ways. Even 'old' forms of media such as television have become less singular texts and more a technological movement and mediation of culture. The extension and intensification of 'teletechnology' has moved television well beyond a broadcast model (Clough, 2000: 96). Shows can be viewed online, on DVD, through Wii, or downloaded onto iPods. Soundtracks for television shows have moved from the background to centre stage; popular music now has a regular and important place in the soundtracks of primetime network television. Consider that iTunes sells both television shows and their soundtracks. Yet perhaps more consequentially, television provides, and draws upon, cultural resources for more than immediate audiences. Consider how key phrases from media creep into the vocabularies of people who have never seen the media that produced the expressions. For example, the phrase 'You're fired!' entered the US media and conversations in ways that were no longer anchored to the television show (*The*

Apprentice) that produced it. Mediated forms of cultural knowledge circulate through and are reproduced by a broad range of contexts. In this sense, television collapses distinctions between production and reproduction, between production and circulation, and between text and context (Clough, 2000).

New technologies, marketing strategies and social relations converge in the production of transmedia texts and expand the notion of intertextuality. Consider how the film *The Matrix* broke new ground. It opened in theatres but also became available by DVD, online, on television, and by ipod; in addition, it was produced in two different game forms (*Enter the Matrix* and *The Matrix*), as a series of comics, and in several animated videos, all of which textually interact with the film. Changes in media content and circulation embody processes that are simultaneously technological and social. Yet social science research remains constrained by a philosophy of science that cannot begin to address the changing nature of social interaction or the porosity of mediated relationships.

In an ever-increasing media landscape, with new forms of media constantly emerging, former distinctions between culture, politics, and economics come to seem less relevant than they once were. Consider that what first started as a campy joke in Dino Ignacio's bedroom as he assembled a collage combining Sesame Street's Bert with Osama bin Laden (to 'prove' Bert was truly evil) quickly became part of an international controversy when the collage appeared on thousands of posters across the Middle East, some of which appeared in anti-American protests (Jenkins, 2008: 1–2). New media, including wikkis, blogs, vlogs, video-conferencing, text messaging, facebook, and twitter have helped to shift the meaning of interaction itself. Arguably, they have collapsed what had been imagined historically as a local interactional context. From the privacy of our homes, we can enter an endlessly public space. Truth, authenticity and reality are no longer easily assumed or clearly apparent.

The advent of TiVo and other similar recording devises are contributing to the decreasing value of 30-second commercials and causing marketing strategists to rethink possibilities for generating media that blur the lines between marketing and entertainment. Beyond the most obvious product-placement techniques, MTV Video, American Idol, Virgin Airlines media come immediately to mind as new genres created by this blurring of advertising and entertainment. Social science needs specific capacities for deciphering the complex layers of media intertextuality and consumer participation.

If audiences were once understood as passive spectators of television, film, or other forms of media, today audiences must be understood as participatory cultures. Increasingly youth are not only consuming media but also producing it. An elementary-school-aged child being home-educated began *The Daily Prophet*, a student written and run newsletter dedicated to bringing the world of Harry Potter to life; the paper now has a staff of 102 children around the world who have never met face-to-face but who form a community that writes, edits, and reads the paper (Jenkins, 2008). This is not to say that all participatory cultures are equal but to indicate how quickly social interactions and social relations are transforming in ways that pose profound problems of data collection and analysis for the social sciences.

In the 21st century, social research must be able to consider the technological mediation of social relationships. While many scholars would argue that the physical sciences never presented a good model of social research, the complexities of social life in the 21st century render the 19th century model of physical science even less useful. Not only do changes in media content and circulation embody processes that are simultaneously technological and social, changes in technology and computerization also continue to blur the distinction between manual labor and mental activity.

It has long been argued that consumers have always purchased not just products, but also symbolic value. In the 21st century, however, the symbolic value of products seems strikingly disproportionate. The increased symbolic value of products has come to erode what once seemed to be obvious distinctions among economic processes, products and systems of representation. If this seems implausible, consider how the presence (or absence) of a Nike swoosh affects the price of running shoes. Even on otherwise identical shoes, the swoosh can increase the market value of a pair of shoes five times; clearly we are not buying the physical characteristics of the Nike symbol but its symbolic effect, its meaning (Ives, 2004: 13). It is impossible to separate the value of the Nike swoosh from the advertisements that give it social value. Yet the research paradigms of the social sciences have not adjusted to be able to address effectively the complex issues of representation in the proliferation of media, social relationships, and economic processes. The philosophical foundations of social research methods make it impossible to examine 21st century media effectively using only social science methods.

Social epistemologies

The pervasive epistemology in Sociology, at least in North America if not also much of Europe, is a Cartesian framework adopted from the physical sciences in which the goal of research was to produce an objective and accurate representation of an external reality. This remains widely true today, yet some things have changed. Sociologists have largely stopped treating people in our studies as mere objects; we long ago abandoned the search for the social equivalent of 'physical laws' such as gravity; and many of us, if not all, recognize the agency of material objects. The discipline has changed. And it continues to change.

We need, though, to help it to change a little more. While the physical sciences might rely more or less comfortably on Cartesian paradigm (and this too is a matter open to dispute), social sciences need *social* ontologies and *social* epistemologies. In a Cartesian ontology, events and phenomena are singular, isolated moments that can be more or less accurately studied. Evidence exists as tangible, objective phenomenon to which one can point and which can be 'discovered' in localized contexts. Cartesian epistemology is individualistic; it concerns the ability of subjects to know objects and consequently focus on issues of truth and error. As the dominant Cartesian paradigm directs researchers to study localized practices, it simultaneously denies the cultural relationality of knowledge production. While analyses of local practices can document meaning-making practices in interaction, the demands of science currently force these practices to stand apart from the society that make them possible.

By contrast, in a social ontology, events and phenomena exist as constellations of relationships that are discerned in temporal and spatial relationship to other events and phenomena. Communities are understood not as groups of individuals, but as interdependent, relational environments. Evidence in this framework is a heuristic – a rule of thumb – for understanding the production of knowledge. If interdependent relationships form the ontological *basis* of sociology, and evidence is freed from a narrow context, then a social epistemology enables us to examine *social routes* to knowledge.

A social epistemology requires that identities and subject locations be analysed in the relational contexts that make them possible and which give them meaning. Knowledge, cognition, and perception are necessarily cultural productions as well as individual ones; they are historical as well as contemporary. Even one's relationship to oneself must be understood largely in terms of broader social relationships and cultural histories. Consequently, the basic concepts of a social ontology and a social epistemology are systems of representation, particularly narratives and discourse.

There are myriad ways of conceptualizing social epistemologies. Here I want to advance the case for studies of language, broadly construed as systems of representation as an effective means for articulating a social epistemology that is distinctly sociological in the way it links together structure and agency, history and local interaction. Historically sociologists have treated language simply as a tool for communication. Glyn Williams (1999: 294) argued that sociology's emergence as a feature of modernism necessitated the discipline's insistence on separating research on language from research on social life. The development of sociology actively excluded language even as scholars worked to understand social interaction and broader issues of culture. This is truly remarkable. The concept of language as a mere tool of communication assumes an extraordinary degree of separation among people, language, and culture that is absolutely unwarranted (Ng, 2009).

Within the past 40 years, sociology has been willing to include (after much struggle) some sociolinguistics and the highly technical analyses of situated, turn-by-turn management of conversation that fit comfortably within the prevailing discourses of science. If it is possible to study conversation in very narrow contexts, language use is never fully realized in localized contexts. Language is made of living, constitutive practices that reach back to the past and forward to the future, practices that inaugurate both individual sentiment and cultural disposition. Even so, the discipline has been reluctant to accept sociological research regarding broader processes of language and meaning, largely because these have been regarded as something other than scientific and therefore something other than sociological.

Some of the most influential intellectual movements of the 20th century have focused on language; here I think of structuralism, poststructuralism, postmodernism, and deconstruction. Despite the broad intellectual impact of the Cultural Turn, sociologists in the United States who study language continue to labour at the margins of the discipline. US sociology has remained largely disinterested in exploring the deeply rooted relationships between language and society – what must be understood as research based on truly social epistemologies.

This is quite surprising considering that language use is a thoroughly social practice, embodied, intuitive and habitual. Through language we come to know and to make sense of the social world. Our most private experiences are constructed through language, as are our abilities to distinguish among truth, illusion, and falsity. The individual, as such, does not exist prior to language. Without language there is no social interaction, no social structure, no culture. It is easy to understand why studies of language and discourse have much to offer to sociology. Yet the resistance to such studies is rooted not only in cultural dispositions, but more importantly in the narratives of science that continue to shape U.S. sociology.

With changing and contested notions of what constitutes a social science, and with deeper appreciation for the inseparability of symbolic practices and material realities, more sociologists are re-considering the sociological importance of language. For example Steinberg (1999) demonstrated how material and discursive forces conjoin in shaping inequalities. Similarly, Bourdieu (2003) argued that the potency of symbolic power is the capacity of systems of meaning and signification to strengthen relations of oppression and exploitation. In addition, scholars have been broadening conceptions of 'mixed methods' to refer also to efforts to combine interpretive and critical qualitative strategies of empirical analysis with more theoretical strategies such as deconstruction, genealogy and poststructural discourse analysis (cf Clarke, 2005; Denzin, 2003; Pascale, 2007; Saukko, 2003).

Of course, the incompleteness of understanding and of interpretation is inevitable. Everything is already an interpretation; there is no primary moment that stands apart from the chain of interpretation. There is always a strategic place where the chain of interpretation is cut off from its origins in order to be analysed. Yet scholars must always ask, not only who determines where and when this chain of interpretation is cut off from its origins but also, to what effect? In sociology, a 19th-century Cartesian paradigm continues to truncate this chain of interpretation at a localized context, which prevents any complex analysis of the phenomenon's conditions of emergence. Yet how we relate to ourselves and to each other is dependent upon not only the words we exchange but also upon the conceptualization that language makes possible. Language itself is *epistemic*: language makes 'reality' real.

Concluding comments

To call social life into question without also calling into question our conception of an adequate explanation of social life makes research vulnerable to intensely ideological and unconscious conclusions. A philosophy of science must question the presuppositions that constitute both the foci of social research and the research methods to address them.

What is the value of a social science that cannot meaningfully apprehend and account for technological mediation, symbolic value, and the intertexuality of social relationships? Is this ineffectiveness a reasonable price to pay to maintain the boundary of 'science'? Should social sciences continue to concede media studies to the humanities? Clearly the answer to these last two questions is 'no,' *if* we believe that all experience is intensely personal, profoundly inter-subjective, and culturally mediated. Efforts to expand the discourse of science – to provide what de Certeau (1984) called the as yet undrawn map – offer the possibility of conceptualizing social life in the 21st century differently from social life in other eras.

Expanding the discourse of science offers the possibility of developing analytical tools for effectively exploring relations of power and privilege, examining porous relationships among social phenomena, thinking about the nature of evidence differently, and situating localized contexts in the broader cultural and historical context from which they emerged. To broaden the paradigms for social research requires challenging the dominant binaries through which the social sciences are constructed including: art/science, objective/subjective, theory/method, and scientific/ideological. A more inclusive social science would recognize multiple styles of inquiry that use a variety of processes of systemization, each best suited to its purpose.

Producing knowledge is always a political act, one in which cultural ideologies are both rationalized and naturalized. What researchers in dominant cultures have tended to see when looking at social life is the product of classificatory systems that embody logics that express hegemonic views of social life. The more effective scholars become at revealing the processes and terms of knowledge production – the foundation of cognitive authority – the more effective we will be at minimizing the effects of ideologies. Research will never be an ideal process, but it can be a more effective and a more accountable one.

While the social sciences have changed dramatically in the last 40 years, our transformation is incomplete. Indeed, precisely because it can never *be* complete, we must continue to examine the theoretical foundations of research methodologies that determine what counts as valid knowledge and consequently limit what can be known.

As researchers, we know that 'knowledge' and 'truth' are polemical, strategic relations of power; our social research paradigms will always be imperfect, but we can do better.

Acknowledgments

I thank Rolland Munro for his thoughtful comments for revision. I also want to acknowledge colleagues in RC 25 Language & Society of the ISA for the sustained and sustaining conversations on this topic. Since this article draws on parts of my forthcoming book, *Cartographies of Knowledge*, I would also like to acknowledge the contributions of Vicki Knight and the Sage editorial team.

Notes

1 Comte is also widely recognized as the founder of positivism and of the discipline of sociology.
2 Positivism, driven by the paradigm of the natural sciences, still appears to many researchers as the most legitimate form of social research. 'Assumptions guiding positivism derive from the study of largely inanimate or biological phenomena that lack the capacity for self-reflection and cultural production. . . . By contrast social sciences are inevitably concerned with social, economic, and cultural worlds that are constituted by the human capacity for meaningful understanding and action. According to Flyvbjerg (2001), this human capacity for interpretation incessantly thwarts the social science dream of becoming the mirror image of the natural sciences. Furthermore, such a dream is not merely impossible, it is also pointless inasmuch as positivism is ill equipped to answer many questions of interest to social science. These include questions such as why organizational reform efforts are frequently met with resistance; which cultural features are most responsible for the collapse of corporate ethic; or how organizations socialize their members' (P. Prasad, 2005: 5).

References

Alcoff, L. M., (2007), Epistemologies of Ignorance: Three Types, in Sullivan, S and N. Tuana, (eds), *Race and Epistemologies of Ignorance*, Albany: State University of New York: 39–58.

Bonilla-Silva, E., (2003), *Racism without Racists: Color-Blind Racism and the Persistence of Racial Inequality in the United States*, Lanham: Rowman & Littlefield Publishers, Inc.

Boothman, D., (1995), Introduction, in Boothman, D., (ed.), *Further Selections from the Prison Notebooks*, Minneapolis: University of Minnesota Press.

Bourdieu, P., (2003), *Language and Symbolic Power*, Cambridge: Harvard University Press.

Clarke, A., (2005), *Situational Analysis: Grounded Theory After the Postmodern Turn*, Thousand Oaks: Sage Publications.

Clough, P. T., (2000), *Autoaffection: Unconscious thought in the age of teletechnology*, Minneapolis: University of Minnesota Press.

de Certeau, M., (1984), *The Practice of Everyday Life*, Rendall, S. (trans.), Berkeley: University of California Press.

della Porta, D. and Keating, M., (2008), Introduction, in della Porta, D. and M. Keating, (eds), *Approaches and Methodologies in The Social Sciences: A Pluralist Perspective*, Cambridge: Cambridge University Press: 1–16.

Denzin, N., (2003), Cultural Studies, in Reynolds, L. T. and N. J. Herman-Kinney, (eds), *Handbook of Symbolic Interactionism*, New York: AltaMira press: 997–1019.

Flyvbjerg, B., (2001), *Making Social Science Matter: Why social inquiry fails and how it can succeed again*, Cambridge: Cambridge University Press.

Foucault, M., (1977), *Discipline and Punish: The birth of the prison*, Sheridan, A., (trans.), New York: Vintage Books.

Gordon, A., (1997), *Ghostly Matters: Haunting and the sociological imagination*, Minneapolis: University of Minnesota Press.

Gramsci, A., (1995), *Further Selections from the Prison Notebooks*, D. Boothman (trans.), Minneapolis: University of Minnesota Press.

Hawkesworth, M., (2007), Truth and Truths in Feminist Knowledge Production, in Hesse-Biber, S. N., (ed.), *Handbook of Feminist Research: Theory and Praxis*, Thousand Oaks: Sage: 469–491.

Hoagland, S. L., (2007), Denying Relationality: Epistemology and Ethics and Ignorance. in Sullivan, S. and N. Tuana, (eds), *Race and Epistemologies of Ignorance*, Albany: State University of New York: 95–118.

Ives, P., (2004), *Language and Hegemony in Gramsci*, London: Pluto Press.

Jenkins, H., (2008), *Convergence Culture: Where Old and New Media Collide*, New York: New York University Press.

Ng, K. H., (2009), *The Common Law in Two Voices Language, Law, and the Postcolonial Dilemma in Hong Kong*, Stanford: Stanford University Press.

Pascale, C.-M., (2007), *Making Sense of Race, Class, and Gender: Commonsense, Power, and Privilege in the United States*, New York: Routledge.

Pascale, C. M., (2010), *Cartographies of Knowledge: Exploring Qualitative Epistemologies*, Thousand Oaks: Sage.

Prasad, P., (2005), *Crafting Qualitative Research: Working in the Postpositivist Traditions*, New York: M.E. Sharpe.

Russell, B., (1938), *Power: A New Social Analysis*, New York: Routledge.

Saukko, P., (2003), *Doing Research in Cultural Studies*, Thousand Oaks: Sage Publications.

Scott, J. W., (1991), The Evidence of Experience,*Critical Inquiry*, 17, 4: 773–97.

Smith, L. T., (2004), *Decolonizing Methodologies: Research and Indigenous Peoples*, London: Zed Books Ltd.

Somers, M. R. and G. D. Gibson, (1996), Reclaiming the Epistemological 'Other': Narrative and the Social Constitution of Identity, in Calhoun, C., (ed.), *Social Theory and the Politics of Identity*, Cambridge, MA: Blackwell Publishers: 35–99.

Steinberg, M., (1999), *Fighting Words: Working-Class Formation, Collective Action, and Discourse in Early 19th Century England*, Ithaca: Cornell University Press.

Steinberg, S., (2007), *Race Relations: A Critique*, Stanford: Stanford University Press.

Sullivan, S. and N. Tuana, (eds), (2007), *Race and Epistemologies of Ignorance*, Albany: State University of New York.

Williams, G., (1999), *French Discourse Analysis: The method of post-structuralism*, New York: Routledge.

Zuberi, T., (2001), *Thicker Than Blood: How Racial Statistics Lie*, Minneapolis: University of Minnesota Press.

Zuberi, T. and E. Bonilla-Silva, (eds), (2008), *White Logic, White Methods: Racism and Methodology*, Lanham, MD: Rowman and Littlefield.

Part 4
Discourse

Populist elements in contemporary American political discourse

Ritchie Savage

Abstract: Granted that it would be absurd to characterize Obama as a populist president, this paper proceeds from Ernesto Laclau's conception of populism as consisting of 'the formation of an internal antagonistic frontier separating the "people" from power' and 'an equivalential articulation of demands making the emergence of the "people" possible' (2005:74). In the 2008 election, Obama was able to articulate a series of empty signifiers, found in such slogans as 'Yes We Can,' which came to represent a new collective identity of the 'people', thus constituting an instance of populism *par excellence*. As support for this theory of populism and its implications for contemporary American political discourse, this paper deconstructs the previously held functionalist assumptions and modernization theories – especially those propagated within Latin American case studies – that consign populism to a developmental stage in the capitalist mode of production or a historical outcome of underdeveloped democratic institutions in order to imagine a new science of rhetoric capable of analysing the synecdochical, metaphorical, and metonymical components (Laclau, 2005) in the discursive construction of 'the American people'.

Introduction

There has been a marked resurgence in the usage of the concept of populism both in the literature of the social sciences and in the media. Whereas the term was originally used to refer to the classical late 19th century cases of The People's Party in America and the Russian *Narodnichestvo*, and the mid 20th century Latin American cases of Perón's rule in Argentina and Brazil's Vargas, populism has also received substantial attention in recent Latin American scholarship with the rise of political figures such as Menem, Fujimori, Collor, Bucaram, Chávez, and Evo Morales among others. So, too, it has been employed to characterize an element of certain reactionary political currents in Western Europe and other political regimes around the world.

Yet even in the media coverage of the United States' 2008 presidential election, the label 'populist' was applied to candidates from both the Democratic and Republican parties, such as Edwards and Huckabee, and one could even argue that the American populist heritage was a salient theme in the vice presidential campaigns of Biden and Palin. And with the current economic crisis and proposed bailout, the media has recently turned its attention to what it has termed as the reemergence of an economic populism,[1] depicted as a surge of hatred targeted at 'Wall Street fat-cats' and CEOs that has its historical roots in the anti-big business discourses articulated in the Progressive era, the present incarnation of which can be found both in popular sentiment and in certain rhetorical appeals utilized by Barack Obama. One might also consider the recent emergence of the conservative anti-government discourse of the Tea Party, which was highly successful in mobilizing support for Republican candidates in the US 2010 mid-term elections.

Given the current resurgence of the term, 'populism', to describe aspects of political phenomena in cases both abroad and in the United States, this paper poses the following questions. What is populism? Why is the usage of the concept proliferating in both the media and academic literature, but always in an ambiguous manner that seems to resist sociological or analytical classification? Does populism still function as a prominent component of current American politics? And is this new American populism similar only to its historical counterpart in the 1890s or is it possible to link the seemingly divergent cases of populism now occurring in the United States and Latin America. Finally, is it possible to locate starkly populist elements in the political discourse articulated by Barack Obama, and does his political discourse involve a strategic positioning that mirrors instances of populism in Latin America?

Dislocation and terrain

In order to analyse the populist elements in Obama's presidential campaign, this paper focuses on aspects of Obama's rhetoric utlilizing Laclau's discursive model of populism. This model bears a host of theoretical and empirical advantages with regard to this project. First of all, insofar as the type of populism found in Obama's campaign is both rhetorically charged and principally based on rhetoric, a model that treats populism as discourse and pivots around elements such as signifiers and chains of articulated demands is specifically oriented to the object of my analysis.

Another advantage of Laclau's model is its ability to allow for the conception of populism as a *universal* discursive formation. There are many instances of political phenomena designated as 'populist' all around the world and in different time periods. After a review of the literature concerning the US, Latin American, and Western European cases, it will become evident that many theorists construct limited definitions of populism that exclude or discount cases of populism occurring in other regions. The attempt to isolate cases of populism based on region and subsequently tie these cases to historical, economic, and political conditions specific to these regions reveals theoretical problems, empirical inconsistencies, and forecloses the possibility of a comparative-historical approach to populism. In order to suggest a comparison between aspects of Obama's populism and those of Latin American cases, it is useful to employ Laclau's ontological model of populist discourse, which provides the abstract discursive components of hegemonic identity formations applicable across cases.

In his discursive model of populism, Laclau articulates a conception of society drawn from the Lacanian conception of the Other or symbolic order. Society is analogous to a fragile symbolic order which, Lacan (2006) argues, following the tenants of Saussurean structural linguistics, is always subject to the 'incessant sliding of the signified under the signifier' (419). For Laclau (1990), 'society is an impossibility' because it is based on a model of social cohesion and stable identity formation that is always subverted by antagonisms between different social groups as well as the instability of signification and reference within the symbolic order which is society (90). Populist discourse thus emerges as a way partially to stabilize the symbolic order and provide for the formation of political identities. In the articulation of an empty signifier, such as the 'people', a political identity is formed around a chain of democratic demands temporarily stabilized within a discourse.

This model of populist discourse allows for an analysis of Obama's campaign rhetoric as well as other instances of populist discourse occurring around the world. However, there is one problem with Laclau's conception of populist discourse from a sociological perspective, which is related to the way in which Laclau privileges the political over the social. Even though I will argue that theorists run into problems in their attempt to attribute the emergence of populism to specific and isolated historical, economic, and political conditions, this is not to say that instances of populism do not emerge from any sociological conditions whatsoever. In this sense, it is evident that the current 'rising tide' or increased frequency of instances of populist discourse is related to the current global economic crisis. Therefore, I would like to suggest a critique of Laclau, which is that his privileging of the political over the social creates problems for empirical and comparative-historical sociological analyses of populism and that a stride toward overcoming these problems can be made by placing more emphasis on Laclau's concept of 'dislocation' than Laclau does himself.

Consider the following passage from the preface of Jacob Torfing's *New Theories of Discourse*:

> Discourse theory, as developed by Ernesto Laclau, Chantal Mouffe and Slavoj Zizek, draws our attention to the implication of postmodernity for the way we conceive of the relation between the political and the social. Postmodernity urges us to take into account the open and incomplete character of any social totality and to insist on the primary role of politics in shaping and reshaping social relations (1999:vii).

This social totality is viewed by Laclau as an essentially discursive totality or differential ensemble that always exists as a failed or impossible totality. Thus political struggles are privileged in which demands linked into equivalential chains make possible empty signifiers or hegemonic identities, such as the 'people', which, in a sense, partially fix the social/discursive totality in 'a stable system of signification' (Laclau, 2005:74).

In other words, political struggles are privileged insofar as they momentarily construct and stabilize the social totality. Furthermore, Howarth (2004) writes that Laclau's 'central claim that "society is an impossible object of analysis" seeks to exclude essentialist, objectivist and topographical conceptions of social relations (whether put forward by positivists, materialists, or realists), while developing a relational conception of society in which concepts such as antagonism and dislocation are constitutive' (266).

In the rest of this paper, I maintain that Laclau's adoption of a relational conception of society, as a discursive entity comprising language and social action, *is* reconcilable from a sociological perspective, as is his claim that social totalities are shaped by politics. I argue, however, that his claim that 'society is an impossible object of analysis' goes too far and that the social and political should be viewed as coextensive discursive planes in order to resolve contradictions already present in Laclau's theory of dislocation.

Howarth (2004) sums up Laclau's (1990) notion of dislocations put forward in *New Reflections on the Revolution of Our Time*:

> Dislocations are thus defined as those 'events' or 'crises' that cannot be represented within an existing discursive order, as they function to disrupt and destabilize symbolic orders (NR 72–8). This enables Laclau to inject an 'extra-discursive' dynamism into his conception of society, and his later writings suggest that late- or post-modern societies are undergoing an 'accelerated tempo' of dislocatory experiences (Howarth, 2000a: 111). *This 'accelerated tempo' is caused by processes such as commodification, bureaucratization, and globalization . . .'* (261, my emphasis).

It seems that the dislocations that Laclau refers to are the effect of precisely those social phenomena and sociological processes which, as they belong to society, he paradoxically thinks are an impossible object of analysis. Howarth (2004) writes that these dislocations open up a space in which there is 'a greater role for political subjectivities' (261). Thus, I argue that it is the primarily *social* terrain of dislocations which fragments the discursive/symbolic order opening the space for political identities to reconstitute the discursive/social totality. In this sense, there is always a reciprocal interplay between the social and political. As I approach the end of this paper, this understanding of dislocations will be integral to the development of what I refer to as the 'accelerated tempo' of populist outbreaks.

Epistemological contours

First, though, in order to argue for Laclau's model of populism for understanding Obama's rhetoric against other models presented in the literature, it is necessary to elucidate the problems with traditional theoretical conceptions of populism and trace out the epistemological contours of how populism has come to be an increasingly ambiguous and highly contested analytical construct in the literature of the social sciences.

The term 'populism' has been used to refer to a variety of different levels of political phenomena including regionally based political movements themselves, certain types of political leaders, specific types of political campaigning and administration, forms and styles of rhetoric employed by political actors, and politically fostered conceptions of identity oriented around a notion of the 'people' opposed to an oppressive elite. It follows that an analysis of the historical case studies generated within the social sciences, which seek to characterize certain movements or political leaders as populist, reveals a whole host of conceptual problems in the subsequent attempt to delineate the general theoretical components of populism as an ideal type or classificatory schema of sociopolitical phenomena.

The first problem one encounters and which is generally referred to by authors who analyse the wide array of political movements labeled populist is that those movements corresponding to different regions (i.e. Russia, United States, and Latin America among others) and different time periods (i.e. mid to late 19th century, mid 20th century, and the present) share little in common other than the fact that they have all been labelled as populist. Laclau (1977) writes about populism, 'it is that 'something in common' which is perceived as a component of movements whose social bases are totally divergent' (146).

This divergence in social bases is one of the main features that divides the classical cases of populism, including the Russian *Narodnichestvo* movement of the mid nineteenth century and The People's Party movement in America during the 1890s, insofar as the Narodniks were primarily composed of an urban intelligentsia who exalted and appealed to peasant farmers in an anti-capitalist and utopian ideology (Walicki, 1969; Worsley, 1969), while The People's Party began as a grassroots organization initiated by commercial farmers who harboured discontents with the crop lien system, monetary deflation, and the role of big business and the two-party political system in furthering their economic hardships (Goodwyn, 1978; Hofstadter, 1969).

Thus, just as one sees this demographic divide between urban and rural social bases in the classical Russian and American cases respectively, further discrepancies emerge with the later developments of Latin American populisms, which hinder and obscure comparisons with these classical cases. The first substantive difference apparent in the most prominently cited Latin American cases – regarding the political rule of Cárdenas in Mexico (1934–40), Perón in Argentina (1946–55) and Vargas's second term in Brazil (1951–54), and the more contemporary cases of Menem in Argentina, Fujimori in Peru, Bucaram in Ecuador, and Chávez in Venezuela – is that these movements are attempts at political mobilization and incorporation initiated by political candidates and leaders, not organic movements fostered by groups of farmers or intellectuals. It follows that a second crucial point of divergence from the United States and Russian cases is that the social bases appealed to by figures such as Perón and

Vargas, although primarily urban in their demographic composition, tend to transcend a solid base in any particular social class and thus constitute multiclass coalitions (Conniff, 1999:4).

But one must make a distinction here between the more traditional cases of *Peronism* and *Varguismo* and the newly emerging form of populism exemplified in the leadership of Menem, Fujimori, and Bucaram. This emergent form of populism is referred to as 'neopopulism' by authors such as Kenneth Roberts (1995) and Kurt Weyland (1999, 2003) and differs from traditional Latin American populism both in the adoption of a neoliberal economic stance, as opposed to the more traditionally advocated nationalist policies that relied on import substitution industrialization and restricted markets, and in the demographic makeup of the social bases appealed to: 'The base of support for neopopulism, for example, includes alliances between emergent elites with the very poor, excluding the industrial bourgeoisie and the organized working and middle classes, which were the advocates of classical populism' (de la Torre, 2000:113). Chávez's rise to power is also commonly associated with the emergence of neopopulism, and the label somewhat fits insofar as his appeal is made to the 'unorganized subaltern sectors of the population' (Roberts, 2003:55) and to 'the impoverished and politically inarticulate section of society, in the shanty towns of Caracas, and in the great forgotten regions of the interior of the country' (Gott, 2000:21). However, his economic stance represents a backlash against neoliberal reforms intitiated by one of his predecessors, Pérez. Roberts (2003) writes that Chávez 'posed a vigorous challenge to the regional trend toward neoliberal reform, countering Latin America's embrace of the political and economic models sanctioned by US hegemony' (71).

These unique features common to Latin American populism observable in the grand scale mobilization efforts initiated by political elites have led some scholars to construct refined definitions of populism that causally link its emergence solely to social, economic, and political conditions specific to these regions – such as processes of modernization, the marginal position Latin American countries occupy with respect to the global market and the resulting dependent capitalist development, and the clientelist legacies inherited from the colonial past. These theoretical frameworks delimit populism as an emergent phenomenon only possible in nation-states that can be historically linked to 'underdeveloped' economic and political structures and foreclose any possible comparison with forms of populism that, one could argue, are emerging in the United States.

Populism and Latin America

The classic approach to situating the emergence of Latin American populism within broader economic and political processes of transformation accompanying modernization was pioneered in the work of Gino Germani. Germani provides a functionalist account of the transition from traditional to industrial society in which processes of modernization are coextensive with and directly tied to processes of social mobilization. It follows that the main process concomitant with social mobilization for Germani (1978) is the 'extension of legal, social, and political rights to all inhabitants, that is, their incorporation into the nation as citizens rather than subjects' (13). Thus, one can imagine a process of industrialization, urbanization, and economic concentration occurring in Latin American countries in which rural agrarian peoples are transformed into an urban mass – a process which is accompanied by changes in their aspirations for economic prosperity and political participation insofar as their sociopolitical positions and expectations change from being subjects dominated by a landed oligarchy to the desire for political incorporation into society as citizens.

This process, then, creates a susceptibility to populist forms of leadership insofar as the political structures and institutional means of integration, which serve the purpose of incorporating these masses into modern society, lag far behind the process of mobilization. Hence, the essential predicament, which leads to populism in this functionalist framework, is that of people entering modern society without modern means of integration. In this sense, Germani (1978) gives us a view of populism as a sort of intermediate form of political organization between authoritarianism and full democratic participation insofar as it 'includes contrasting components such as a claim for equality of political rights and universal participation for the common people, but fused with some sort of authoritarianism often under charismatic leadership' (88).

In a general sense, many of the analyses that seek to account for the emergence of populism in Latin America rely on the historical legacy of dependent capitalist development in order to explain the rise of populism as a type of aberrant political phenomenon. Paul Drake (1982), writing at a time after the initial wave of Latin American populism extending from the 1930s through the 1970s, but before the advent of neopopulism in the late 1980s, views populism in this way as a transient form of political organization that was made possible by the rise of the export economy and the resulting urban demographic explosion after which industrialization developed at a slower pace (236).

Other authors, such as James Malloy (1977), formulate a comparative-historical perspective, referred to as a 'modal pattern,' in which they see Latin American countries as passing through successive phases relative to transformations in the economic market. Roxborough (1984) succinctly sums up the three historical stages posited in this approach: once again, starting in the late 19th century, Latin American countries first produced 'primary products for the world market,' which was interrupted by World War I, the depression, and World War II (3). This initiated a second phase of import-substitution industrialization in which 'Latin American economies turned in on themselves and industrialized . . . meeting domestic demand for manufactured goods from internal production, rather than through export revenues' (Roxborough, 1984:3). A third phase follows with 'the massive penetration of Latin American economies by multinational manufacturing corporations,' which Roxborough (1984), following O'Donnell (1973), refers to as 'bureaucratic authoritarianism'

(3). Thus, it is the second phase of import substitution industrialization that is usually associated with the emergence of populism:

> The period of ISI was accompanied by a displacement of the old agrarian oligarchies from state power and by the mobilization of previously excluded classes and strata. A heterogeneous coalition of industrialists, the urban middle class, urban workers and migrants to the cities led this assault on the oligarchical state. Frequently with the aid of sections of the military, this coalition led to the installation of populist or Bonapartist regimes and to a new level of state autonomy from direct class pressures. Industrial expansion, growth in employment, and widespread rises in living standards were the material bases for the widespread support enjoyed by these populist governments (Roxborough, 1984:7).

Another set of causal factors linked to the emergence and success of populist regimes in Latin America is derived from an emphasis on the clientelist political culture inherited from the colonial past and other problems associated with the development and effectiveness of democratic political institutions. Following Roxborough (1984), I will refer to this as the 'essentialist' model (3). With reservations about the explanatory value of this cultural model, Drake (1982) describes the historical roots of the 'patron-client' relationship and alludes to possible affinities with populist forms of leadership:

> A cultural approach to Latin American populism would emphasize the paternalistic bond between the leader and the masses. According to many analysts, this reciprocal but hierarchical relationship grows out of the rural, seigniorial, Roman Catholic, Ibero-American heritage of ingrained inequality with at least 500-year old roots (220).

Other authors, such as Claudio Véliz (1980), explain the problem of underdeveloped democratic institutions and the persistence of authoritarian forms of government in reference to the tradition of centralized colonial rule extending back to the Spanish and Portuguese monarchies. Carlos de la Torre (2000) also points to problems concerning democratic institutions, especially the extension of citizenship and the gap between civil society and the dominant power structures in countries like Ecuador, suggesting that these problems help to explain the appeal of populist leaders and the relative feasibility of populist forms of political organization (9,10).

Each of these paradigms for explaining the emergence of Latin American populism (i.e. the modernization paradigm, the 'modal pattern' paradigm, and the 'essentialist' paradigm) have encountered rigorous critiques in academic literature and reveal a whole host of theoretical shortcomings and inconsistencies when measured against the multitude of cases that are associated with or labelled as forms of populism in Latin America and elsewhere. For instance, Laclau (1977) provides a common critique of the modernization paradigm insofar as it 'implies highly questionable assumptions' that 'greater economic development' would result in 'less populism' and that societies affected by populism 'will necessarily advance towards more 'modern' and 'class' forms of channelling popular protest' (153,154).

These problematic functionalist assumptions endemic in the modernization paradigm, which asserted that increases in levels of modern integration would ultimately decrease instances of populism, led to the formation of the aforementioned 'modal pattern' paradigm. Once again, with this paradigm authors O'Donnell (1973) and Malloy (1977) attempted to provide a more 'structuralist argument that linked populism with import substitution industrialization' (de la Torre, 2000:5). However, Roxborough (1984) argues that the empirical data corresponding to the rise of the political regimes of Peron, Vargas and Cárdenas does not reveal a significant correlation with the advent of import substitution industrialization (16).

Similar inconsistencies arise in the attempt to create theoretical models that posit a unified historical account of the impact of inherited practices of corporatism, clientelism, and centralized colonial rule on the emergence of authoritarian regimes of either a militaristic or populist type and the underdevelopment of democratic institutions. Regarding these inconsistencies, Roxborough (1984), citing Cammack (1983), refers to a pertinent contradiction in the model of traditional continuity that Véliz (1980) attributes to the influence of colonial rule on authoritarian military regimes insofar as Véliz himself points to a 'liberal pause' in his own model between colonialism and military rule that 'covers virtually the entire period of national independence' in Latin America (Roxborough, 1984:5). And in order to refute any comparative-historical argument that would link the emergence of Latin American populism to a continuous tradition of underdeveloped democratic institutions, one has only to consider the history of stable democratic institutions in Argentina for seventy years prior to the military coup of 1930 (Germani, 1978:125).

From this analysis of the literature on Latin American populism it is apparent that there are serious limitations and inconsistencies that arise in the attempt to create a unified historical model of the economic and political conditions that led to the emergence of populism and in the attempt to delineate the essential characteristics that populism entails. The following examination of the literature on populism in the United States also reveals attempts to link up the emergence of populism with social, economic, and political conditions. And similar to the literature on Latin American populism, there are disagreements among scholars about the historical conditions, social bases, ideological content, and other essential characteristics of populism in the United States.

Populism in the United States

One of the more prominent historical accounts of populism in America is provided by Lawrence Goodwin. Similar to most other analysts of American populism (Hicks, 1961; Hofstadter, 1969; Szasz, 1982; McMath, 1992; Kazin, 1995), Goodwin historically situates the emergence of populism in the economic destitution experienced by farmers in the post-Civil War period as they found themselves facing an increasing and insurmountable debt as a result of being bound to the crop lien system.

Goodwyn (1978) suggests that populism in America consisted of a movement culture that really began when the farmers of Lampasas County, Texas, reacting against the hardships of the crop lien system, banded together in 1877 to form the 'Knights of Reliance', a group which later became known as 'The Farmers Alliance' (25, 26). This movement culture was a complex and multilayered set of ideologies and practices that consisted of three sets of processes often intermingling: the farmers' emphasis on self-help, education and the formation of cooperatives; the farmers' view that they were part of a larger industrial class leading to boycotts and coordination of efforts with other movements such as the Knights of Labor; and the acceptance of the greenback doctrine calling for the introduction of fiat currency in conjunction with C. W. Macune's subtreasury system.

Goodwyn's historical account of the formation of the Populist Party has encountered substantial critiques. Concerning the emphasis that Goodwyn places on the greenback ideology, Clanton (1991) comments, 'Not all historians of Populism would agree that greenback ideology was quite that fundamental, but it figured prominently in the thought of a significant segment of the leadership, in Texas and elsewhere' (18). McMath (1992) has suggested that Goodwyn's analysis of the origins of populism is too narrowly focused on a radical type of Alliance action exhibited in the formation of cooperatives, which occurred only to a large extent in Texas, and that Goodwyn's study overemphasizes a distinctive and local movement culture that dismisses the broader reception of populism by the nation (15).

Whereas Goodwyn suggests that the core of the populist movement revolved around the attempted formation of cooperatives and the dissemination of the greenback ideology, Szasz (1982) argues that it was the moment at which cooperatives proved unsuccessful and the Populists began to support other issues that populism began to broaden its appeal as a movement. Thus, as the issues that the Populists supported became diversified so did their social base of support. The Populist party 'provided the only real political alternative to the Republicans or Democrats . . . In addition to agrarians, the famous 1896 Populist convention at St. Louis bounded with Single Taxers, Bellamyite Nationalists, Socialists, Prohibitionists, Greenbackers, and Suffragettes' (Szasz 1982:194). And the fact that 'much of the Populist vote in the western mining states of Colorado and Montana relied on labor support' lends support to Szasz's (1982) claim that, not unlike Latin American forms of populism, populism in the United States could be described as 'multiclass, expansive, electoral, socially reformist, and led by charismatic figures' (195,191).

Authors such as Szasz and Kazin build from a historical account of the populist movement of the 1890s to show that this political heritage, in the form of a rhetoric of the 'people', has been adopted by a myriad of political figures in the subsequent decades of American history, extending all the way to the present. Although exhibiting some basic rhetorical affinities with the initial movement, insofar as there is always an appeal to the common people, the history of populist discourse in America, much like in Latin America, reveals an articulation of diverse ideological contents that oscillates between Left and Right: 'thus, the Populist heritage has been ambiguous: it provided ammunition for both liberals and conservatives' (Szasz, 1982:203). Accordingly Szasz and Kazin have traced a populist discourse that runs through the rhetoric of such diverse political figures as Bryan, McCarthy, Wallace, Nixon, Reagan, and Bill Clinton. However, most analysts agree that there is still a common element in American populism, which Kazin (1995) defines as 'a language whose speakers conceive of ordinary people as a noble assemblage not bounded narrowly by class, view their elite opponents as self-serving and undemocratic, and seek to mobilize the former against the latter' (1).

Unpicking populism and other movements

In the final section of this paper, I argue that Laclau also analyses populism from a discursive perspective, although he has a very different conception of discourse, and that this is the only definition that remains tenable in a comparison of the Latin American cases, let alone a comparison between US and Latin American cases, insofar as the models of modernization, modal patterns, and political institutions reveal vast divergences and inconsistencies in the Latin American cases, and in both U.S. and Latin American cases, the ideological contents of populist discourse are always shifting.

Ahead of this, a brief examination of the academic literature on current populist trends in Western Europe will be useful in further debunking the already well refuted claim that the emergence of populism is tied to the processes inherent in economic and political modernization and in creating a space for the analysis of other contemporary cases of populism in 'developed' Western nations, such as the United States.

Considering the recent emergence of a new form of populism in Western Europe beginning in the 1980s, Paul Taggart (1995) has linked a series of nascent party developments to 'a rising tide of right-wing extremism' and coins the term 'New Populism' to distinguish these movements[2] from neo-fascist trends, despite a few ideological similarities (34). In delineating the distinguishing features of this form of populism, Taggart provides us with three essential characteristics that allow for comparisons to the other instances of populism previously discussed. First of all, Taggart (1995) notes that 'all these parties have combined elements of nationalism with neo-liberal economic policies' (35). Thus, in terms of economic stance, there is a parallel to the upsurge in neopopulist leadership in Latin America; however the nationalist anti-immigration and racist sentiments that characterize New Populism, and the fact of its occurrence in well-established and institutionalized democratic regimes, represent stark contrasts.

A second aspect of New Populism that is coextensive with more general definitions of populism and neopopulism is its anti-system ideological orientation. Taggart (1995) writes, 'New Populism is on the right, against the system, and yet defines itself as in the "mainstream" . . . It is of the people but not of the system. The growth of the New Populism is itself the repudiation of any idea that politics as usual is a politics that works . . . It enjoys breaking the rules because they are the rules of a system it sees as defunct' (36, 37). In this sense, New Populism represents what has been commonly referred to as the 'politics of anti-politics' 'as politicians and political parties become the "other" of the people' (Panizza, 2005:12). The 'politics of anti-politics' discourse is a common element in many instances of populism ranging from The People's Party in the United States to the description of Fujimori's 'antielitest and antiestablishment rhetoric' given by Roberts (1995). From Panizza's perspective, the people's disenchantment with institutionalized politics has led to the emergence of populist leaders as diverse as Berlusconi and Chávez. Both these factors of the people's disenchantment with institutionalized politics and the anti-system/ 'outside politics' orientation shed light on such phenomena as the brief electoral success of Ross Perot in the United States (Westlind, 1996).

A third aspect of New Populism that mirrors forms of Latin American populism and neopopulism is its centralized organizational structure and the reciprocal relationship between this organizational structure and reliance on charismatic leadership. Taggart (1995) writes,

> New Populist parties have two qualities that pertain to their organization: they are very centralized and they set great store in the leadership which is both personalized and charismatic . . . they can reconcile anti-systemic elements with organizational elements that ensure their institutional and electoral survival. They are also the organizational articulation of key elements of their ideology (40).

Thus, the fact that these parties rely on centralized charismatic leadership as opposed to typical institutionalized bureaucratic structures expresses precisely their anti-system ideology. Many analysts of Latin American populism have pointed to similar centralized organizational structures and personalistic styles of leadership (Conniff, 1999:16).

Thus, despite the right-wing, anti-immigrant and racist content of New Populist ideology, this emergent form of populism in Western Europe has many of the same characteristics attributable to populism in Latin America, especially neopopulism, insofar as it supports a neoliberal economic stance, articulates an anti-system, anti-political ideology, and rests on personalized and centralized organizational structures. And given the fact that New Populism proves a powerful force in countries with well-developed and institutionalized democratic structures, it becomes increasingly difficult to maintain the position that the economic and political conditions specific to Latin American countries are ripe for the emergence of populism in general and certain types of populist regimes in particular.

In the light of the aforementioned problems encountered in the attempt to relegate populism to a specific set of regional and historical processes, I argue that only Laclau's theory of populism as a unitary discursive formation retains explanatory value across cases insofar as the empirical evidence provided by the Latin American and Western European cases counters any essentialist link between the emergence of populism and modernization processes, import substitution industrialization, and a continuous trend of underdeveloped democratic institutions.

Laclau's conception of discourse

Laclau conceives of populism as a discursive phenomenon in which hegemonic political identities are constructed through 'empty signifiers,' which link together popular demands in a chain of equivalence or stable discourse. This stability of the chain of equivalence is achieved through the differentiation of an excluded element, which forms the basis of an antagonism. In order to render a detailed explanation of this process, it is important to understand Laclau's conception of discourse itself. Laclau (2005) writes, 'By discourse, as I have attempted to make clear several times, I do not mean something that is essentially restricted to the areas of speech and writing, but any complex of elements in which relations play the constitutive role' (68).

In an earlier work, Laclau and Mouffe (1985) refer to Wittgenstein's concept of language games in order to elaborate this theory of discourse that moves beyond a purely cognitive scope to include the forms of social action which correspond to a given discursive formation: 'The theory of speech acts has, for example, underlined their performative character. Language games, in Wittgenstein, include with an indissoluble totality both language and the actions interconnected with it . . . The linguistic and non-linguistic elements are not merely juxtaposed, but constitute a differential and structured system of positions – that is, a discourse' (108). It follows that the other integral aspect of this conception of discourse besides its extension beyond language is its relational character.

This relational character of discourse is derived from Saussure's conception of language as a system of signs[3] in which signifiers only acquire meaning in their relation, in terms of differences, to other signifiers within the linguistic system. Laclau (2005) then extends this conception of language as a system of differences to other 'signifying elements' and actions:

> And what is true of language conceived in its strict sense is also true of any signifying (ie objective) element: an action is what it is only through its differences from other possible actions and from other signifying elements – words or actions – which can be successive or simultaneous. Only two types of relation can possibly exist between these signifying elements: combination and substitution (68).

Laclau uses this conception of discourse as language and action encompassed in a 'differential ensemble' to privilege the discursive terrain as the primary level in which social and political relations are constituted; this then allows for the analysis of the operations of rhetorical tropes, which were previously the exclusive domain of language, to be applied to social relations and political discourse and identities. Laclau and Mouffe (1985) reveal this tropological orientation in writing, 'Synonymy, metonymy, metaphor are not forms of thought that add a second sense to a primary, constitutive literality of social relations; instead, they are a part of the primary terrain itself in which the social is constituted' (110).

Laclau's concepts of difference, antagonism, and equivalence are developed from this notion of discourse as a 'differential ensemble'. Once again, if the primary level of analysis is discourse as a 'purely differential ensemble, its totality has to be present in each act of signification. Consequently grasping the totality is the condition of signification as such. Secondly, however, to grasp that totality conceptually, we have to grasp its limits – that is to say, we have to differentiate it from something other than itself' (Laclau, 2005:69).

Laclau goes on to argue that the differentiated element would only constitute another internal difference within a system of differences and would thus prevent the grasping of the totality necessary for the act of signification. For this reason, the differentiated element, which constitutes the limit of the signifying totality, must be excluded and externalized. This expelled difference forms the basis of the antagonism upon which populist identities depend. Laclau, (2005) writes, 'the only possibility of having a true outside would be that the outside is not simply one more, neutral element but an *excluded* one, something that the totality expels from itself in order to constitute itself (to give a political example: it is through the demonization of a section of the population that a society reaches a sense of its own cohesion)' (70).

It follows that the differentiated element, as the excluded element from the totality, causes all other internal differences to be equivalent to each other 'in their common rejection of the excluded identity' (Laclau, 2005:70). Because of this 'tension' between difference and equivalence, the totality represents an 'impossible' and 'failed' totality (Laclau, 2005:70). The totality is impossible because it is precisely the act of expelling one difference – in order to form the limit of the totality and thus constitute it as totality – that transforms the differences within the differential ensemble into equivalences thereby subverting the differential ensemble or totality itself. For Laclau then, 'This totality is an object which is both impossible and necessary. Impossible, because the tension between equivalence and difference is ultimately insurmountable; necessary, because without some kind of closure, however precarious it might be, there would be no signification and no identity' (70).

Hegemony is thus achieved when one of the differences within the differential ensemble or totality comes to represent the totality as a whole, and in this act of representing the 'incommensurable totality,' the particular difference or 'hegemonic identity' takes on the role of 'empty signifier, its own particularity embodying an unachievable fullness' (Laclau, 2005:70,71). David Howarth (2004) traces out the development of Laclau's conception of the empty signifier in *Emancipations* as 'a signifier without a signified', and notes:

> 'the hegemonic relationship' refers to the way in which a particular signifier ('people', 'nation', 'revolution') is emptied of its particular meaning and comes to represent the 'absent fullness' of a symbolic order. Thus, in social terms, the empty signifier comes to play the universal function of representing an entire community or social order' (261, 262).

In this hegemonic moment 'social demands' are linked together in an equivalential chain. Laclau thus refers to the demands of social groups as the elemental units upon which his theory of populism rests. In order to explain how these demands can be transformed into populist claims, Laclau makes a distinction between 'democratic demands' and 'popular demands.' If the demands that social groups articulate are satisfied, they obviously pose no problem, and if the demands are either satisfied or not, but remain isolated, they are simply democratic demands. However, 'if the situation remains unchanged for some time, there is an accumulation of unfulfilled demands and an increasing inability of the institutional system to absorb them in a *differential* way (each in isolation from the others), and an *equivalential* relationship is established between them' (Laclau, 2005:73).

These demands inscribed in an equivalential chain thus become popular demands and can lead to 'a widening chasm separating the institutional system from the people' (Laclau 2005:74). It follows that the 'two clear preconditions of populism' are '(1) the formation of an internal antagonistic frontier separating the 'people' from power; and (2) an equivalential articulation of demands making the emergence of the 'people' possible' (Laclau, 2005:74).

The Obama election

With this understanding of Laclau's definition of populism, the theoretical ground is set for an analysis of Obama's election and how it represents an instance of populism based on a reading of Laclau. As I approach an analysis of Obama's election as an instance of populism from a Laclauian perspective, it is important to note that there is nothing novel in utilizing Laclauian discourse theory to analyse aspects of American political discourse. This terrain has already been charted by many theorists: the comparison of Ross Perot and Sweden's New Democracy by Westlind (1996); the study of George Wallace by Lowndes (2005); the brief analysis of Bush's anti-terrorist discourse by Panizza (2005) [to name a few]. However, as I will simply and briefly demonstrate, the Obama case is just as amenable to such a discursive analysis.

A good starting point would be the dislocation: the 'event' or 'crisis' that 'disrupts the symbolic order'. Many political analysts have argued that the event that really led to Obama's ascendancy over McCain in the polls was the devastating impact of the financial crisis felt in September 2008. The economic crisis 'fragmented the symbolic order' and opened up the space for new political identities; it revealed many flaws with the Republican administration in the minds of the American people. There were many democratic demands, which until well into Bush's second term of office, remained isolated democratic demands, such as ending the war in Iraq, fixing problems with the healthcare system, cracking down on CEOs and the irresponsible financial practices of lending firms, etc.

The institutional order, represented by the Republican administration, revealed its inability to absorb these democratic demands by isolating or satisfying them. These demands were thus linked into an equivalential chain and became popular demands. This equivalential chain of popular demands continued to persist, creating an antagonistic rift between 'the American people' and the power bloc. Barack Obama articulated a series of empty signifiers, found in such campaign slogans as 'Yes We Can,' 'Hope' and 'Change You Can Believe In,' which transformed the social totality and equivalential chain of demands into 'a stable system of signification' oriented around the hegemonic identity of 'the American people'.

One particular slogan of the Obama campaign, which reveals the capacity of political discourse to organize forms of social action with respect to grassroots campaigning and fundraising, is 'We Are the People We've Been Waiting For.' This slogan made it possible to signify a conception of 'the American people' that engendered the potential for collective political action. It was not Obama that 'we' were waiting for, but ourselves. 'We' had the power, through online donations, social networking sites, grassroots campaigning, t-shirts, and buttons, to participate actively in ushering in an administration that would satisfy our popular demands. Whether or not the campaign funds raised contributed directly to votes, the felt experience of popular participation did. Thus, these slogans were important not just as empty signifiers, but in the role they play as empty signifiers in this language-game. For after all, what I am describing here, following Laclau's usage of Wittgenstein, is a discourse which simultaneously involves both language and forms of social action and presupposes their inextricable connection.

Conclusion

I want to argue that this instance of populism conceived within Laclau's theoretical framework is comparable to instances of populism in Latin America, but first I will suggest a theory of the forces within academic discourses that hinder comparisons of instances of populism occurring in the US and Latin America. Using the theories of Wittgenstein (1958) and Foucault (1972), I argue that the academic discourses of US and Latin American populism constitute 'language-games' comprised of social norms that govern, regulate, and restrict the usage of the term, 'populism', relegating its usage to their own respective 'fellowships of discourse'.[4]

There is also a set of discursive forces suggesting that such comparisons should be made, and Bakhtin gives us a model of the interrelationship of both sets of forces. Bakhtin (1981) argues that there are centripetal forces, mirroring sociopolitical and linguistic processes of centralization, which seek to merge diverse languages and their accompanying ideological perspectives on the world into a standardized unitary language. Unitary language is thus an abstraction reinforced by philosophical, linguistic, and poetic discourses, which denies the reality of heteroglossia – that there are multiple, diverse languages and points of view existing in the world. These diverse languages and points of view are given expression in the carnivalesque discourses inherited by the novel and represent centrifugal forces which seek to pull languages apart.

I would argue that there are similar sets of forces at work in the academic discourses of populism: forces which seek to pull cases apart and reveal the reality of multiple populisms and forces which seek a standard and unified conception of populism. And we have seen these forces at work in literature on both regions and in between them. My work thus represents both forces: on the one hand, I want to distance the case of Obama's populism from the type of American populism present in the 1890s, which was ultimately unsuccessful but, on the other hand, I would like to make comparisons between the populism present in the Obama election and that of Latin American cases.

There are many features of Latin American populism that make it difficult to compare with the populism present in the Obama campaign. Latin American populism is often associated with a top-down power structure, centralized leadership and organization, links to authoritarianism, and disrespect for the rule of law. Obama's populism has none of these characteristics and corresponds more closely to what Canovan (1980) has termed 'polititicans' populism': 'broad, nonideological coalition-building that draws on the unificatory appeal of "the people"' (13). But the fact of the matter is, 'against the assumptions of political modernizers, populist leaders are not anachronistic figures to be superseded by the political institutions and rational debate of modern democracy . . . populism is here to stay' (Panizza, 2005:19). And even though Obama's populism is considerably more benign and moderate than the populism of Chávez, I *imagine* that we will see more instances of populism in 'developed' Western nations in the future – perhaps taking on more dangerous forms. This bleak prediction is perhaps warranted, given the manner in which mainstream American politicians have begun to placate the problematic and reactionary demands of the Tea Party.

In one of the plenary sessions of the Sociological Review 100th Anniversary Conference, Randall Collins presented a paper entitled, 'Technological Displacement and Capitalist Crisis,' in which he argued that, due to the increasing severity of crises surrounding finance capitalism and the displacement of the middle class, we will soon see a movement toward more forms of socialism.

Thus far, however, it seems that we are witnessing more movements toward forms of populism than socialism. I argue that Collins is correct in positing a phenomenon that is similar to Laclau's 'accelerated tempo' of dislocations. As capitalism runs out of 'escape routes' in Collins' formulation, we will experience more dislocatory crises, which I believe will result in an exponential increase in populist outbreaks.

In comparing Obama's populism to populism in Latin America, we can see that despite the specific character of the dislocation – whether it follows a modal pattern, essentialist model, or economic recession – the aspects of antagonism, equivalence, and hegemonic identity formation remain constant. My argument is that from the perspective of a populist study, we should not analyse Obama at all; rather, there is something present in the language of his campaign, and how it so easily sutured the present dislocation and averted a confrontation with the unavoidable Lacanian Real that is worthy of interrogation.

Notes

1 See 'For Populism, A Return to Economic Roots,' John Harwood, *New York Times*, March 23, 2009, and articles by Michael Kazin and Fareed Zakaria in *Newsweek*, March 30, 2009.
2 Some of the movements Taggart refers to as parties that fit within his ideal type of 'New Populism' include: Haider and The Austrian Freedom Party, the Northern Leagues and Berlusconi's Forza Italy, the Ticino League and Automobilist Party in Switzerland, the Danish and Norwegian Progress Parties, Sweden's New Democracy, the Flemish Bloc of Belgium, Le Pen's French National Front, the Republicans in Germany, etc. To these we can now add Pim Fortuyn in the Netherlands – and beyond Europe, Preston Manning's Reform Party in Canada and Pauline Hanson's One National Party in Australia (Canovan, 2005). This classification also retrospectively fits political figures such as George Wallace in the United States.
3 For Saussure, the sign is composed of a signifier (sound-image) and signified (concept), which the signifier refers to.
4 See the appendix, 'The Discourse on Language,' in Foucault's *The Archaeology of Knowledge*. 'A rather different function is filled by 'fellowships of discourse', whose function is to preserve or reproduce discourse, but in order that it should circulate within a closed community, according to *strict regulations*, without those in possession being dispossessed by this very distribution' (225, my emphasis).

References

Bakhtin, M., (1981), *The Dialogic Imagination*, Austin: University of Texas Press.
Cammack, P., (1983), Review of Véliz, 'Centralist Traditon in Latin America,' *Durham University Journal* 75, 2: 118–19.
Canovan, M., (1980), *Populism*, New York: Harcourt Brace Jovanovich.
Canovan, M., (2005), *The People*, Malden: Polity Press.
Clanton, G., (1991), *Populism: The Human Preference in America, 1890–1900*. Boston: Twane Publishers.
Conniff, M., (1999), 'Introduction,' in Conniff, M. (ed.), *Populism in Latin America*, Tuscaloosa: The University of Alabama Press: 1–21.
de la Torre, C., (2000). *Populist Seduction in Latin America: The Ecuadorian Experience*. Athens, Ohio: Ohio University Center for International Studies.

Drake, P., (1982), 'Requiem for Populism?' in Conniff, M., (ed.), *Latin American Populism in Comparative Perspective*, Albuquerque: University of New Mexico Press: 217–45.

Foucault, M., (1972), *The Archaeology of Knowledge and The Discourse on Language*. New York: Pantheon Books.

Germani, G., (1978), *Authoritarianism, Fascism, and National Populism*. New Brunswick, NJ: Transaction Books.

Goodwyn, L., 1(976), *Democratic Promise: The Populist Movement in America*. New York: Oxford University Press.

Goodwyn, L., (1978), *The Populist Movement: A Short History of the Agrarian Revolt in America*. New York: Oxford University Press.

Gott, R., (2000), *In the Shadow of the Liberator: Hugo Chavez and the Transformation of Venezuela*. London: Verso.

Hicks, J., (1961), *The Populist Revolt: A History of the Farmer's Alliance and the People's Party*. University of Nebraska Press.

Hofstadter, R., (1969), 'North America,' in Ionescu, G. and E. Gellner, (eds), *Populism: Its Meaning and National Characteristics*, New York: The Macmillan Company: 9–27.

Howarth, D., (2000), *Discourse*, Buckingham: Open University Press.

Howarth, D., (2004), 'Hegemony, Political Subjectivity, and Radical Democracy,' in Critchley, S. and O. Marchart, (eds), *Laclau: A Critical Reader*, New York: Routledge: 256–76.

Kazin, M., (1995), *The Populist Persuasion: An American History*, Ithica: Cornell University Press.

Lacan, J., (2006), *Écrits*. New York: W.W. Norton & Company.

Laclau, E. and C. Mouffe, (1985), *Hegemony and Socialist Strategy: Towards a Radical Democratic Politics*, New York: Verso.

Laclau, E., (1977), *Politics and Ideology in Marxist Theory*, London: Humanities Press.

Laclau, E., (1990), *New Reflections on the Revolution of Our Time*, New York: Verso.

Laclau, E., (2005), *On Populist Reason*, New York: Verso.

Lowndes, J., (2005), 'From Founding Violence to Political Hegemony: The Conservative Populism of George Wallace.,' in Panizza, F., (ed.), *Populism and the Mirror of Democracy*. New York: Verso: 144–71.

McMath, R., (1992), *American Populism: A Social History, 1877–1898*, New York: Hill and Wang.

Malloy, J., (1977), 'Latin America: the Modal Pattern,' in *Authoritarianism and Corporatism in Latin America*, Pittsburgh, University of Pittsburgh Press.

O'Donnell, G., (1973), *Modernization and Bureaucratic-Authoritarianism*. Berkeley: Institute of International Studies, University of California.

Panizza, F., (ed.), (2005), *Populism and the Mirror of Democracy*, New York: Verso.

Roberts, K., (1995), 'Neoliberalism and the Transformation of Populism in Latin America. The Peruvian Case,' *World Politics* 48,1: 82–116.

Roberts, K., (2003), 'Social Polarization and the Populist Resurgence in Venezuela,' in Ellner, S. and D. Hellinger, (eds), *Venezuelan Politics in the Chavez Era*, Boulder: Lynne Rienner Publishers: 55–72.

Roxborough, I., (1984), 'Unity and Diversity in Latin American History,' *Journal of Latin American Studies* 16:1–26.

Szasz, F., (1982), 'United States Populism,' in Conniff, M., (ed.), *Latin American Populism in Comparative Perspective*, Albuquerque: University of New Mexico Press: 191–215.

Taggart, P., (1995), 'New Populist Parties in Western Europe,' *West European Politics*, 18, 1: 34–51.

Torfing, J., (1999), *New Theories of Discourse: Laclau, Mouffe, and Zizek*. Malden: Blackwell Publishers.

Véliz, C., (1980), *The Centralist Tradition in Latin America*. Princeton: Princeton University Press.

Walicki, A., (1969), 'Russia,' in Ionescu, G. and E. Gellner, (eds), *Populism: Its Meaning and National Characteristics*, New York: The Macmillan Company: 62–96.

Westlind, D., (1996), *The Politics of Popular Identity: Understanding Recent Populist Movements in Sweden and the United States*, Lund: Lund University Press.

Weyland, K., (1999), 'Populism in the Age of Neoliberalism.'. in Conniff, M., (ed.), *Populism in Latin America*, Tuscaloosa: The University of Alabama Press: 172–90.

Weyland, K., (2003), 'Neopoulism and Neoliberalism: How Much Affinity?' *Third World Quarterly*, 24,6: 1095–115.

Wittgenstein, L., (1958), *Philosophical Investigations*, Upper Saddle River, New Jersey: Prentice Hall.

Worsley, P., (1969), 'The Concept of Populism,' in Ionescu, G. and E. Gellner, (eds), *Populism: Its Meaning and National Characteristics*, New York: TheMacmillan Company, 212–50.

Released from gender? Reflexivity, performativity, and therapeutic discourses[1]

Kateřina Lišková

Abstract: My paper is an analysis of contemporary Czech expert discourses on love and coupledom, framed within ongoing feminist discussions of sociological theory's emphasis on the individualization, reflexivity and detraditionalization of gender. Using Bourdieu's notion of symbolic violence, I argue for understanding therapeutic discourses as perlocutionary speech acts that authoritatively enact gendered norms and heteronormative assumptions. This performative approach both challenges heightened reflexivity theory by pointing to its flawed voluntarism, and also allows for grasping transformation through fissures between a perlocutionary act and its reception.

Introduction

'Increasingly, the individuals who want to live together are, or more precisely are becoming, the legislators of their own way of life, the judges of their own transgressions, the priests who absolve their own sins and the therapists who loosen the bonds of their own past,' wrote Beck and Beck-Gernsheim 15 years ago (1995: 5). Have love, coupledom and gender been freed from patterns dictated by modernity? Do we fully negotiate the terms of our 'being-togetherness'? Or else, how is our understanding of intimacy and gender constrained symbolically?

In this paper, I consider one terrain of expert discourses which informs our understanding of love and coupledom – therapeutic discourses. I will analyse Czech discourses of partner psychotherapy and sexology as conceived in two recent books.[2] How are the norms regulating gender, sexuality and love constructed in expert therapeutic discourses? My aim is to account for the symbolic avenues structuring gender and intimacy.

First, I want to analyse therapeutic accounts in light of the debates on the detraditionalization of intimate life and gender started by Giddens (1992) and Beck and Beck-Gernsheim (1995). Can we identify detraditionalization traits in therapeutic discourses? Are therapeutic discourses consistent with the detraditionalization theory of changing intimate landscapes? In this section, I interrogate feminist critiques of Giddens and further explore the claim of Giddens's compatibility with therapeutic discourses (Jamieson, 1999). As a counter argument to Giddensian accounts of reflexive transformation, sociologists usually use Bourdieu's notion of habitus. However, this approach has its pitfalls as it does not account for social change (Butler, 1999). To remedy this, I propose to focus instead on Bourdieu's concept of symbolic violence which captures the reproduction of hierarchical social structures while theoretically allowing for (thinking) change via the notion of performatives.

Second, I will examine the efficacy of therapeutic discourses in the context of power, social reproduction and change. I want to argue that therapeutic discourses functions like a performative speech act. Performatives, as introduced by Austin (1962), include so-called perlocutionary performatives which act in social reality through action following a particular performative speech act. I propose to view expert therapeutic discourses as a form of performative shaping what is socially intelligible. Here I draw on Bourdieu's notion of symbolic violence as a form of power that circumscribes the social through rendering it intelligible in a certain way. Symbolic violence is powerful in structuring the social; however, if we understand it in performative terms, we begin to see its limits and structural openness to failure and thus change.

Reflexivity, detraditionalization and gender

Giddens and Beck and Beck-Gernsheim famously set out to describe and explain the changes that have occurred in intimacy, and subsequently gender, since the inception of modernity and especially during the decades leading up to the end of the 20th century. According to Giddens (1992), we have witnessed the 'transformation of intimacy'. Historically, the changes were set into motion by the emergence of romantic love, a modern phenomenon that is voluntary, egalitarian, communicative and satisfying (Giddens, 1992: 58). The narrative of romantic love is long-term and future-oriented, attributing special meaning to a particular relationship, thus outlining a trajectory towards 'an anticipated yet malleable future.'

Giddens somewhat unproblematically assumes that romantic love, as a restructuring of intimacy, gives rise to 'pure relationship' defined as:

> a situation where a social relation is entered into for its own sake, for what can be derived by each person from a sustained association with another; and which is continued only in so far as it is thought by both parties to deliver enough satisfactions for each individual to stay within (Giddens, 1992: 58).

In his view, people move through a series of relationships throughout their lifetimes, the norm of lifelong commitment becoming considerably weakened. Giddens suggests that the pure relationship 'is in some causally related ways parallel to the development of plastic sexuality' (Giddens, 1992: 58), a decentred form of sexuality freed from reproduction that signals variability and ever-broadening forms of sex in contemporary societies. To navigate the shifting terrain of intimacy, high levels of reflexivity must be exercised by an individual.

Similarly, Beck and Beck-Gernsheim assert that the traditional constraints and obligations of pre-modern times have vanished; instead one is increasingly faced with a vast scope of questions where 'socially prescribed answers' used to be (Beck and Beck-Gernsheim, 1995: 47). With so many options to choose from, individuals confront a social landscape requiring heightened reflexivity. In this tumultuous world, individuals turn towards romantic love in search of a source of personal stability. However, with structural demands, it becomes exceedingly difficult to reconcile a relationship with work and claims to individual autonomy.

The accent on the broadening scope of options available, and the subsequent pressure to choose the right one, is apparent in both accounts. Some authors have criticized theories of transformative reflexivity for conflating symbolic ambivalence with social detraditionalization (McNay, 2000: 69), questioning the amount and meaning of expressive possibilities open to women and men. Is there symbolic ambivalence in therapeutic discourses? And if so, to what extent does it allow for change?

Critics of theories of reflexive transformation (Jamieson, 1999) have identified an easy fit between the so-called 'transformation of intimacy' and therapeutic literature. Jamieson argues that by definition therapy works with highly individualized accounts, thus mirroring its patterns leads to impoverished analysis divorced from sociological focus on structures and institutions. To what extent does the therapeutic discourses I analyse correspond to the idea of transformation of intimacy? What institutional and structural underpinnings are there in therapeutic discourses?

Habitus and social reproduction

While Giddens and Beck and Beck-Gernsheim have suggested that identity is increasingly reflexive, such accounts are arguably problematized by theories stressing the social 'mooring' of our dispositions and aspirations. It has been pointed out that Bourdieu's understanding of social practice offers a counterargument to theories of reflexivity, individualization and detraditionalization. In particular, his concept of habitus suggests that identity may be less prone to reflexive alteration than theorists such as Giddens have proposed (Sweetman, 2003; Adams, 2006; Skeggs, 2004; Adkins, 2004; McNay, 1999 and 2000; Lovell, 2000; Evans, 2003).

Often, the argument against heightened reflexivity and its vast restructuring of gender emphasizes that gender reproduction is tied to the reproductive work of women. For example, Mary Evans (2003: 52) points to women's involvement in childrearing that 'returns our couple of late modernity to the constraints of a previous era'. Caring, symbolically and empirically connected to childrearing, as well as emotional labour more generally, has been identified as a factor chiefly underscoring the tendency towards gender reproduction. Based on empirical findings, some authors indicate that within heterosexual intimate relationships it is still women who perform most of the emotional labour (Duncombe and Marsden, 1996; Langford, 1999), and go on to explain how this emotional work carries over into their occupations in the public realm, where it further reproduces the hierarchical gendered status quo (Hochschild, 2003; Ehrenreich and Hochschild, 2004). Reproduction, typical of the gendered condition of women, is antithetical to change. Thus the idea that reflexivity functions equally for both men and women is undermined.

Other authors have refuted the almost synonymic pairing between individualization as a simple withering away of gender norms on one hand, and reflexivity conflated with detraditionalization on the other. Lisa Adkins (2004) suggests that reflexivity is intrinsic to our everyday action and as such is hardly exclusively transformative. Reflexivity reflects and tends to reproduce existing inequalities rather than being a simple vehicle of gender detraditionalization. Gender seems to be a pre-reflexive structure that is rather less open to reflexive interpretation since it is rooted habitually and thus linked to the reproduction of norms. However, norms can never be fully occupied by subjects – there is always a gap; it is this very ambivalence that allows for social change.

Arguably the most elaborate feminist critique of detraditionalized accounts of gender was presented by Lois McNay (1999, 2000). McNay criticizes voluntaristic tendencies embedded in the theories of reflexive modernization that re-instate rather than undo androcentric views of an unconstrained subject typical of modern epistemologies. Gender changes have undoubtedly arisen but their character is rather discontinuous, uneven and conflictual. For MacNay, change might emanate from the incongruity between the fields of action. Unexpected changes within or movements between various fields might bring about reflexivity and thus social change (McNay, 1999: 106–7).

It is the somatization of gender norms that renders agents resistant to social change. For most critics, Bourdieu's concept of habitus has served as the basis for refuting the detraditionalization accounts. From the other side, however, habitus has also been criticized for its perceived blindness to change (Jenkins, 2002; Butler, 1999). Butler has questioned the usefulness of the concept, claiming that it subscribes to the 'normativity that governs the social game' (Butler, 1999:115) and as such is biased towards conformity and conventions. My analysis of expert therapeutic discourses and their relevance for gender follows the findings that gender is habitually grounded and thus exceedingly difficult to alter reflexively (Adkins, 2004; McNay, 1999, 2000), while at the same time trying to tackle the criticisms that habitus allows little, if any, space for (explaining) change (Butler, 1999). In this theoretically contradictory situation, I propose to utilize Bourdieu's concept of symbolic power or symbolic violence (Bourdieu, 1991). Not only is it relevant for studying expert therapeutic discourses, I will argue that it also structurally allows for change.

Through the concept of symbolic power, Bourdieu refers not so much to a specific form of power, but rather to a quality characteristic of any type of power exercised in social reality. For power to be smoothly accepted, it has to be legitimate, which means the power relations remain obscured and domination is experienced as justified. Legitimacy, Bourdieu argues, is achieved through imposing structures of meaning upon social agents. The radical inescapability of the formative influence of symbolic violence is expressed in Bourdieu's maxim: 'the whole social order is present in the very way that we think about that order' (Bourdieu, 2000: 83). The objective structures of the social world form the incorporated structures of social agents, and the established congruence between both types of structures ensures the social reproduction of the status quo. At the same time, incorporated structures modelled through symbolic violence serve as a way of making sense of the world, or – in Bourdieu's terms – doxa, taken-for-granted understandings of the world and ourselves in it. Thus, symbolic violence can only be exercised with an agent's complicity or, viewed from the other side, cannot be rejected at will. Bourdieu speaks of an 'insurmountable *submission* which binds all social agents, whether they like it or not, to the social world of which they are, for better or worse, the products' (Bourdieu, 2000: 173, emphasis in original). One cannot deliberately jettison the structures formed by symbolic violence for they profoundly shape the subject's self.

Symbolic power and performativity

The operations of symbolic violence can be understood through the concept of performatives. Performatives as a linguistic category were coined by J. L. Austin (1962). Austin famously shifted scholarly attention from verifying the truth claims of constative sentences to exploring felicitousness, that is the efficacy, of utterances that do not state or describe anything but rather act in social reality. Austin focused on what he named performative speech acts and distinguished between two kinds of performatives: perlocutionary and illocutionary (Austin, 1962: 94). The latter kind acts and thus accomplishes what it says in the saying, ie it acts in the moment of utterance; it is itself a deed. Classic examples of illocutionary speech acts are 'I bet' 'I promise' and – fitting our focus on gender, intimacy and coupledom – the 'I do' pronounced during a wedding ceremony.[3] The former kind, perlocutionary performatives, produces effects as their consequence. By saying something, certain effects ensue – perlocutives are followed by a sequel distinct from the speech itself. Typical examples of perlocutives are convincing, getting to obey, persuading, etc. (Austin, 1962: 109–20).

While Austin tried to enumerate the linguistic conditions for felicitous performatives – an effort he ultimately failed at – he overlooked a fundamental quality of language, its socialness.[4] This analytical deficiency was pointed out by Bourdieu (1991). For Bourdieu, the efficacy of performatives, and thus of symbolic power, is a function of their belonging to a social institution. The power of speech acts to act is delegated by the social institution of which a speech act is part. In other words, speech acts participate in the authority of the institution.

I propose to study sexological and psychotherapeutic utterances on intimacy and coupledom as performative speech acts backed by the powerful institution of expertise. Therapeutic discourses does not function like an illocutionary speech act. Nothing happens *in* the pure fact of saying/writing about love, sex and intimacy. But it is possible to claim that *by* saying/writing something, therapeutic discourses triggers effects in social reality. Thus we can conceive of expert therapeutic discourses as a form of perlocutionary performative acts. It is then important to ask, what is the structure of meaning these utterances (re)produce? Are they detraditionalized, and if so, to what extent?

Romantic love? Yes. Pure relationship? Not so much

Psychologist and therapist Ivo Plaňava (1998) writes about vast changes that have occurred in the Czech relationship landscape. These are characterized by a loosening of norms and regulations; transformations in value orientation;[5] lower binding power, higher expectations;[6] marriages based on affection, not reason;[7] and changes in gender roles, accompanied by changes in sexual behaviour.[8] When Plaňava describes the pairing process, he writes about mutual attraction, shared interests, values and attitudes. He highlights 'spontaneous communication, positive experiencing of a relationship, and rapport between a girl and a boy – as well as self-validation through the other' (Plaňava, 1998: 92). Even though Plaňava is not using the term, these descriptions of the current state of 'affairs of the heart' correspond to what Giddens calls romantic love.[9]

Plaňava acknowledges the precariousness of our contemporary intimate lives. Surprisingly, he suggests marriage to be 'one of the communities, maybe the most important one' (Plaňava, 1998: 14) protecting people from the uncertainties of the outside world. Marriage as an anchor in an ever-changing world belongs to an index of romantic love (Beck and Beck-Gernsheim, 1995: 49–51). On one hand, the therapist acknowledges a right to divorce, he recognizes that a person might have two life partners: one for bringing up children with, the other for sharing the rest of their life with (Plaňava, 1998: 17). On the other hand, he still sees divorce as a 'paranormative' phenomenon:

> And what about divorce? There have been a lot of books, mainly of transatlantic production, that classify the dissolution of marriage as so-called normative situations (. . .). It comes out of the statistical understanding of normalcy: what is frequent, is normal, and thus in good order. That would mean that if over half of the population gets the flu in fall, it is alright and nothing special is taking place. I do not endorse this understanding of normalcy, I conceive of divorce as a paranormative event; it is a swerving from the road and a situation of loss, full of burden and frustration; one has to deal with similarly as if someone close leaves them forever (Plaňava, 1998: 77–78).

Concessions should be made and partners are encouraged to adapt and compromise. This imperative is in sharp contrast with the trend towards 'conscious separation' identified by Beck and Beck-Gernsheim in therapeutic literature since the late 1960s (Beck and Beck-Gernsheim, 1995: 53–56).

Plaňava's understanding of intimate relationships tends to be normative. He advises prospective partners to ask themselves questions such as: 'Do I wish this lover of mine (who is attractive to me and with whom I share a lot of ideas, values and interests) to be a father of our child or children?' (Plaňava, 1998: 97) Although he recognizes the importance of mutual attraction and sharing of ideas and values within a couple, he is focused on lifelong commitment and creation of a conventional biological family. He talks about the 'normative cycle of a life together' (Plaňava, 1998: 79) and devotes a fifth of his book to explaining successive stages of marriage organized around childbearing (Plaňava, 1998: 104–46).[10] Within this framework, women are assigned the role of a primary caretaker and emotional binder of a family, while men's task is to navigate a family towards the outer world.

Even after children have 'left the nest,' Plaňava has nothing but disdain for people looking for new partners, thus effectively undermining his previous claim about two (serial) life partners:

> Both in work and non-work-related settings I meet these perennial youngsters of middle and advanced age. And it is striking that in their arduous fight against marital stereotype, they forever repeat the same, albeit with a different partner; only every time they leave more ruins behind. By that, I mean all these insecure seekers of eternal happiness who cannot sustain any human relationship after the delusional air of novelty wears off (Plaňava, 1998: 141).

For Plaňava, marriage has clearly not 'veered increasingly towards the form of a pure relationship' as Giddens (1992: 58) would have it.

With Plaňava's rather contradictory account of qualities classifiable as belonging to the pure relationship, it is not surprising that the instances of plastic sexuality in his writings tend to be similarly antagonistic. Eroticism and sex have changed greatly, Plaňava recognizes, sex is primarily for pleasure, not reproduction (Plaňava, 1998: 60). However, when comparing the situation of contemporary 20-year-olds with their counterparts from the 1970s, he states:

> Their problems and worries were of all kinds, often similar to the current ones. But one question of then young girls is seldom asked in the therapists' offices these days. I hope that in the minds of girls this question is not too rare: Should I sleep with him – or not yet? (Plaňava, 1998: 85)

Despite highlighting new sexual ethics, Plaňava cannot abandon the imperative of virgin purity for women. His contradictions are revealed when he discusses pre-marital sex: 'It seems, as research and statistics say, that people today have sex very often before marriage in couples that will be eventually married, *but even* in couples that *might perhaps break up*' (Plaňava, 1998: 95, emphasis added). He goes on to repeat his metaphor about normalcy and fall flu, and continues by reassuring that sex is, in 99.8 per cent of cases, performed for pleasure and people will probably be having more of it. 'And I only hope and wish that the feelings of guilt are diminishing. Which does not mean that everyone should sleep with everyone else, just like that' (Plaňava, 1998: 96). Plaňava's account of sexuality is riddled with inconsistencies. He champions what Giddens calls plastic sexuality while cautioning against casual sex.

What is interesting here is that Plaňava's account manifestly fits with Giddens' transformative agenda. The therapist stresses the character of love and intimacy transformed towards mutuality, affection and equality, characteristics typical of Giddens' romantic love. Plaňava's account of uncertainty, successive partnerships and sex primarily for pleasure meets the criteria for pure relationships as described by Giddens. However, the therapist's message about the malleability of intimacy is severely curtailed by his normative insistence on life-long commitment with the ultimate aim of bearing children in a biological family defined by strict gender divisions.

In Giddens' account, romantic love historically evolves into a pure relationship. The therapist's account, however, is ambivalent on this issue. Or more precisely, he acknowledges and even condones the qualities of pure relationship, only to contradict himself later by reasserting the normative narrative of intimacy confined to the boundary lines of procreative nuclear family.

Sexuality is plastic, gender is rigid

Unlike therapist and family counsellor Plaňava, sexologist Radim Uzel is unequivocally pro-sex. He perceives sexuality as good, pleasurable and 'immensely heterogeneous' (Uzel, 2000: 29). In this variability, he refuses to identify norms and pathologies, a drive that is typical of his discipline (see Weeks, 1985):

> No wonder it is archaic to set boundaries to sexuality. No one is infallible and artificially set moral norms could change within a couple of years into useless junk, and thus be ridiculous to future generations (Uzel, 2000: 25).

Uzel also refuses the majority principle for the assessment of normalcy because it is not tolerant of minorities 'without whose existence our sexuality would be deprived of individuality, similar to the carnal lives of bees or ants, dull and insipid' (Uzel, 2000: 26). The best definition of what is normal sexually is 'every activity that satisfies me, my partner and possibly other participants and does not cause any physical or mental harm to anyone' (Uzel, 2000: 27). Human relationships for Uzel are defined by both emotions and sexuality, understood as an infinitely pliable and consensual activity, thus corresponding to Giddens' concept of plastic sexuality.

Uzel appears to release sexuality from the confines of exclusively coupled and exclusively heterosexual activity, particularly stressing the pleasure women derive from sex.[11] While talking about women and orgasms, the sexologist advises that 'virtually any kind of titillation that is pleasurable for a woman and leads to sensual climax is normal and coupled sexual activity should accommodate to it. For that, complete openness is necessary' (Uzel, 2000: 98). However, not only did he not discuss men and orgasm, thus implying the uncomplicated nature of male climax, he continues his positive-sounding account of female orgasm in a paragraph opening with this sentence: 'Within this discussion of malfunctions of female sex life . . .' (Uzel, 2000: 98–9). This phrasing exposes a sexological inclination to perceive women as defective and essentially pathological (Jamieson, 1999; Bauer, 2008; Marcus, 2007; Irvine, 2005; Duggan, 2001; Bland and Doan, 1998; Sedgwick, 1990; Weeks, 1981 and 1985; Faderman, 1981).

Plastic sexuality is supposed to connote the democratization of intimate relationships, including changes in gender patterns towards greater equality. Changes in gender would be especially hard to find in Uzel's writings.[12] He perceives gender to be founded in biology and thus identifies allegedly different sexual strategies of men and women based in their differing sex cells (Uzel, 2000: 11, 51). Despite his previous sex-is-for-pleasure claims, here he conflates the sexual with the reproductive. When trying to answer the question 'why sex at all?', he quickly slips into naturalist discourses:

> This (sexual) part of our activity presents spice to our life. In short, sex is a pleasurable thing. Various scientists have always been getting their heads around the question of how sex could have originated, without being able to answer it unequivocally up to this day. The sexual act brings a male embryonic cell to fertilize a female egg (Uzel, 2000: 33).

From 'spice' and 'pleasure' in the first and second sentences, Uzel gets to procreation in the fourth sentence. Interestingly, the discursive bridge between the two is 'science'.

Naturalist discourses performs a double-step consisting of the socialization of nature, describing the life of animals in terms of social institutions, and naturalization of society.[13] Having shown that nature operates quite like humans, Uzel proceeds to suggest that, naturally, people's desires, sexuality and gender are best understood as part of nature. When talking about 'males and females', Uzel (2000: 95) holds a 'genuinely biological perspective on the categorization of humans as primates'; a perspective that appears to inform his conclusion that there exists an irreconcilable difference between men and women regarding sexuality:

> While for a man coitus occupies a high rank in his value orientation', a woman prefers rather an emotional relationship to her partner and the feeling of security that this union brings to her. This is a usual source of disputes and quarrels because not every man can understand female sexuality and vice versa (Uzel, 2000: 96).

Here, the naturalist discourses is complemented by 'Mars-and-Venus' rhetoric underscoring supposedly insurmountable differences between 'animals' from 'different planets'.

Uzel acknowledges social changes that would be compatible with Giddens' account of pure relationships, such as 'changes in the patriarchal character of family, the emancipation of women and their higher education, feminist movement' (Uzel, 2000: 30), only to contradict himself in a subsequent paragraph where he says: 'In all this ever-changing world, it is a prosperous family that remains the cornerstone of society' (Uzel, 2000: 30). His account of sexuality as plastic is compromised both by naturalism and by occasional endorsement of the conventional family.

Giddens' account expects a seamless causality between romantic love, pure relationships and plastic sexuality, all of which bring about deep changes in gender patterns. Plaňava acknowledges profound transformations of gender: women exhibit traditionally masculine characteristics, they can 'assert themselves, be tough, dominate, compete, not care about cleanliness but about their wellbeing' (Plaňava, 1998: 42), while men can be 'sensitive, adaptive, submissive' (Plaňava, 1998: 42). He perceives androgyny as an 'interesting vision of a not so distant future. This idea means the freedom of every individual to cultivate in themselves both masculine as well as feminine aspects of their personality and behaviour – disregarding what is traditionally considered male and female' (Plaňava, 1998: 44). However, a page earlier he rejects 'sameness, that is fading away of differences between men and women as completely as possible' (Plaňava, 1998:43). He deems it anachronistic to perceive women as the weaker sex[14] and men as (always) strong. Only several paragraphs later he negates himself:

> If God had the intention or natural selection the need for us to be the same, then we would be. Masculine and feminine gender would disappear, our grammar would be easier[15] and we would reproduce all alone by partition like protozoa (Plaňava, 1998: 39).

Gender difference is invoked in the name of procreation. It is reproductive capacity that in Plaňava's view preordains woman's gender fate.[16] In his account, gender follows rigidly from sex, perceived as given, anatomical and physiological. Anatomy is destiny, specifically for women. When Plaňava discusses sexuality in both men and women, he describes orgasm as follows: 'In men it is connected with a fast and sharp draining, that is something is going away from him – in women with filling, accepting' (Plaňava, 1998: 41). Gender is sexual and as such different and complementary, frozen into the universal polar opposites of yin and yang.

Discussion

Very little in the therapeutic texts I analysed suggests that 'the individuals who want to live together are (. . .) the legislators of their own way of life' (Beck and Beck-Gernsheim, 1995: 5) or that 'large areas of a person's life are no longer set by pre-existing patterns' (Giddens, 1992: 75). My analysis tends to support claims made by feminist theorists such as Lynn Jamieson (1999), Lisa Adkins

(2004) and Lois McNay (1999, 2000) that question the seamless concepts of reflexive self-transformation, especially as applied to gender. Contrary to the claims of Giddens and Beck, gender remains a more complex structure than the detraditionalization accounts would have it.

Giddens was criticized that his account feeds on and into therapeutic discourses (Jamieson, 1999). My findings reveal discrepancies within both psychotherapeutic and sexological narratives with regard to the central categories of Giddens's analysis, thus complicating the claim of an easy fit between Giddens and therapy.[17] Romantic love does not have to, as Giddens assumes, 'carve open a way to the formation of pure relationships' (Giddens, 1992: 58), at least not on the symbolic level of Czech therapeutic discourses.

Therapeutic accounts of contemporary love can coexist rather easily with the imperatives of normative heterosexuality and the gendered status quo. Authors focusing on Western discourses on heterosexual relationships stress the women's (expected and effected) rootedness in emotional labour (Hochschild, 2003; Jackson and Scott, 2004; Duncombe and Marsden, 1996; Langford, 1999) that reproduces their gender inequality. Paradoxically, the connection between women, romantic love and gender conservatism was noticed by Giddens himself.[18] In his Introduction to *The Transformation of Intimacy* Giddens writes:

> The ethos of romantic love has had a double impact upon women's situation. On the one hand it has helped to put women 'in their place' – the home. On the other hand, however, romantic love can be seen as an active, and radical, engagement with the 'maleness' of modern society (Giddens, 1992: 2).

Refining men and softening the edges of androcentric society is not only a weak weapon (as the weapon of the weak; Bourdieu, 2001), it is also imposing responsibility for the oppressive state of things on the shoulders of the dominated. However, as I argued, there is no necessary symbolic connection between romantic love and pure relationship. Thus the androcentric character of modern society can easily stay untouched and the matters can remain as in Giddens's 'one hand', that is to say, women staying 'in their place'.

Emotionality is almost exclusively ascribed to women in therapeutic discourses – women are responsible for the emotional well-being of the nuclear familial unit and their sexuality is expressed and experienced as emotional. This is in contrast, and complementary to, men. Gender difference is thus presented as complementarity between men and women. It is the same complementarity that is intrinsic to the notion of romantic love, here underscored by procreative and naturalistic tones. Whereas Giddens observes the trend towards 'the decline of perversion' (Giddens, 1992: 32–34) and argues that it has brought about sexual diversity, I would argue that the shift in focus away from perversion does not necessarily mean appreciation of sexual variety. In the therapeutic texts I analysed, heterosexuality with reproduction as its focal point continues to occupy the centre and reinstate the norm.

The theory of heightened reflexivity builds on a notion of symbolic ambivalence presenting a plethora of possible subject positions, thus supposedly leading to unprecedented reflexive self-awareness. In therapeutic discourses, gender positions are not uniform or simply conventional. The structure of the therapeutic narrative moves in waves from acknowledging and endorsing changes in intimate relations (so highlighted and praised by the theorists of transformative reflexivity), to questioning new patterns and discrediting arrangements of intimacy and gender that are deemed not 'normal' and 'natural.'

The ambivalence and instability does not unequivocally yield transformation and change. The manifestly detraditionalized rhetoric of therapeutic discourses has not undermined the dominant view of a 'couple' as a heterosexual reproductively oriented unit, or of 'sex' as an activity shaped by the forces of nature. Instead, its rather confounded utterances about intimacy and gender are biased towards upholding the status quo. Challenging some but reasserting most gender and sexual stereotypes, therapeutic discourses unwittingly lapses into reproducing the gender binary.

Therapeutic discourses seems to be rather a powerful tool in forming and naturalizing heteronormative coupledom. Social agents cannot be unstructured by prevailing discourses of love. The expert discourses of the personal are highly political and as such circumscribe the re-imagining of social reality. Therapeutic discourses yields symbolic violence that re-establishes the boundaries not only of what can and cannot be thought (Foucault, 1972) but more specifically what is and is not socially intelligible (Butler, 1997b).

While critics of heightened reflexivity theories point to the deeply embedded structures of habitus (Adkins, 2003; Skeggs, 2004; McNay, 1999 and 2000), I have stressed instead the operations of symbolic violence as an avenue for understanding how gender is deployed (and embodied). In so doing I have adopted the perspective of comprehending therapeutic discourses as a performative speech act yielding symbolic violence. As a form of symbolic power, expert discourses on intimacy bestow intelligibility and social recognition upon subjects, making them invested in embracing the law.[19]

Bourdieu asserts that it is by definition impossible to break through symbolic violence, for it structures one's very self. Perlocutives uttered from the authoritative position of expert discourses co-constitute and structure our collective imagery. What is expressed through therapeutic discourses which endorse some forms of conduct, decision-making and patterns of intimacy while deprecating or disregarding others is not insignificant. In Bourdieu's words, 'symbolic power does not reside in 'symbolic systems' in the form of an 'illocutionary force'' (Bourdieu, 1991: 170) but emanates from 'the field in which *belief* is produced and reproduced' (Bourdieu, 1991: 170, emphasis in original). The power of words is a function of 'belief in the legitimacy of words and those who utter them' (Bourdieu, 1991: 170). In this sense, expert discourses enjoy a great deal of legitimacy and thus power.

However, it is this very perlocutive character of therapeutic discourses that, structurally, allows for displacement. In this sense, understanding symbolic violence in terms of performatives can help us move away from the overly static account of social structure for which Bourdieu's theory has been criticized. Butler (1999) claims that Bourdieu freezes the social in its status quo by limiting the function of performatives to the extent to which they derive from existing authority. In other words, Bourdieu conflates the 'authority to speak' with 'speaking with authority.' Thus, Bourdieu operates within a fixed environment where authority escapes questioning and social agents remain subjected to what Butler calls 'social magic,' a situation in which authority is collectively recognized and accepted.

I would argue, however, that Bourdieu accounts for a predominant motion within societies, and that is the motion toward social reproduction. As we have seen with the two therapeutic discourses examined in this paper, perlocutionary performatives disproportionately tend towards upholding the norm and reproducing the gendered status quo. Despite their lack of uniformity, therapeutic utterances incline towards underscoring heteronormativity. Central to the structure of contemporary societies, expert discourses, and particularly their therapeutic rendition, have a tendency to endorse the social structure in its contemporary form.

Contrary to Bourdieu's accent on authority propelling social reproduction, Butler stresses the 'expropriability' of authorized discourses. Where Bourdieu limits the notion of performative speech acts to 'official state speech and official discourses in general' (Butler, 1999: 120), Butler suggests focusing on the emergence of authoritative discourses from de-authorized places. While this is certainly one avenue accounting for social change, I would stress that there is structural potential for alteration *within* the functioning of perlocutionary performatives themselves.

Performatives can fail to achieve what they intend.[20] Perlocutionary performatives, the model on which I have examined the effects of expert discourses, require a reaction on the part of social agents. And the concordant reaction does not have to arrive. Or at least the reaction does not have to be reflexive in the Giddensian sense. To account for change only or predominantly through reflexivity would overemphasize the reflexive level of everyday social action or its transformative potential, and more importantly, exclude any non-reflexive, performative action.

The fissures between perlocutive speech acts and responses to them create a space for agency and for the transformation of gender order. Similarly, incorporated structures of social actors are not simple copies of objective structures forming the social order. Neither performative action nor incorporated structures line up smoothly with perlocutives, or objective structures respectively. However, we cannot perceive social actors as the sovereign agents of their lives, 'norms and morality as varying from individual to individual and from relationship to relationship' (Beck and Beck-Gernsheim, 1995: 5) or optimistically disregard the political nature of discourses organising intimacy (Giddens, 1992). Sociological theory which rests on these assumptions would appear to be unreflective of the prevailing heteronormative organization of the symbolic universe, as expressed, among other places, in therapeutic discourses.

Kateřina Lišková

Notes

1 This paper was originally presented at the Sociological Review 100th Annual Conference in Stratford upon Avon in June 2009 as a paper entitled *Love as the Political: Imagining Connections between Past, Present and Future.*

2 The first book, entitled in an intentionally contradictory fashion *Together Everyone by Themselves. In Marriage and Family (Spolu každý sám. V manželství a rodině,* 1998), was written by an influential therapist, psychologist and university professor, a founder of the Czechoslovak marital and partner therapy movement, Ivo Plaňava. The second book, entitled *Sexual Menagerie (Sexuální zvěřinec,* 2000), was written by the popular Czech sexologist Radim Uzel. Both authors are trusted experts in their disciplines and their views are widely accepted.

3 Judith Butler pointed out the essential significance of Austin's prominent example of performatives, his so often stressed nuptial 'I do', to the heteronormative layout of our societies (Butler, 1997b).

4 Only in passing was Austin able to hint at social embeddedness of language and speech acts in particular: 'Strictly speaking, there cannot be an illocutionary act unless the means employed are conventional (. . .). But it is difficult to say where conventions begin and end' (Austin, 1962: 119). To the detriment of his theory of language, he did not follow up on this 'complication.'

5 These changes, according to Plaňava, carry democratization as well as increased egoism. Plaňava sees the shift in value orientation towards hedonism: 'So: the important and widespread value orientation of today has become: to have, to have some more, and enjoy' (Plaňava, 1998: 70).

6 Transformed expectations of coupledom are encapsuled in the following: 'From marriage, and especially from the other, we expect most of all constant fulfillment and satisfaction of personal needs: we want to be happy, satisfied, loved, to have an oasis of unproblematic well-being at home' (Plaňava, 1998: 71).

7 Transformation of intimacy, in a very Giddensian fashion, is depicted in Plaňava's observation: 'Today, we enter marriage or cohabitation usually based on mutual affection, attraction and love – love we called amorous' (Plaňava, 1998: 70).

8 Transformation in sexuality includes 'the so called sexual-erotic ethics, that is what is considered to be right or at least acceptable' (Plaňava, 1998: 73).

9 Other instances support my claim about paradigmatic 'romantic love' in Plaňava's writing. Love according to him can happen between 'people of equal status, because only then one can satisfy each other's needs' (Plaňava, 1998: 100). His descriptions of individuals in love involve their self-interrogation (how do I feel about the other?), perception of intimacy as incompatible with lust (see Giddens, 1992: 44–5) and destructive *amour passion,* shift from patriarchal authority towards maternal affection, etc. (Plaňava, 1998: 67–79).

10 Plaňava explains the characteristic of the first stage as follows: 'Generally speaking, to create a new viable unit out of two individuals, and to prepare an environment (. . .) for the reproduction of humankind' (Plaňava, 1998: 105).

11 He writes about masturbation and non-coital sex as forms not only equal to classical intercourse but for many even more preferable. In this respect, he writes about women for whom non-coital sex might be more pleasurable and who can thus become more involved and not be ashamed of sex. In this manner, Uzel refuses the term 'foreplay' for non-coital activities because it presumes that there is some 'play', some real thing to follow (Uzel, 2000: 22).

12 More about Uzel on gender and sexuality in Lišková, 2009.

13 Uzel thus talks about the 'family relations of mites' (Uzel, 2000: 60), 'courtship of higher animals that is similar to that of humans' (Uzel, 2000: 64), 'orgasmic facial expressions' in macaques (Uzel, 2000: 80), 'monogamy or promiscuity' in primates (Uzel, 2000: 80), etc. His sociobiological explanations of gender identify 'typical female traits' in seeking rich and powerful men and the complementary male preference for young, healthy and beautiful women is 'given by the rules of natural and genetic selection' (Uzel, 2000: 11). Masculine protectiveness of women is triggered

by feminine resemblance to children that is analogous to the childish features of some favourite animals such as Pekinese dogs or koala bears (Uzel, 2000: 101).

14 Interestingly, he refuses to perceive women as the 'more tender, vulnerable *or even more oppressed sex*' (Plaňava, 1998: 38, emphasis added). Many feminists have shown how misguided it is to ground feminist politics in feminine vulnerability (Snitow, 1983; Brown, 1995). It is ill-conceived, though, as Plaňava suggests, to argue that women are not vulnerable, *and thus* are not oppressed.

15 Czech grammar is gender-specific.

16 He writes: 'Every parent soon notices that his progeny come to this world equipped as either a future man or woman. Anatomical uncertainties are rare. That to a certain extent predetermines what is expected of this progeny. At least, if it is of feminine gender and if everything goes as it should, she will give birth to a new individual, so that we do not die out' (Plaňava, 1998: 41).

17 However, I am in agreement with most of Jamieson's criticisms of Giddens.

18 However, to the detriment of his analysis, he did not engage this thought further.

19 Judith Butler highlights the interconnectedness of social intelligibility, recognition and embodying the law in her *Psychic Life of Power* (1997a). Butler refuses to see power as an external force or as something merely internalized; in her view 'one's very formation as a subject, is dependent upon that very power'. Her argument here resembles that of Bourdieu (1991), despite the disagreements Butler voiced with Bourdieu's analysis (see Butler, 1999).

20 The work of Austin himself reads at times like a list of failed performatives.

References

Adams, M., (2006) 'Hybridizing Habitus and Reflexivity: Towards an Understanding of Contemporary Identity?' *Sociology*, 40(3): 511–28.

Adkins, L. and B. Skeggs, (eds), (2004). *Feminism after Bourdieu*, Oxford: Blackwell Publishing.

Adkins, L., (2004). 'Reflexivity: Freedom or habit of gender?' *Sociological Review*, 52(2): 191–210.

Austin, J.L., (1962), *How to Do Things With Words*, Cambridge: Harvard University Press.

Bauer, H., (2008), 'Theorizing Female Inversion: Sexology, Discipline, and Gender at the Fin de Siècle', *Journal of the History of Sexuality*, 18(1): 84–102.

Beck, U. and E. Beck-Gernsheim, (1995), *The Normal Chaos of Love*, Cambridge: Polity.

Beck, U., (1992), *Risk Society: Towards a New Modernity*, London: Sage Publications.

Bland, L. and L. L. Doan, (1998), *Sexology in culture: labelling bodies and desires*, Chicago: The University of Chicago Press.

Bourdieu, P., (1991), *Language and Symbolic Power*, Cambridge: Polity Press.

Bourdieu, P., (2000), *Pascalian Meditations*, Stanford: Stanford University Press.

Bourdieu. P., (2001), *Masculine Domination*. Cambridge: Polity Press.

Brown, W., (1995), *States of Injury. Power and Freedom in Late Modernity*, Princeton: Princeton University Press.

Butler, J., (1997a), *The Psychic Life of Power: Theories in Subjection*, Stanford: Stanford University Press.

Butler, J., (1997b), *Excitable Speech: A Politics of the Performative*, London: Routledge.

Butler, J., (1999), 'Performativity's Social Magic' in Shusterman, R., (ed.), *Bourdieu: A Critical Reader*, Oxford: Blackwell.

Duggan, L., (2001), *Sapphic Slashers: Sex, Violence, and American Modernity*, Durham, NC: Duke University Press.

Duncombe, J. and D. Marsden, (1996), 'Whose Orgasm is it Anyway? "Sex Work" in long-term couple relationships', in Weeks, J. and J. Holland, (eds), *Sexual Cultures*. London: Macmillan.

Ehrenreich, B. and A. Hochschild (eds) (2004), *Global Woman: Nannies, Maids, and Sex Workers in the New Economy*, Metropolitan Books.

Evans, M., (2003), *Love: An Unromantic Discussion,* Cambridge: Polity.

Faderman, L., (1981), *Surpassing the Love of Men: Romantic Friendship and Love between Women from the Renaissance to the Present,* London: Junction.

Foucault, M., (1972), *The Archaeology of Knowledge,* New York: Pantheon Books.

Fowler, B., (eds), (2000), *Reading Bourdieu on Society and Culture,* Oxford: Blackwell Publishers/ The Sociological Review.

Giddens, A., (1992), *The Transformation of Intimacy: Sex, Love and Eroticism in Modern Societies,* Cambridge: Polity.

Hochschild, A., (2003), *The Commercialization of Intimate life: notes from home and work,* Berkeley: University of California Press.

Irvine, J.M., (2005), *Disorders of desire: sexuality and gender in modern American sexology,* Philadelphia: PA, Temple University Press.

Jackson, S. and S. Scott, (2004), 'Sexual Antinomies in Late Modernity', *Sexualities,* 7(2): 233–48.

Jamieson, L., (1999), 'Intimacy Transformed?' A Critical Look at the 'Pure Relationship', *Sociology,* 33 (3): 477–94.

Jenkins, R., (2002), *Pierre Bourdieu,* London and New York: Routledge.

Langford, W., (1999), *Revolutions of the Heart,* London: Routledge.

Lišková, K., (2009), 'Defining Pornography, Defining Gender: Sexual Citizenship in the Discourses of Czech Sexology and Criminology', in Oleksy, E.H. (ed.), *Gender and Intimate Citizenships: Politics, Sexualities, and Subjectivity,* New York: Routledge.

Lovell, T., (2000), 'Thinking feminism with or against Bourdieu', in Fowler, B., (ed.), *Reading Bourdieu on Society and Culture.* Oxford: Blackwell Publishers/The Sociological Review.

Marcus, S., (2007), *Between Women: Friendship, Desire and Marriage in Victorian England,* Princeton, N.J.: Princeton University Press.

McNay, L., (1999), 'Gender, Habitus and the Field: Pierre Bourdieu and the Limits of Reflexivity', *Theory, Culture and Society,* 16(1): 175–93.

McNay, L., (2000), *Gender and agency: Reconfiguring the subject in feminist and social theory,* Cambridge, UK: Polity Press.

Plaňava, I., (1998), *Spolu každý sám. V manželství a rodině,* Praha: Nakladatelství Lidové noviny.

Sedgwick, E.K., (1990), *Epistemology of the Closet,* Berkeley: University of California Press.

Skeggs, B., (2004), 'Context and Background: Pierre Bourdieu's analysis of class, gender and sexuality' in Adkins, L. and B. Skeggs, (eds), *Feminism after Bourdieu,* Oxford: Blackwell Publishing.

Snitow, A., (1983), 'Mass Market Romance: Pornography for Women is Different', in Snitow, A., (ed.), *Powers of Desire. The Politics of Sexuality.* New York: Monthly Review Press.

Sweetman, P., (2003), 'Twenty-first century dis-ease? Habitual reflexivity or the reflexive habitus', *The Sociological Review,* 51(4): 528–49.

Uzel, R., (2000), *Sexuální zvěřinec,* Praha: Ikar.

Weeks, J., (1985), *Sexuality and Its Discontents. Meanings, Myths and Modern Sexualities,* London and New York: Routledge and Kegan Paul.

Weeks, J., (1981), *Sex, Politics and society: the regulations of sexuality since 1880,* London and New York: Longman.

Embracing dependency: rethinking (in)dependence in the discourse of care

Bernhard Weicht

Abstract: This article analyses and challenges the categories of dependency and independence as they feature in discourses on care for older people in two countries, Austria and the UK. Using critical discourse analysis of newspaper extracts and transcripts of focus group discussions, I demonstrate how independence and self-sufficiency are constructed as ideals for human existence. Being dependent, on the other hand, is seen as the expression of an inferior state of life. Three possible challenges to the ideal of independence in the literature on care are then discussed. The paper shows how, through their focus on empowerment, mutuality and reciprocity, they each reproduce aspects of dependency as anathema to contemporary ideas of personhood, to fall short of a fruitful critical intervention into orthodox discourses on older people and care. In contrast, this article argues for embracing a notion of dependency built upon new conceptualizations of the body, of relating and of the conditions of a good life.

Introduction

> The myths and the clichés put out by bourgeois thought aim at holding up the elderly man as someone who is different, as another being (de Beauvoir, 1972: 3)

In an article in the *Guardian* on the laws on assisted suicide, Polly Toynbee (2009: 31) mentions beside other motivations 'the loss of independence and becoming a burden to others' as 'a valid part of the reason why someone feels life has become undignified and past bearing'. From an individual's perspective it is completely understandable to evaluate and reconsider one's own life and the possibility of assisted dying. However, the discursive theme which links the wish to die to 'the loss of independence' and 'becoming a burden' bears important consequences for society in general, and older people and the need for care in particular.

Independence – constructed as an ideal – is penetrating all levels of modern society (e.g. within families or in relation to the welfare state). Commensurately,

Bernhard Weicht

becoming dependent is associated with being a burden on others; and is thus feared and rejected. Discourses on care for older people have particular difficulty in moving beyond the utopic thrall of independence. Critically, within such discourse, independence functions as an ideal representing what is considered as a good life (Harrefors *et al.*, 2009). Specifically, the goal of intervention into the lives of older people (through public policies or delivery of care) is to enhance the older person's independence (Harlton *et al.*, 1998) and enable 'independent life styles' (López and Domènech, 2009).

But what does independence mean? And how can its prominence as an ideal for our existence be explained? Is there a possibility of challenging the persistence of this ideal? The literature on care recognizes the importance of ethical considerations (Skoe, 1995; Karniol *et al.*, 2003) and the experience of care itself (Twigg, 2000, 1997) for the understanding of the meaning of being in need of help. Gender identities and family relations are also seen as the basis of how people in care settings define their own situation (Ungerson, 1987; 2000; Guberman *et al.*, 1992). In each of these accounts, ideologies, ideas and attitudes about care play an important role in defining the situation and people's understanding of giving and receiving care. Specifically, notions of caring change over time (Jamieson, 1998) and Bowlby *et al.* (2010: 15) rightly state that:

> [the] ways in which we experience care reflects our age, gender, ethnicity, health and social status, and will be influenced by our beliefs and values about families and relationships, and hence by where and when we live.

What is important here is to draw attention to the political implications that are often masked by focusing on social and cultural factors. Hughes *et al.* (2005), for example, emphasize care's meaning as both an activity and a culture in order to explain the feminized status and the subordination of carers. A similar argument is presented by Winch (2006: 6–7) who focuses on 'an interplay of political structures and ethical attitudes and practices' based on a carer discourse and a 'morality of caring' (see also Paoletti, 2002). These studies imply that practices and experiences of care need to be understood as 'effects': enactments of broader discursively arranged conceptualizations of care; and of what being old and in need of care means.

This article moves beyond the acknowledgement and recognition of the role of the social and cultural construction of care in constituting and reproducing clearly defined identities and separations, important though this is. Rather, I emphasize the existence of underlying dichotomies and divisions, and assess how the political relevance of these dichotomies remains largely unchallenged. Specifically, the dichotomy of dependence and independence lies at the roots of a public construction of care, leading to an *othering* of older persons and a totalizing of people's identities.

The question of how independence has been established as such a powerful ideal and a dominant paradigm of current care and welfare state arrangements (Mittelstadt, 2001) where control, choice and self-governance are penetrating discussions of more and more fields of social life and social policy (Power, 2008;

Glendinning, 2008) deserves greater attention. Independence as an ideal and principle has a long history in philosophy (Held, 1990), economics and policy making but also in everyday public discourses. Fraser and Gordon (1994) show that the concept of dependency has changed from an economic classification to a moral/psychological category according to ideological and political demands, meaning that those being dependent on others are constructed as morally inferior to the idealized independent person. Especially during the Enlightenment the values of independence and rationality have led to an idealization of the white, male, middle-aged, able-bodied autonomous subject as the quintessential social actor (Watson *et al.*, 2004; Shakespeare, 2000; Chantler, 2006). One site in which to examine how the dominance of independence is produced and reproduced is in popular and professional discourse on care and older people.

Even though Fink (2004: 15) highlights that 'the delivery and receipt of care (. . .) is a dynamic process in which the lives of both parties are woven together, disrupting any simplistic division between dependence and independence', an analysis of the discourses on care demonstrates the persistence of such general distinctions between the dependent recipient of care and the independent carer. In other words, even though personal experiences might suggest otherwise, societal attitudes hold on to a problematic, simplifying and exclusionary construction of care, that of being old and needing help. Through categories and dichotomies, participants in care relationships are constructed as 'other to the masculine subject of modernity' (Hughes *et al.*, 2005: 265).

In order to identify the processes of the creation of the ideal of independence I analyse discourses on care for older people. I will demonstrate the persistence of this fundamental dichotomy by looking at various sites in which dependency and the ideal of independence are negotiated. I will then ask whether and how this dichotomy and idealization can be challenged. Three perspectives will be evaluated which try to contest specific aspects of the dichotomy; all three however still maintain the notion of a dichotomous understanding of care and what it means to be human. The main aim of this article is to depict the ideological fear of dependency and to suggest embracing dependence as a foundation of personhood (Dean, 2004). It will be shown that independence as an ideal can only be challenged in all its interlinked nuances (from the imperative of physical and mental capabilities to the conception of old age as a dependent stage in life) by embracing dependency. There is a critical politics here: the way dependency is constructed in theory strongly impacts on the political possibilities for intervention. At the same time the political importance of independence influences the articulation of how we understand the discourses on old age and older people.

Methodological remarks

This article emerged from a study of the discursive construction of elderly care, carried out in two countries, Austria and the UK. Discourse here is understood as the way people construct and make sense of their everyday lives and experiences, 'in a specific setting determined by social rules, norms and conventions' (Wodak, 2008: 5). To identify dominant discourses, I utilize critical discourse analysis to analyse relevant texts in their particular historical, cultural, political and material context (Reisigl and Wodak, 2001), starting with samples of British and Austrian newspapers. In order to generate an exemplifying but nevertheless representative sample aimed at reflecting the political and class spectrum, the selection was composed of the most popular newspapers (Reisigl and Wodak, 2001; Bednarek, 2006), and included a combination of 'tabloids' and 'broadsheets', ranging from what are considered to be working-class and rather sensationalist papers, through middle range papers to quality newspapers, and from conservative to liberal papers. Specifically, the sample consisted of six British (*The Sun, Daily Mirror, Daily Mail, The Guardian, The Times, Daily Telegraph*) and four Austrian newspapers (*Kronenzeitung, Kurier, Die Presse, Der Standard*), which were analysed over a period of one year (August 2006–August 2007). In a pilot study, covering July–August 2006, I familiarized myself with the field and constructed preliminary categories for the analysis. The second step was a text search enabling the identification of a vast range of articles on care from which I extracted recurring themes, narratives, terms and concepts. In a third step I focused on relevant 'typical' texts in their original settings. For this endeavour I used the newspaper archives of the Austrian National Library in Vienna and the British Library in London. The texts studied in detail were then always related back to the whole sample of articles referring to care.

Following Richardson (2007), I started with the micro-textual level (the use, choice and meaning of certain words and sentences) followed by a mid-level analysis (the speakers' / writers' attitudes, judgements and evaluations). The last step consisted of an evaluation of the narratives and plots being used to tell a story, to report news or to construct a commentary. The categories and narratives identified in the newspapers, together with materials such as pictures or statements, were then used in ten focus group discussions which are, as Bloor *et al.* (2001) put it, the ideal method for identifying *group* norms and understandings. Krzyżanowski (2008: 169) emphasizes focus groups' potential to analyse how 'the public sphere influences . . . individuals' views . . . and how, conversely, the ideas crucial to the 'social' (individual) level penetrate . . . into . . . the public sphere'. I worked with both pre-existing groups and groups of people unknown to one another. The participants were recruited through local organizations, clubs, church groups, political parties and informal networks. The focus groups consisted of three to seven participants and lasted up to two hours and allowed for both group discussion and personal accounts to emerge. The focus groups took place in various public and private venues in the UK and Austria. A widespread representation of participants was achieved in terms of gender, age, socio-economic background and their history of care or caring commitments.

The main aim of the analysis was to identify which narratives people use to describe care and ageing. Who are the subjects and in which kinds of stories? I was interested in the construction of categories, such as 'carer', 'elderly', 'dependent', 'independent', and in how these categories are being used. The discursive accounts below are representative of the discourses in question. As can be expected people usually refer to their own experiences when talking about care; the categories and narratives they use, however, represent broader societal features. People draw on a discursively constituted moral, ideological, cultural and social understanding of what it means to live a good life. Through public discourse this consensus is shaped and continuously reproduced, impacting on how people make sense of ageing and care. In the next section I present analysis of how independence and dependence are constituted by discourses on care.

The ideal of independence

In discourses on care the construction of the ideal of independence is constituted in three different, interrelated ways. First, care is established as a dichotomy between the young, active, independent actor and the old, passive, dependent non-actor. Secondly, the older body is identified as the manifestation and representation of what it means to be dependent. Thirdly, the dependent person is constructed as the general and totalized other, which in turn fosters an understanding of the self as independent. Fourthly, the othering has consequences for how people imagine being cared for and is expressed as anxiety over becoming a burden on others.

Dichotomy

The literature on care has identified how dominant dichotomies, such as emotional relating-professional work, formal-informal, public-private or state-society (Fine, 2005; Fine and Glendinning, 2005), underpin and define understandings of care. Because of its correlation with contemporary definitions of what independence means to be human, the embedding of the dichotomy of dependence and independence in discourses of care is of equal, or, perhaps, even greater significance. Clearly the framing of social phenomena as dichotomies is based on social and cultural constructions, but they gain meaning from their dominance in public discourses (Fine and Glendinning, 2005). How care is talked about mobilizes a dichotomy of independent and dependent actor(s), with one person being active in the process and another being passive and dependent on the former.

Care is often seen as the logical reaction to dependency. For example, Eva Kittay starts her highly influential book *Love's Labor* with the sentence: 'Dependence requires care' (1999: 1). Alternatively, Lloyd (2004: 247) describes care as taking 'into account the needs and rights of those too young or too old to be the active 'independent' adult citizen'. Both accounts represent the general understanding of care as being based on a dichotomy of 'polar opposites' of dependence and independence (Chantler, 2006). If there is care there needs to be someone who is dependent on someone else. A dichotomy is created in which older people are portrayed as passive, totally dependent non-actors who are in need of care and whose life is determined by others. Dependency, once essentialized in this way, becomes associated with an indecent, undesirable way of being in the world. In fact, as agency-less, infantile and burdensome, older persons in need of care are being figured as the antithesis of the good citizen.

Dependency is hence constructed as the *other* way of existence, one which is prefigured already as undesirable, feared and rejected. In this sense, the passive older person is made into *the Other* – against which their own life circumstances are judged, as also exemplified in my research by Paul's[1] statement:

> Paul: She was in [care home] for seven years, and she has hardly recognized her daughter then. And is, so to say, kept alive by law (. . .) That really wasn't a life in the sense, how we imagine it, or, how we, or what we understand by it.

Interestingly, when people reflect on their future old age, further divisions come into play. In Will's statement below, for instance, there is a clear creation of a binary between *us* and *them*; where the *us* is defined by choice, decision-making and active involvement, and the *them* is represented by passivity and dependency:

> Will: I mean, fortunately (. . .) we will be able to do that, and I thank God, I have been given that choice, because I've had a good life and it's given me (. . .). The people we are really talking about are those that can't help themselves. And (. . .) have lost out on life, for whatever reason, some have not bothered (. . .) and you say, well, they don't deserve it, but you still gotta look after them.

It must be noted that the clear dichotomy of (independent) actor and (dependent) non-actor reflects ideological constructions rather than subjectively experienced situations.

The dichotomy of dependence and independence is deeply embedded in people's understanding of care. As such personal relations may bridge the dichotomy on a subjective level; they do not, however, challenge the societal meaning of care.

The body as a signifier

The dichotomy of dependence and independence is played out in various aspects of how care is imagined. The care home, for example, is a material manifestation of dependency (Andrews and Phillips, 2005; Milligan, 2003) and the (old, vulnerable) body is the physical expression of dependency, both representing the absence of individual choice and autonomy. Ingrid's comment below illustrates how the care home is both symbol and manifestation of dependency and loss of personhood:

> Ingrid: That's the bad thing, I think. In the home they not only take their (. . .) individuality, they also take their dignity.

In addition, people's stories of care homes often circulate images of cold, smelly and dirty places in ways that reinforce dependency as the antithesis of a desirable state of being. For instance, John's statement captures the associations that many people share:

> *John: And then slowly, you start getting a picture. . . I suppose if I go into a care home and (. . .) if I smell, unfortunately can't but say urine – that immediately puts me off.*

The young, healthy body (and mind) is linked to decent (active) behaviour and the older body is linked to vulnerability signifying dependency. The ill and/or vulnerable body is more than just a body, it is a signifier of the other and thus, in consequence, a signifier of the self (White, 2009). The old person's body represents what one is not; it signifies the *improper* way to live, to exist and to appear.

Breaks in narratives of the body (cf. Munro and Belova, 2009) threaten the ontological security, which O'Neill (2009) describes as *ur*-trust. Changes in bodily features are therefore associated with changes in one's personality and one's self. Rudge (2009) for example demonstrates how patients with burns signify human vulnerability, reminding us of our frailty and mortality, destabilizing our sense of security. Mitteness and Barker's (1995) work reveals how incontinence is related to frailty, disintegration and a loss of moral and social competence, arguing that the emphasis placed upon self-reliance and self-control leads to a situation in which incontinence is seen as incompatible with adulthood.

Bodily 'failures' challenge the image of the proper person functioning in society. A loss of bodily strength and health coincides with and is symbolized by 'loss of activity, productivity, rationality, and self-determination' (Latimer, 1999: 204). As a second factor, bodies are linked to the value of a person for and in society (Shilling, 1993). Old age and related vulnerabilities bring decline in the symbolic value of the body. This means that vulnerability and disability are seen as individual pathology based on a medicalization of everyday life and of society (Oliver, 1990). The normativity of a healthy body and a good life, however, influence all people, whether young or old. The stigma of the not-healthy body reinforces the general normativity of 'vitalism' (Greco, 2009), in which dependency and vulnerability challenge the social norms of a good life.

Without doubt the body represents both physical reality and socially constructed connotations at the same time (Grenier and Hanley, 2007) and these associations are intrinsically related to self and identity. The old, vulnerable body is described in the discourses as signifying an *other* identity, an *other* self than one's own, the 'tragedy' being the idea that one's former self is gone.

Othering

Choices and decisions taken by oneself are often presented in opposition to an image of old age, in which older people are dependent, passive, infantilized and vulnerable to abuse and neglect. The following newspaper extract reproduces the idea of old age as being closely related to dependency and shows a distancing of the self against this *other*:

> It wasn't just the sociable nature of the enterprise that appealed [of moving into a home together]. It was the thought that we were going to be one bunch of oldies in charge of our destiny. We will choose everything from menu to morphine and thumb our nose at the cruel convention that the elderly are to be treated like children. We will show the curious visitors that you can be in your sunset years and still be interested in the news or in seeing a good play (*The Observer*, 9 Sep 2007).

This extract refers to the different features that are persistently associated with being old, adding emphasis through contrasting these associations with an image of self-determination and control. Due to a social construction of certain bodily characteristics people are infantilized, disempowered and degraded in public social, cultural and political discourses (Bowlby *et al.*, 2010; Hughes *et al.*, 2005; see also Sennett, 2003). Hockey and James (2003) point out that certain periods in the life course are seen as metaphors for stages of dependence/ independence (for a similar argument see Dean and Rogers, 2004). While Shakespeare identifies a construction of a 'polarity between dependent, vulnerable, innocent, asexual children and competent, powerful, sexual, adult citizens' (2000: 15), older people in need of care are associated with children, even infants. The following focus group extract exemplifies this:

> Barbara: And on the other hand, somebody has given me this recommendation (. . .) that you can indeed also scold the ill person a bit, and also the person in need of care (. . .) and not having to always do everything for them, and having to give in. Because they forget it, that you have told them off, this they forget again anyways, but somewhere, something remains with them, that it isn't entirely fine, what they're doing (. . .) So you can really once, of course not all the time, but you can really once also have a strict word with them.

> Vanessa: And they, I think, like small children, test the boundaries.

Infantilization and othering (Oakley, 2007) are underpinned by the dichotomy between dependence and independence. Bobbio in his description of what it means to be old argues that old age marks an end, a final stage, and is 'mainly depicted as decadence and degeneration: the downward curve of an individual' (2001: 24). In the discourses of care that I have analysed this feeling of old age as an end is very prominent. Old age is very easily equated with dependency (Plath, 2008) and old people are seen as passive victims of life who ought to be grateful for being looked after, as the following quote also illustrates:

> Helma: Because I really believe (. . .) and I also know old people, who are like that, adorable, quiet, grateful, not that they are now dismissive (. . .) but, dignified grateful, yes, that you like to have them with you, and that you like to be there for them (. . .) Now, (. . .) the whole caring would be much easier, because they, yeah, they simply would also be there.

De Beauvoir (1972: 4) concludes that older people are imagined as different due to public associations: 'either by their virtue or by their degradation they stand outside humanity'. Differences in degrees of dependency (see Shakespeare, 2000; Oliver, 1990) are not recognized in discourses on elderly care. Rather, the identity of being the other, i.e. the dependent person, is essentialized. The dichotomy created between the dependent older person and the independent active, agentic individual enables a reaffirmation of all that is most valued. The Other is used, by way of comparison (cf Strathern, 1997), to define what a reasonable life is; the Other is used to define one's own independence.

Imagining one's dependency – being a burden

Some participants expressed extreme anxiety about becoming this dependent, helpless Other, as someone in need of care. Euthanasia is frequently discussed in this context as the idea that needing care cannot be combined with a dignified life.

> *Andy: So, I have in that sense thought about it . . . that I say, right, I don't want to get that old. If it doesn't go anymore, then away, away, away. And there, I think, I'm agreeing with my mother. She also ran until the last moment. And then, when it got critical, she gave up. Then she died within 2 days . . . So, of care, she was horrified, that she will be in need of care, that she would be dependent on other people. And I do understand that very well. I don't want that either. Then, I rather want to go before that . . . So, care, no, then I'd really like to go.*

People express their unwillingness to live a life of *being a burden* and effectively of being dependent on others. This leads to a wish to die healthily without needing any care (*Neil: My prayer is that I keep healthy, till the day I die . . . And I never need looking after*) but also includes a discourse in which euthanasia is repeatedly thought and talked about (see also Traphagan, 2004). Ingrid for example declares that she would consider ending her life in response to a discussion on the possibilities of being in a care home:

> *Ingrid: If I'm able to do it, to understand my situation, and I can't see a way out, then I would make use of my right, to determine the point of my death.*

The important political and societal discursive intervention of recognizing the work of carers has sometimes led to an emphasis on the idea of care as burden in ways that reinforce and institute the negative connotations of dependency. As a consequence the discourses show that while people value caring, and even express their willingness to care for their relatives, friends or neighbours, they themselves do not want to be cared for by anyone close to them:

> *Pamela: I would never ask my children, to look after me*
>
> *Walter: No, and I've made that clear*
>
> *Pamela: I know that very clearly (. . .) because I just don't think it's fair.*

The fear of becoming a burden is fed by two care-related associations. Firstly, as Clarke points out, that there is 'evidence that the current generation of elderly people prefer care from independent sources rather than from the family' (1995:

45), challenging the 'traditional Western normative preference structure' (Qureshi and Walker, 1989: 123). While Pickard (2010) shows how people involved in care have to juggle two diverse discourses; of individualization on the one hand and the family ideal on the other. Secondly, a focus on individual fulfilment and success has led to a situation in which people want to make the decision to care and to be there for others (representing the heroic, sacrificial, selfless, virtue of giving), but in which they do not want to be in need of care (the horror of taking) (see also Dean and Rogers, 2004). The worry about being the reason that others (usually people close to oneself) have to carry out undervalued and unrecognized work is obviously part of the fear; however, conceptions of oneself and the strong aversion against becoming the *other* are also reproduced. Imagining oneself through the narrative of care in a situation of helplessness and dependency is understood as something different from life 'as we know it'.

The ideal of independence in combination with a wish to 'help' dependents has also featured prominently in political discourses (Harris, 2002; Doheny, 2004). Since independence is both an individual characteristic and an 'artefact of market-directed liberal democracies' (Chantler, 2006: 29) the fear of becoming a burden needs to be understood as an expression of the demands on people to live happy, fulfilled lives on their own (Pickard, 2010; Beck and Beck-Gernsheim, 2001). On a personal level, people express a fear of being seen as someone who is having to rely on others (Latimer, 1999) or the welfare state (see Latimer, 2000; Misra *et al.*, 2003; Scott *et al.*, 2002). Thus a strong interrelation between personal and societal dependency can be found which expresses itself as a fear of becoming a burden on others. Dependency is a sign of not being healthy, of being passive, of not being self-reliant and not being a 'proper' person in society. Capitalist society is an arrangement of/for able-bodied individuals (Oliver, 1990) in which those who are a burden are *the other*. As the discourses of independence and competitive individualism strongly correlate (Oliver, 1990; Chantler, 2006) the dependent Other is the quintessential non-actor in society.

Challenging the independent actor

> It is almost impossible to contest the concept of independent living, as it is hard to challenge motherhood and apple pie (Oldman, 2003: 45).

The foregoing analysis of the creation of the dichotomy of dependency and independence has investigated the various playing fields on which the othering of those who are seen as dependent manifests itself. It has been demonstrated that the ideal of independence penetrates thinking about personhood and what it means to live a good life. A dichotomy is created in which the active, independent, healthy citizen is constructed in opposition to the passive, dependent, old and ill non-actor. Reflecting on their own lives, focus group participants expressed anxiety about becoming dependent and being a burden.

The culturally normative meaning of independence (Power, 2008) requires that one is active and healthy and dismisses personal and social dependency. But to what extent can the idealization of independence and the independent actor be challenged? Do the discourses on care show any questioning of the dichotomy presented above? In this section three possible counter-discourses will be discussed. The first emphasizes how older people are not by definition dependent and that there are older people who are very active. In the second approach *practices* of care are critiqued for (re)producing dependency; instead notions of help, support and empowerment are seen as preferable. The third approach recognizes the mutuality of interdependencies. All three positions, however, entail shortcomings in challenging the ideal of independence by only disputing and reformulating specific aspects of the construction of dependency. By leaving the constitutional dichotomy intact, they inevitably lead to a reproduction of the very ideal they set out to challenge.

Elderly but fit

In some of the focus group discussions, participants (here volunteers at a luncheon club) emphasize how some older people are very active and witty:

Patricia: Our favourite lady at the moment is 98

Nathan: She said she wants to go to Australia

Patricia: next year

Nathan: For a holiday (. . .), at 99

John: It's amazing

Patricia: And she came in the other week and she said 'Patricia, I'm a bit worried', I say 'Why (. . .), what's the matter?' She says: 'I'm beginning to feel my age' [laughing]. And I: 'I'd worry about it when you start acting your age' [laughing].

The emphasis of people's liveliness takes up the academic discussion on the distinction between the third age as characterized by personal fulfilment and new social roles (Hazan, 2009; Duncan, 2008) and the fourth age illustrated by the image of the 'frail, dependent and disabled body, the body in decline' (Whitaker, 2010). Again a dichotomy is installed in which, against the background of a third age culture, the infirmities of old age (fourth age) are totalized (Gilleard and Higgs, 2010) and the dependence-independence dichotomy is only postponed and reproduced. Due to the emphasis that some older people are still fit and healthy, the negative associations of dependency are perpetuated. By representing some older people as independent, self-reliant actors, they are brought into opposition with those who really are in need of care and support. The positive image of the third age is contrasted with the decline, vulnerability and incompleteness of the fourth age (Baltes and Smith, 2003). Similarly Walter, in the following extract, emphasizes the engagement with the 'modern world' as a praiseworthy character trait:

Walter: my neighbour (. . .), he's now 91, but at the age of 90 he bought himself a brand new (. . .) car, he bought himself a computer [some laugh]. He's got a mind like, and, I visit him obviously and it's always a pleasure, it's never a chore, because his conversation, you know (. . .) ok, he's got his aches and pains, but he maintains a 3 bedroom detached house, no cleaner, no, he cooks for himself and everything (. . .). He's 91, and he's, but he's got, the essential thing is he's got his brain

Pamela: And he's got a mental attitude.

While the image of the fourth age is one of decline, the third age brings back the possibility of agency and functioning in and for society for older people. The important attempt (see Edmondson and von Kondratowitz, 2009) to highlight how older people are far from passive (and how the dichotomy carer-cared for denies them agency) must, however, also be seen as reproducing yet a further dichotomy. This is the exclusion of some people from the category of the valued older person still living a decent and valuable life. A public norm in which the '"normal" healthy body is a moral obligation' (Oakley, 2007: 117) is created where the very positive representation of older people as being fit, healthy, smart, funny and active reinforces the moral responsibility to stay independent. Lloyd (2004) emphasizes that the concept of 'active ageing' also ignores aspects of the general human condition and only tries to approximate the ideal of the independent citizen. Harris (2002: 277–78) rightly argues that while these strategies are important in rejecting the image of older people as burden they also 'reinforce a concept of citizenship which defines people's status according to their contribution to the economy' (see the discussion of interdependency below) 'as well as reinforcing a sharp distinction between the young-old/old-old'. I agree with Phillips when she argues that '[k]eeping older people "independent" has been translated into a message of keeping them fit and active' (2007: 135). What is needed is a challenge to the idealized version of the subject.

Empowerment and support

Built upon the denial of dependency and the emphasis of activity and healthiness of older people, Williams (2001) identifies a more general new discourse on care which focuses on support and help instead of on the practice of caring. The construction of care is seen as preventing the ideal of personal assistance as a normal component of a relationship (Henderson and Forbat, 2002) and friendship (Bowlby *et al.*, 2010). The idea of support and help replacing care is also seen as enabling people to stay in control of their identity and their circumstances of life (Smith, 2005). This perspective, also developed by the Disabled People's Movement (Shakespeare, 2000), sees care not only as an answer to, but also as a cause of dependency (Hughes *et al.*, 2005). The understanding of care-receivers as passive recipients, and not active, 'independently' acting people is thus rejected. The main aim is to discard notions of pity and victimization (Smith, 2005) and instead focus on emancipating and empowering people. John, in the following extract, discusses a photo of a young man fitting new light bulbs and an older man standing beside him:

John: And the greatest thing that a carer can do in that situation is actually . . . not lord it over them . . . He's still taking part, and inviting him, even to hold something, . . . 'can you hold that for me', . . . just not exclude them from the activity but make them feel as though they are part of it, and in fact that they're the boss.

Undoubtedly, the importance of rejecting this objectifying notion of care cannot be overestimated. A notion of support instead of care, however, also (re)produces dilemmas in the conceptualization of dependency. Firstly, as Oliver and Barnes (1998) emphasize, there is an inherent contradiction in being empowered by someone else. Secondly, Watson *et al.* (2004: 339) raise the question whether the term assistance does actually 'capture the combination of emotional and practical care'. Thirdly, and fundamentally, the focus on help, instead of care, can reproduce the dichotomy between independent and dependent recipients of assistance even further. The dichotomy does not vanish; it is only reconfigured. The societal emphasis on independence and self-determination has led to a focus on empowerment of people and participation in public life. As was the case with the emphasis on the activity of people in the third age, these discussions also carry the danger of exclusion and discrimination of those left out. An alternative view of the subject as relational, as embedded and embodied (Reindal, 1999) is crucial for a rethinking of old age, care and the individual that transcends the persisting dichotomy.

Recognizing interdependence

The third possible challenge to the reproduction of the dependence-independence dichotomy is presented by accounts that emphasize reciprocity and mutuality as significant aspects of relationships. Representations of society, especially in their meritocratic conception, are constructed in ways that favour individual contributions. In the study people recurrently talk about the worth of older people in terms of their contribution to society and their value for others. In the following extract the importance for one's feeling of self-worth as a consequence of 'fulfilling tasks' is emphasized:

Barbara: here in [town] there [was] this elderly home (. . .) and even then, I don't know, 200 years ago (. . .) people had to do simple tasks (. . .)

Vanessa: yes, that just keeps fit

Barbara: Yeah, and this was actually very smart, intelligent from this founder, who has ordered that they are asked to do simple tasks (. . .) that you are not feeling useless. Because that's a very heavy burden (. . .) a psychological burden.

What is of note here is a recognition that some people need help or care but that they also give something back to society. *Feeling useless* and not contributing anything is seen as *a very heavy burden*. In that sense older people's contribution to others (in relationships) and to society is highlighted. Several writers in the ethics of care tradition (e.g. Groenhout, 2004; Noddings, 2003) argue for

Bernhard Weicht

replacing both dependency and care with the concept of interdependence, describing a process of 'reciprocity between partners, exchanges between dependent actors over time, and the networking of these relations of dependence' (Fine and Glendinning, 2005: 612). Interdependence and a sense of self in reference to others are positioned against the (masculine) ideals of independence and individualism. The moral relations between people are characterized by the absence of generalizable, independent actors but happen as social relations between concrete others (Kittay, 1999; Smith, 2005). Stocker (2001) even argues that mutuality needs to be understood as a moral normative which prevents oppression; and Bowlby *et al.* (2010) describe interdependency as a necessary part of human flourishing. However, even though interdependence seems more promising for an understanding of social relations and human relationships (Dean, 2004: 193), there is still a questionable tendency to emphasize aspects of mutuality, reciprocity, and therefore, potentially, deservingness. As long as contributing, giving and exchanging are emphasized as fundamental features of the human condition, not only are some people who cannot fulfil these prerequisites (Kittay, 1999) excluded, but the glorification of independence, and thus the construction of the human condition itself is not challenged satisfactorily. Also, in practice, care relationships are usually between unequals (Kittay, 2007). Any challenge to this hegemony must not simply identify people's mutual contributions, but might be better based on a 'theory of equality that embraces dependency' (Kittay, 1999: xii).

Embracing dependency

The analysis of the discourses on care has demonstrated that the construction of the dichotomy of dependency and independence needs to be understood as penetrating every aspect of what it means to be human. The dichotomy (and with it the valorisation of independence) is crucial to the dominant definition of care, it manifests itself in the conceptualization of the old body and it cumulates in the repulsion against becoming a burden on others. Three challenges that can provide possibilities for moving beyond a simplified distinction of the carer and the cared-for have been evaluated. They all, however, remain focused on integrating people in the fellowship of independent actors. Emphasizing active engagement during the third age, the possibility of empowerment through support, and the existence of mutuality and reciprocity, respectively, demonizes dependency. A conceptualization of embracing dependency needs to incorporate several crucial foci. Firstly, dependency needs to be recognized as a neutral and normal aspect of human existence (Kittay, 2007) and any normative valuation needs to be rejected. It has been noted that many people in the focus groups expressed a willingness to care for others but rejected the image of being cared for themselves, as being the independent actor upon whom others can rely is seen as superior to being dependent on others. Since dependency understood as a neutral condition also allows the disentanglement of the need for care from

© 2011 The Author. Editorial organisation © 2011 The Editorial Board of the Sociological Review

being a burden, people's perception of the ideal self can be altered. Recognition of the human nature of dependencies can challenge both the stigma attached to the need for care and the hierarchy within care relationships.

Secondly, a neutrality of dependency also renounces a transfiguration of old age and illness. Vulnerability of the body and the mind and suffering do exist and create real difficulties for people and should not be romanticized (Groenhout, 2003; Sevenhuijsen, 1998).

Thirdly, it has been shown that the old body is used as a signifier for dependency and that the creation of the dichotomy of dependency and independence is played out on the normativity of the (healthy) body. Embracing dependency entails an integration of the body in the human and a rejection of its objectivization (see Garland-Thompson, 2005). Shilling (1993) highlights the fact that bodies are not something we *have*, but something we *are* (see also Latimer, 2009; Munro and Belova, 2009).

Fourthly, the discourses show that because the construction of the dichotomy of dependency and independence is penetrating every aspect of what it means to be a proper person, intrinsically related to an understanding of the self and identity (Grenier and Hanley, 2007), the human condition itself needs to be reformulated. With Kittay I argue that an approach which embraces dependency can manage an integration of care and autonomy in the sense of relational autonomy (Ellis, 2004), 'where the self is viewed as situated in a matrix of relationships' (Kittay, 2007: 66). By situating the ontological – not in different types of people (explaining how human beings *are*) but as being in the relations people have with each other – allows an inclusive and open approach to emancipation of disabled and old people. Following authors such as Nussbaum (2002) and Tronto (1993) who try to integrate ideas of justice and equality into an ethics of care, there is a need to reject demands of mutuality and reciprocity in relationships and to alternatively embrace the inevitability of everyone being dependent. This might enable a conception of dependency which is not an 'evil state of existence' (Groenhout, 2003) but which allows for 'accepted dependency'.

Finally, embracing dependency requires one to be conscious of the fact that care discourses are a representation of broader societal structures and that foci on 'person-centred care, empowerment and independence' are instrumental 'to suit political and ideological ends' (Phillips, 2007: 156). That also means that an attack on the ideological creation of the dichotomy of dependency and independence needs to include an analysis of the latter's association with the ideal actor in capitalist society (Kittay, 2001). As long as the independent, healthy, able-bodied market participant represents the quintessential actor in society, every real situation is judged against this standard. Pickard (2010) has demonstrated that the possibility of rejecting or challenging current discourses on care is closely related to power and status. Promoting a notion in which the dependent person is understood as a proper person and as a social and political actor, therefore, also has to challenge those hierarchies of social status and power.

Concluding comments

In this article I have analysed public discourses on care as exemplified in two European societies. In so doing I have emphasized the extent to which the ideal of independence underwrites the construction of care, the thinking about care and the narratives about care for older people. As has been discussed, the construction of the ideal of independence is based on a creation of politically- and normatively-charged dichotomies. Even though people show some awareness of that the status of care is ambiguous (Bowlby *et al.*, 2010), their representation of care remains situated within sets of traditional oppositions. Specifically, descriptions of the older body typically help to reinforce the split between active and passive, or independent and dependent; the latter one of each of these being constructed as the quintessential other.

Possible challenges designate a more inclusive notion of independence but fall short of challenging the main conceptualization of dependency. Care in these conceptualizations remains based on a normative dichotomy of dependency and independence. The analysis has illustrated how the ideal of independence penetrates all levels and aspects of care discourses. Academic, political and social discourses are complicit not only in the 'making' of older people, but also in the construction of what it means to be human itself (Edmondson and von Kondratowitz, 2009). In all this we come face to face with the possibility of confronting the old as no longer 'human' (see also Latimer, 1999). In formulating an alternative of 'embracing dependency' I have argued that a reconceptualization of what it means to be human is necessary. The deconstruction of the ideology of independence is thus not a minority concern for disability studies or gerontology, but an issue for mainstream sociology (Barnes *et al.*, 1999). Contemporary society fosters a fear of becoming a burden on others and on the collective. The discourses on care illustrate how difficult it is for people to escape the construction of 'depending' as a negative state of existence. Embracing dependency as both an interpersonal and a political project connects to Groenhout's (2004) image of a 'dance of intimacy', in which both caring *and* promoting independence become possible. Although for some, an engagement with others is mainly based on being dependent, it does not follow that their not leading the dance entails an inevitable reduction in the possibility of experiencing and enjoying the social relations underlying it.

Note

1 All names have been changed.

References

Andrews, G.J. and D.R. Phillips, (eds), (2005), *Ageing and Place: Perspectives, Policy, Practice*, Abingdon: Routledge.

Baltes, P., and J. Smith, (2003), 'New frontiers in the future of aging: From successful aging of the young old to the dilemmas of the fourth age', *Gerontology*, Vol. 49: 123–35.

Barnes, C., G. Marcer and T. Shakespeare, (1999), *Exploring Disability: A Sociological Introduction*, Cambridge: Polity Press.

Beck, U., and E. Beck-Gernsheim, (2001), *Individualization: Institutionalism and its Social and Political Consequences*, London: Sage Publications.

Bednarek, M., (2006), *Evaluation in Media Discourse: Analysis of a Newspaper Corpus*, London: Continuum.

Bloor, M., J. Frankland, M. Thomas and K. Robson, (2001), *Focus Groups in Social Research*, London: Sage Publications.

Bobbio, N., (2001), *Old Age and Other Essays*, Cambridge: Polity Press: 3–31.

Bowlby, S., L. McKie, S. Gregory and I. MacPherson, (2010), *Interdependency and Care over the Lifecourse*, Abingdon: Routledge.

Chantler, K., (2006), Independence, Dependency and Interdependence: Struggles and Resistances of Minoritized Women within and on Leaving Violent Relationships, *Feminist Review*, Vol. 82: 27–49.

Clarke, L., (1995), Family Care and Changing Family structures: Bad News for the Elderly?, in Allen, I. and E. Perkins, (eds), *The Future of Family Care for Older People*, London: HMSO: 19–49.

Dean, H., and R. Rogers, (2004), Popular discourses of dependency, responsibility and rights, in Dean, H., (ed.), *The Ethics of Welfare: Human Rights, Dependency and Responsibility*, Bristol: The Policy Press: 69–88.

Dean, H., (2004), Reconceptualising dependency, responsibility and rights, in Dean, H., (ed.), *The Ethics of Welfare: Human Rights, Dependency and Responsibility*, Bristol: The Policy Press: 193–209.

de Beauvoir, S., (1972), *The Coming of Age*, translated by P. O'Brian, New York: Putnam's Sons.

Doheny, S., (2004), Responsibility and welfare: in search of moral sensibility, in Dean, H., (ed.), *The Ethics of Welfare: Human Rights, Dependency and Responsibility*, Bristol: The Policy Press: 49–66.

Duncan, C., (2008), The dangers and limitations of equality agendas as means for tackling old-age prejudice, *Ageing & Society*, Vol. 28: 1122–58.

Edmondson, R. and H-J. von Kondratowitz, (eds), (2009), *Valuing Older People: A Humanistic Approach to Ageing*, Bristol: The Policy Press.

Ellis, K., (2004), Dependency, justice and the ethic of care, in Dean, H., (ed.), *The Ethics of Welfare: Human Rights, Dependency and Responsibility*, Bristol: The Policy Press: 29–48.

Fine, M., (2005), Individualization, risk and the body: sociology and care, *Journal of Sociology*, Vol. 41, 3: 247–66.

Fine, M. and C. Glendinning, (2005), Dependence, independence or inter-dependence? Revisiting the concepts of 'care' and 'dependency', *Ageing & Society*, Vol. 25: 601–21.

Fink, J., (2004), Questions of Care, in Fink, J. (ed.), *Care: Personal Lives and Social Policy*, Bristol: Policy Press: 1–42.

Fraser, N. and L. Gordon, (1994), A Genealogy of *Dependency*: Tracing a Keyword of the US Welfare State, *Signs*, Vol. 19, 2: 309–36.

Fraser, N., (1989), *Unruly Practices: Power, Discourse and Gender in Contemporary Social Theory*, Cambridge: Polity Press.

Garland-Thompson, R., (2005), Feminist Disability Studies, *Signs*, Vol. 30, 2: 1557–87.

Gilleard, C. and P. Higgs, (2010), Aging without agency: Theorizing the fourth age, *Aging & Mental Health*, Vol. 14, 2: 121–28.

Glendinning, C., (2008), Increasing choice and control for older and disabled people: A critical review of new developments in England, *Social Policy & Administration*, Vol. 42, 5: 451–69.

Greco, M., (2009), On the art of life: a vitalist reading of medical humanities, *The Sociological Review*, Vol. 56, 2: 25–45.

Grenier, A. and J. Hanley, (2007), Older Women and 'Frailty': Aged, Gendered and Embodied Resistance, *Current Sociology*, Vol. 55, 2: 211–28.

Groenhout, R., (2003), *Theological Echoes in an Ethic of Care*, Occasional Papers of the Erasmus Institute: 2.

Groenhout, R., (2004), *Connected Lives: Human Nature and an Ethics of Care*, Oxford: Rowman & Littlefield.

Guberman, N., P. Maheu, and C. Maillé, (1992), Women as Family Caregivers: Why Do They Care?, *The Gerontologist*, Vol. 32, 5:. 607–17.

Harlton, S.-V., N. Keating and J. Fast, (1998), Defining Eldercare for Policy and Practice: Perspectives Matter, *Family Relations*, Vol. 47, 3:. 281–88.

Harrefors, C., S. Sävenstedt and K. Axelsson, (2009), Elderly people's perceptions of how they want to be cared for: an interview study with healthy elderly couples in Northern Sweden, *Scandinavian Journal of Caring Sciences*, Vol. 23, 2: 353–60.

Harris, J., (2002), Caring for Citizenship, *British Journal of Social Work*, Vol. 32: 267–81.

Hazan, H., (2009), Beyond dialogue: entering the fourth space in old age, in Edmondson, R. and H.-J. von Kondratowitz, (eds), *Valuing Older People: A Humanistic Approach to Ageing*, Bristol: The Policy Press: 91–104.

Held, V., (1990), Feminist Transformations of Moral Theory, *Philosophy and Phenomenological Research*, Vol. 50, Suppl: 321–44.

Henderson, J. and L. Forbat, (2002), Relationship-based social policy: personal and policy constructions of 'care', *Critical Social Policy*, Vol. 22, 4: 669–87.

Hockey, J. and A. James, (2003), *Social Identities Across the Life Course*, Basingstoke: Palgrave.

Hughes, B., L. McKie, D. Hopkins and N. Watson, (2005), Love's Labours Lost? Feminism, the Disabled People's Movement and an Ethic of Care, *Sociology*, Vol. 39, 2: 259–75.

Jamieson, L., (1998), *Intimacy: A Personal Relationship in Modern Societies*, Cambridge: Polity Press.

Karniol, R., E. Grosz and I. Schorr, (2003), Caring, Gender Role Orientation, and Volunteering, *Sex Roles*, Vol. 49, 1/2: 11–19.

Kittay, E.F., (1999), *Love's Labour: Essays on Women, Equality, and Dependency*, London: Routledge.

Kittay, E.F., (2001), A Feminist Public Ethic of Care Meets the New Communitarian Family Policy, *Ethics*, Vol. 111, 3: 523–47.

Kittay, E.F., (2007), Beyond Autonomy and Paternalism: The Caring Transparent Self, in Nys, T., Y. Denier and T. Vandevelde, (eds), *Autonomy & Paternalism: Reflections on the Theory and Practice of Health Care*, Peeters Publishing: 23–70.

Krzyżanowski, M., (2008), Analysing Focus Group Discussions, in Wodak, R. and M. Krzyżanowski, (eds), *Qualitative Discourse Analysis in the Social Sciences*, Basingstoke: Palgrave Macmillan: 162–81.

Latimer, J., (1999), The Dark at the Bottom of the Stairs: Performance and Participation of Hospitalized Older People, *Medical Anthropology Quarterly*, New Series, Vol. 13, 2: 186–213.

Latimer, J., (2000), *The Conduct of Care: Understanding Nursing Practice*, Oxford: Blackwell Science.

Latimer, J., (2009), Introduction: body, knowledge, worlds, *The Sociological Review*, Vol. 56, s2: 1–22.

Lloyd, L., (2004), Mortality and morality: ageing and the ethics of care, *Ageing & Society*, Vol. 24: 235–56.

López, D. and M. Domènech, (2009), Embodying autonomy in a Home Telecare Service, *The Sociological Review*, Vol. 56, s2: 181–95.

Milligan, C., (2003), Location or dis-location? Towards a conceptualization of people and place in the care-giving experience, *Social & Cultural Geography*, Vol. 4, 4: 455–70.

Misra, J., S. Moller and M. Karides, (2003), Envisioning Dependency: Changing Media Depictions of Welfare in the 20th Century, *Social Problems*, Vol. 50, 4: 482–504.

Mittelstadt, J., (2001), 'Dependency as a Problem to Be Solved': Rehabilitation and the American Liberal Consensus on Welfare in the 1950s, *Social Politics*, Vol. 8, 2: 228–57.

Mitteness, L.S. and J. S. Barker, (1995), Stigmatising a 'Normal' Condition: Urinary Incontinence in Late Life, *Medical Anthropology Quarterly*, New Series, Vol. 9, 2: 188–210

Munro, R., and O. Belova, (2009), The body in time: knowing bodies and the 'interruption' of narrative, *The Sociological Review*, Vol. 56, s2: 87–99.

Noddings, N., (2003), *Caring: a feminine approach to ethics and moral education*, 2nd edn., London: University of California Press.

Nussbaum, M., (2002), Introduction to the Symposium on Eva Kittay's *Love's Labor: Essays on Women, Equality and Dependency*, *Hypatia*, Vol. 17, 3: 194–99.

Oakley, A., (2007), *Fracture: Adventures of a Broken Body*, Bristol: The Policy Press.

Oldman, C., (2003), Deceiving, theorizing and self-justification: a critique of independent living, *Critical Social Policy*, Vol. 23, 1: 44–62.

Oliver, M. and C. Barnes, (1998), *Disabled People and Social Policy: From Exclusion to Inclusion*, London: Longman.

Oliver, M., (1990), *The Politics of Disablement*, Basingstoke: Macmillan.

O'Neill, F.K., (2009), Bodily knowing as uncannily canny: clinical and ethical significance, *The Sociological Review*, Vol. 56, s2: 216–32.

Paoletti, I., (2002), Caring for older people: A gendered practice, *Discourse & Society*, Vol. 13, 6: 805–17.

Phillips, J., (2007), *Care*, Key Concepts, Cambridge: Polity Press.

Pickard, S., (2010), The 'Good Carer': Moral Practices in Late Modernity, *Sociology*, Vol. 44, 3: 471–87.

Plath, D., (2008), Independence in Old Age: The Route to Social Exclusion?, *British Journal of Social Work*, Vol. 38: 1353–69.

Power, A., (2008), Caring for independent lives: Geographies of caring for young adults with intellectual disabilities, *Social Science & Medicine*, Vol. 67: 834–43.

Qureshi, H. and A. Walker, (1989), *The Caring Relationship: Elderly People and their Families*, Basingstoke: Macmillan.

Reindal, S.M., (1999), Independence, Dependence, Interdependence: some reflections on the subject and personal autonomy, *Disability & Society*, Vol. 14, 3: 353–67.

Reisigl, M. and R. Wodak, (2001), *Discourse and Discrimination: Rhetorics of Racism and Antisemitism*, London: Routledge.

Richardson, J.E., (2007), *Analysing Newspapers: An approach from Critical Discourse Analysis*, Basingstoke: Palgrave Macmillan.

Rudge, T., (2009), Beyond caring? Discounting the differently known body, *The Sociological Review*, Vol. 56, s2: 233–48.

Scott, E.K., A.S. London and N.A. Myers, (2002), Dangerous Dependencies: The Intersection of Welfare Reform and Domestic Violence, *Gender & Society*, Vol. 16, 6: 878–97.

Sennett, R., (2003), *Respect: The Formation of Character in a World of Inequality*, London: Penguin Press.

Sevenhuijsen, S., (1998), *Citizenship and the Ethics of Care: Feminist Considerations on Justice, Morality and Politics*, London: Routledge.

Shakespeare, T., (2000), *Help*, Birmingham: Venture Press.

Shilling, C., (1993), *The Body and Social Theory*, London: Sage Publications.

Skoe, E.E., (1995), Sex-Role Orientation and its Relationship to the Development of Identity and Moral Thought, *Scandinavian Journal of Psychology*, Vol. 36, 3: 235–45.

Smith, S.R., (2005), Equality, identity and the Disability Rights Movement: from policy to practice and from Kant to Nietzsche in more than one uneasy move, *Critical Social Policy*, Vol. 25, 4: 554–76.

Stocker, S.S., (2001), Disability and Identity: Overcoming Perfectionism, *Frontiers: A Journal of Women Studies*, Vol. 22, 2: 154–73.

Strathern, M., (1997), Gender: Division or Comparison, in Hetherington, K. and R. Munro (eds), *Ideas of Difference: Social Spaces and the Labour of Division*, Sociological Review Monograph, Oxford: Blackwells.

Toynbee, P., (2009), The 1961 Suicide Act is an instrument of state torture, *The Guardian*, 01/08/2009.

Traphagan, J.W., (2004), Interpretations of Elder Suicide, Stress, and Dependency among Rural Japanese, *Ethnology*, Vol. 43, 4: 315–29.

Tronto, J.C., (1993), *Moral Boundaries: A Political Argument for an Ethic of Care*, London: Routledge,

Twigg, J., (1997), Deconstructing the 'social bath': Help with bathing at home for older and disabled people, *Journal of Social Policy*, Vol. 26: 211–32.

Twigg, J., (2000), *Bathing – the Body and Community Care*, Routledge, London.

Ungerson, C., (1987), *Policy is Personal: Sex, Gender, and Informal Care*, London: Tavistock Publications.

Ungerson, C., (2000), Thinking about the Production and Consumption of Long-term Care in Britain: Does Gender Still Matter?, *Journal of Social Policy*, Vol. 29, 4: 623–43.

Watson, N., L. McKie, B. Hughes, D. Hopkins and S. Gregory, (2004), (Inter)Dependence, Needs and Care: The Potential for Disability and Feminist Theorists to Develop an Emancipatory Model, *Sociology*, Vol. 38, 2: 331–50.

Whitaker, A., (2010), The body as existential midpoint – the aging and dying body of nursing home residents, *Journal of Aging Studies*, Vol. 24: 96–104.

White, P., (2009), Knowing body, knowing other: cultural materials and intensive care, in *Un/knowing Bodies*, Monograph, Oxford, Blackwells: 117–37.

Williams, F., (2001), In and beyond New Labour: towards a new political ethic of care, *Critical Social Policy*, Vol. 21, 4: 467–93.

Winch, S., (2006), Constructing a Morality of Caring: Codes and Values in Australian Carer discourse, *Nursing Ethics*, Vol. 13, 1: 5–16.

Wodak, R., (2008), Introduction: Discourse Studies – Important Concepts and Terms, in Wodak, R. and M. Krzyżanowski, (eds), *Qualitative Discourse Analysis in the Social Sciences*, Basingstoke: Palgrave Macmillan: 1–29.

Part 5
Social movements

Part 5
Social movements

Curious cases: small island states' exceptionalism and its contribution to comparative welfare theory

Zoë Irving

Abstract: While the size of states and the significance of 'islandness' have been of mild interest within the comparative study of politics and economics, the theoretical frameworks that operate within contemporary comparative analyses of welfare and social policy rest upon a largely unremarked assumption that population size does not matter. Explanations of and predictions for the development of welfare relations are undertaken in the belief that it is the ideological essence of welfare states that is important, and this national 'character' is established through concentration on the politics of class, sometimes gender, and occasionally ethnicity. However, it is often from the study of the small that important insight is generated and variation in universals can be found. Focusing on exemplars of the smallest national units, Cyprus, Iceland and Jersey, this article explores the significance of size and 'islandness' in welfare analysis. The findings of these country case studies expose aspects of the relationship between economics, geo-political strength and weakness, welfare state exceptionalism and hybridity and the social basis of welfare regime types which are less visible when size is not featured as an explanatory variable.

Introduction

In explaining welfare state development (eg Esping-Andersen, 1990) and welfare reform (eg Heidenheimer *et al.*, 1990; Esping-Andersen, 1996, 1999; Pierson, 2001), contributions from political sociology routinely overlook the significance of population size in the processes and outcomes identified.[1] In large part this is due to both the geopolitical focus on powerful western economies or 'the global', and the focus on universal policy processes that are assumed to operate similarly in industrially advanced countries whatever their population size. Thus a comparative interest in the US, Netherlands, Sweden, Germany and so on can be sustained on the basis that it is the political composition of actors, coalitions and governments – their ideological essence – that is important, not the size of their constituencies. Alternatively, as Heidenheimer *et al.* (1990: vi) suggest, size is unimportant because 'the options for pursuing strikingly unique policies have been reduced for many countries, large and small' as a consequence of the global economy's logic of convergence. At first glance, the lack of a 'size matters' approach to complement those of 'politics matters', 'history matters' and 'institutions matter' used in cross-national comparative political sociology is thus unremarkable. However, this article argues that neglect of the question of 'size' impoverishes a comparative understanding of national welfare relations in two significant ways.

Firstly, because although not explicitly recognized in welfare state comparison, many of the insights and research avenues pursued are drawn from the study of small states. A notable example is Peter Katzenstein's work (1985; see also 2003), which has generated important observations in relation to both industrial relations and the wider study of politics (Iversen, 2001) but also ideas that clearly feed into welfare regime theory. In the study of welfare relations and policy change, the themes of 'adaptability' and 'vulnerability' developed in such political economy and international relations literature on small states, are analytically valuable in investigating the two key problematics for welfare typologies: exceptionalism and hybridity, as well as the consequential question of path dependency and its impact on the form and success of welfare reform. The second reason for focusing on size as a factor of explanation in the consideration of difference and similarity in the development of welfare arrangements, is best illustrated through reference to the world of Biology where John Tyler Bonner argues that 'Size dictates the characteristics of all living forms. It is the supreme and universal determinant of what any organism can be and do' (2006: 3–4). While size is simply 'a description, a property' (Bonner, 2006: 147) and does not in itself confound any general laws of nature, attention is drawn to the differential importance of these laws when they are mediated through size. Without taking the analogy too far, it can be recognised that in the comparative study of social policy and society, exploration of the extent to which the operation of established affective factors and processes are similar in the smallest polities, can add support to or raise questions regarding their universal significance; it can in addition, reveal the greater and lesser significance of particular factors and processes within general explanatory schema when accounting for size.

One such factor might be the ideational and social make-up of the national ideological character which is represented in a 'regime type', how it develops and to what extent the abstract 'national' representation reflects actual social relations (some interest has developed in this area and is presented in the collection edited by van Oorschot *et al.*, 2008). It is essentially the historical cumulation of the day to day reality of the social relations of welfare that is assumed to be captured in macro-sociological national typologies, but the circumstances of familiarity and anonymity within which relations take place has not hitherto figured in these accounts. If it were possible to establish a link between the size of a welfare state population (and consequently the proximity of social relations) and the 'niceness' of its policy arrangements (arguably features such as egalitarianism, reciprocity, support for the vulnerable and so on) then we could explain very simply, and without recourse to Katzenstein's (1985: 206) 'audaciously commonsensical' notions relating to national culture, why the US is unable to learn from the small states, and why the social democratic states which score most highly on indices of welfare effort are all small. This article seeks to engage with the question of nation state size as a factor of difference in the evolution of welfare relations and, in a more tentative way to explore whether such an engagement can open up opportunities for a productive theoretical exchange between anthropological and micro-sociological studies and those of the political-institutional oriented comparative political economy.

As a starting point and an alternative to the analytical preoccupation with geopolitical giants, this article draws attention to the gains to be made from the study of the most diminutive national units: small island states. In terms of their analytical attraction, islands, particularly those that are small and remote, are alluring as ready-made 'laboratories' and have been widely studied as such in the natural sciences. In the social sciences, although significant in the emergence of sociological theory (Goffman, 1959; Cohen, 1987), much contemporary knowledge and understanding of islands is, in fact, generated by development studies infused with anthropological insight and economic theory. Alongside romantic and exotic notions of island life, the features that have been of interest to both natural and social scientists are insularity, homogeneity and isolation, and what analyses of these can tell us about wider processes of development. In terms of social policy study, their attraction is found in the propensity to social cohesion evidenced in political research. There has also been critique of the 'distinctiveness' of small island states in comparison to small states more generally however, and Selwyn (1980) argues for example, that such a distinction panders to the inappropriate status of 'oddity' ascribed to small island states, when it is peripherality not 'islandness' that is important as an explanatory factor in politics and economics. Read (2004: 369) also suggests that they are more usefully studied as 'a discrete subset of small states in general'. Undoubtedly, the significance of 'islandness' depends on what aspects of the human condition are of interest, and in contrast to Selwyn's view that 'neither social structures nor social trends can usefully be discussed in this context' (1980: 950), the discussion here posits a significant role for size as well as islandness in the development of welfare relations and policy. The remainder of this article presents a preliminary excursion into the comparison of economically advanced small island states[2] to demonstrate how a contribution to traditional comparative theory might be developed.

The discussion to follow begins with a summary of the ways in which size has contributed to understanding of social, political and economic relations and goes on to examine the ways in which the study of small island states can bridge the theoretical gaps between micro-sociology and political-institutional analysis. Case studies of social welfare development and change in three small island states, Cyprus, Iceland and Jersey, are presented as a means to illustrate the contention that size matters. These three islands provide contrasting geopolitical exemplars but would also be expected to fit broadly within the *Three worlds of welfare capitalism*, the conservative, social democratic and liberal respectively, established by Esping-Andersen (1990) and embellished by others (see Arts and Gelissen (2002) for a review of such typologies). The case study analyses provide an assessment of the evolution of welfare provision with reference to the traditional concerns of welfare state analyses such as key historical events, the political complexion over time, characteristics of the welfare mix, the significance of familism in policy architecture and indicators of gender equality. Examination of these features gives insight into the formal basis for welfare relations and a sense of how social divisions are articulated in social policy. From consideration of these dimensions of development, it is possible to comment upon the social relations of welfare and the place of key values in welfare arrangements. Examining the nature of more recent welfare transition in these contrasting polities also reveals interesting dilemmas in the layering of the values associated with global competitiveness and the marketization of the social upon the existing contours of small and historically inter-reliant societies. Finally, the three case studies make possible critical reflection on the place of small states in comparative analytical frameworks, and the more abstract question of size as an underestimated factor in explaining the shape of welfare relations.

The significance of size in comparative study

Katzenstein's (1985) comparative study *Small states in world markets* stemmed from an interest in explaining why, during the 1980s, standards of living were higher in the smallest European states (Austria, Belgium, Denmark, the Netherlands, Norway, Sweden, and Switzerland) than they were in the USA, ostensibly the world's most powerful state. Historical analysis led him to conclude that democratic corporatism, which characterizes the political structures in all the small states, allows them to simultaneously maintain the mutually contingent 'political stability and economic flexibility' (1985: 9, 191) required to compete successfully in the world economy. The openness of small states' economies (their vulnerability) is counter-balanced by a form of 'social' protectionism – state welfare expansion achieved via the high levels of trust in political institutions generated by proportional representation, and an ideological preference for unity (Katzenstein, 2003). Despite critique of Katzenstein's work (eg Iverson, 2001; Jones, 2008), it is his main themes of small state vulnerability and adaptability that have renewed resonance in the current economic climate. If the global order is one where all states are 'Icelandic' now, Katzenstein's contention that in the context of economic adjustment big states can learn from small ones, and that cutting 'social fat . . . to stop the atrophy of economic muscle' (1985: 20) is not the only road to competitiveness, is all the more prescient. In terms of economic measures, while small states don't always 'do better' than large ones (Katzenstein, 2003; Schmidt, 2003), in terms of welfare concerns they do tend, generally, to score more highly (with inevitable exceptions). Size matters then, because one feature of small states' responses to their vulnerability is argued to be the drive to consensus – an 'ideology of social partnership' (Katzenstein, 2003) or emphasis on 'national cohesion' (Kosonen, 2003) which, particularly in the Scandinavian small states, is linked to arrangements for social provision. Thus, if there is interest in exploring why social policy is 'nicer' in some countries than in others, size becomes a crucial variable and sociologizing or even anthropologizing political economy, invaluable.

The impetus for national cohesionist strategies in both 'large' small states and small island states is global competitiveness and heightened exposure in the world market, often in juxtaposition to powerful neighbours in patterns of dependence (Kosonen, 2003). At the same time, it has to be recognized that small size does not equal powerlessness, and an assumption of small state weakness is problematic. Katzenstein calls this 'a traditional paradox in international relations concerning the strength of the weak' (1985: 21). Vulnerability is very much context specific and not necessarily a disadvantage. Small states can use 'vulnerability' as a bargaining tool to negotiate preferential economic and political terms, for example in subsidies and aid packages, military protection, and trade agreements (Prasad, 2007). In a global economy increasingly reliant on markets characterised by an absence of the need for physical space and labour, small states can actually represent significant actors able to manipulate the global situation through specialisation in financial services for example. This survivalist strategy requires the policy flexibility or adaptability admired by Katzenstein and others, and attention to social context in order to explain it. In the past it tended to direct small island states into more individualist protectionist policies, often with strong bi-lateral and post-colonial ties. This has given way to less dependent relationships (Srebrnik, 2004), but for economically advanced small island states, the shape of the contemporary global market in the latter half of the 2000s has more recently required a national rethink of regional interests. The economic vulnerability (and strength) of small states reflected in the openness of their economies is somewhat trumped by the kind of vulnerabilities associated with small island states, where domestic production is acutely specialized, import reliance greatest and growth is dependent on a service sector – and ideally one which is not labour intensive. As Read (2004) points out, therefore, wealth does not necessarily bring security, and it is human capital which forms a key part of small island states' comparative advantage. From a world-systems perspective advanced small island states are also problematic, existing somewhere in the semi-periphery but often as mice that can roar. As Baldacchino (2004: 237) observes, representing 64 per cent of all sovereign states with populations under 1.5 million, the political alliances of small islands both at UN and EU level bear witness to the need for overdue academic recognition of their significance on the world stage. What is also indicated however, is the overdue scholarly attention to the ways in which small island states comply and conflict with current understandings of patterns of welfare development: whether their character suggests exceptionalism is actually the rule and hybridity the ideal and what their study reveals about 'national' welfare systems.

The significance of size to the social relations of welfare

Small island societies are argued to exhibit a number of national characteristics that correspond to their geopolitical position and population experience. Some of the social characteristics attributed to small island states are central to an analysis of the operation of welfare. These include levels of socio-political tolerance, unity and the 'strong sense of locality the bounded island context breeds' (Dommen, 1980: 942). These ascriptions are reminiscent of the romantic themes established in community studies, such as Göran Rosenberg's 'warm circle' of tolerance, trust and reciprocity, associated with the supposed shared understandings held by communities (cited in Bauman, 2001: 10–20). Nevertheless, the study of the relationship between size and democracy also reports favourably on smallness. A review of political philosophy confirms that the small state was believed to deliver many of the objectives with which social policy is concerned: equality, friendliness, dedication to peace and the common good, for example (Srebrnik, 2004: 329). In explanation of their exceptional strength of democratic values, Ott's (2000) study indicates that there is more to the 'democratic-ness' of small island states than absence of armed conflict. Her study foregrounds some of the issues that are here regarded as central to the development of welfare relations: that small size enables more direct political participation and more cooperative political relationships. Supporting this, other research also suggests that in small states 'politics are friendlier' (Dommen, 1980: 931, also Schmidt, 2003) and that policy-making is more flexible because there are 'shorter distances and deeper links between economic agents' (Read, 2004: 370). Drawing attention to the accessibility of political structures, the expression of social responsibility and strength of social bonds raises questions such as whether the more socially proximate people are, the less likely it is that processes of othering will inform domestic policy; whether the 'vibrant civil societies' attributed to small island states (Srebrnik, 2004) and the concomitant social capital, maintain national cohesion and lead to a disinclination to bowling alone or, more importantly for this article, an inclination to welfare stateness in the Esping-Andersen (1990) sense. Ways in which varying welfare relations that could be linked to size, 'islandness' and international vulnerability, are played out over time are examined in the case study analyses that follow.

Cyprus: welfare at the crossroads

Cyprus occupies 'crossroads' in senses other than its geographical position between countries of Europe, Africa and the Middle East. As a former British colony, which gained independence in 1960 following numerous historical invasions, and with both Greek and Turkish traditions, Cyprus has influences beyond those attributed to the other Mediterranean welfare states. The island was still considered a 'developing country' in the mid 1970s, but one whose heritage includes strands of both feudalism and Catholicism (Pantelli, 2005). Formal social welfare provision was first introduced in Cyprus in the inter-war period but was less progressive than even the British residualist model from which it drew. In the decade following the Second World War, key factors for welfare state development included the establishment of the British welfare state and the growth and action of the Cypriot Trade Union and Left movement, combined with the aspirations of demobilized Cypriots, and with Bismarckian logic, Britain's desire to mollify political agitation for union with Greece. Farmers were never a political force in Cyprus as urbanization began before the rural peasantry was able to organize itself separately from the Communist Party, and rural poverty remained despite improvements in the urban quality of life. It is interesting then that in politics, Cyprus presents a case of social democracy at its most left, combined with what Triseliotis (1977: 143) describes as 'apathetic communities' in terms of struggles for welfare. Following independence, Cyprus has experienced disproportionate alternative struggles that revolve around its geopolitical significance in the middle of the east-west oil-shipping lanes, US suspicion that it represents a Mediterranean 'Cuba' and its partition following the Turkish invasion in 1974, leading to substantial reliance on state aid amongst the Greek refugee population (Pantelli, 2005).

Contrary to the general findings on small states, politics have been far from friendly in Cyprus. In the 1950s, conflict between right and left in both Greek and Turkish communities, particularly in approach to anti-colonialism and union with Greece, seriously hampered the capacity of the left (namely, AKEL)[3] to focus on seeking social rights. In the early 1950s Cyprus set up a social welfare department which Triseliotis declares 'imaginative and advanced for its kind' (1977: 23) but over the subsequent two decades patterns of social development reflect the post-colonial dependency and aid relationships which have stunted democratic development of state welfare in most developing countries. Health care followed a residual and means-tested route, combined with status-related concessions, and municipal housing schemes were transcended by state policies to create 'owner rented housing'[4] and private land speculation. The public assistance programme introduced in 1953 represents an unusual hybrid of discretionary payments based on less eligibility, household means and the existence of liable relatives, tempered by a non-stigmatizing social casework approach to those in need, reminiscent of approaches found in continental countries. Viewed alongside the family orientation of other elements of the contemporary insurance system in place since 1980, there is indication of both the British Beveridgean influence, but also Cypriot cultural values of self-sufficiency and kinship obligations. Public assistance was not rights-based in its early formulation and it was the 1957 social insurance scheme and subsequent amendments that established social protection. In spite of its colonial legacy, Cyprus rapidly recovered its economy through the 1990s and acceded to the

European Union (EU) in 2004. Spending on public assistance rose from 0.4 per cent of GDP in 1992 to 1.4 per cent in 2001, much of this in respect of old age, illness and disability (MLSI/EC, 2003). Despite the social and economic costs of the Turkish invasion, Cyprus ranks 28th in the Human Development Index for 2005, with life expectancy which has risen from 66.2 years in 1960 to 70 in 2005. It has also rapidly urbanized with the urban population representing 47.3 per cent in 1975 and projected to be 71.5 by 2015 (UNDP, 2008).

The Cypriot economy is dominated by services, mainly in tourism, property and the financial sector, which was liberalized in 2000. Cyprus has joined the single European currency, but EU membership has not provided a resolution to the Cyprus 'question', and the *Acquis Communitaire* does not apply to the North. Much social policy development undertaken over the last decade has been led by preparation for EU accession. Thus the tone and content of joint memoranda and assessments, produced by the Cypriot Ministry of Labour and Social Insurance and various EU representatives, reflect the EU social policy agenda, which has been grafted easily onto the relatively skeletal existing arrangements. In terms of values and principles, the casework approach developed in public assistance now fits well with the EU social inclusion agenda for example. In other areas, especially employment, there is pressure to align with the European employment strategy. This indicates policy development towards 'maximum participation', employability and activation measures, and a flexible labour market. In terms of the first point, although women still make up three quarters of family workers, the female labour market participation rate is 53.7 per cent, comparable with the UK and higher than other continental and Mediterranean countries (UNDP, 2008). Increasing women's employment rates was a key aim established in the Joint assessment of employment priorities produced in 2001 (MLSI/EC, 2001), but family unity is also a longer-standing objective for family services. Like the other continental states, Cyprus will have to address the demise of the breadwinner model and a declining fertility rate (2.5 in 1970–75 to 1.6 in 2000–05). This may not be so difficult however, as women's employment has been promoted, especially since the 1980s, the tax system is more individualized and childcare provision is well established and subsidized (MLSI/EC, 2003; Ministry of Labour and Social Insurance, 2004). These features of Cypriot welfare diverge from the Mediterranean model, so it is interesting that according to data for 2000, Cyprus still clustered with other Mediterranean countries, Poland and Slovakia in terms of its conventional patterns of family formation and family forms (Hantrais, 2004: 64, Figure 3.1). There are indications that family structure is changing though, and this has significant implications for the family focused welfare mix that currently maintains low social spending. Triseliotis (1977) concludes that partly due to the strength of the church, state intervention was limited in the various social welfare fields, and three decades later, there remains a very strong reliance on the voluntary sector albeit state subsidized. Reform of the health system to create a national health insurance system has taken longer than planned and reflects a general structure and mix of state/private/voluntary involvement that is standard fare for 'marketizing' European economies (see Health Insurance Organization, 2008).

Part of AKEL's governmental success has to be its placing of national unity and self-determination at the pinnacle of its ideological and policy package. In his February 2009 inauguration speech as General Secretary, Andros Kyprianou stated that as the governing party, AKEL would 'promote the strong social character of the government and its support to social policies in a way that will advance social justice' and that 'it will attempt to restore values, principles and ideals in Cypriot society' (AKEL, 2009). The pre-EMU austerity drive may well be revisited, in the light of the global economic downturn and its potential effect on tourism and construction. In a subsequent speech in March, Kyprianou hinted that there might be an impact on social spending plans included in the 2009 budget but reassured that 'for us what is of utmost importance is that these measures have a strong social character', concluding that 'the future and the hope of Cyprus lie in the Left' (AKEL, 2009a and b). Clearly, Cyprus is facing difficult times as a socialist state in a neo-liberal world. Despite accession to the EU, AKEL retains its 'unreconstructed' critique of EU/US global economic policy. The government is committed to the improvement of socio-economic conditions through social provision but will have to pursue the logic of Cyprus's comparative advantage to achieve welfare aims. Whether it is possible to reconcile high rates of pensioner poverty with the government actuary's recommendations for reductions in pension entitlement for example (MLSI/EC, 2003) will demonstrate Cyprus's capacity to maintain its tradition of intergenerational solidarity. The fact that AKEL achieved the presidency in 2008 suggests that even with a gini coefficient close to the EU average, popular desire for redistributive policies remains.

Iceland: policy inconsonance within the Nordic model

Although included within the Nordic family of nations, propinquity to social democratic welfare regimes has not determined the development of welfare arrangements in Iceland. The island has a rich and unique medieval political history, but it was a late European industrializer and, following independence from Denmark in 1944, its economy was relatively closed until the 1960s. With a change of foreign economic policy in 1960 and improved relationships with western Europe (Palmarsdottir, 1991), Iceland developed rapidly from an impoverished agrarian ex-colony to a flourishing maritime economy, ranked top in the UNDP Human Development Index in 2005. In contrast to other Nordic countries, however, performance on quality of life indices is more attributable to social cohesion and full employment than to any state redistributive impulse, although Pálsson and Durrenberger (1996) provide anthropological accounts which qualify this view. It is suggested that an 'imagined political unity' exists in Iceland which echoes its medieval politics and imbues political discourse with both collectivist sentiments and the idea that

Iceland's good society hinges on its sovereignty, the ultimate goal of government activity (Halfdanarson, cited in Thorhallsson, 2002: 355), but more recent critical analysis points to an unhappy and ineffectual marriage between Icelandic politics and advanced capitalism (Boyes, 2009; OECD, 2009; Special Investigation Commission, 2010).

Politics has mattered in Iceland however. Despite a lack of conformity to the principles and goals of the 'Scandinavian model' (Ólafsson, 1993, 2005; Siaroff, 1994; Sveinsson, 1996; Jonsson, 2001), the strength of left parties at strategic points in the 1930s and 1940s ensured the establishment of solidaristic social and health insurance. Universalism is nevertheless fragile within the Icelandic welfare state, and this is linked both to the coalition-dependent political system dominated by the centre-right Independence Party, combined with affinity towards other more liberal 'settler' states (such as New Zealand), and to strong US relations. This hybridity of influence on the operationalization of welfare values has permitted the erosion of early collectivist elements within welfare provision. Unsurprisingly then, public spending in Iceland has been low compared to that of the other Nordic countries and historically, the highest labour market participation rate amongst OECD countries (exceptionally high for those aged over 65) has hitherto removed the pressure for policy debate around work incentives. Thus, from the 1990s, the neo-liberal policy agenda was able to take root in relatively fertile ground and alongside the liberalization of financial markets and the pursuit of a low-tax international identity, a far-reaching programme of public sector privatization and management reforms was undertaken (Jonsson, 2001; Kristmundsson, 2003). Despite these developments, Icelandic idiosyncrasy in policy response is also distinguishable in inconsonant reforms, hidden in the general shift to the right in welfare provision, most obviously in the direction of housing policy. This latter reflects a preponderance of often self-built home ownership that has been assisted by low levels of personal taxation (Ólafsson, 1993), state preference for 'social owner-occupation', and more significantly the 'nationalization' of mortgage lending. In contrast to the liberal welfare states where the residualization of social housing dominated policy from the 1980s, Iceland's path evidences what Sveinsson (1996) calls a process of 'Scandinavianization' in housing policy.

In the early 2000s, in line with other small states, Iceland made banking and finance its sector of choice in the global market, and was promoted amongst banking audiences as the fifth most competitive economy in the world (Asgrimsson, 2005). Prime Ministerial speeches at this time reflect elements of expansionary zeal, and the widespread policy reforms in areas of tax and business show Iceland attempting to recreate itself as a high tech financial player. Financial overindulgence and corruption reaped bitter rewards in October 2008 when the three main banks collapsed with losses of over US$ 100 billion, and Iceland requested International Monetary Fund (IMF) intervention. Along with further foreign loans, the IMF rescue package is expected to stabilize the financial sector, but cannot prevent the serious economic, and social repercussions (OECD, 2009). The impact on solidarity of the current recession is potentially injurious. The IMF reports that Iceland's progress is 'broadly in line' with the recovery plan (IMF, 2009) but the unemployment rate, which peaked at 5 per cent in 1995, rose from 2.5 to 7.1 per cent between 2008 and 2009. In addition, spending on social security and welfare increased from 4.4 per cent of treasury expenditure in 2008 to 46.5 per cent in 2009. The crisis has impacted on the entire population, with levels of personal borrowing very high and a generally inflated housing market.

Popular anger at Iceland's economic collapse culminated in the 'pot and pan revolution', and the fall of the conservative Independence Party government, which had governed the country more or less since independence in 1944. In many ways Iceland spent the years following independence resisting the Scandinavian social model represented by its previous rulers (Denmark and Norway). In his commentary on Icelanders as 'Scandinavian' or 'American' Ólafsson (2003) suggests a tilt to the 'east', but subsequent elections in May 2009 evidence an historic swing to the left in Icelandic politics, with a ruling coalition made up of the Social Democratic Alliance (29.8 per cent) and the Left-Green Movement (21.7). The coalition government's first statement, released on 10th May 2009, includes the following:

> In the national elections just concluded, a majority of voters gave social democratic and left-wing parties a clear mandate to continue, and to prioritize new values of equality, social justice, solidarity, sustainable development, gender equality, moral reform and democracy in Iceland. The new government, guided by these values, aims at creating a Nordic welfare society in Iceland, where collective interests take precedence over particular interests.

> (Prime Minister's Office http://eng.forsaetisraduneyti.is/news-and-articles/nr/3706)

The new government's *First 100 days Planned Actions* includes a 'cost-cutting drive launched in public administration, involving employees, managements and users of services' (Prime Minister's Office, 2009). Given earlier administrative reforms in the civil and welfare services and the previous government's concern with 'focused government administration' and 'restraint' (Prime Minister's Office, 2007), it is hard to see how further cost-cutting exercises will deliver the welfare outcomes desired in a social democratic regime. It is possible that the standard OECD advice around workforce rationalization, privatization and competition in health services and education (OECD, 2009) will seem more attractive as a cost-saving option, perhaps with a market model more similar to that of Denmark.[5] The OECD has also been critical of the role of the publicly owned Housing Financing Fund, which it views as an anti-competitive obstacle to sound economic policy. Its recommendation, unsurprisingly, is that the HFF's government apron strings should be cut and its social role become targeted. As noted above, however, housing is the most 'Scandinavian' element of the Icelandic welfare state and this latter advice may now be unwelcome.

Other planned actions in the welfare arena include 'proposals for a new social insurance system' and measures to address unemployment, which are high on the agenda given the increase in numbers registering for benefit. Since this is a relatively undeveloped area of policy, the choices again will reflect battles of ideas between those promoting 'workfare' (the neo-liberal approach) and those preferring 'activation' (the approach preferred within the EU). The revisions to the social insurance system, and particularly pensions, are most interesting from the point of view of welfare 'regime change' as the committee appointed to develop these reforms is indeed aiming to streamline pensioner provision and reduce the means-tested elements[6] in line with the Nordic model. In terms of welfare relations, Iceland is now facing a real dilemma, in that the principles of state obligation and intervention, solidarity and egalitarianism have come to the fore just at the time when there is less scope to devote resources to supporting them. One strategy to square this circle is the imminent submission of Iceland's application to join the EU. Accession will ultimately be decided in a referendum, and while popular support for EU membership has always been stronger than that of the political elite (Thorhallsson, 2002), with the current support of two thirds of MPs, and of the IMF according to Prime Minister Sigurðardóttir (2009), the longstanding worry that Iceland would be 'inhaled' by the EU (Palmarsdottir, 1991: 10) seems to have evaporated. As Iceland seeks safety in an insecure world, the parameters of both its social model and its notion of sovereignty are being redrawn.

Jersey: welfare without the social?

Exploiting its geographical position between France and England, Jersey has a history of independence from both major powers that has allowed it to pursue a very idiosyncratic path to competitiveness with very little interference. As the smallest of the island states considered here, it is also the most exceptional in both political development and social welfare provision, and as such, it fits least comfortably in relation to welfare models. There is little comparative data covering Jersey or the Channel Islands, and where it crosses the OECD radar, Jersey is of interest only as a global offshore finance centre and tax haven. It is this position however, which enables the States of Jersey to maintain and exert sovereign power regardless of its status as a British Crown Protectorate. The most significant element of Jersey's economy (about half of output) continues to be the provision of international financial services, but tourism (a quarter) and agriculture also account for a substantial proportion of GDP, most of the latter being exported to Britain. Taxation is extremely light relative to other European countries, and it is Jersey's low tax identity which attracted wealthy settlers in the post-war period of decolonization and economic boom, and its nurturing of UK tax-avoidance potential which has consolidated its appeal (Hampton, 1998). Le Hérissier (1998) argues that the rapid population growth experienced between the 1960s and 1980s, as the finance industry expanded, has been a source of contention which continues in the realm of immigration policy, over which the UK retains control. Instead, housing policy has been used as the means to control Immigration (States of Jersey, 2004), and linking settlement to wealth, it is highly restrictive. It is only since 2005 that measures have been phased in to address some of the economic effects of global competition and subsequently the recession, measures which, while attractive for businesses and foreign investors, required increases in the domestic tax burden to make up a potential £100 million annual shortfall.

Jersey has no political parties or cabinet and underwent significant governmental reform in 2005 when ten new ministries were created and Departments replaced Committees. Prior to this the executive had only become 'representative' in 1947 and the social significance of the 'parish' as a political unit remains strong (Le Hérissier, 1998). Policy is still formed and enacted via 'committees' that operate in a highly fragmented and under-strategized environment that lacks the mechanisms for accountability found in traditional democracies. The 2005 reforms were clearly intended to address the increasing complexity of policy-making in the global context and as Le Hérissier (1998: 183) observes 'the [previous] system has almost connived to make change a slow, incremental process'. This is nowhere more obvious than in the area of social policy.

In the early 2000s Jersey began to seek change in the operation of social security policy, intending to streamline and integrate a number of separate means-tested benefits. Included in this review were commissioned surveys around budgetary standards and income distribution which compared Jersey's provisions to those of other European countries (Kellard *et al.*, 2001; States of Jersey, 2004). The reforms to income support provisions were largely concerned with the operation of work incentives and poverty traps and the impact of the introduction of a general sales tax. The report on Income Support (IS) also notes 'a mixed response' to proposals to make income support a 'passport to free primary healthcare', where it was felt that 'requiring a co-payment, however little, was a prudent thing to do' in order to ensure that benefit recipients were 'incentivized' to save for health costs (States of Jersey, 2004: 7). Clearly then, there is a moral dimension to decision-making and an explicit desire to retain both the 'discipline' of the market and control over the expenditure patterns of low-income households. Housing policy in Jersey epitomizes the internal contradictions afflicting a polity that is attempting to modernize, while retaining existing values. The manipulation of property purchase to limit immigration has priced much of the population out of the housing market, and consequently 40 per cent of households rent property and one fifth of households are in receipt of rent subsidies. Social insurance is restricted to old age, disability, sickness and maternity benefits, although there is no right to maternity or parental leave unless offered by an employer. All other benefits are means-tested, including the universal family allowances. There is no insurance-related unemployment benefit and unemployment is dealt with via the welfare grants system, which provides means-tested support on an individual case basis. Cases are put to the Parish authorities for assessment and award along the lines of the English poor laws. In consequence perhaps, labour market participation rates are comparable to those of other European countries: 60 per cent for women and 70 per cent for men, (although this latter is slightly lower than most) and unemployment low at 2.3 per cent.

Reminiscent of the changes in British social provision as more women and working class members were voted onto the poor law boards, Jersey is gradually adapting to the welfare needs of a changed population in a different world. Policy documents suggest that although strands of less eligibility continue to be woven through the social security reforms, having commissioned social research and reviews, the committees and States have been partly persuaded by arguments in favour of social rather than individual risk. Nevertheless, there is also a greater desire to move towards targeting of benefits alongside administrative simplification and a distrust of 'centralization', and an uncertainty in policy language which switches from discussion of the 'beneficiary' to the 'customer' (States of Jersey, 2004). It was only in 2002 that the States debated abolishing the law of obligation from children to parents as 'out of step with modern day life', and while this illustrates both the influence of French and English law in the Jersey system, it is also symptomatic of the welfare conundrums Jersey faces. A simultaneous desire for freedom and guarantees can also be identified in public opinion.

In line with most advanced countries, the question of pension sustainability looms large in policy discussion in Jersey. In the 2008 Social Survey 22 per cent of respondents did not have either private or occupational pensions and 24 per cent stated that they would be relying on the state pension in retirement. In terms of the potential policy options preferred by the population, most chose increased contributions over either reduced payments or raising of the pensionable age (with a predictable age effect in responses), but three quarters agreed that a voluntary tier in the state pension should be provided and 55 per cent that this should be compulsory. With regard to the funding of long-term care a high proportion (20–25 per cent) of respondents 'don't know' what their views are on the state/private mix. This might suggest a lack of informed public debate on this topic, but of those who did express an opinion, 81 per cent were in favour of a publicly organized scheme (either via insurance or tax), over half thought the scheme should be compulsory, three quarters that it should be funded by those of working age only, half that contributions should be progressive and three quarters that the scheme should enable private top-ups for more expensive care (States of Jersey Statistics Unit, 2008). In terms of values it appears that while the traditional liberal economic principles remain strong, there is popular demand for state intervention in the area of pensions and care, and this reflects both the changing labour market in Jersey and greater recognition of the contingency of social diswelfare.

Jersey's identity as a tax haven is crucial in its global position of power and influence and with regard to its domestic welfare relations; it is highly protectionist and dominated by the interests of the finance industry. Clearly then, changes in welfare values need to be evaluated in a unique context where 'democracy' exists in the absence of political movements, and where at the key historical point for welfare development, politics were dominated by the interests of wealthy settlers. In spring 2009 the Director General of the OECD confirmed the organization's support for more stringent regulations of tax havens, and Jersey has begun to bow to peer pressure by developing Tax Information Exchange Agreements with 13 countries. In mid May 2009, the chair of Christian Aid UK in Jersey resigned in protest at Christian Aid's public critique of Jersey's tax status and consequent role in sustaining global inequality and poverty. This indicates the dominance of local rather than international politics in wider welfare debates. Jersey is certainly an actor on the world stage, but is able to manage its global relationships mostly out with the advisory interventions of international organizations such as the OECD, and without the domestic electoral pressures impinging upon modern welfare states.

Concluding comments

The study of small states has contributed important observations to general schema of politics and economics, but welfare state theorizing has not yet fully accounted for the challenges of being and not being a 'micro state in a macro world' (Harden, 1985; cited in Ott, 2000: 3). The case studies of social policy development set out above suggest that exceptionalism is the main characteristic of the place of small island states in traditional frameworks of comparative welfare research. Their hybridity of welfare influences connected with geopolitical vulnerability (smallness) problematizes the notions of national 'regimes', and the resultant policy landscape can tell us much about the establishment and strength of 'path dependency' as a means to understand policy development. These characteristics create both political processes and frameworks for social relations that are crucial for welfare development and redevelopment. While all states are unique, it seems some are more unique than others, and the three islands considered here exhibit sharp contrasts with both large states, 'large' small states and each other in their political history, colonial and cultural influences as well as in their smallness. Their 'islandness' however, has led them to adopt similar economic survival strategies that attempt to minimize reliance on natural resources but carry a heavy price in terms of exposure to and integration in the global. Contemporary global pressures however, are mediated in ways that reflect surprisingly versatile social politics, ready and able to accommodate policy dissonance. Housing policy in Iceland, marketization of healthcare in Cyprus and even the limited public preference for socialized care insurance in Jersey illustrate this point. It is not yet clear whether this results from welfare state hybridity and the wider range of policy options this presents, the localized and negotiable political routes which characterize the policy process, or a tendency to privilege national unity whatever the party political cost. The discussion here indicates a combination of all three. Although they do display regime type characteristics, within their families of nations, these small island states are very much the long-lost relatives; they may attend the family events but no one is quite sure to whom they are related. As such, they are indeed theoretical thorns and neglected outliers of comparative research; but the retention of their exceptionalism makes them all the more interesting, both sociologically and in terms of policy learning. Given the small size but significance of all three islands in the world-system, it is important that these curious 'exceptions' are understood in terms of their capacity to act in arenas which are not of their own making. The sociological concern, here framed as one of unearthing the social basis of regime types, requires much fuller exploration than these policy case studies allow. What is established is that all three polities exhibit strength and weakness in characteristics consistent with the varying worlds of welfare but not in any consistent or predictable way. Solidaristic social policy values are obviously present in Cyprus and Iceland and there is a hint that popular support for collectivist solutions to public problems is emerging in Jersey but further testing of the relationship between size and more 'social' social policy will be necessary to state this with more confidence. Equally, the question of policy learning, which first raised the interest of Katzenstein in the 1980s has to be approached with a degree of equanimity based on the evidence presented here. In a recent volume with the sub-title *Small states big lessons*, Obinger *et al.* (2010) argue that there is much that can be learned by the large from the small. However, it is unlikely that the greater breadth and lesser depth of social, political and economic relationships in large states could allow the degree of policy flexibility and adaptability to international and global change exhibited by the island states considered here.

In privileging size as an independent variable, the study of island states as national units does however reveal much about scalar relationships and 'the importance of considering the differential cultural *interpretations* of the modern global circumstance' (Robertson and Lechner, 1985: 110) that is missed in analyses of big, internationally powerful nations. As discussed in the introduction, the preceding case studies do expose aspects of the relationship between economics, political strength and social relations which are less visible when considering policy change in larger states. Accounting for size does change perspective. In the cases here, external policy influences are less diffuse and more readily identifiable, and internal idiosyncrasies more obvious. Small island states may well be the places where more socially responsive or experimental forms of interpretation of the global circumstance can be found. Adding such a layer of understanding to historical and institutional analysis can provide a fuller picture of welfare relations in circumstances of crisis, transition and innovation, and in so doing contribute much to the development of welfare theory.

Acknowledgements

Thanks to Richard Jenkins, two anonymous reviewers and the editors for comments on an earlier version of this paper.

Notes

1 A notable exception is Kosonen (2003).
2 It is something of a paradox given critique of the global Northern focus of cross-national welfare state research that in the study of small island states there is much less interest in those that are not considered to be 'developing'.
3 The Progressive Party for the Working People, founded in 1941 and merged with the then illegal Communist Party of Cyprus in 1944.
4 In 2001 68.4 per cent of households were owner occupied (MLSI/EC, 2003).
5 Iceland spent 8.3 per cent of GDP on public health expenditure in 2004, a global high (UNDP, 2008).
6 Personal communication, Office of Social Security, MSSS, May 2009.

References

AKEL (2009a), *Greeting at the reception following the election of comrade Andros Kyprianou to the post of General Secretary of the CC of AKEL Release Date: February 2, 2009* http://www.akel. org.cy/ngcontent.cfm?a_id=5907&tt=graphic&lang=13
AKEL (2009b), Speech of G.S. of AKEL Andros Kyprianou for the International Women's Day *at the mass meeting organized by the WOMEN'S MOVEMENT OF POGO, Release Date: March 8, 2009* http://www.akel.org.cy/ngcontent.cfm?a_id=5884&tt=graphic&lang=13
Arts, W. and J. Gelissen, (2002), 'Three worlds of welfare capitalism or more? A state-of-the-art report', *Journal of European Social Policy*, 12 (2): 137–58.
Asgrimsson, H., (2005), *The Icelandic Economy*, Prime Minister's speech, Landsbanki Islands, March 14th 2005 http://eng.forsaetisraduneyti.is/minister/Speeches_HA/nr/1732
Baldacchino, G., (2004), 'Editorial introduction', *World Development*, 32 (2): 327.
Bauman, Z., (2001), *Community: Seeking Safety in an Insecure World*, Oxford: Blackwell.
Bonner, J., (2006), *Why Size Matters, From Bacteria to Blue Whales*, Princeton: University of Princeton Press.
Boyes, R., (2009), *Meltdown Iceland*, London: Bloomsbury.
Cohen, A.P., (1987), *Whalsay: Symbol, Segment and Boundary in a Shetland Island Community*, Manchester: Manchester University Press.
Dommen, E., (1980), 'Some distinguishing characteristics of island states', *World Development*, 8: 931–43.
Esping-Andersen, G., (1990), *The Three Worlds of Welfare Capitalism*, Cambridge: Polity.
Esping-Andersen, G., (1996), *Welfare States in Transition*, London: Sage.
Esping-Andersen, G., (1999), *Social Foundations of Postindustrial Economies*, Oxford: Oxford University Press.
Goffman, E., (1959), *The Presentation of Self in Everyday life*, London: Penguin (Reprinted 1990).
Hampton, M., (1998), 'Mapping the Minefield: Theories of Island Offshore Finance Centres with reference to Jersey' in M. Bowe, L. Briguglio and J.W. Dean (eds), *Banking and Finance in Islands and Small States*, London: Pinter.
Hantrais, L., (2004), *Family Policy Matters, Responding to Family Changes in Europe*, Bristol: The Policy Press.

Health Insurance Organization (2008) 'Strategy' http://www.hio.org.cy/en/strategy.html

Heidenheimer, A., H. Heclo and C.T. Adams, (1990), *Comparative Public Policy, The Politics of Social Choice in America, Europe and Japan*, Basingstoke: Macmillan Education Ltd.

IMF, (2009), *Statement by the IMF mission to Iceland*, Press Release 09/76 March 13, 2009, (http://www.imf.org/external/np/sec/pr/2009/pr0976.htm)

Iversen, T., (2001), 'The Dynamics of Welfare State Expansion: Trade Openness, Deindustrialization and Partisan Politics' in P. Pierson (ed.), *The New Politics of the Welfare State*, Oxford: Oxford University Press.

Jones, E., (2008), *Economic Adjustment and Political Transformation in Small States*, Oxford: Oxford University Press.

Jonsson, G., (2001), 'The Icelandic welfare state in the Twentieth century', *Scandinavian Journal of History*, 26 (3): 249–67.

Katzenstein, P., (1985), *Small States in World Markets, Industrial Policy in Europe*, Ithaca: Cornell University Press.

Katzenstein, P., (2003), 'Small states and small states revisited', *New Political Economy*, 8 (1): 9–30.

Kellard, K., L. Adelman, Y. Hartfree and S. Middleton, (2001). *The 2001 Budget Standards for Different Household Types in Jersey*, CRSP433 Final Report Centre for Research in Social Policy: Loughborough University.

Kosonen, K., (2003), 'Small and large welfare states in the face of internationalization and globalization', Paper available at http://palissy.humana.univ-nantes.fr/msh/costa15/pdf/nantes/kosonen.pdf

Kristmundsson, Ó., (2003), *Reinventing Government in Iceland, A Case Study of Public Management Reform*, Reykjavik: University of Iceland Press.

Le Hérissier, R., (1998), 'Jersey: Exercising executive power in a non-party system', *Public Administration and Development*, 18: 169–84.

MLSI/EC, (2001), *Joint Assessment on Employment*, Brussels: European Commission.

MLSI/EC, (2003), *Joint Memorandum on Social Inclusion of Cyprus*, Brussels: European Commission.

Ministry of Labour and Social Insurance, (2004), Annual Social Welfare Report 2004, Cyprus, http://www.mlsi.gov.cy/mlsi/sws/sws.nsf/dmlannualrpt_Archive_en?OpenForm

Obinger, H., P. Starke, J. Moser, C. Bogedan, E. Gindulis and S. Leibfried, (eds) (2010), *Transformations of the Welfare State: Small States Big Lessons*, Oxford: Oxford University Press.

OECD, (2009), *Economic Survey of Iceland 2009*, Policy Brief, September 2009, Paris: OECD.

Ólafsson, S., (1993), 'Variations within the Scandinavian model: Iceland in the Scandinavian perspective' *International Journal of Sociology*, 22 (4): 61–88.

Ólafsson, S., (2003), 'Contemporary Icelanders – Scandinavian or American?' *Scandinavian Review*; Summer 2003; 91, 1; Academic Research Library: 6–14.

Ólafsson, S., (2005), 'Normative foundations of the Icelandic welfare state: On the gradual erosion of citizenship-based welfare rights' in Kuhnle S. and N. Kildal, *Normative Foundations of the Nordic Welfare States*, London: Routledge.

Oorschot, W., van, M. Opielka and B. Pfau-Effinger, (eds), (2008), *Culture and Welfare State*, Cheltenham: Edward Elgar.

Ott, D., (2000), *Small is Democratic, An Examination of State Size and Democratic Development*, New York: Garland Publishing.

Palmarsdottir, B., (1991), *Independence and Interdependence: Iceland and the EC*, Reading Papers in Politics, Occasional Paper No 8, Department of Politics: University of Reading.

Pálsson, G. and E.P. Durrenberger, (eds.), (1996), *Images of contemporary Iceland, everyday lives and global contexts*, Iowa: University of Iowa Press.

Pantelli, S., (2005), *The History of Modern Cyprus*, New Barnet: Topline Publishing.

Pierson, P., (ed.), (2001), *The New Politics of the Welfare State*, Oxford: Oxford University Press.

Pierson, P., (2004), *Politics in Time*, Princeton: Princeton University Press.

Prasad, N., (2007), *Research Proposal and Project Document: Social policies in small states*, A joint project of the Commonwealth Secretariat & United Nations Research Institute for Social Development (UNRISD).

Prime Minister's Office (2007), *Policy Declaration of the Government of the Independence Party and the Social Democratic Alliance 2007*, 23 May 2007 (http://eng.forsaetisraduneyti.is/news-and-articles/nr/2646)

Prime Minister's Office, (2009), *The first 100 days planned actions* 10 May 2009 (http://eng.forsaetisraduneyti.is/news-and-articles/nr/3702)

Read, R., (2004), 'The implications of increasing globalization and regionalism for the economic growth of small island states', *World Development*, 32 (2): 365–378.

Robertson, R. and F. Lechner, (1985), 'Modernization, globalization and the problem of culture in world-systems theory', *Theory, Culture and Society*, 2 (3): 103–118.

Schmidt, V., (2003), 'How, where and when does discourse matter in small states' welfare state adjustment?' *New Political Economy*, 8 (1): 127–46.

Selwyn, P., (1980), 'Smallness and islandness', *World Development*, 8 (12): 945–951.

Siaroff, A., (1994), 'Work, welfare and gender equality: A new typology' in Sainsbury, D., *Gendering welfare states*, London: Sage.

Sigurðardóttir, J., (2009), *Address Delivered at the AGM of the Central Bank of Iceland*, 17 April 2009. http://eng.forsaetisraduneyti/minister/JS_speeches/nr/3669

Special Investigation Commission, (2010), Report of the SIC, Delivered to Althingi 12th April at: http://sic.althingi.is/

Srebrnik, H., (2004), 'Small island nations and democratic values', *World Development*, 32 (2): 329–341.

States of Jersey, (2004), *Income Support System*, Report presented to the States on 2nd November 2004 by the Employment and Social Security Committee (http://www.statesassembly.co.uk/documents/reports/31482-13840-2112004.htm)

States of Jersey Statistics Unit, (2008), *Jersey Annual Social Survey*, States of Jersey Statistics Unit.

Sveinsson, J.R., (1996), 'Main trends of Icelandic housing in the 1980s and 1990s', *Scandinavian Housing and Planning Research*, 13: 215–220.

Thorhallsson, B., (2002) 'The skeptical political elite versus the pro-European public: The case of Iceland', *Scandinavian Studies*, 74 (3): 349–78.

Triseliotis, J., (1977), *Social Welfare in Cyprus*, London: Zeno Publishers.

UNDP, (2008), *Human Development Report 2007–8*, New York: United Nations Development Programme.

The political-opportunity structure of the Spanish anti-war movement (2002–2004) and its impact

Isis Sánchez Estellés

Abstract: This paper contributes to the study of social movements and their impact by approaching the topic through a discussion of the framework of political-opportunity structure. While there is a lack of research on the impact of movements, and few theories have yet been developed, there is a healthy debate on the elements that configure a movement's political-opportunity structure. This paper aims to contribute to these debates by first analysing the political opportunities of the anti-war movement in Spain (2002–2004) and, second, noting its impact in terms of the subsequent withdrawal of troops from Iraq after the elections in March 2004. After reviewing the literature on impact in social movement theory, the analysis then presents the elements of a movement's political-opportunity structure, explaining which elements should be considered variable and which stable. The paper closes by exploring which of these elements explains most powerfully the policy impact of movements.

Introduction

This paper analyses how the Spanish anti-war movement achieved its goal of troop withdrawal from Iraq in March 2004. In November 2002, agreement was reached at the European Social Forum to launch a campaign against the war in Iraq, to coordinate an international anti-war movement, and to consult on possible protest dates such as February 15th or March 20th 2003. There followed a moment of climax in Spain between February 15th and 20th, when more than 5 million people demonstrated in several Spanish cities. The protests continued during the spring, summer and autumn and even into the beginning of 2004, although their intensity diminished.

On March 11th 2004, however, there was a terrorist attack by Al Qaeda in Spain on the Atocha trains. The following day prime minister José María Aznar called for a demonstration defending Spain against the terrorism of ETA (Euskadi Ta Askatasuna, the nationalist-terrorist organization of the Basque Country), but his calls backfired. On March 13th, part of the citizenship spontaneously demonstrated against Aznar and his centre-right party, the Popular

Party (PP) in front of its offices. The next day, elections were held and the centre-left Socialist Workers Party of Spain (PSOE) won. The new prime minister, José Luis Rodríguez Zapatero, withdrew the troops from Iraq. This decision to withdraw the troops was considered a success for the anti-war movement. So what were the conditions for such a success? Is there any theory that can account for this process?

In Schumaker's typology (1975), this success or impact can be understood as 'policy responsiveness'; in Kitschelt's (1986) typology, it can be understood as a 'substantive' impact; in Kriesi's (1991), a 'proactive' impact; and in Giugni's (1999) and Rochon and Mazmanian's (1993), a 'policy change' impact. All of these types thus refer only to changes in policy. Much research has focused on policy outcomes, because it is easier to measure such an impact than assess wider social or cultural impacts (Giugni, 1999). In particular much research has focused on the policy impact of movements by relating their actions to changes in legislation, or to some other manifest indication of policy change (Amenta, Carruthers and Zylan, 1992; Banaszak, 1996; Burstein, 1985, 1979; Tarrow, 1993; Kitschelt, 1986).

By contrast Gamson (1990) suggests two critical aspects of a movement's success: the acceptance of a group as a valid representative of a legitimate set of interests by its antagonists; and the same group winning advantages for its benefit. This categorization is generally useful, but omits something critical: the political process itself that occurs between a movement's initial challenge and a subsequent substantive political change (Burstein, Einwohner and Hollander, 1995). It is here, as is discussed in what follows, where the concept of the political-opportunity structure can play a role, explaining the process of how the political environment provides the conditions for a movement to attain its goals.

Theories of social movement impact

The impact of social movements has still not been theorized systematically (Giugni, 1999). Movements, and their impacts, have long been the subject of study, but the theoretical focus of this work has tended to be somewhat narrow (Amenta, Dunleavy and Bernstein, 1994; Banaszak, 1996; Giugni *et al.*, 1999). Evaluating what is to be considered to be an outcome is also an open debate (Amenta and Young, 1999). What stand out are two debates within the study of the impact of social movements: the disruption/moderation debate (discussion about the (un)successful use of violence) and the internal/external debate (Giugni, 1999). Both issues are addressed by Gamson (1990) in *The Strategy of Social Protest*. In this paper, I focus my attention on the internal/external debate, because the anti-war movement in Spain considered itself to be pacifist and did use violence in its tactics.

The internal/external debate relates to whether variables are endogenous or exogenous to the movement and which better account for its success. More specifically, the debate involves disagreement between those authors who argue that social movements are capable of achieving their aims independent of external support, and those who see external support as a precondition for success. The former perspective is identified with the resource mobilization theory, which has been translated into a perspective that stresses the importance of 'bargaining' for the movement's impact (see Burstein, Einwohner and Hollander, 1995). The latter perspective is identified with political-process theory and it is this perspective I propose to analyse alongside the theoretical elements associated with political-opportunity structures.

A number of studies stress the importance of the political environment and the context for the success or otherwise of a social movement (Goldstone, 1980; Kitschelt, 1986; Jenkins and Perrow, 1977; McAdam, 1982; Schumaker, 1975). Kitschelt (1986) in his comparison of anti-nuclear movements in four Western democracies argues that a movement's impact strongly depends on the existing political-opportunity structure. Similarly, Tarrow (1998) explains the crucial role of political opportunities in shaping the long-term effects on the individual, institutional and cultural levels. Piven and Cloward (1979), in their research on the unemployed workers' movement, the industrial workers' movement, the civil rights movement and the welfare rights movement, demonstrate that the impact of protest movements is shaped by the prevailing social structure, specifically the features of institutional life that shape the opportunities for action, model its forms and limit its impact.

There is, then, an ongoing interest in which factors are most important in affecting the impact of movements (Giugni, 1998). Amenta and his colleagues (1992, 1994, 1996) provide the most recent systematic attempt to understand the determinants of a movement's impact. They present a 'political mediation model', whereby a movement's impact typically requires mediation by supportive actors across various political institutions. In particular, they look at the presence of sympathetic regimes and state bureaucracies that benefit from protest outcomes, in addition to the importance of strong organization within movements. For example, Amenta *et al.* (1996) suggest that disruptive tactics may be less important in a strongly sympathetic political context, but note that the same context may require strong organization. Thus, the importance of the factors does not rest solely on the strength of their association with a particular outcome but, in a more complex way, how they interact with each other in relation to the type of impact (Cress and Snow, 2000).

This point leads to an important idea: that the factors associated with a movement's impact may vary in their importance depending on the type of impact. As mentioned already, there are several typologies of impact, including those suggested by Schumaker (1975), Kitschelt (1986), Kriesi (1995), Rochon and Mazmanian (1993) and Giugni (1999). In general, the types of impact depend on: whether the impacts are in the political arena or in other arenas including the social and cultural; whether the impact is external or internal (i.e. inside or outside the movement); and whether the impact affects the fundamental relationship between political elites and the people, or only changes policy.

Methodology

I follow Miles and Huberman's (1994) 'transcendental realism' as a means of qualitative analysis with three interrelated elements: the reduction of the data, the treatment of the data and the development of conclusions. It involves the processes of coding, taking notes and developing explanations.

My methodology includes analysis of data with a constructivist approach (Silverman, 2006) of 45 open standardized interviews (Patton, 1990) with experts, more specifically with activists in the anti-war movement and with politicians of the two most important left-wing parties in Spain, the United Left (IU) (the third most important party in votes) and the Spanish Socialist Workers Party (PSOE); also the main trade unions, the Workers Commission (CCOO) and the Workers General Union (UGT). The constructivist perspective focuses on documenting the way in which accounts are part of the world that they describe.

I also analysed news from two main newspapers in Spain, *El Pais* and *El Mundo*, particularly their coverage of the anti-war movement, and documented analysis on the main organizations (Madrid Social Forum, Stop the War in Catalonia, Culture Platform against the war, Committee of Solidarity with the Arab Cause). I coded and analysed the data using MaxQDA software. I focus on these two main newspapers with opposing ideologies, one from the right (*El Mundo*), and one from the left (*El Pais*), because I am interested in how they deal with topics related to the war.

This paper adopts a qualitative methodology to complement the statistical analyses that other authors have undertaken relating the anti-war movement in Spain with electoral turnout and the mobilizations of left-leaning abstainers following the 2004 terrorist attacks (see Lago and Montero, 2005; Montero and Lago, 2007; Sanz and Sierra, 2005; Font and Mateos, 2007; Barreiro, 2004). The aim is to discover the sociological routes that helped the movement make an impact though a major change in foreign policy.

Political-opportunity structure and the impact of social movements

Tarrow (1994) outlines the problems of assessing the impact of social movements since their influence is often indirect and mediated by conventional political processes (Andrews, 1997). Identifying a direct causal relationship is often extremely difficult. However, the elements of political-process theory can give an account about the opportunities and constraints for a social movement. In fact, the political-process approach appears the most appropriate for providing an account of the reasons and conditions for when movements achieve a policy change. The wisdom, creativity and outcomes of activists' choices are perhaps only understood and evaluated by looking at the political context and the rules of the games in which the choices are made (Sawyers and Meyer, 1999).

The most suitable concept for analysing this process is the political-opportunity structure. It has been used in previous studies of social movements as a key explanatory variable in relation to two dependent variables: the timing of collective action and the outcomes of movement activity (McAdam, 1996).[1] It is the latter that is of concern in this study. High mobilization does not necessarily lead to impact if the political-opportunity structure is not open to change. In contrast, lower mobilization may have an important impact, owing to properties of the political-opportunity structure (Kitschelt, 1986; Kolb, 2007). In this paper, I therefore analyse those elements of the political-opportunity structure that are more suitable to explaining the impact of social movements, in particular policy change.

To start with the definition of political-opportunity structure, Tarrow defines this as '*dimensions of the political environment that provide incentives for people to undertake collective action by affecting their expectations for success or failure*' (Tarrow, 1994: 85).[2] Tarrow points out that this is a dynamic set of variables that varies from time to time and from place to place (Tarrow, 1994).[3] Different authors have conceptualized this set of variables in different ways (see McAdam, 1996), such as Brockett (1991), Kriesi *et al.* (1992, 1995), Rucht (1996) and Tarrow (1994).

Basically, all four authors have distinguished the formal institutional or legal structure of a given political system from the more informal structure of power relations (McAdam, 1996: 26). Meyer and Minkoff (2004) have further noted the difficulty of determining which elements contribute to the emergence, development and influence of protest movements. They also distinguish between the more stable elements in the socio-political structure and the more unstable elements. The present paper attempts to clarify which elements can be considered more stable in the political structure or more variable, and also clarify which elements have best explained the attainment of the Spanish anti-war movement's goal.

Starting with the variable elements, there are four which can be readily identified: 1) the opening up of political access, 2) shifts in ruling alignments, 3) the availability of influential allies, 4) cleavages within and amongst elites. As explained below, I add to these number 5), repression and faciliation. A brief explanation of each element now follows.

1) The opening up of political access

Authors such as McAdam (1996) have named this element *the relative openness or closure of the institutionalized political system*. McAdam claims (1996) that this first dimension emphasizes the importance attributed to the formal legal and institutional structure of a given polity by all of the authors.

Expanding access is expressed more clearly through elections, in the case of democratic regimes. However, I consider another element which can explain the possibility of access to participation, which is in my explanation of the emergence and impact of the anti-war movement. *It is the consequences of the government responses* to the 3/11 attacks in Spain. When there is a terrorist attack in a country, it creates a new environment in which government's response, and the citizens' reaction to that response can be crucial for a movement's impact. The result can be considered as an issue-specific opportunity ie not translatable across social movements (Meyer and Minkoff, 1993, 2004).

2) Unstable alignments

Changes in government and opposition parties, especially when they are based in new coalitions, create uncertainty among supporters, and may lead elites to compete for support outside the polity (Tarrow, 1994). This element of the opportunity structure is more likely to have a causal effect on the emergence and development of a movement than the movement's own subsequent impact (Meyer and Minkoff, 2004).

3) Influential allies

Political parties are important allies for dissidents in representative systems. Generally speaking, the parties of the left are more favourable to the dissidents than the moderate or conservative parties (Tarrow, 2004). If the Social Democrats in particular are in opposition, they profit from the challenges new social movements direct at the government. This is especially true of moderate challenges that are considered legitimate by a large part of the electorate. By extension, Maguire (1995) claims that if a party is a potential party of government it could offer a successful movement an opportunity to realize its goals. This element is likely to be crucial for a movement's impact on policy.

4) Divided elites

Conflicts within and amongst elites encourage unrepresented groups to engage in collective action. Tarrow argues that elite-level divisions encourage non-represented groups, as well as those elites who are out of power, to seize the 'role of the tribunes of the people' (Tarrow, 2004: 119). This element of the political-opportunity structure encourages a process of legitimisation by the movement that spreads its demands through the population.

5) Repression and facilitation by the state

While Tarrow (2004) places this in the variable elements, he then talks about it again in the stable elements. I am going to place this firmly in the variable category as a fifth element as it changes depending on who is in government.

Repression and facilitation are better seen as two separate continua than as polar opposites, characteristic of different types of states. (Tilly, 1978).[4] I base my analysis of repression/facilitation on the interpretive framework of Donatella della Porta (1996), which includes the following dimensions: a) 'repressive' versus 'tolerant', according to the range of prohibited behaviours; b) 'selective' versus 'diffuse', according to the range of groups subject to repression; c) 'preventive' versus 'reactive', according to the timing of police intervention; d) 'hard' versus 'soft' according to the degree of force involved ; and c) 'dirty' versus 'lawful', according to the degree to which respect for legal and democratic procedures is emphasized. For example, a softer style of policing favours the diffusion of protest (Della Porta, 1996). This diffusion of protest attracts people to the cause.

Stable elements in political-opportunity structures

The aspects mentioned above can be considered as the dynamic aspects of political-opportunity structures, but there are other elements that can be considered as stable. Authors such as Peter Eisinger, William Gamson, David Meyer, Hanspeter Kriesi and Herbert Kitschelt have argued about the stable elements of the political-opportunity structure.

The structure of the state is a useful dimension in predicting whether and where the movements will find opportunities to engage in collective action. As states deal differently with strong and weak contenders, they show a different face in different sectors and vary their strength over time. Consequently, it is more useful to specify particular aspects of an institutional structure that relate directly to movements than to situate the state as a predictor of collective action[5] (Tarrow, 2004).

For this reason, I prefer to use more operational and concrete concepts. Where I am trying to explain the more stable elements, I prefer to use two concepts of Kitschelt (1986): political input structures and political output structures. Political input structures refer to how some elements of the political system are more open or closed to receiving and absorbing demands. Political output structures refer to how the system implements policies.

According to Kitschelt (1986) there are at least four factors that determine the openness of the political system to new demands. Firstly, the number of political parties that effectively articulate different demands in electoral politics influences openness (Kitschelt, 1986). Where there are large numbers of parties, social movements will be more likely to find allies within the system (Kriesi, 1995). In addition, Kriesi (1995) remarks that the *electoral system* plays a role. Proportional representation allows easier access for challengers than plurality or majority methods. New social movements, and in fact I would extend this to all kinds of movements, are more likely to find allies within the party system in proportional representation systems (Kriesi, 1995).

The second element in the input structures of Kitschelt is the independence of the legislatures. Openness increases with the capacity of the legislatures to develop and control policies independently of the executive (Kitschelt, 1986).

The third element is patterns of intermediation between the interest groups and the executive branch. Where fluid links are dominant, access for new interests are facilitated.

The fourth element refers to the mechanism of aggregation of demands. In fact, demands must actually find their way '*into the processes of forming policy compromises and consensus*' (Kitschelt, 1986: 63).[6]

To these stable elements, I also add the *structure of mass media*. In fact the more open the structure of the mass media is in a country, the more visible the movement is for the people (more coverage) and the more likely it is that the social movement can achieve its political objectives. '*The mass media play a crucial role in defining for movement actors whether they are taken seriously as agents of possible change*' (Gamson and Meyer, 1996).

The importance of the media

The media spotlight validates the movement as an important player. This suggests that the opening and closing of media access and attention is an important element in determining the political opportunities for movements (Gamson and Meyer, 1996). Media norms and practices and the broader political economy in which they operate affect the opportunities and constraints under which movements operate. Key organizations in the media system confer the standing of actors. They put them into the public sphere, suggest other media, refer to elites and publicly explain who the serious players are (Gamson and Meyer, 1996). By putting them into the public sphere and pointing out who the serious players are, the mass media help to legitimate a social movement. This process can shape the public preferences (Burstein, 1985) and this can lead to a change in voting behaviour.

Gamson and Meyer (1996) distinguish between a stable element of the mass media, which they call organizational and political economy of the mass media, and the other more volatile one which they call mass media access. I consider this as a stable element, as I am going to demonstrate certain aspects of how the media works in the country independently of who is in power. The structure of the mass media is interrelated with the rules of the political system.[7]

Analysis of the Spanish anti-war movement

In this section, I analyse the political-opportunity structure of the Spanish anti-war movement in order to identify those elements that best explain its policy impact. Meyer and Minkoff (2004) claim that movement-related policy outcomes are unequivocally determined by structural elements in the polity. The case of the Spanish anti-war movement suggests otherwise; instead, my reading of events supports Rucht's (1990) argument that structural political opportunities are not very helpful in understanding dynamic processes. I analyse the importance of both variable and stable elements to see which of these claims holds up best and identify whether there are some stable elements that help to explain the final outcome.

Although the first dimension in the variable elements is *the opening up of political access,* I relate this to the consequences of the terrorist attacks. Therefore, I analyse what the immediate consequences of the attacks were. The consequence of the attacks had an immediate influence on the impact of the anti-war movement, especially the events of March 13th, in other words the spontaneous demonstration in front of the offices of the PP just one day before the elections.

After the attacks Aznar, the prime minister, tried to construct a new discourse, pointing to ETA as the instigator of the attacks. After receiving information about the possible role of Al Qaeda, the government chose to deny it and place the blame on ETA. The first socio-political consequence of the attacks was the lie about the instigators, but there was another consequence that followed from this lie: the anger and mobilization of the people. I present below some of the quotations that illustrate the consequences of the attacks.

Pilar Masana from Aturem la Guerra explains why the lies of the government tried to protect it from an election defeat:

> *It was the lies that made many people go to vote. People voted against the PP(...) My perception is that Acebes until the last moment was defending the theory of ETA, because they knew the terrorism was linked with the war in Iraq which could lead them to lose the elections*

Montse, also from Aturem la Guerra, explains the reaction of the people to the lies:

> *People are not stupid, they know that ETA exists, who they kill and the style and type of attacks, and they are saying no, it is ETA, it is ETA, and that caused a huge spontaneous demonstration, all the people against the PP on the 13th March and the police hardly appeared.*

In all the interviews the same idea is repeated: the immediate consequence of the attacks was the lie, the lie produced anger and the spontaneous mobilization. This lie attracted the political tension that had been generated during those years (2001–2004) and connected with previous mobilizations, especially the anti-war movement as the second participant explains.[8]

Sara, an activist and organizer of alternative information (information for social movements) explains:

> *I always consider the 13th as a culmination of a cycle of four years, which started with the LOU[9] followed by a series of events until the final straw demanding no more lies, after the Prestige. You are not going to lie with 200 dead people on the table, the sequence was clear. The slogans of the 13th March during the whole night in the PP central office of Genova were the same as those we had been shouting for four years 'They call it democracy and it is not', 'Liars'.*

Jose Luis Gordillo, a pacifist from Aturem la Guerra, explains how citizens had learnt from earlier mobilizations:

> *People had been demonstrating for around two years. It is such a long process that was developing and culminated with the attacks and the government's lie. Without the mobilizations of 2003 the other (referring to 13th March) could not happen.*

254

The government's management of the lies about the ownership of the attacks reminded citizens of problems from the past, regarding lies about ecological prestige and weapons of mass destruction in Iraq (Sánchez, 2006; Sánchez and López, 2007). Also the response to the attacks was perceived to be a deceit. In response, a large portion of the citizenry angrily demonstrated in front of the offices of the PP on March 13th. During the protest, the public chants included: 'Who did the attacks? Europe knows already'; 'Liars, liars'; 'Aznar does not know it has been Al Qaeda'; 'He knows it, he knows it'; 'Television, manipulation'; 'you should not play with the deaths'; 'Do not use death to manipulate'; 'The people do not believe in the liars of the PP'; 'Aznar is guilty, you are responsible'; 'there is a lack of 200 votes because of you'; 'No to war'; 'We want information before the elections'; 'Today more than ever. Right of Information'; and 'We want to know now!' (Gómez, Ordaz, and Perejil, 2004; Rodriguez, 2004; Cue, 2004; Artal, 2004; Alvarez de Toledo, 2004). The public anger and the anticipation of a change in government constituted a process of 'cognitive liberation', in which people *'define their situation as unjust and subject to change to group action'* (McAdam, 1982: 51). The anger and the hope of change interacted to produce a movement (Aminzade and McAdam, 2001), in this case a protest. This protest had two objectives: to get the government to tell the truth about the attacks; and/or to punish the government the next day.

The demonstration on March 13th and the resulting press coverage, especially by *El Pais*, helped to unite the anger of the anti-war mobilizations of 2002–2003 with a wider desire to oust Aznar's PP from government. The government's deceit was transformed into an opportunity by the movement, and the opportunity for the movement was the possibility of changing the government in the next day's election. The party most likely to be the beneficiary was PSOE, a factor which leads us to the following aspect of political opportunities: the presence of influential allies.

Influential allies are an important factor in the success of social movements. The key influential ally of Spain's anti-war movement was the PSOE, a party that has been historically opposed to war.[10] This was no exception in the case of the Iraq war in 2003. It positioned itself against the war along with IU and the main trade unions, CCOO and UGT. The four political actors PSOE, IU, CCOO and UGT were central allies for the movements and they made up the Madrid Social Forum along with other organizations.

Of all these actors, however, the most influential ally was the PSOE. In fact, the PSOE has strong influence in the media group PRISA, of which the radio station SER and the newspaper *El Pais* made an important contribution to the movement. *El Pais* called for demonstrations and announced the demonstrations with the dates and places, as well as the route. *El Pais* also announced all kinds of actions, in the form of camping, sit-ins, rallies, pickets, demonstrations, boycotting, banging pots and pans and human mosaics (*El Pais*, 11/4/2003).

Jose Luis Gordillo, the pacifist from Aturem la Guerra quoted earlier, says that thanks to the support of PSOE they had the mass media in their favour, and the people on the ground accepted that the only message could be NO TO WAR, without any additional message of NO To NATO or BASES OUT. He says '*In exchange we thought it was worth it because that way we reached more people*'. Given the opportunity of having the PSOE as allies, the movement aimed to broaden its appeal and make more general demands in order to attract the support of more people.

Vicky, a student activist, explains how she and others were conscious of the influence of the PSOE on the population:

> When the PSOE participates, it makes the issue appear in newspapers, on TV, so there is more visibility for the movement which already exists. Thanks to this the issue appeared on every TV news broadcast.

As Carlos Girbau from IU says, the support of the parties, especially the PSOE contributed to the impact of the anti-war movement:

> There was a connection between the position of the parties (referring to IU and PSOE) and the movement, because it later helped to transform the rejection of the demonstrations into votes against Aznar.

The mobilizations on March 13th, and the others that preceded it, revealed the people's anger towards the PP, but if there had not been a party in position to win the election such as the PSOE, there would have been no way of transforming those mobilizations into votes against the PP. In turn, there would have been no possibility of withdrawing the troops from Iraq, as Zapatero did. Not only was the existence of important allies a key variable, but so too was the legitimacy this garnered for the cause. This leads us to consider the aspect of *division of elites*.

It is known that during 2003 the movement against the war on Iraq influenced some sectors, and some people in the PP distanced themselves from the executive. This was the case for Adriano del Moral in Montmelo (Catalonia), candidate to the council of the town, who put up a banner saying 'No to war, no to the weapons of mass destruction, no to hunger'. Francisco Marisca, councillor of the PP resigned because of his disagreement about the position of the PP in the war on Iraq. (*El Pais*, 11/4/2003, '*Barcelona se moviliza de nuevo el dia siguiente a la toma de Bagdad?*').

In Santa Coloma de Gramenet, Juan Manuel Ruiz Garcia resigned as a member of the Municipal Group for the Plenary of the town council. He resigned with colleague Concepción Fernandez in order to vote 'without problems of conscience' in favour of a motion against the war on Iraq that was presented in that plenary session. Ruiz claimed that the Iraq conflict was immoral and unethical as there was not enough time for the inspectors (*El Pais*, 2/4/2003).

The councillors of the PP in the two towns of Andalucia where the US bases were installed distanced themselves from the official line of the PP. In the case of Moron de la Frontera (Seville), the five town councils of the PP voted in favour of a motion rejecting the war and the use of the installations of the aerial bases in the military conflict. They also supported the anti-war mobilizations. Three of these five councillors of the PP announced that they would leave the party because of their opposition to the war on Iraq (*El Mundo* 26/03/2003). In Rota (Cadiz) all the councillors of the municipal corporations, including the PP ones, had a sit-in to plead for a peaceful solution in the conflict. (*El Pais*, 15/2/2003 'Los concejales del PP de Moron y Rota se desmarcan de su partido').

The city council of Segovia, where the PP governs, sent a resolution against the war on Iraq to the Congress (El Mundo, 14/3/2003). During the months of March and April 2003 resolutions approved by the support of the PP were sent to the Congress. This occurred with Lezuza (Albacete), San Vicente de la Sonsierra (La Rioja) and Los Barrios (Cadiz) (*El Mundo* 20/3/2003).

In addition, a deputy from the PP, who was the president of the Commission of Justice of the Congress distanced himself from his party. He said that peace has preference over security and that a war 'against all the people' cannot be based on 'some suspicions' even if its president (referring to Saddam) is 'bloodthirsty' (*El Mundo* 31/3/2003). He explained that he is one of the sensitive ones in the PP who think that peace is a more important value than security. Also present in the demonstrations against the war on Iraq were part of the Bureau of the councils of the PP in Andalucia (*El Pais*, 16/02/2003).

All these actions within the PP propelled the movement forward with different actions and presented the image to the public that the anti-war movement was taking hold. This supports the argument of Piven and Cloward (1979) that the opportunities for the challengers are limited to times of widespread discontent when there is a division among elites. In such cases, certain elites may ally themselves with the concerns of challengers to shore up their own power base, ultimately helping to legitimate the movement's claims. In this case, the increasing legitimacy of the Spanish anti-war movement by another part of the electorate strengthened the movement. There was also another element that helped to legitimate the cause of the anti-war movement: the low level of repression by the State.

In line with Dela Porta framework (1996) I can say that in the case of the anti-war movement in Spain, it was tolerant, selective, reactive, soft and lawful. Tolerant because the majority of the demonstrations were peaceful, selective because any actions were mooted by specific leftist groups, reactive because it was always following demonstrations and actions, gentle in general because repression from the government forces consisted of fines to the demonstrators,[11] and more or less lawful because the demonstrators respected the laws of the government.

The most common form of repression was soft because it consisted of fines, for instance in cases in some towns in Spain: Palma de Mallorca, Valladolid, Leon, Madrid, and Tenerife. However, the denomination of lawful came hand-in-hand with harsher aspects because lawsuits were also used to shut down the freedom of expression of some groups.[12]

Despite this repression, the anti-war movement continued to demonstrate until the end, because the image of the movement was soft and legal and was not distorted, and so people continued to demonstrate without fear. Of great significance here is the fact that there was no police repression after the attacks on the 13th of March. Robert Gonzalez from Aturem la Guerra explains: '*Also the police did not charge. It was all a bit odd. It was strange that we were demonstrating illegally on the day of reflection before the elections and nothing happened and the police did not charge anyone*'. Regarding the repression in the anti-war movement Robert from the Space of Universities, explains: '*It was a selective repression, that it was focused on the more radical streams of the movement.*'

All this made the anti-war movement more attractive for potential protestors as they had less fear of demonstrating. The tolerant and soft style of policing favoured the diffusion of protest. Also selective and legal protest policing isolated the violent wings of the movement and helped the integration of the more moderate activists (Della Porta, 1996). This kind of repression facilitated the integration and participation of all kinds of people who might otherwise never have been enrolled.

Interventions by the media

As I pointed out before, the opening or closing of media access and attention is an important element in defining political opportunities for movements (Gamson and Meyer, 1996). The first thing to note about the political economy of the mass media is that during the years of democracy in Spain, the government has had a strong influence on public and private television. (Fernández and Santana, 2000). Since the beginning of the years of transition to democracy (1977–1978 and 1978–1982), the executives showed a concern for the control of television in their politics. The general directors of RTVE (the public television network) are appointed by the executives, demonstrating the strong link between the government and the public TV.

There are messages promoting the government in the public radio stations and in the private sector in favour of the Administration. The rest of the private media adopt views critical of the executive, even creating media platforms that have given impulse to changes in government, such as the arrival of the PP to the government in 1996. (Jerez, Sampedro and Baer, 2000)

It is important to note that during the Aznar administration (2000–2004) this was no exception. TVE-1 (the public television network) proved to be more in favour of the government and the work of TVE at that time distorted the role of public television. In fact, news was presented with evaluations that were favourable to the executive and the PP. As an example, the PSOE denounced the media for not directly reporting the mobilizations of February 15th. In a summer musical show, TVE also censored criticism of the politics of Bush, the mobilizations against the war on Iraq and the Gescartera case (El Pais, 1/7/2003).

TVE and Antena 3 are the channels which dedicated less time to providing information about the numerous protests against the invasion of Iraq (8.5 per cent corresponding to TVE and 12.3 per cent to Antena 3).[13] TVE-1 was the channel that gave more voice to the government at the beginning of the conflict (43.6 per cent). One of the significant actions of TVE was not to broadcast the well-known Max Awards. After the ceremony of the Goya Awards, the Participants of the Culture Platform claimed that this was censorship from the government and they did not agree with it.[14] It is important to note that a committee was created against manipulative information, composed of 351 workers of the public body. The first analysis that they made was on the period from 28th February to 5th March 2003. It shows that those at the top of RTVE performed actions in which '*the minimum criteria of veracity, pluralism and independence were not respected*'. (Culture Platform against the War).

Since the time when the socialist party was in government (1982–1996), two media groups were created that still exist nowadays. One which was made up of the newspapers *ABC*, *El Independiente*, *El Mundo* and the radio station COPE as well as sometimes Diario 16, and which was in favour of the opposition at the time, the PP. The other group was composed of the Newspaper *El Pais*, SER radio, *El Siglo* and Canal Plus, and was more closely linked to the government at that time, the PSOE. In general, the first group supports the PP and the second PSOE, regardless of whether they are in the government or in the opposition. (Fernandez and Santana, 2000; Reig, 1998).

At the time that we are analysing, with the PP in government and PSOE in the opposition, El Pais[15] as well as El Mundo gave coverage to the anti-war movement. During the years 2003–2004 there are 100 news stories from El Mundo and 251 from El Pais. As I pointed out before, El Pais and the Group Prisa were important allies of the movement.[16]

In relation to the 11th and the attacks, the public media did not question the official theory of ETA as an author, although also they did not rule out Islamic responsibility. On the other hand, there were other media that sided with the idea of Islamic authorship and accused the government of withholding information. (Arroyo and Roel, 2006).

We can see from this, that part of the mass media was critical of the government and gave more visibility to the anti-war movement. This influenced public opinion. In fact, 90.8 per cent did not agree with the military intervention in February 2003 and mantained this opinion until March 2004 (CIS, Centre for Sociological Research. In Spanish Centro de Investigaciones Sociologicas).[17]

Concluding comments

Despite the difficulty of studying the impacts of social movements, and despite the lack of theory surrounding the subject, the foregoing analysis of political-opportunity structures can shed some light on the topic of a movement's policy impact. Specifically there is an ongoing debate surrounding the elements that ought to be considered as part of a political-opportunity structure, and this paper has sought to contribute to this discussion.

Meyer and Minkoff (2004) ask the question 'political-opportunity for what?' – recognizing that the political environment provides consistent and variable influences. The consistent elements of the political structure in the present Spanish case are closed: they include a legislative branch with limited independence from the executive, and one that was dominated by one party (PP) due to the electoral law; interest groups that do not really interact fluidly with the government; and a judicial system closed to citizen's demands and with limited independence in the resolution of conflict (for details of these more specific factors, see Appendix).

Among the stable elements, the current party system in Spain provided the possibility of different party allies such as the IU, PSOE, and mass media helping to spread the cause of the movement and legitimate their demands. However, these stable elements have one feature in common, the PSOE, which is connected to the variable elements: the presence of influential allies.

The other variable elements include the government's response to a terrorist attack, the patent lies which were essential for triggering a protest, in this case the March 13th protest which united the anti-war protests with the demand for a change in government. Also, the division of elites in the PP and the recourse to soft repression (even on March 13th) both helped to legitimate the anti-war movement's cause. All this suggests that the structural obstacles of a political system, coupled with one-party majority rule in Congress (PP), can be overcome if there is coverage of the movement by the media and a main party supports the movement's cause.

This said, we should not forget that the protest of 13th March (and its coverage) was crucial in linking past mobilizations with a diminution in support for the government a day before a general election. Emotions and memories were united by the possibility of change and the attainment of the movement's goals. In contrast to the argument offered by Meyer and Minkoff (2004), all this supports the idea that that the variable elements of political-opportunity structure, along with the stable element of the mass media's structural role, were crucial factors in determining this particular movement's impact not only on policy but also on events.

Appendix: Background to a discussion of stable elements and unstable alignments

Concerning the variable elements, it is worth highlighting the importance of unstable alignments. There were no unstable alignments, because the PP (the right-wing party) was in government with an absolute majority, and it did not need any support or coalitions of other parties. Also it was the second legislature in government. This leads us to analyse the features of the political system that created the possibility of one party governing on the basis of an absolute majority, as well as other elements that can explain the outcome of the movement. I differentiate between input (how much the system is open to new demands) and output structures (how the policies are implemented) (Kitschelt, 1986).

Recalling the elements of the political system's openness to new demands, we firstly have to consider the *structure of the political parties*. The name that it is attributed to the parties of the political system is *moderate pluralism* or *moderate multipartidism*, composed of two majority parties PSOE (centre-left), PP (centre-right), one which is less significant in the national sphere, IU (United Left), and the constant presence of two nationalistic parties of the centre-right, the PNV (Nationalist Basc Party) in the Basque country and the CIU (Convergence and Union) in Catalonia.

As there are a wide range of parties, movements find it easy to find different allies. As I explained, the PSOE and the IU were allies of the movement. Generally speaking, with regards to the political parties, we can consider Spain to have a system which is open to new demands.

Regarding the *electoral system,* Spain has a proportional system with majority correction. The province is the electoral circumscription. For the assignment of seats in the Congress of deputies there is a legal barrier related to electoral circumscription.[18] The formulas of conversion of votes into seats are simple in the two chambers (The Congress and the Senate). For the composition of the Congress of Deputies, the D'Hondt formula is used. In the distribution of seats, this method tends to over-represent the parties with the highest number of votes, especially in the small circumscriptions. In the case of the Senate, the process of conversion of votes into seats is simpler. A majoritarian system is applied in which candidates who obtain the most votes are elected until the total of number of senators assigned to that circumscription has been filled. (Crespo, 1997). The system which favours the big parties, has encouraged the formation of parliamentary majorities that have created strong and stable governments. (Laiz Castro, 2002).

As an effect of the element indicated, parliamentary representation has been concentrated on the two major parties, PP and PSOE.[19] The openness of the party system to demands contrasts with the electoral system. This makes use of the 'useful vote', the election of one of the majority parties instead of the party that is closest ideologically in the spectrum. This especially tends to happen to the IU in relation to the PSOE. A high percentage vote goes to the PSOE instead of the IU, as it is more likely to govern. This means that although the IU was an important ally of the anti-war movement, PSOE is the only ally with potential to govern. This 'useful vote' restricted the outcome of the anti-war movement. The alternative for change was therefore focused on the PSOE and not the IU, although the IU has had a more clear position against the war since the beginning than PSOE.[20]

The second element in the input structures of Kitschelt is the *independence of the legislatures.* The more the legislatures develop and control policies independently of the executive, the more open the system. In the case of Spain, the process of compiling the budget law, the amendments which are aimed at increasing or decreasing the budget require the approval of the government. The Parliament can delegate legislative competence in the government through the law of the rules for articulating texts. The Parliament then approves a general principle (in the rules outlined) that are subsequently developed in texts (laws with articles). The Congress also decides the validation or repeal of the law decrees that the government dictates in cases of urgent necessity (Sanchez de Dios, 2002).

Generally speaking, we can say that legislative production is low compared with the Italian or German parliament. Although the committees do a very good job, some of the culture of our political elites is orientated towards giving the capacity of legislating to the executive branch (Sanchez de Dios, 2002).

It is important to note that the Spanish system of legislative-executive relations has been defined as the most pro-government system in Europe, as a system of the hegemony of the prime minister (Lopez Nieto, 1997). In the context of the anti-war movement, the legislature was even more connected with the executive because of the PP's absolute majority in Congress. This is partly due to the features of the electoral system in Spain which privileges major parties and majorities as stated above.

The third element refers to the patterns of intermediation between interest groups and the executive branch.[21] In Spanish political-administrative history, the relations between the groups of interest and the Public administrations has been significant. Neither were the Public Administration interested in having contact with the diverse individual interests that exist in society, nor would they contemplate a relation different from 'favouritism'. A radical separation was established between the 'general interests' represented in the Administration and the 'private interests' of the individuals. Parallel to this concept, the channels of communication between the private interests and the Administration worked in an informal way in the tradition of 'favouritism' (Molins, 1997).

In general, the density of affiliation to different groups is very low. There is a certain mistrust amongst the citizens in relation to their capacity to influence public policies through their integration in organized groups. This is connected with a political culture of delegated participation, where the generic trust in the representative organizations of interest is compatible with a minimum link to them. Besides, the Public administrations prefer to have privileged relations with certain groups to which they in turn give certain privileges (Molins, 1997).

Taking all this into account, we can say that the relationship with the executive branch through the public administration with the interests groups is not transparent and does not promote openness within the system. The closeness of the system encouraged the two main trade unions as groups of interests (CCOO and UGT) to collaborate as allies rather than as interlocutors of the public administration.

The fourth element is the existence of mechanisms that aggregate demands. In this regard, the first mechanism that aggregates demands from society is political parties, an aspect which has already been discussed.

Kitschelt (1986) also points out three operational dimensions to characterize the capacity of political systems to implement policies. However, I disregard the first two because they are not relevant for my analysis as I said before. The third element that Kitschelt points out is the relative independence and authority of the judiciary system in the resolution of political conflict. In Spain, the General Council of the Judiciary Power is elected in an indirect manner by the legislature. In practice, the General Council of the Judiciary Power has been elected because of party criteria rather than professional knowledge. Interest from parties has halted the job of the General Council of the Judiciary Power due to the lack of consensus between the majority parties in renewing the positions. The General Council of the Judiciary power is not subjected to any political control. The relation between the General Council of the Judiciary Power and the Ministry of Justice is based on the principle that it is the former who studies and designs public policy and then proposes it to the government and the parliament. It seems that there is certain independence of the judiciary in relation to the executive, but in practice there have been many connections between the role of the judiciary and the political sphere (Alcántara and Martínez, 1997). Regarding the antiwar case, the Platform culture against the war, together with the free association of lawyers, decided to submit a lawsuit against Aznar in April 2003, and the public was invited to sign up to it. Many people took the opportunity to sign up, but the High Court in Spain decided to shelve this lawsuit in January 2004. This shows how the judicial system is closed to citizens' demands and it is very connected with the executive.

Finally there is one stable element that exerts a greater influence than all the other stable elements that are usually theorized (Eisinger, 1973; Kitschelt, 1986) and for this reason this is discussed at length in the text of the paper.

Notes

1 The idea of political-opportunity structure, implicitly developed by Lipsky (1968), was made more explicit in the 1970s: first by Eisinger (1973) who operationalized it cross-sectionally using local political institutions, then by Piven and Cloward (1979), who claimed that electoral instability is the major source of political-opportunity. After that Jenkins and Perrow (1977) paid particular attention to the external resources of farm workers. The concept was then developed more formally by Tilly (1978), McAdam (1982), Tarrow (1994, 1996, 2004)) and Kitschelt (1986). The concept of political-opportunity structure has been used to study women's movements (Katzenstein and Mueller, 1987), antinuclear movements (Kitschelt, 1986) and Civil Rights movement (McAdam, 1982). It has been used in Tarrow's research on religious insurgency (1988) and in his study on the cycle of protest in Italy 1965–1975 (1989). Other authors have also done case studies using POS (Brockett, 1991; Costain, 1992; della Porta, 1995; Duyvendak, 1995; Kitschelt, 1986; Koopmans, 1995; Meyer, 1993; Rucht, 1994; Tilly, Tilly and Tilly, 1975).

2 Another useful definition is suggested by Brockett (1991: 254) '*the configuration of forces in a (potential or actual) group's political environment that influences that group's assertion of its political claims*'.

3 The concept of political-opportunity structure goes back to the last upheaval of The West, the 1960s. (Tarrow, 2004: 111).

4 Tilly defines repression as '*whatever action by part of a group that elevates the cost of collective action of the contending. One action that reduces the cost of collective action is a form of facilitation*' (Tilly, 1978: 100).

5 This perspective of the State as a predictor of collective action is explained in Kriesi *et al.* (1995)

6 Kitschelt (1986) also points out three operational dimensions to characterize the capacity of the political systems to implement policies. However, I disregard the first two on the grounds that they are not relevant to my analysis. In fact, centralization vs. decentralization does not affect the implementation of policies when we are talking about foreign policy. Secondly, government control over market participants again does not affect foreign policy. The third element that Kitschelt points out is the relative independence and authority of the judiciary system in the resolution of political conflict.

7 In this sense, my view is different from Crossley (2002) who considers what he calls 'the media opportunities structure' to be unstable.

8 There were previous mobilizations against the new education law (LOU) 2002, against the labour reform 'el decretazo' in 2002, against the ecological disaster of the Prestige and finally against the war and the attacks. For an analysis of this see Sánchez, I 'Why the PP lost the general elections? A discursive analysis', from the University of Essex, MA Dissertation.

9 LOU stands for Organic Law of Universities passed in the Congress by the PP majority.

10 Especially during the period when it had a Marxist ideology until 1979. For the socialists, whilst they had a Marxist ideology, the war resulted from the clash of interests between two blocs of capitalist societies who disputed by forcing the markets and sourcing cheap raw materials. The war is a consequence of the competitive capitalist system (Gómez Llorente, 1972: 162). After abandoning the Marxist ideology the Socialist Party has distinguished between just and unjust wars. A war is considered just when it is approved by UN resolutions such as the case of Afghanistan (2001- onwards), unjust wars are those not approved by UN such as the case of Iraq.

11 There were only a few cases of violence, which were in Alicant in action by Colectivo Tortuga, Bilbao (Basque Country) and some demonstrations in Madrid at the beginning of March 2003. In this case the strategy of the demonstrators was to carry video cameras to record these violent events. But it is important to note that the majority of demonstrations resulted in no incidents.

12 For instance the lawsuit interposed by the PP (government party) against a website called www.noalaguerra.org was publicly known, as was the incident of the professor at the Complutense University, Carlos Monedero, because students were involved who said that deputies of the PP were 'murderers' and 'accomplices to murders' in that website created by the professor. This was also the case with the investigation by the Security Forces of a website of social movements called www.nodo50.org because there were campaigns threatening leaders of the PP.

13 However, the channels that dedicated more time to the spontaneous demonstration of the people were Barcelona Television who dedicated 42.9% of time to the conflict, followed by TV-3 (also from Catalonia) with 26.9%. (*El Pais*, 29/3/2003, La Guerra de Irak dispara el consumo de informativos).

14 It is important to note the demonstration of 500 students in the RTVE offices to denounce the manipulation of RTVE by the government. The Goya Awards ceremony on the TV was the starting point of the anti-war movement, from which public opinion started to rise against the war. In the ceremony the actors wore bands saying 'No to war' and some of them spoke about it.

15 It is important to note that El Pais is the most read newspaper during the democracy. (Arroyo and Roel, 2006).

16 There are also other media groups which were born from newspapers. Prisa started from El Pais, Correo from El Correo Español-El Pueblo Vasco, Godó from la Vanguardia, Recoletos from Marca and Actualidad Económica, 16 from Diario 16 and Zeta from El Periodico de Cataluña, Tiempo. (Arroyo and Roel, 2006: 215). Generally speaking, in Spain we can distinguish between Telefónica Group, RTVE, Prisa, Zeta, Correo, Godó, Prensa Española, Voz, Moll, Semana, Joly, Nuevo Lunes, Negocios and MAJ. The first three are more relevant and influential (Reig, 1998).

17 CIS, Centre for Sociological Research, located in Spain.

18 To specify, the list of candidates that cannot surpass the minimum of 3% of valid votes in their circumscription are not taken into account.
19 Between 1977 and 1996 the two major parties obtained 69.7% of the votes which translated into 83.7% of the seats (Crespo, 1997: 240).
20 It is important to note that at the beginning there were doubts as to whether the PSOE should participate on the streets or not, 'there was an internal debate about if it was convenient to support the action on the streets or not' (Javier Dolz, International Secretary of CCOO). Finally Zapatero opted for supporting the action in the streets. It was after the Goya Awards (February 1st 2003) and after the action in Congress (5th February 2003) when the PSOE also called for the demonstration on 15th February 2003. In the war on Afghanistan there was no involvement from the PSOE. The position of the IU (United Left) against the war was clearer from the beginning, but they do not have the power of influence on the mass media the PSOE has. The IU was born from the anti-NATO mobilizations in 1984–86 when the PSOE in the government sided with the Spanish participation in the NATO alliance.
21 There are several interest groups in Spain. The enterprises are organized around the Spanish Confederation of the Enterprise Organizations (CEOE). The trade unions are organized around two majority organizations, the General Union of Workers (UGT) and Workers Commissions (CCOO). Other groups connected with cattle and farming are: the National Confederation of Farmers and Cattle (CNAG), the National Centre for Young Farmers (CNJA), The Coordinator of Organizations of Farmers and Cattle (COAG) and the Union of Small Farmers (UPA). Other interest groups are the professional schools and also the Catholic Church and other religious organizations.

References

Alcántara, M. and A. Martínez, (1997), *Política y gobierno en España*, Valencia: Tirant Lo Blanch (1997), 'El poder de los jueces' in Alcántara, M. and A. Martínez, (eds), *Política y Gobierno*, Valencia: Tirant lo Blanch.

Amenta, E., B. Carruthers and Y. Zylan, (1992), 'A Hero for an aged? The Townsed movement, the political mediation model and US Old-Age policy, 1934–1950, *American Journal of Sociology*, 98: 308–39.

Amenta, E., K. Dunleavy and M. Bernstein, (1994), 'Stolen Thunder? Huey Long's Share Our Wealth, Political Mediation and the Second New Deal', *American Sociological Review*, 59: 678–702

Amenta, E., R. Tamarelli and M. Young, (1996), 'The Old Folks at Home: Political Mediation Theory and Impact of Towsend Movement in California' Unpublished manuscript

Amenta, E. and P. Young, (1999), 'Democratic States and Social Movements: Theoretical Arguments and Hypotheses', *Social Problems*, 57: 153–68.

Aminzade, R. and D. McAdam, (2001), 'Emotions and Contentious Politics', in Ronald R. Aminzade, Jack A. Goldstone, Doug McAdam, Elizabeth J. Perry, William II Sewell, Jr. Sidney Tarrow and Charles Tilly, (eds), *Silence and Voice in the study of Contentious Politics*, Cambridge: Cambridge University Press.

Andrews, K., (1997), 'The Impacts of Social Movements on the Political Process: the civil rights movement and black electoral politics in Mississipi', *Americal Sociological Review*, 62: 800–819.

Arroyo, M. and M. Roel, (2006), *Los medios de comunicación en la democracia (1982–2005): prensa, radio, televisión e Internet y grupos de comunicación*, Madrid: Fragua.

Artal, R. M. (2004), *11M-14M. Onda expansiva*. Madrid: Espejo de Tinta

Banaszak, L. A., (1996), *Why movements succed or fail: Opportunity, Culture and the Struggle for woman suffrage*, Princeton: Princeton University Press.

Barreiro, B., (2004), '14M: Elecciones a la sombra del terrorismo,' in *Claves de la Razón Práctica* 141, April 2004.

Brockett, C., (1991), 'The structure of Political Opportunities and Peasant Mobilization in Central America' *Comparative politics*: 253–74.

Burstein, P, R. Einwohner and J. Hollander, (1995), 'The success of political movements: a bargaining perspective' in Jenkins, C. and B. Klandermans, (eds), *The Politics of Social Protest*, Minneapolis: University of Minnesota Press.

Burstein, P., (1979), 'Public opinion, demonstrations and the Passage of Antidiscrimination Legislation', *Public Opinion Quarterly*, 43: 157–72.

Burstein, P., (1985), *Discrimination, Jobs and Politics*, Chicago: University of Chicago Press.

Costain, A., (1992), *Inviting Women's Rebellion: A Political Process Interpretation of the Women's Movement*, Baltimore: John Hopkins University Press.

Cress, D. and D. Snow, (2000), 'The Outcomes of Homeless Mobilization: The influence of Organization, Disruption, Political Mediation and Framing', *American Journal of Sociology*, 105: 1063–104.

Crespo, I., (1997), 'El sistema electoral' in Alcántara, M. and A. Martínez, (eds), *Política y Gobierno en España*, Valencia: Tirant lo Blanch.

Crossley, N., (2002), *Making sense of Social Movements*, Buckingham, Philadelphia: Open University Press.

Cue, C. (2004), *Pásalo! Los cuatro días de marzo que cambiaron un país*, Barcelona: Editorial peninsula.

de Toledo, A., (2004), *Los cuatro días de Marzo. De las mochilas de la muerte al vuelco electoral*, Barcelona: Ed Planeta.

Della Porta, D., (1995), *Social Movements, Political Violence and the State*, Cambridge: Cambridge University Press

Della Porta, D., (1996), 'Social movements and the state: Thoughts on the policing of protest' in McAdam, D., J. McCarthy and M. Zald, *Comparative Perspectives on Social Movements*, New York: Cambridge University Press.

Duyvendak, J. W., (1995), *The power of politics: new social movements in France*, Boulder, Colo: Westview Press.

Eisinger, P., (1973), 'The conditions of protest behaviour in American cities', *American Political Sciene Review*, 67: 11–28.

Fernández, I. and F. Santana, (2000), *Estado y medios de comunicación en la España democrática*, Madrid: Alianza.

Font, J. and A. Mateos, (2007), 'La participación electoral' in Montero, J., I. Lago and M. Torcal, (eds), *Elecciones generales 2004*, Madrid, CIS.

Gamson, W., (1990), *The Strategy of Social Protest*, 2nd edn., Belmont, CA: Wadsworth.

Gamson, W. and D. Meyer, (1996), 'Framing political-opportunity' in McAdam, D., J. McCarthy and M. Zald, (eds), *Comparative perspectives on Social movements*, New York, Cambridge University Press.

Giugni, M., D. McAdam and C. Tilly, (1999), *How movements matter*, Minneapolis: University of Minnesota Press.

Giugni, M., (1998), 'Was it worth the effort? The outcomes and Consequences of Social Movements', *Annual Review of Sociology*, 24: 371–93.

Giugni, M., (1999), 'How social movements matter: past research, present problems, future developments' in Giugni, M., D. McAdam and C. Tilly, (eds), *How Social Movements Matter*, Minneapolis: University of Minnesota Press.

Goldstone, J., (1980), 'The weakness of Organization: a new look at Gamson's the Strategy of Social Protest', *American Journal of Sociology*, 85: 1017–42.

Gómez-Llorente, E., (1972), *Aproximación a la historia del socialismo español (hasta 1921)*, Madrid: EDICUSA.

Gómez, L., P. Ordaz and F. Perejil, (2004), 'Las crónicas del 11M', Special edition *El Pais*. http://www.elpais.com/especiales/2004/cronica11m/docs/lacronica_11m_h.pdf

Holstein, J. and J. Gubrium, (1997), 'Active interviewing' in Silverman, D., (ed.), *Qualitative Reseach: Theory, Method and Practice,* London: Sage.

Jenkins, C. and C. Perrow, (1977), 'Insurgency of the powerless: Farm Worker movements (1946–1972)', *American Sociological Review,* 42: 249–68.

Jerez, A., V. Sampedro and A. Baer, (2000), *Medios de comunicación, consumo informativo y actitudes políticas en España,* Madrid: Centro de Investigaciones Sociológicas.

Katzentesin, M. and C. Mueller, (1987), *The Women's Movement of the United States and Western Europe: Conciousness, Political-opportunity and Public Policy,* Philadelphia: Temple University Press.

Kitschelt, H., (1986), 'Political Opportunities structures and Political Protest: Anti-nuclear movements in four democracies' *British Journal of Political Science,* 16: 57–85.

Klandermans, B. and S. Goslinga, (1996), 'Media discourse, movement publicity and the generation of collective action frames: Theoretical and empirical exercises in meaning construction' in McAdam, D., J. McCarthy and M. Zald (eds), *Comparative Perspectives on Social Movements,* New York, Cambridge University Press.

Kolb, F. (2007), *Protest and Opportunities. The Political Outcomes of Social Movements,* Chicago: University of Chicago Press.

Koopmans, R., (1995), *Democracy from below: New Social Movements and the political system in West Germany,* Berlin: Westview Press.

Kriesi, H., (1991), 'The Political-opportunity structure of New Social Movements: Its impact on their mobilization', WZB, 91:103.

Kriesi, H., (1995), 'The political opportunity structure of new social movements: its impact on their mobilization', pp. 167–98 in J. C. Jenkins and B. Klandermans, (eds), *The Politics of Social Protest.* Minneapolis: U. of Minnesota Press; London: UCL Press.

Kriesi, H., R. Koopmans, J. Duyvendak, and M. Giugni, (1992), 'New Social Movements and Political Opportunities in Western Europe,' *European Journal of Political Research,* 22: 219–44.

Kriesi, H., R. Koopmans, J. Duvvendak and M. Giugni, (1995), *New Social Movements in Western Europe. A comparative analysis,* USA: University of Minnesota Press.

Kornhauser, W., (1959), *The Politics of Mass Society,* Glencoe, III: The Free Press.

Lago, I. and J. Montero, (2005), 'Los mecanismos del cambio electoral del 11M and 14M' in *Claves de la Razón Práctica,* 149, January/February 2005.

Laiz, C., (2002), 'Las elecciones y los sistemas electorales' in Román, P., (ed), *Sistema Político Español,* Madrid: McGraw-Hill.

Lipsky, M., (1968), 'Protest as a political resource,' *American Political Science Review,* 62: 1144–58.

Lipsky, M., (1970), *Protest in City politics,* Chicago: Rand McNally.

Lopez, N. L., (1997), 'El Parlamento' in Alcántara, M. and A. Martínez, (eds), *Política y Gobierno en España,* Valencia: Tirant lo Blanch.

Maguire, M., (1995), 'Similarities between social Movements and Political Parties' in *The Politics of Social Protest,* Jenkins, C. and B. Klandermans (eds), Minneapolis: University of Minnesota Press.

McAdam, D., J. McCarthy, and M. Zald, (eds) (1996), *Comparative perspectives on social movements,* New York, Cambridge University Press.

McAdam, D., (1982), *Political Process and the development of black insurgency, 1930–1970,* Chicago: University of Chicago Press.

McAdam, D., (1996), 'Conceptual Origins, current problems and future directions' in McAdam, D., J. McCarthy and M. Zald, (eds), *Comparative Perspectives on Social Movements,* New York: Cambridge University Press: 23–40.

Meyer, D., (1993), 'Peace protest and Policy: Explaining the rise and decline of Antinuclear movements in Postwar America,' *Policy Studies Journal,* 21: 29–51.

Meyer, D. and D. Minkoff, (2004), 'Conceptualizing Political-opportunity,' *Social Forces,* 82: 1457–92.

Miles, M. and A. Huberman, (1994), *Qualitative Data analysis: an expanded sourcebook* (2nd edn), London and Thousand Oaks, CA: Sage.

Molins, J., (1997), 'Los grupos de interés' in Alcántara, M and Martínez, A, *Política y Gobierno en España*, Valencia: Tirant lo Blanch.

Montero, J. and I. Lago, (2007), 'Del 11M al 14M: terrorismo, gestión del gobierno y rendición de cuentas', in Montero, L. and M. Torcal, (eds), *Elecciones generales 2004*, Madrid: CIS.

Patton, M., (1990), *Qualitative evaluation and research methods* (2nd edn), Newbury Park, CA: Sage.

Piven, F. and R. Cloward, (1979), *Poor People's movement*, New York: Vintage.

Rochon, T. and D. Mazmanian, (1993), 'Social Movements and the Policy Process', *Annals of the American Academy of Political and Social Science*, 528: 75–87.

Rodriguez, P., (2004), *11M. Mentira de Estado. Los tres días que acabaron con Aznar*. Barcelona: Ediciones B.

Reig, R., (1998), *Medios de comunicación y poder en España: radio, prensa, televisión y mundo editorial*, Barcelona: Paidos.

Román, P., (2002), (ed.), *Sistema político español*, Madrid: Mcgraw-Hill.

Román, P., (2002), 'Los partidos y los sistemas de partidos' in Román, P., (ed.), *Sistema Político Español*, Madrid: Mcgraw-Hill.

Román, P., (2002), 'El Gobierno' in Román, P., (ed.), *Sistema Político Español*, Madrid: McGraw-Hill.

Rucht, D., (1994), *Modernisierung und neue soziale Bewegungen, Deutchland, Frankreich un USA mi Vergleigh.* Frankfurt am Main: Campus.

Rucht, D., (1990), 'Campaigns, Skirmishes and Battles: Anti-nuclear movements in the USA, France and West Germany', *Industrial Crisis Quarterly* 4: 193–222.

Rucht, D., (1996), 'The impact of national contexts on social movements structures: a cross-movement and cross-national comparison' in McAdam, D., J. McCarthy and M. Zald, (eds) *Comparative perspectives on social movements*, New York: Cambridge University Press.

Sanchez de Dios, M., (2002), 'Las Cortes, el Congreso de los Diputados y el Senado' in Román, P., (ed.), *Sistema Político Español*, Madrid: Mcgraw-Hill.

Sánchez, I., (2006), 'The four days that change Spain?: a discourse theory response' Master Dissertation, University of Essex.

Sánchez, I. and S. López, (2007), 'De la LOU al 14M: actores sociales, opinion pública, poder político', IX Spanish Congress of Sociology, Research Commitee of Political Sociology, Completed Papers.

Sanz, A. and A. Sierra, (2005), 'Las elecciones generales de 2004 en España: Política exterior, estilo de gobierno y movilización. Working paper 48, Universidad Autónoma de Madrid.

Sawyers, T. and D. Meyer, (1999), 'Missed Opportunities: Social Movement Abeyance and Public Policy', *Social Problems* 46: 187–206.

Schumaker, P., (1975), 'Policy Responsiveness to protest-group demands', *Journal of Politics*, 37: 488–521.

Selznick, P., (1960), *The Organizational Weapon*, New York: The Free Press.

Silverman, D., (2006), *Interpreting Qualitative data*, London: Sage Publications.

Tarrow, S., (1983), *Struggling to Reform: Social Movements and Policy Change During Cycles of Protest, Western Societies Program Occasional* Paper n°15. Cornell University, Ithaca NY: New York Centre for International Studies.

Tarrow, S., (1988), 'National Politics and Collective Action: Recent theory and Research in Western Europe and United States', *Annual Review of Sociology*, 14: 421–40.

Tarrow, S., (1989), *Democracy and disorder. Protest and Politics in Italy 1965–1975*, Oxford: Oxford University Press.

Tarrow, S., (1991), 'Struggle, politics and reform: collective action, social movements and cycles of protest' Cornell studies in International Affairs. *Western Societies Paper* n°21.

Tarrow, S., (1993), 'Social Protest and Policy Reform: May 1968 and the Loi d'Orientation in France', *Comparative Political Studies*, 25: 579–607.

Tarrow, S., (1994), *Power in movement, Social Movements, Collective action and mass politics in the modern state*, Cambridge: Cambridge University Press.

Tarrow, S., (1996), 'States and opportunities: The political structuring of social movements', in McAdam, D., J. McCarthy and M. Zald, (eds), *Comparative Perspectives on Social Movements*, New York: Cambridge University Press.

Tarrow, S., (1998), Power in Movement: Social Movements and Contentious Politics, Cambridge: Cambridge University Press.

Tarrow, S., (2004), *El poder en movimiento, Los movimientos sociales, la acción colectiva y la política*, Madrid: Alianza Editorial.

Tilly, C., (1978), *From Mobilization to Revolution*, Reading Mass: Addison-Wesley.

Tilly, C., L. Tilly and R. Tilly, (1975), *The Rebellius Century 1830–1930*, Cambridge, Mass: Harvard University Press.

Internet sources:

www.elpais.es
www.elmundo.es
www.cis.es
www.noalaguerra.org
www.culturacontralaguerra.org

Between mobility and mobilization – lifestyle migration and the practice of European identity in political struggles

Michael Janoschka

Abstract: Lifestyle migration, such as the temporary or permanent movement of European citizens to coastal areas in Southern Europe, widely responds to the freedom of movement that EU citizenship provides to all its members. Although this migration can be evaluated as an individual and rather apolitical expression of a politically intended mobility within the European Union, it may seriously alter political life within destinations. The following article presents a case study about the political mobilization of lifestyle migrants living on the Spanish Mediterranean coast. It is based on empirical research and explores narrative interviews with members of a transnationally active political pressure group that campaigns against misapplications of local and regional land use policies. The central aim of the text consists of evaluating how central actors draw on European identity within conflict negotiations that traverse diverse scales including the European level. Referring to this, the article engages with key issues in contemporary sociological debates addressed in this monograph, namely the question of how sociologists approach the study of the political in general and how imaginations of Europe and European identity are strategically appropriated within political debates.

Introduction

Lifestyle migration and leisure-oriented mobilities – conceived as (temporary or permanent) spatial mobilities of relatively affluent persons of all ages moving between meaningful places with an imagined and collectively perceived potential to provide a better quality of life (Benson and O'Reilly, 2009: 2) – have, in recent years, been undertaken by an increasing number of people moving to and from places all around the world. The emergence of this social phenomenon as a topic of academic enquiry has resulted in a lively and multifaceted discussion in interdisciplinary fields such as Social Anthropology, Sociology, Tourism Studies, Human Geography and Urban Planning (Croucher, 2009; Hall, 2005; Jackiewicz and Craine, 2010; Janoschka, 2009; Korpela, 2009; McIntyre, 2009; Moss, 2006; Oliver, 2007; O'Reilly and Benson, 2009; Warnes, 2009).

Much attention is paid to exploring the motivations, the mobility paths, transnational experiences and social capital of such mobile citizens, especially in the European case (Benson, 2010; Casado-Díaz, 2009; Gustafson, 2008; King *et al.*, 2000; Oliver and O'Reilly, 2010; O'Reilly, 2000, 2009; Rodríguez *et al.*, 2004; Williams and Hall, 2002). Within the European Union, lifestyle migration can be interpreted as a practice reflecting the freedom of movement that EU citizenship provides to its members (Schriewer and Encinas, 2007). At first glance, this appears to be primarily an apolitical expression of a politically intended mobility within the European Union. Although they bring important investment to an area and their preference includes a long-term commitment to the place (Hall *et al.*, 2009), lifestyle migrants may be considered as outsiders and even invaders by local inhabitants and politicians. As a result there is the potential for them to be resented by members of the native population (McWatters, 2008), with the consequence of being at least symbolically deprived of the access to participate in political questions (Hall and Müller, 2004). However, as this article argues, if they achieve political participation within the destinations, they have the potential to seriously alter political life. The right of EU citizens to vote and stand as candidates in local elections even if they do not hold citizenship of their country of residence, creates the space for such intra-European migrants to establish distinctive social relations, instigate claims and challenge established political regimes (Durán, 2010; Janoschka, 2010). Such a commitment proves to be of theoretical interest, especially as it contradicts the predominant image of intra-European migrants as individuals devoid of major political concern in respect to their chosen place of residence (Favell, 2008).

This article provides an analysis of the political mobilization of lifestyle migrants living on the Spanish Mediterranean coast. It is based on empirical research carried out in the province of Alicante, Spain (also known as the *Costa Blanca*) and explores the discursive strategies of a pressure group who have been campaigning against serious misapplications of local and regional land use policies. In a geographical setting that is the destination of the largest number of lifestyle migrants from across Europe (Huete, 2009; Rodriguez *et al.*, 2010), a group of alarmed expatriates protest to challenge the regional planning legislation (LRAU, in spanish *Ley Reguladora de la Actividad Urbanística*, enforced since 1995) that permits alleged abuses.

Theoretical considerations

An emergent strategy has been the attempt to de-localize the conflict by making use of supranational European institutions (eg, the European Commission, the European Parliament and the European Court of Human Rights). Additionally, activists refer to themselves strategically, drawing on a collectively shared idea of 'Europe' and meanings ascribed to 'European identity'. In this regard, a central aim of this article consists of evaluating how actors centrally involved in protesting against the abuse of particular regulatory mechanisms assume European identity as they engage in a struggle that traverses diverse scales, including the European level. It is of major conceptual interest to analyse whether such negotiations, with a strategic reference to social constructions of European identity, can be interpreted as an embodiment of European citizenship. Hence, this article questions what the politics of identity and difference can reveal about contentious politics and political mobilization in lifestyle migration destinations.

To address this question, two assumptions will be initially clarified: First, following Leitner *et al.*, (2008: 157), 'contentious politics' will be used here as a term to 'describe the phenomenon of organized social resistance to hegemonic norms [. . .] in which differently positioned participants come together to challenge dominant systems of authority, in order to promote and enact alternative imaginaries'. In this regard, it is interesting to analyse how the conflict that my respondents in Spain take part in, 'inhabit[s] a political space outside of formal national politics [. . .] and address[es] a range of institutions across a variety of geographic scales' (Routledge, 2008: 336). Recognizing the centrality of politics of identity and difference in this conflict allows such an analysis to become apparent.

The term 'politics of identity' initially emerged from the experiences of new social movements within Western capitalist societies (Benhabib, 1999) and refers to identity as a power-laden construct that enables individuals to engage in collective political action. Identity is considered to be an invention that is expressed in and through practices and relations. But it also includes non-relations, absences, interstices and other continuous, more or less self-conscious positions in the social world (Calhoun, 1993). This means that identity is always established in relation to a series of differences – an idea that also applies to European identity, another highly disputed term addressed in Sociology and Political Science (Bruter, 2005; Checkel and Katzenstein, 2009; Delanty, 1995; Delanty and Rumford, 2005; Herrmann and Brewer, 2004; Rumford, 2009; White, 2010).

Identities, including European identity, are rarely defined in a satisfactory way. In this regard, this article primarily presents some constitutive elements of what European identity refers to in this specific and paradigmatic political conflict that has an array of European dimensions. My argument will be developed in three central sections: first, a short discussion of the research methodologies, widely based on qualitative approaches. This will be followed by an empirical analysis of political mobilization in eastern Spain, including the strategic reference to politics of identity and European identity. Finally, I will introduce a conceptual framework for understanding how European identity can provide an inspiring perspective for the analysis of politics of identity. In this regard, key issues in contemporary sociological debates addressed in this monograph will be discussed, namely the questions of how sociologists approach the study of the political in general and how imaginings of Europe and European identity are strategically appropriated within political debates.

Research methodology

This article provides a contribution to the extensive debates regarding European identity, as it reconstructs and interprets the constructions and ascriptions of European identity in a political protest amongst lifestyle migrants in eastern Spain. Hence, it follows a perspective that evaluates the situated practice and discourse in the conflict as key for the understanding of politics of identity. Such empirical research that reconstructs individual and collective meanings of European identity and refers to subject-bound practices as a main analytical category should concentrate on interpretative methodological approaches.

In the course of this study, more than 90 narrative interviews were conducted with a total of 64 politically engaged persons, a vast majority of them lifestyle migrants living in Spain. These interviews were held in three languages (English, Spanish and German) and carried out with representatives belonging to Canadian and nine European nationalities. Interviewees were not chosen for belonging to specific age groups, status, nationality or other socio-demographic characteristics, but in regard to active involvement in local political issues. Many interviewees were directly suffering the consequences of the application of the land use law LRAU and participated actively in the mentioned protest. Although the age of respondents ranged from 36 to 84, a vast majority of the informants were older individuals who live permanently in Spain.

Some of the interviewees have lived in Spain since the late 1970s, while others moved during the last decade. It is important to consider that the people interviewed are not a representative sample, but belong to a minority: lifestyle migrants who are politically active. As a consequence, the subsequent analysis primarily reflects identity expressions in the political field, which can vary substantially from identity constructions and feelings of belonging articulated in other circumstances of daily life (Huber and O'Reilly, 2004; Oliver, 2007).

Although the narrative interviews were intended to focus on individual biographies (Rosenthal, 2004), many of the interviewed activists were so concerned about the land use law that they immediately narrated their involvement in the protest movement, relegating biographical issues to a later stage of the interview. In addition, 15 problem-centred interviews were carried out with central actors including representatives of different European embassies and the regional government. Interviews were transcribed and analysed with MAXQdA software to permit the application of hermeneutic and reconstructive analytical methods (Rosenthal, 2004). Furthermore, internal protest meetings were attended to get an insight into the protest movement and its internal debates. Additionally, official documents and parliamentary debates as well as media covering the conflicts were studied.

Lifestyle migration and real estate development – the emergence and configuration of a political conflict

During the decade preceding the financial and economic crisis triggered by the 2008 credit crunch, Spain experienced an economic boom that was determined through an over-alignment to the construction industry: by late 2007, more than 2.7 million persons were employed in this sector – an eighth of all occupied workers countrywide (INE, 2010). In certain areas such as the province of Alicante, a region that combines investment in mass tourism and residential building, this focus was even stronger. Amongst others, this extraordinary real estate boom was nourished by European lifestyle migrants: for instance, more than 90,000 Britons moved to this area, known colloquially as the *Costa Blanca*, between 2001 and 2008, with the consequence that many formerly remote rural areas were transformed into literally 'vibrant' and urbanized areas, doubling their population in less than a decade. As O'Reilly (2007) stresses, retirement is not the only source of lifestyle migration to Spain; it is increasingly the case that there are a rising number of younger people, families and other individuals of working age that recently moved from Britain, Germany or Scandinavian countries to Spain in search of a better life. Rodriguez *et al.* (2010) shows that hardly one third of these EU-15 free movers in Spain are aged 55 or more.

Indeed, one can find a variety of wide-reaching explanations for such a frenetic urbanization process. For example, global capitalism and the financial industry imply major social transformations and challenge certain viewpoints about the role of the individual in postmodern and ageing societies. Lifestyle migration widely responds to the freedom of movement within the European Union and the possibility to settle, work and purchase properties in any part of the common market. However, Korpela (2010), in line with O'Reilly and Benson (2009), points out that this mobility also means an escape from the hectic and consumer-oriented lifestyles in Western and Northern Europe. Additionally to such broader trends, the disproportionately high account of lifestyle migrants moving to the *Costa Blanca* might also be associated with specific regional policies related to urban development. For instance, in other destinations such as coastal areas in Costa Rica, the establishment of a development regime was reported (Janoschka, 2009), and in eastern Spain politicians, state-owned saving banks and real estate entrepreneurs also laid the foundations for and promoted frenetic real estate development. The basic legal framework for this regime was the enforcement of the regional land use legislation named LRAU (adopted in 1995) and the legislative update LUV (dating from late 2005). Both laws regulate social practice in the field of urban politics within this region, especially the development of new residential estates. In summary, the law enables local authorities to change the zoning plan of the municipality whenever a developer presents a new plan for urbanization. This means that, aside from protected landscape and technically irreclaimable land, real estate development is allowed anywhere in a municipality. Additionally, it can be implemented against the will of the owners (Soriano and Romero, 2004). The original purpose of the law was to give municipalities the legal authority to force (unwilling) landowners to cede portions of their property, with the aim of providing space for affordable housing (Sánchez de Madariaga, 2003). However, it has become increasingly evident that the municipalities have widely mishandled the expropriation power of this law.

The consequences of the LRAU law remain barely comprehensible at a first sight: one problem is that the law refers not only to agricultural land but also to semi-urbanized and consolidated areas with detached houses. In this regard, it is surprising that the promoters do not necessarily have to buy the land they want to urbanize. A system of forced concessions implements a situation where the private owner has to pay all costs deriving from urbanization and infrastructure to the investor. Additionally, he must concede up to two thirds of the total area to the developer (Soriano and Romero, 2004). For example, Alfred T., a German pensioner who has lived in the region since 1983, lost his appeal when his property became part of a development plan intended to densify an area with ten pre-existing villas that would be complemented with more than 60 new houses. He did not agree to the application of the law and appealed – but after six years of legal conflict, he was ordered to cede more than 1,000 square metres of his property and to pay 65,000 euro to the investor. This case is only one of several thousand cases that have occurred since 1995.

The application of such a law infringes the individual property rights guaranteed in the Spanish constitution, the EC Treaty and the Charter of Fundamental Rights. In 2002, some of the supposed victims of the land law decided to fight for their rights in a different way and founded an NGO named '*Abusos Urbanísticos No*' (No to Urbanistic Abuses) with the aim of achieving a moratorium for similar development plans in several municipalities via the establishment of political pressure. As local and regional authorities did not respond to their claims, they decided to de-localize the conflict and organized petitions addressed to the European Parliament and the European Court of Human Rights. The embeddedness of several members of the NGO in transnational political networks led to success, and the activists were able to convince several delegations from the European Union of the failures of the law. By vote of the Euro-Parliament on December 13, 2005, infringement proceedings against Spain were opened, and consequently a new law (LUV) replaced LRAU legislation by the end of December 2005. Although small changes were implemented, similar abuses followed under the new law. According to the reports of the EU institutions dating from June 2007 and March 2009, the planning legislation established an 'endemic form of corruption' that makes citizens suffer an 'abuse of rights and obligations enshrined in the EC Treaty, in the Charter of Fundamental Rights, in the ECHR and in the relevant EU Directives, as well as in other conventions to which the EU is a party' (European Parliament, 2009). The case drew major national and international media attention, and the British government issued official warnings to its citizens against buying properties in the region and regularly updates the online information that they provide about property-related issues in Spain (British Embassy Madrid, 2010). At the same time, the regional government accused the NGO of 'damaging the image of the region in Europe', claiming that 'European lobbies likely want to decide our future' (Corts Valencianes, 2005). Such a reaction may respond to the hardened front-lines between the movement and the regional government at a crucial moment – the day after the decision of the European Commission to open infringement proceedings against Spain in the LRAU cause. Nevertheless, it is a good example of how certain imaginings relating to the social construction of Europe were central to the negotiation of this conflict. Furthermore, the statement also reminds us that the recourse to European institutions to resolve a locally embedded political conflict is an unconventional method of contestation that, in this case, attacks the hegemonic way of conceiving urban development politics. I will come back to this argument, but at first a brief look into the extremely important consolidation process of the NGO *'Abusos Urbanísticos No'* will be provided.

Collective memory and the consolidation of a political movement through politics of identity

Social practice that is embedded in historical and symbolical meanings ascribed to imagined communities has commonly been approached through the discussion of the social construction and invention of modern nation-states (Anderson 2006 [1983]). Preceding this, Emile Durkheim's descendant Maurice Halbwachs had developed a framework that refers to traditions originated in families, within a class specific habitus or any other coherently originated group: the collective memory (Halbwachs, 1992). The development of collective memory takes place via two intertwined and mutually enforcing aspects. First, the 'rule of division' means that a common history can be duplicated at different specific places. Second, the 'rule of accumulation and concentration' implies that different meanings can be ascribed to a specific place or occurrence. Both aspects occurred during the early phase of the protest movement in question and led to the mutually reinforcing establishment of a coherent founding myth of the NGO. The movement started its trajectory when a Canadian-Swedish couple became affected by a development plan. Unlike many other individuals, they understood from early on that taking legal steps would not provide them any guarantee of winning the struggle for their own land. However, this couple not only questioned the legal Spanish instances; they also possessed the social capital to articulate their objection and were fortunate enough to live in an environment with people who shared their ideas. In such a social field they were able to set up the initiative, pursuing legal advice from novel actors such as the embassies of different European countries. In retrospect, this sounds like quite an easy issue – but at that time, it proved to be a completely different approach to handling the LRAU problem.

With regard to the collective memory of the movement, the founder himself and his initial movements play an important role, a point confirmed by many of the interviewees. But it is additionally interesting that in the course of their narratives many of the interviewees placed themselves very close to the founder, reinforcing the initially mentioned 'rule of division'. The following two examples state this issue:

> *Abusos Urbanísticos* is really the best example of how to make a grassroots organization. It works perfectly now, so we do not have to help. We only organized in the very beginning and told them who they could call. It would not have been possible without Chuck [the founder of the NGO], whose life was managing this kind of thing. This is the elite living there; every one of them knows important people in London, Brussels, Washington, everywhere, and they can activate them with one call. So only under these circumstances could Chuck do this, just because there are so many people with power.
>
> (Interview with a representative of the British consular service in Spain)

> Nowadays many people say they helped *Abusos Urbanísticos* in the very beginning. But it was here, in this office, that a man came in and asked me to assist him with regard to the urban abuses. And I explained to him how to found the NGO. This was the very beginning of *Abusos Urbanísticos No*.
>
> (Interview with a representative of the German consular service in Spain)

Independently of the concrete circumstances of the foundation itself, there is a symbolical founding myth of the NGO, namely, the first public consultation carried out in the convention room of a restaurant in late 2002. Many interviewees, especially those affected by development plans, recognize this afternoon as a crucial moment:

> There were so many people there, there were people standing, there were people in the corridor, there were people, who couldn't even get in the door. They reckoned that there were 700 people at that meeting. And that was really the start of the whole movement of *Abusos No* and their support for people like us basically.
>
> (Tessa D., affected property owner)

Following the conceptualization of the collective memory carried out by Halbwachs (2003), only those incidents that at the same time represent a lesson and a future model of attitude are remembered. In the case of this protest, the establishment of a coherent founding myth enabled the group to develop a specific 'movement habitus' (Crossley, 2005) and subsequently facilitated the symbolically important reference to a collectively shared political identity. In this regard, a second aspect of the meeting mentioned is important: one of the official representatives invited to the presentation was the British ambassador. As a spontaneous reaction to the apparently shocking complaints reported, he expressed diplomatic assistance and announced an initiative of all embassies of the EU-15 states in Spain, to be carried out within the following weeks. By this time and through this initial European dimension, the movement

277

originated under an expanded attachment to politics of identity that refers to 'Europe'.

European identity as an analytical tool for conflict analysis – an empirical discussion

It is important to consider that the establishment of the protest movement raises concern in questions referring to the field of identity – and this happens among both adversaries. In this regard, the original economic problems of the property owners are brought forward strategically to a culturally-interpreted sphere that relates to politics of identity. It is explicitly the fading out of internal differences on the basis of identity constructions that empowers the actors to set up an effective support for such political action. Politics of identity reproduce and reify alleged cultural boundaries between artificially constructed groups (eg, 'affected foreigners' vs. 'Spanish politicians and avaricious promoters') and refer to constructions of 'Europe' and 'European identity'. This context is interesting as the founder of the NGO, a Canadian national, and the activists made important efforts to include initially passive Spaniards who are also affected. Given the nature of a conflict that refers to EU institutions and that is backed by 15 ambassadors and several EU parliamentarians from different countries, the reference to questions of European identity seems to be a winning strategy to express and unify the political claims amongst a group of activists that gained more than 10,000 members from different nationalities in a few months. This is especially the case as the founders – initially two dozen foreign senior residents from a handful of European countries and Canada – 'invented', in the words of Stuart Hall (1997), the spectacle to refer to discursive constructions of European identity. Given the non-European nature of the founder and president of the protest movement and the subsequent implication of more and more Spanish activists, such an effort deserves special interest. During their struggle, the participants established a complex relation of identities and differences that referred not only to individual and collective experiences in the political struggle, but also to a political invention named 'Europe'. How can this be explained?

First, it is of major interest that many participants of the political movement were used to occupying positions of social power during their former professional trajectories. These experiences make them well-prepared for challenging the *modus operandi* of local development politics commonly regarded as incomprehensible and unjustified. Furthermore, as many of them have been active in political issues on different hierarchical levels and in different social and geographical environments for many years, they have the know-how to trigger emotions in reference to the addressed target group and to apply politics of identity strategically. In interviews, public appearances and official media releases, as well as through the website of the NGO, reference to a constructed abyss between a 'Spanish' or 'Valencian' reality and 'European' norms, beliefs and ways of political and juridical action was permanently reified. Such politics of identity establish discursive contexts that enable collective political action through temporary fixations of social constructions regarding Europe. This strategic use of identity and difference aims at a depreciation of the political opponent: any positive construction of one's own reference group is inevitably entangled with negative attributes regarding the other.

Such politics of identity have been widely discussed in other contexts and, as Penrose and Mole (2008) state, any construction of such a self-related identity ('me' and 'us') implies at least a tacit knowledge of the 'other' ('you' and 'them') that does not form part of oneself and one's 'own' reference group. This means that identity is always established in relation to a series of differences – it requires this difference and converts it into otherness to secure its own self-cer-tainty (Connolly, 2002). The acceptance of the relational character of identity and its internal multiplicities implies an interesting perspective for the analysis of political movements that constantly 'play' with changing ascriptions and challenge established scales (Massey, 2004). Nevertheless, this strategic use of identity in political contexts does not mean that 'essentialist' representations and ascriptions do not exist. Quite the contrary, the necessity to position one's 'own' (subject, group, idea, practice, act) against 'other' (subjects, groups, ideas, practices, acts) in a political conflict at least temporarily requires, for instance, 'fragile' fixations of the meanings (Glasze, 2007). As a consequence, politics of identity conceived as representations of social and spatial meanings, provide a basis for action. As Nicholls (2009) discusses, identities are projected by the actors involved in political struggles and resistance, in order to legitimate claims and silence internal differences. This is clearly evident in the case of the described political involvement of lifestyle migrants: the activists play efficiently with identity and difference to set up a political movement against the legal abuses they are supposed to have suffered in Spain. But how can one conceive of this context with reference to European identities?

For this purpose, it is important to think about the chosen political embed-ding of the protest which gives rise to semantic strategies that refer to Europe. The petition process at the European institutions helps to establish a coherent identity construct, based on the successfully defended assumption that the polit-ical adversaries permanently infringe supposed 'European' principles. But it is now of interest which content and discursive ascriptions are applied to refer to European identity versus the alleged 'otherness' of the political opponents. The analysis of the empirical data highlights the strategic application of four central social constructions:

- *First*, the political activists interpret Europe as a 'community of values' and demand the compliance of basic civic principles such as democracy, human rights, tolerance and freedom – ethical values that are interpreted as a sub-stantial element of European identity. The argument also asserts that due to the application of the planning law, promoters and the regional political elite repeatedly disregard these basic assumptions of the European community. By means of such an argument, the political sphere is discursively devalued and charged with 'otherness' – for the activists it is clear that their opponents do not share the 'European' community of values. The following example shows how this argument is enforced in a common discourse:

If you want to explain this to someone and say, you don't have any rights here – they do not believe you. I just received a visit from Hungary, they told me: 'This cannot be true!' – They thought we were crazy, they told us: 'This did not happen even in communism.' And it is strange that there is no property protection in a democratic country, especially after the Spaniards signing the European constitution that explicitly says that property rights, human rights are defended in Europe.

(Günter, local activist)

– *Second*, Europe is evaluated as a 'community of modernity'. This dimension responds to the legal and moral empowerment the group receives through the European institutions. Amongst other points, the activists refer to the legal certainty modern states guarantee their citizens. With regard to this aspect, the imagining and construction of Spain as a non-modern society – a profoundly embedded assumption among lifestyle migrants – is tied to the political sphere and thus reinforced politically. The activists claim to introduce a 'European' way of modern thought via the recourse to European institutions. The following argument exemplifies the dialectical method for establishing otherness and political identity when Spain and Europe are contrasted:

It seems the spirit of the conquistador is still alive, but in reverse. Rather than brigands sailing to their victims in other lands, the casualties now are many of those of us who have brought their life savings to Spain's fair shores. And the abuses under the laws have truly become, in their turn, 'weapons of mass construction'. Is it for us to cry out? Yes, because those we speak for should not suffer the denial of rights and privileges modern Europe is supposed to offer. Grateful though we may be to live in Spain, there are limits to what is acceptable.

(Charles S., former president of the NGO, at a petition committee meeting in Brussels)

– *Third*, the protest group refers to a discursive field that embeds Europe as a 'community of communication'. This signifies that European identity is constructed among the common basis of a shared economic, political and juridical system. Many discourses of the protest movement refer to issues of democracy – not as a superior ideal but as practical assumptions of how current debates are structured in a public sphere. Hence, local and regional politics in Spain are described as underdeveloped, thus fixing the otherness of the political opponent.
– *Fourth*, the political activists also refer to an aspect which is related to a framing originated from the category 'Christendom'. This argument needs further explanation as Spain is a country rooted in Catholic tradition and holds bishops and other religious leaders who tend to influence debates. The members of the movement claim that the application of the land use regulation violates basic Christian values and the human rights underlying

these values. The infringement of constitutional aspects of European values such as questions of burglary and the status of property unifies the political identity of the activists and sets up recognizable lines of conflict. It portrays the coalition between politicians and real estate developers as 'the fall of man' that may only be redeemed by a superior moral institution, which is embodied in this case by the European Union. As the following two examples show, this powerful moral reference is used both in common communication and official statements of the initiative.

> Worse yet, for a nominally Catholic country, at least two of the Commandments of God Almighty, those which state 'thou shalt not steal' and 'thou shalt not covet thy neighbours's property, nor shall be false witness against him' appear to fail into sinful disregard with regularity as the Report suggests. A sunny country with so many shady dealings, so some say.

> (Charles S., former president of the NGO, at a petition committee meeting in Brussels)

> One of the affected owners was literally 'crucified'. They planned a road junction, and on the map you see a cross on his property. He would have to cross the street to go from his house to the garden, to cross the street to use his pool.

> (Günter K., local activist)

These four basic principles represent a distillation of the empirical data gathered in many interviews and expressed in official statements. Although these dimensions of European identity remain here analytically separated, individual political statements usually entangle several of them at a time. The empirically observed references to European identity thus establish antagonistic categories of identity and difference, of inclusion and exclusion, that permanently frame and reframe one's 'own' reference group as well as the constitutive 'other'. It is of major interest that Spain is discursively excluded from such constructions of European identity. In order to gain strength and establish coherent collective political identities in the battle against the land use law, the entangled notions of European identity are permanently reified among the members, while other possible identifications with Europe are largely faded out. This can be explained by the need for establishing a coherent and unifying frame to actors who are widely rooted in different reference systems within Spain, Europe and non-European countries. Several theoretical threats emerge from this case study, and we will address them in the following article against the background of debates regarding the social construct of European identity.

Political mobilization of lifestyle migrants and European identity – a conceptual framework

The increasing proliferation of lifestyle migration in a European context is one facet of major social trends in the course of individualization and a growing

Michael Janoschka

desire for self-realization (O'Reilly and Benson, 2009). In this regard, lifestyle migrants embody a challenge for conceptions regarding migration, tourism, home, community and identity that are predominantly constituted on the presumption that people only have one residential place. One aspect belongs to the reconfiguration of the political life in places shaped by lifestyle-oriented mobility. As discussed in different contexts, this may happen through participation in structures of representative democracy at the local level such as municipal parliaments (Collard, 2010; Durán, 2010; Janoschka, 2010). However, given its prototypical situation, it is especially the political protest outside the representative political system that can be evaluated as a major force of social innovation. The empirical discussion shows how intra-European migrants, who have the privilege of freedom of movement within Europe, are capable of challenging a local and regional political regime in at least one specific area. Collective action and contentious politics that contest hegemonic norms respond in this case to alternative imaginings of territorial development and to questions of the implementation of a constitutional state and the rule of law at a specific spatial setting in the European Union. Such a challenge stirs strong emotions among the individuals affected and thus proves an interesting subject for the discussion of politics of identity and difference – and the debate about European identity.

Although the concepts of identity and European identity are not easy to deal with, they provide both analytical and conceptual interest. Politics of identity as a research perspective recognizes the possible transformations, mobility and flows inherent to a conceptualization of identity as a powerful and meaningful social construction that is constantly destabilized and reinvented. As the empirical discussion reflected, politics of identity and the reference to European identity can be a powerful discursive mechanism within political struggles. But in the meantime, scientific discourse acknowledges that European identity, as well as the imaginations and meanings ascribed to Europe, are widely disputed concepts. This is in the nature of a term which is used in different frameworks, ie, in economic, political and philosophical debates. Hence, any attempt fully to discuss and reproduce the discourse on Europe and European identity does not suit the wider scope of this article. In consequence, the following conceptual ideas will focus on only three central aspects that are relevant to the discussion of European identity among lifestyle migrants and might give new insights into the practical uses of European identity in political conflicts.

First, in very different contexts, empirical and theoretical debates, Europe is considered a useful example for exploring the nature of 'cosmopolitan realism' (Pichler, 2008: 1110). Cosmopolitan realism responds to a conceptualization of European identity as a cosmopolitan project, a vision that is defended by an array of key theorist (Beck and Grande, 2007; Calhoun, 2009; Rumford, 2007; Stevenson, 2005). This correlates with the proposition of Delanty and Rumford (2005: 54 f) that we should think of European identity in constitutive cultural terms instead of following the traditional division between individual and collective identities. At the same time, this perspective also enables the viewpoint that EU institutions and EU law promote a European identity that is being fulfilled and expressed by officers in the heart of the EU administration (Herrmann and Brewer, 2004; Laffan, 2004; Wodak, 2004). This idea is rejected and criticized by different authors, as if European identity was an exclusively top-down process steered by European institutions (Checkel and Katzenstein, 2009; Mayer and Palmowski, 2004), suggesting an engagement with the articulations and negotiations of European identity. As proposed in this article, politics of identity may have a meaningful importance within collective political action, responding to both the complex accounts of space and the contexts included in dynamic and often unstable constructions of contested European identities when applied to political disputes. In consequence, if political cosmopolitanism is understood as an expression of multiple affiliations, attitudes and dispositions, practices and competences (Vertovec and Cohen, 2002), the political engagement of lifestyle migrants can be considered as a practical experience of cosmopolitanism that focuses on symbols, 'material practices and identities associated with border crossings, nationalisms, hybridity, and the connections between travelling and locatedness' (Mitchell, 2007: 707). Such a conceptualization of cosmopolitanism goes hand in hand with the array of studies regarding transnationalism and transnational social formations in post-modern societies (Appadurai, 2008; Faist, 2008), providing a framework for the political consequences that cosmopolitan individuals and transnational elites evoke in global cities and European centres of political and administrative command and control (Beaverstock, 2005; Favell, 2008).

Second, discussions about European identity should reflect on methodological approaches for gauging the existence (or non-existence) and the character of European identity. For instance, much emphasis is drawn to the transformations of national identities by 'European' values and beliefs (Blokker, 2008; Eder, 2006; Kantner, 2006). This kind of research is often, although not exclusively framed by quantitative studies that analyse, amongst others, cross-country surveys such as the *Eurobarometer* (Grundy and Jamieson, 2007; Hooghe and Marks, 2007; Kohli, 2000; Pichler, 2009). Such studies tend to simplify European identity and thus might fail to attend to the shape and significance of its discursive and symbolical dimensions (Bruter, 2009). In contrast, the central aim of this article responds to the question of how imaginings of Europe and European identity are strategically appropriated within political debates.

The empirical discussion presented in this article has provided much-needed evidence of the strategic use and appropriation of European identity in political conflicts, which is a different issue from the weak and fragile European attachment and identity observed among lifestyle migrants in daily life (Oliver and O'Reilly, 2010). This goes hand-in-hand with findings regarding the everyday meanings ascribed to Europe among 18–24 year-old residents in Edinburgh, Scotland, carried out by Grundy and Jamieson (2007). They report rather low levels of European attachment, and that feelings of being European were only shared by a small proportion of the young population. Additionally, Grundy and Jamieson stress that even those individuals who have an explicit interest in European topics do not automatically develop an attachment to European identity. This poses the question of whether such an attachment is a necessary precondition when a politics of identity referring to Europe is strategically established. As the empirical data presented here shows, the claiming of European identity for political purposes, concrete experiences, emotions and meaningful (political) communication can be considered of greater importance than expressions of European identity in other fields of daily life.

Third, returning to conceptual concerns, it is important to mention that the references to European identities follow the same constructions that characterize all politics of identity, namely the principle of establishing discursively antagonistic categories of inclusion and exclusion that establish the 'own' and the constitutive 'other'. Such an approach is compatible with the aforementioned idea that European identity is one possible attachment among multifaceted strategies of identification (Bruter, 2005). In this rendering, the conceptualization of European identities can be thought of as a dynamic and contested negotiation process that, lacking a hegemonic narrative, permits a range of disputed and sometimes contradictory interpretations of Europe. As a consequence, it is explicitly a conflict over meaning and the condition of indeterminacy that can be evaluated as a constitutive element of all identities regarding a Europe that is ambiguous and a mere expression of the development from unity through diversity (which is another highly disputed 'idea' see for example: Delanty, 1995; Kraus, 2008; Pinxten *et al.*, 2007).

While it is theoretically inspiring that European identities can be nourished and constructed in many ways, however, in daily practices of politics of identity they are seemingly only applied within evocative and meaningful situations. Hence, a starting point for the analysis of European identity can again be the conceptual difference between 'us' and 'them' and the ways group definitions are accomplished with reference to Europe. In the case of lifestyle migrants in Spain, many people define themselves as 'European residents', which is a political statement expressed independently of national origin. To a certain degree, this responds to the unconscious necessity lifestyle migrants feel to avoid defining themselves with categories such as 'immigrants' (Croucher, 2009; Oliver and O'Reilly, 2010; O'Reilly, 2007). However it also shows that for these individuals whose everyday life is bound to a variety of different identification processes, Europe is one of various identities that they cling to with certain attachment. Additionally, in political conflicts the indeterminacy of European identity can provide a framework for an active application of this category.

Responding to the elusiveness of European identity, different authors advocate a definition of the contents European identity may include. For instance, Mikkeli (1998) introduces a semantic field that includes aspects such as democracy, civilization, Christendom, freedom, white skin or the 'west' as constitutive constructs for European identity. In an antagonistic way, these concepts are contrasted with a semantic field of 'otherness' which centres on terms such as barbarism, despotism, slavery, non-white skin or the 'Orient'. Based on similar differentiations and the acknowledgement of the constitutive idea of identity-difference as a semantic couple, Quenzel (2005) introduces a perspective that distinguishes two different degrees of otherness for European identity: internal and external others. External otherness reflects the conceptual efforts to differentiate Europe from something else that is 'not Europe'. By contrast, internal otherness represents and inscribes the manifold differentiations included within European identity constructions, for example the ascriptions related to the slogan 'unity in diversity'. In cases where identity is negotiated against an external subject, such internal otherness is usually suspended. However, internal otherness becomes the dominant construction if internal queries are negotiated. If such a conceptualization is carried over to the political struggle in southern Spain, interesting insights into the politics of identity can be gained.

The politics of identity applied by the protest movement target two aspects: first, the establishment of a coherent group and second, the discursive exclusion of all opponents from this group. As the opponents definitely remain European, such a process happens thus through the negotiation and expression of internal otherness. Such otherness was generated with the help of a coherent founding myth of the movement and its permanent re-inscription in the collective memory of its members. Additionally, through the concept of internal otherness we may also explain why the members made use of four categories of identification: Europe as a community of values, Europe as a community of communication, Europe as a community of modernity and Europe as a community with a common idea of man based on the Christian faith. These categories simultaneously express the most striking differences between themselves and political opponents – and much equivalence between themselves and some of the constitutive ideas of Europe. The case study bears in mind that a vague idea such as European identity can easily be re-framed, transformed and filled with significance – at least if essential issues such as individual property and with it one's life savings are endangered.

Concluding comments

Lifestyle migration, conceptualized here as an inherently intra-European mobility, can be considered to shed light on the practical consequences of the European unification process. Many such citizens move out of their country for the first time in their life, while for others migration and mobility have developed as one of the constant concomitants of their daily life. Although such mobility is common within the European Union, different studies pronounce rather critical conclusions regarding the evolution of a commonly shared European attachment or identity even among these free movers (Oliver and O'Reilly, 2010) – transnationalism is often strictly reduced to a transnational mobility (Gustafson, 2008).

This issue gains a different meaning, however, if we analyse political mobilization among mobile citizens such as in the case against the LRAU legislation. Within this political conflict, the practical use of EU citizenship rights such as the possibility of presenting petitions and requesting legal action and support from European institutions is entangled with a discourse referring to Europe and European identity. Indeed, the political field of contention presents specific circumstances that, for instance, radicalize certain habitus dispositions or even entail the suppression of habitus (Janoschka, forthcoming). It enables the practical use of identity and in this case, the discursive appropriation of European identity, conceived as an expression of politics of identity that aim at destabilizing hegemonic relations.

One of the key elements aimed at inscribing differential identity constructions was to combine cultural and national identities with the authoritative framework the European Union offers in order to establish a coherent identity discourse that serves for the daily practice of political contention. However, the case of European identity provides further insights into the evolving spatialities of Europe. If mobility and flux is stressed in detriment to stability and permanence, European identities can be conceptualized as relational, multiple and mobile (Sassatelli, 2010). This responds to a political sociology of mobility as demanded by Aradau *et al.* (2010) with reference to new accounts towards European citizenship. The practical use of European identity in political contest reveals that the Union is strategically appropriated and filled with significance by its inhabitants, when European identity is thought of as a practical experience and meaningful communication. Such expressions of practising European identity and enacting European citizenship demonstrate that the political may contribute and promote novel expressions and imaginations of Europe and European identity for which lifestyle migrants can be conceptual precursors.

Acknowledgements

This research was supported by a Marie Curie Intra-European-Fellowship within the 7th European Community Framework Programme (PIEF-GA-2008–220287), hosted at the Centre of Human and Social Sciences of the Spanish National Research Council in Madrid (CCHS-CSIC). I am grateful to Rafael Durán Muñoz and Heiko Haas for critical reading of the manuscript, as well as to the peer reviewers and editors whose remarks and suggestions helped improving the quality of this contribution.

References

Anderson, B., (2006 [1983]), *Imagined Communities: Reflections on the Origin and Spread of Nationalism*, London: Verso.
Appadurai, A., (2008), Global Ethnoscapes: Notes and Queries for a Transnational Anthropology, in Khagram, S. and P. Levitt, (eds), *The Transnational Studies Reader. Intersections and Innovations*, London, New York: Routledge: 51–63.
Aradau, C., J. Huysmans and V. Squire, (2010), Acts of European Citizenship: A Political Sociology of Mobility, *Journal of Common Market Studies*, 48: 945–65.

Beaverstock, J., (2005), Transnational Elites in the City: British Highly-Skilled Inter-Company Transferees in New York City's Financial District, *Journal of Ethnic and Migration Studies*, 31: 245–268.

Beck, U. and E. Grande, (2007), *Cosmopolitan Europe*, Cambridge: Polity Press.

Benhabib, S., (1999), Strange multiplicities: The politics of identity and difference in a global context, in Samatar, A., (ed.), *The Divided Self: Identity and Globalization*, St. Paul (MN): Macalester College: 27–52.

Benson, M., (2010), The context and trajectory of Lifestyle Migration, *European Societies*, 12: 45–64.

Benson, M. and K. O'Reilly, (2009), Migration and the search for a better way of life: a critical exploration of lifestyle migration, *The Sociological Review*, 57: 608–25.

Blokker, P., (2008), Europe 'United in Diversity'. From a Central European Identity to Post-Nationality? *European Journal of Social Theory*, 11: 257–74.

British Embassy Madrid, (2010), Property issues. http://ukinspain.fco.gov.uk/en/help-for-british-nationals/living-in-spain/property-issues/ (Last accessed 25 October, 2010)

Bruter, M., (2005), *Citizens of Europe? The emergence of a mass European identity*, Houndmills: Palgrave Macmillan.

Bruter, M., (2009), Time Bomb? The Dynamic Effect of News and Symbols on the Political Identity of European Citizens, *Comparative Political Studies*, 42: 1498–1536.

Calhoun, C., (1993), Civil Society and the Public Sphere, *Public Culture*, 5: 267–80.

Calhoun, C., (2009), Cosmopolitan Europe and European studies, in Rumford, C., (ed.), *The SAGE Handbook of European Studies*, London: Sage: 637–54.

Casado-Díaz, M. A., (2009), Social Capital in the Sun. Bonding and Bridging Social Capital among British Retirees, in Benson, M. and K. O'Reilly, (eds), *Lifestyle Migration Expectations, Aspirations and Experiences*, Surrey: Ashgate: 1–14,

Checkel, J. and P. Katzenstein, (2009), The Politicization of European identities, in Checkel, J. and P. Katzenstein, (eds), *European Identity*, Cambridge: Cambridge University Press: 1–25.

Collard, S., (2010), Lifestyle Migrants or European Citizens? Communicating European Citizenship to British Residents in France. Conference Paper presented at the UACES academic conference 'Communicating European Citizenship, available at: http://www.uaces.org/pdf/papers/1002/Collard.pdf (Last accessed 27 April 2010).

Connolly, W., (2002), *Identity\Difference: Democratic Negotiations of Political Paradox, Expanded Edition*, Minneapolis: University of Minnesota Press.

Corts Valencianes, (2005), Diario de Sesiones. Sessió plenària realitzada el dia 22 de desembre de 2005. (http://www.cortsvalencianes.es/CIC3/BASIS/DSCV/WEB/DSCV_PDF/DDD/VI%20% 20001220.pdf)

Crossley N., (2005), How Social Movements Move: From First to Second Wave Developments in the UK Field of Psychiatric Contention, *Social Movement Studies*, 4: 21–48.

Croucher, S., (2009), *The Other Side of the Fence. American Migrants in Mexico*, University of Texas Press: Austin.

Delanty, G., (1995), *Inventing Europe. Idea, Identity, Reality*, London: Routledge.

Delanty, G. and C. Rumford, (2005), *Rethinking Europe. Social theory and the implications of Europeanization*, London: Routledge.

Durán, R., (2010), Residentes extranjeros y corrupción política. Las elecciones municipales de 2007 en España, *Revista Española de Ciencia Política*, 23: 59–79.

Eder, K., (2006), Europe's Borders. The Narrative Construction of the Boundaries of Europe, *European Journal of Social Theory*, 9: 255–71.

European Parliament (2009): European Parliament resolution of 26 March 2009 on the impact of extensive urbanization in Spain on individual rights of European citizens, on the environment and on the application of EU law, based upon petitions received (2008/2248(INI)). Available at: http://www.europarl.europa.eu/sides/getDoc.do?type=TA&reference=P6TA-2009-0192&language=EN (Last accessed 29 March 2009).

Faist, T., (2008), Transnationalization in North and South: Concepts, Methodology and Venues for Research, in Anghel, R., E. Gerharz, G. Rescher and M. Salzbrunn (eds), *The Making of World Society. Perspectives from Transnational Research*, Bielefeld: transcript: 25–50.

Michael Janoschka

Favell, A., (2008), *Eurostars and Eurocities: Free Movement and Mobility in an Integrating Europe*, Malden (MA): Wiley-Blackwell.

Glasze, G., (2007), The Discursive Construction of a World-Spanning Region and the Role of Empty Signifiers: The Case of Francophonia, *Geopolitics*, 12, 656–79.

Grundy, S. & L. Jamieson, (2007), European Identities: From Absent-Minded Citizens to Passionate Europeans, *Sociology*, 41: 663–80.

Gustafson, P., (2008), Transnationalism in retirement migration. The case of North European retirees in Spain, *Ethnic and Racial Studies*, 31: 451–75.

Halbwachs, M., (1992), *On Collective Memory*. Edited, translated and with an introduction by L. Coser, Chicago: University of Chicago Press.

Halbwachs, M., (2003), *Stätten der Verkündigung im Heiligen Land. Eine Studie zum kollektiven Gedächtnis*, Konstanz: UVK Verlag.

Hall, C. M., (2005), Reconsidering the geography of tourism and contemporary mobility, *Geographical Research*, 43: 125–39.

Hall, C. M. and D. Müller, (2004), Introduction: Second Homes, Curse or Blessing? Revisited, in Hall, C. M. & D. Müller, (eds), *Tourism, Mobility and Second Homes. Between elite landscape and common grounds*, Clevedon: Channel View Publications: 3–14.

Hall, C. M., D. Müller and J. Saarinen, (2009), *Nordic Tourism. Issues and Cases*, Bristol: Channel View Publications.

Hall, S., (1997), The Spectacle of the Other, in Hall, S. (ed.), *Representation. Cultural Representations and Signifying Practices*, London: Sage: 223–90.

Herrmann, R. and M. Brewer, (2004), Identities and Institutions, Becoming European in the EU, in Herrmann, R., T. Risse and M. Brewer, (eds), *Transnational identities. Becoming European in the EU*, Lanham: Rowman & Littlefield: 1–23.

Hooghe, L. and G. Marks, (2007), Sources of Euroscepticism, *Acta Politica*, 42: 119–27.

Huber, A. and K. O'Reilly, (2004), The construction of 'Heimat' under conditions of individualized modernity: Swiss and British elderly migrants in Spain, *Ageing & Society*, 24: 327–51.

Huete, R., (2009), *Turistas que llegan para quedarse. Una explicación sociológica sobre la movilidad residencial*, Alicante: Universidad de Alicante.

INE (Instituto Nacional de Estadísticas/Spanish National Statistical Institute), 2010, Labour market – Economically Active Population Survey, http://www.ine.es (last accessed 30 August 2010).

Jackiewicz, E. and J. Craine, (2010), Destination Panama: An Examination of the Migration-Tourism-Foreign Investment Nexus, *Recreation, Society in Africa, Asia and Latin America*, 1: 5–29.

Janoschka, M., (2009), The Contested Spaces of Lifestyle Mobilities: Regime Analysis as a Tool to Study Political Claims in Latin American Retirement Destinations, *Die Erde*, 140: 251–274.

Janoschka, M., (2010), Prácticas de Ciudadanía Europea. El uso estratégico de las identidades en la participación política de los inmigrantes comunitarios. *ARBOR – Ciencia, Pensamiento y Cultura* CLXXXVI (744): 705–19.

Janoschka, M., (forthcoming). Habitus and radical reflexivity: A conceptual approach to study political articulations of lifestyle- and tourism-related mobilities, *Journal of Policy Research in Tourism, Leisure & Events*, 2 (3).

Kantner, C., (2006), Collective Identity as Shared Ethical Self-Understanding. The Case of the Emerging European Identity, *European Journal of Social Theory*, 9: 501–23.

King, R., A. M. Warnes and A. Williams, (2000), *Sunset Lives. British Retirement Migration to the Mediterranean*, Oxford: Oxford University Press.

Kohli, M., (2000), The battlegrounds of European Identity, *European Societies* 2: 113–137.

Korpela, M., (2009), When a Trip to Adulthood becomes a Lifestyle: Western Lifestyle Migrants in Varansi, India, in Benson, M. and K. O'Reilly, (eds), *Lifestyle Migration. Expectations, Aspirations and Experiences*, Surrey: Ashgate: 15–30.

Korpela, M., (2010), A Postcolonial Imagination? Westerners Searching for Authenticity in India, *Journal of Ethnic and Migration Studies*, 36: 1299–1315.

Kraus, P., (2008), *A Union of Diversity. Language, Identity and Polity-Building in Europe*, Cambridge: Cambridge University Press.

Laffan, B., (2004), The European Union and Its Institutions as 'Identity Builders', in Herrmann, R., T. Risse and M. Brewer, (eds),*Transnational identities. Becoming European in the EU*, Lanham: Rowman & Littlefield: 75–96.

Leitner, H., E. Sheppard and K. M. Sziarto, (2008), The spatialities of contentious politics, *Transactions of the Institute of British Geographers*, 33: 157–72.

Massey, D., (2004), Geographies of Responsibility, *Geografiska Annaler*, 86: 5–18.

Mayer, F. & J. Palmowski, (2004), European Identities and the EU – The Ties that Bind the Peoples of Europe, *Journal of Common Market Studies*, 42: 573–98.

McIntyre, N., (2009), Re-thinking Amenity Migration: Integrating Mobility, Lifestyle and Socio-Ecological Systems, *Die Erde*, 140: 229–50.

McWatters, M., (2008), *Residential Tourism. (De)Constructing Paradise*, Bristol, Buffalo, Toronto: Channel View Publications.

Mikkeli, H., (1998), *Europe as an idea and an identity*, Houndmills: MacMillan Press.

Mitchell, K., (2007), Geographies of identity: the intimate cosmopolitan, *Progress in Human Geography*, 31: 706–720.

Moss, L., (ed.), (2006), *The Amenity Migrants. Seeking and sustaining mountains and their cultures*, Cambridge (MA): CABI.

Nicholls, W., (2009), Place, networks, space: theorizing the geographies of social movements, *Transactions of the Institute of British Geographers*, 34: 78–93.

Oliver, C., (2007), *Retirement Migration. Paradoxes of Ageing*, New York: Routledge.

Oliver, C. and K. O'Reilly, (2010), A Bourdieusian Analysis of Class and Migration. Habitus and the Individualizing Process, *Sociology*, 44: 49–66.

O'Reilly, K., (2000), *The British on the Costa del Sol. Transnational Identities and Local Communities*, London: Routledge.

O'Reilly, K., (2007), Intra-European Migration and the Mobility-Enclosure Dialectic, *Sociology*, 41: 277–93.

O'Reilly, K., (2009), The Children of the Hunters: Self-realization Projects and Class Reproduction, in Benson, M. and K. O'Reilly, (eds), Lifestyle Migration. Expectations, Aspirations and Experiences, Surrey and Ashgate: 103–119.

O'Reilly, K. and M. Benson, (2009), Lifestyle Migration. Escaping to the Good Life?, in Benson, M. & K. O'Reilly, (eds), *Lifestyle Migration. Expectations, Aspirations and Experiences*, Surrey: Ashgate: 1–14.

Penrose, J. & R. Mole, (2008), Nation-States and National Identity, in Cox, K., M. Low and J. Robinson, (eds),*The SAGE Handbook of Political Geography*, London: Sage: 271–283.

Pichler, M., (2008), How Real is Cosmopolitanism in Europe? *Sociology*, 42: 1107–26.

Pichler, M., (2009), Cosmopolitan Europe, *European Societies*, 11: 3–24.

Pinxten, R., M. Cornelis and R. Rubinstein, (2007), European Identity: Diversity in Union, *International Journal of Public Administration*, 30: 687–98.

Quenzel, G., (2005), *Konstruktionen von Europa. Die europäische Identität und die Kulturpolitik der Europäischen Union*, Bielefeld: transcript.

Rodríguez, V., G. Fernández-Mayoralas and F. Rojo, (2004), International Retirement Migration: Retired Europeans Living on the Costa Del Sol, Spain, *Population Review*, 43: 1–36.

Rodríguez, V., R. Lardiés and P. Rodríguez, (2010), Migration and the Registration of European Pensioners in Spain, in ARI 20/2010, 1–8. Available at: http://www.realinstitutoelcano.org, (last accessed 14 April 2010).

Rosenthal, G., (2004), Biographical research, in Seale, C., G. Gobo, J. Gubrium and D. Silverman, (eds), *Qualitative Research Practice*, London: Sage: 48–64.

Routledge, P., (2008), Transnational Political Movements, in Cox, K., M. Low and J. Robinson, (eds), *The SAGE Handbook of Political Geography*, London: Sage: 335–349.

Rumford, C., (ed.), (2007), *Cosmopolitanism and Europe*, Liverpool: Liverpool University Press.

Rumford, C. (ed.), (2009), *The SAGE Handbook of European Studies*, London: Sage.

Michael Janoschka

Sánchez de Madariaga, I., (2003), Aktuelle Tendenzen in der spanischen Raumordnung, *Planungsrundschau*, 3: 92–105.

Sassatelli, M., (2010), European Identity between Flows and Places: Insights from Emerging European Landscape Policies, *Sociology*, 44: 67–83.

Schriewer, K. and I. Encinas, (2007), Being Misleading About Where One Resides. European Affluence Mobility and Registration Patterns – Ethnologia European/Journal of European Ethnology 37 (1–2): 98–106.

Stevenson, N., (2005), European cosmopolitanism and civil society, *Innovation: The European Journal of Social Science Research*, 18: 45–59.

Soriano, J. and C. Romero, (2004), *El Agente Urbanizador*, Madrid: Iustel Publicaciones.

Vertovec, S. and R. Cohen, (2002), *Conceiving Cosmopolitanism. Theory, Context and Practice*, Oxford: Oxford University Press.

Warnes, A., (2009), International Retirement Migration, in Uhlenberg, P., (ed.), *International Handbook on Population Aging*, Dodrecht: Springer: 341–63.

White, J., (2010), Europe in the Political Imagination, *Journal of Common Market Studies*, 48: 1015–38.

Williams, A. M. and C. M. Hall, (2002), Tourism, migration, circularity and mobility. The contingencies of time and place, in Hall, C. M. and A. M. Williams, (eds), *Tourism and Migration. New Relationships between Production and Consumption*, Dordrecht: Kluwer: 1–52.

Wodak, R., (2004), National and Transnational Identities: European and Other Identities Constructed in Interviews with EU Officials, in Herrmann, R., T. Risse, and M. Brewer, (eds), *Transnational identities. Becoming European in the EU*, Lanham: Rowman & Littlefield: 97–127.

Notes on contributors

Maria Adamczyk is doctoral student at the Institute of Sociology at the Jagiellonian University, Cracow and holds a teaching assistant position at the Cracow Medical College. Her research areas include stigma and the female body, and social construction of health and illness. e-mail: maria.e.adamczyk@gmail.com

Michaela Benson is the author of *The British in Rural France* (2011, MUP) and various other publications on lifestyle migration. She is currently working in the Centre for Urban Studies at the University of Bristol, and was previously employed as The Sociological Review Fellow (2008–2009). e-mail: M.Benson@bristol.ac.uk

Oscar Forero is a senior researcher at ESRC's Centre for Economic and Social Aspects of Genomics (Cesagen) investigating the relationship of genomic promises, food security and cultural change. He is also a consultant tutor to the Centre for Development Policy and Research at SOAS, University of London, with research focus on the areas of poverty reduction, sustainable development and natural resources management. e-mail: o.forero@lancaster.ac.uk

Barbara Grüning is post-doctorate research associate at the University of Bologna. She has recently published: *Diritto, norma e memoria. La Germania dell'est nel processo di transizione*, Macerata, Eum, 2010; *Luoghi della memoria e identità collettive*, Roma, Carocci, 2010; *Transition, memory and narrations in the urban space. The case of East German cities,* in G. Sonda, C. Coletta and F. Gabbi (eds), *Urban Plots, Organizing Cities*, Farnham, Ashgate Publishing, 2010. e-mail: babsi.gruening@gmail.com; barbara.gruning2@unibo.it

Zoë Irving is Lecturer in Comparative Social Policy in the Department of Sociological Studies, University of Sheffield, UK. Her current research interests are in the social policy of small island states, the impact of financial crises on welfare states, and changes in the patterns of men's work and employment. She has previously published in the area of gender and work and is co-author with Michael Hill of the eighth edition of *Understanding Social Policy* (2009, Blackwell/Wiley). Her latest publication, co-edited, with Kevin Farnsworth is

Editorial organisation © 2011 The Editorial Board of the Sociological Review. Published by Wiley-Blackwell Publishing Ltd, 9600 Garsington Road, Oxford OX4 2DQ, UK and 350 Main Street, Malden, MA 02148, USA

Social Policy in Challenging Times: Economic Crisis and Welfare Systems (forthcoming 2011, The Policy Press). email: z.m.irving@sheffield.ac.uk

Michael Janoschka is graduate geographer from the Humboldt-University of Berlin (2002) and received his PhD in Philosophy at the University of Frankfurt (2007). After carrying out a postdoctoral Marie Curie research fellowship at the Centre of Human and Social Sciences of the Spanish National Research Council (2008–2010), he is now holder of a Ramón y Cajal research chair at the Department of Political Science of the Autonomous University in Madrid. His research interests mainly focus on migration processes in a globalized world, the role of politics of identity and citizenship practice in local political conflicts, and neoliberal citizenship in urban sceneries. Further information: http://www.michael-janoschka.de e-mail: michael.janoschka@uam.es

John Law is Professor of Sociology at the Open University, and a director of the ESRC Centre for Research on Socio-Cultural Change. He uses STS material semiotic approaches to work on social research methods and their performativity, on post-colonial and other asymmetrical knowledge relations, and on human-animal-technology relations. His recent books include *After Method: Mess in Social Science Research, and Aircraft Stories*. e-mail: j.law@open.ac.uk

Lin, Wen-yuan is Associate Professor at the National Tsing-hua University, Taiwan. His research interests are medical sociology, STS, and social theory. He has published papers on medical practices, users of technology, and R&D of ICTs in university context. e-mail: wylin1@mx.nthu.edu.tw

Kateřina Lišková is Assistant Professor in the Gender Studies programme at the Faculty of Social Sciences, Masaryk University, in the Czech Republic. Her research is focused on gender, sexuality, and the social organization of intimacy. She was affiliated with the New School for Social Research as a Fulbright Scholar, and as a Visiting Scholar with New York University. She has lectured at various US universities and her papers have appeared in several monographs published by Routledge and SAGE. In the Czech Republic, her book *Good Girls Look the Other Way, Feminism and Pornography* was published by Sociological Publishing House (2009). e-mail: katerina@fss.muni.cz

Rolland Munro is Emeritus Professor at Keele University and Joint Managing Editor of The Sociological Review and is best known for his ethnographic work on consumption, power and identity. His published articles across a wide range of topics – including accountability, affect, bodies, class, ethics, knowledge, landscape, language, money, polyphony, reason, technology and time – provide a bridge between humanist and anti-humanist perspectives and elaborate an emerging vocabulary of motility, disposal, engrossment and punctualizing. e-mail: rolland.editor@socrev.keele.ac.uk

Celine-Marie Pascale is an associate professor of sociology at American University in Washington, DC. She is the author of *Making Sense of Race, Class and Gender: Commonsense, Power and Privilege in the U.S.* (Routledge, 2007),

Cartographies of Knowledge: Exploring Qualitative Epistemologies (Sage, 2010), and numerous journal articles. She is currently working on a book entitled *Inequality and The Politics of Representation: A Global Landscape* (Sage, 2012). Pascale is active in the International Sociology Association where she serves as President of the Research Committee of Language & Society. e-mail: pascale@american.edu

Wiebke Pohler teaches sociology at Eichstätt University/Germany and Neubiberg University/Germany. Her research interests are STS, Risk Studies and Sociology of Medicine. She is currently working on her PhD thesis, which is about 'Nano-Medical Innovations'. Her most recent publication is '*Weltrisikogesellschaft als Ausnahmezustand*', Velbrück [World-Risk-Society as State of Exception] with Markus Holzinger, and Stefan May. e-mail: wiebke.pohler@soziologie.uni-muenchen.de

Derek Robbins is Professor of International Social Theory in the School of Humanities and Social Sciences at the University of East London. His *On Bourdieu, Education and Society* was published by Bardwell Press in July, 2006. In 2007–8 he was in receipt of an ESRC award to study the work of Jean-Claude Passeron, and he has written an introduction to a translation of Passeron's *Le raisonnement sociologique* which will be published in 2011/12 by Bardwell Press, Oxford, as *Sociological Reasoning*. His book *French Post War Social Theory: International Knowledge Transfer* is due to be published by Sage in 2011. e-mail: d.m.robbins@uel.ac.uk

Isis Sánchez Estellés is assistant professor of Sociology at the University of Castilla-La Mancha (Spain) and PhD candidate at the University of Essex. She got the First National Prize of the Sociology degree in Spain in 2005. Her main areas of research are political sociology, development and impact of social movements, and State and citizenship. She has published in *Nomadas, RIS* (international review of Sociology), *Postgraduate Essex Journal of Sociology* and recently contributed in a book about the women's movement impact in Castilla-La Mancha. She is about to finish her PhD about the impact of the antiwar movement in Spain and the USA (2002–2004). e-mail: isanch@essex.ac.uk, IsisMaria.Sanchez@uclm.es

Ritchie Savage is a doctoral candidate in the Sociology Department at the New School for Social Research. He is currently working on his dissertation, 'A Comparative Analysis of Populist Discourse in Venezuela and the United States: 1945–1954 and 1998–present'. e-mail: savar647@newschool.edu

Michael Schillmeier teaches Sociology and Science and Technology Studies (STS) at the Department of Sociology at Ludwig-Maximilians-University/Germany. Currently he holds a Schumpeter-Fellowship to research 'Innovations in Nano-Medicine'. He has written widely on the material dynamics of societal ordering and change, on bodies, senses and dis/ability, on the societal relevance of objects and the heterogeneity of the social. With Juliane Sarnes he has edited and translated Gabriel Tarde's *Monadology and Sociology* into German. Latest publications include *Rethinking Disability: Bodies, Senses and Things,* published by Routledge, *Un/knowing Bodies* (2009), published by Wiley/Blackwell (with Joanna Latimer), *New technologies and Emerging Spaces of Care* (2010), (with Miquel Domènech) and *Disability in German Literature, Film and Theatre,* published by Camden House (2010), (with Eleoma Joshua). e-mail: m. schillmeier@lmu.de

Graham Smith is a senior lecturer in History at Royal Holloway, University of London. His research and teaching is in oral history, public history and the history of medicine. He is currently chair of the Oral History Society (http:// www.ohs.org.uk/) e-mail: graham.smith@rhul.ac.uk

Bernhard Weicht works as a researcher at CMO Flevoland in the Netherlands and is associated with the University of Nottingham in the UK. He received his PhD from the University of Nottingham with a thesis on the discursive construction of care for elderly people. His research interests include care, morality and ethics, health and ageing, gender structures, migration and discursive constructions. e-mail: bernhard.weicht@nottingham.ac.uk

Index

Editorial organisation © 2011 The Editorial Board of the Sociological Review. Published by Wiley-Blackwell
Publishing Ltd, 9600 Garsington Road, Oxford OX4 2DQ, UK and 350 Main Street, Malden, MA 02148, USA

small states: adaptability of 230, 231;
national cohesion of 229, 231;
vulnerability of 230, 231, 241; welfare
development 227–9, 230, 232–42
Smelser, N.J. 13
Smith, G. 81
Smith, L.T. 154
social, politics and 1–2, 17, 18
social change 192, 198; European 25, 26,
28
social construction 1, 103, 105, 110–12,
212, 272, 276, 279, 282,
social epistemologies 160–2
social movements (*see also* impact of
social movements) 247; organization
and 12–14; participation of lifestyle
migrants 271, 278, 282–5; state
repression and 251–2, 257–8
social policy 7, 232–42
social reproduction 191–3, 201
social sciences 118, 122, 124, 125, 154,
155; Bourdieu and 122, 124, 125–6;
epistemology 160–2; evidence
and 157–8; as power 155;
research 155, 156, 157–8, 159–60,
163
social totality 172, 182
Socialist Workers Party of Spain *see*
PSOE
society 171, 172; science and 124–5
sociology: borders of 2–5; of
education 119–20, 123, 131
Spain (*see also* Popular Party; PSOE):
anti-war movement 246, 253–8;
electoral system 261; General Council
of the Judiciary Power 263; interest
groups-executive relations 262;
legislature-executive relations 261–2;
lifestyle migrants' participation in
pressure group 274–6, 281–5; planning
legislation 274–6; terrorist attacks
(2004) 246–7, 255, 260
speech acts 181; performative 193–4,
200–1
Steinberg, M. 162
Steinberg, S. 156
structuralism 120, 123
subjectivities 136–7, 141, 144, 146, 147
surveillance 11, 12; of women 106, 107

sustainability 27, 31
symbolic power 190, 200; and
performativity 193–6, 200–1
symbolic violence 105, 160, 190

Taggart, P. 179, 180
Taiwan 141–2; gods 143–4;
modernization 141–3; STS
seminars 138–41
Tarrow, S. 13, 248, 249, 250, 251,
263
taste 78–9, 92
television, role of in Spanish anti-war
movement 258–9
theory, critique and 7–9
therapeutic discourses 190, 192, 194–6,
199–200
Thomson, R.G. 107
Thrift, N. 14
Tilly, C. 263
Tivadar, B. 85
Torfing, J. 171
Toynbee, P. 205
trans-local ethnography 37–8
transnationalism 283
Triseliotis, J. 233, 234
Tronto, J.C. 219
Turkle, S. 99

ugliness 97, 98–9, 102; dealing with 110–
11, 112; as disability 107; identity
and 105; self-ascribed 102–3, 111;
social construction of 103–5, 111–12;
as social deviation 107–8; stigma
of 98, 102, 107, 111
Ukraine 36, 80–1
Ukrainian diaspora 80–2, 85; traditional
food of 82–7, 88–91, 92
Ukrainian identity 80, 81, 83, 85, 87, 90,
91, 93
United States of America, populism
in 169–70, 173, 177–9, 183
Uzel, R. 196–8

Vargas, G.D. 169, 173, 174
Véliz, C. 176, 177
Verdès-Leroux, J. 118
Verran, H. 137, 140–1
video-ethnography 38

south essex college

FURTHER & HIGHER EDUCATION
SOUTHEND CAMPUS